Mediating Environmental Conflicts

Theory and Practice

EDITED BY
J. Walton Blackburn
Willa Marie Bruce

Q

QUORUM BOOKS
Westport, Connecticut • London

Library of Congress Cataloging-in-Publication Data

Mediating environmental conflicts : theory and practice / edited by J.
  Walton Blackburn, Willa Marie Bruce.
      p.   cm.
    Includes bibliographical references and index.
    ISBN 0–89930–846–5
    1. Environmental mediation—United States.   I. Blackburn, J.
  Walton.   II. Bruce, Willa M.
  KF3775.M43   1995
  344.73'046'0269—dc20
  [347.304460269]   94–34271

British Library Cataloguing in Publication Data is available.

Library of Congress Catalog Card Number: 94–34271
ISBN: 0–89930–846–5

First published in 1995

Quorum Books, 88 Post Road West, Westport, CT 06881
An imprint of Greenwood Publishing Group, Inc.

Printed in the United States of America

The paper used in this book complies with the
Permanent Paper Standard issued by the National
Information Standards Organization (Z39.48–1984).

10 9 8 7 6 5 4 3 2 1

Copyright Acknowledgment

All figures in Chapter 8 of this volume are copyright © 1994 by Guy and Heidi Burgess.

**For Charles T. Goodsell
Teacher, Mentor, Friend**

May his belief in good government be an
inspiration to all who are concerned with
resolving environmental conflicts

Contents

Figures and Tables

FIGURES

TABLES

Chapter 1

Introduction

J. Walton Blackburn and Willa Marie Bruce

A recent "Report Card on the Nation's Public Works" graded the United States' ability to manage environmental issues as follows: Water Resources—B; Waste Water—C; Solid Waste—C minus; and Hazardous Waste—D (Fragile Foundations, 1988). With grades like this, a college student might have difficulty graduating. With grades like this, the United States has serious environmental problems.

Yet not only do many areas of the country perform poorly on the management of environmental issues, but administrators and citizens disagree on what is proper and effective management of those issues. These disagreements are known as environmental conflicts, and they must be resolved so that our environment will be protected for our children and our children's children. An emerging way of addressing environment-related conflicts is mediation.

The Institute for Environmental Mediation uses the following definition when discussing the mediation process:

> Mediation is a process in which those involved in a dispute jointly explore and reconcile their differences. The mediator has no authority to impose a settlement. His or her strength lies in the ability to assist the parties in settling their own differences. The mediated dispute is settled when the parties themselves reach what they consider to be a workable solution. (Cormick, 1982:16)

Mediation is a relatively new approach to managing conflict over environmental issues. It developed from attempts to apply labor and community mediation experience to environment-related conflicts, with the first documented instance of such mediation dating from 1974. Since then, a literature on the theory and practice of environmental mediation has evolved as practitioners reflect upon the techniques and approaches which have worked best and theoreticians attempt to pull together the key elements of successful environmental mediation activities.

Environmental conflict arises when one or more parties involved in a decision-making process disagree about an action which has potential to have an impact upon the environment. When one or more of these parties is able to block a proposed action of any of the others, a stalemate exists. The traditional method for resolving environmental conflicts was litigation, although protest activities, old fashioned fist fights, and loud shouting matches most surely also occurred.

Alternative dispute resolution (ADR) techniques, of which environmental mediation is one, are emerging as an alternative to litigation in the settlement of environmental disputes. In selecting material to be included in this book, the editors have taken as an article of faith that "people accept what they help to create," thus presupposing that mediated dispute resolution is superior to litigious activities. This assumption is not ours alone, for two federal directives within the last decade have given impetus to replacing traditional litigation with alternative dispute resolution efforts. They are: a policy memorandum, *Final Guidance on Use of Alternative Dispute Resolution Techniques in Enforcement Actions*, issued by the Environmental Protection Agency in 1986, and the federal *Administrative Dispute Resolution Act* (Public Law 101-552, 104 Stat. 2736, November 15, 1990).

Despite our belief in its power, mediation as a conflict resolution technique is not applicable to all environmental conflicts. Practitioners and theoreticians are still attempting to understand which disputes are most amenable to mediation and which practices and approaches are most likely to be successful. Theory development has been slow.

Each environmental conflict has many dimensions and contextual aspects which make it different from other environmental disputes and other public conflicts. Mediators come from a great variety of backgrounds, have differing levels of technical expertise and group management skills, and contrasting philosophies of how to conduct mediation. The great diversity of mediator approaches and starkly differing contexts of environmental conflicts have made both practice and theory development extremely challenging.

The information presented in this book is an attempt to move the practice of environmental mediation forward through discussions of theoretical considerations and descriptions of mediation practices. Just as environmental mediation is applied to a great variety of environmental disputes which differ widely in substance, scope, and number and nature of parties involved, this volume examines environmental mediation from very diverse perspectives. Some chapters are conceptual and general examinations of mediation and its context, while others address the practical problems which need consideration for mediation to be effective. Many address issues of both theory and practice.

In the next chapter, Christine Reed suggests that the new environmental agenda—loss of biodiversity, nonpoint source pollution, global warming, and acid rain—call for new policy tools, including environmental mediation. She argues that these problems extend beyond point-specific sources of pollution or case-by-case listing of endangered species and calls for a more communitarian approach to resolution, an approach aimed at creating "sustainable communities."

Chapters 3 and 4 explore the conceptual foundations of mediation. Rosemary O'Leary provides a comprehensive review of existing research and commentary on environmental mediation, giving special attention to answering the question "how do we know what we know?" Asking if the present approaches to knowledge development in environmental mediation are adequate, she makes suggestions for improving research in the area. Peter Maida argues that law and economics offer viable perspectives from which to study environmental mediation. He suggests that these disciplines can provide a more rigorous and thorough understanding of the dynamics of mediating environmental disputes than the conceptual methodology typically utilized.

After the chapters which address theoretical concepts come chapters 5 and 6, which are relevant to training mediators. John Allen presents a format for environmental mediation training and a discussion of the background information needed for designing and managing mediation efforts. James Dworkin and G. Logan Jordan developed a teaching case which can be utilized in both college classrooms and mediator training activities. Called "Midwest Energy Utilities," it presents real world issues which can facilitate the learning process.

In Chapter 7, Kenneth Klase addresses the special problems of environmental mediation in small communities. He articulates why efforts need to be carefully designed to take account of their unique characteristics and human resource capabilities.

Guy Burgess and Heidi Burgess point out in Chapter 8 that not all environmental conflicts are amenable to mediation. They propose a means for identifying those controversies for which mediation is appropriate, describe the nature of "unmediatable" conflicts, and offer steps to make these confrontations more constructive.

The value of citizen participation in mediation activities is a theme which runs through the case studies contained in Chapters 9, 10, and 11. Bruce Clary and Regan Hornney use the example of determining the site of a low-level nuclear waste facility to suggest that alternative dispute resolution is a means of facilitating citizen input. They argue that the Prenegotiation and Negotiation phases of mediation are essential building blocks to successful resolution of environmental disputes. James Richardson describes a citizen participation process which provided for facilitated negotiation between federal agencies, a project proponent and disparate community interests. Sondra Bogdonoff explains how negotiated rule-making was used as the basis of a process that allowed 50 stakeholders to heal the scars of a bitter referendum and arrive at rules for Maine's new transportation policy, which were accepted by all parties and received public support.

Chapters 12 and 13 explore ethical and social justice concerns. William O. Stephens, John B. Stephens, and Frank Dukes discuss environmental ethics and explain the ethical dimensions of environmental dispute resolution for advocates and third party interveners. They suggest that ethical considerations are due to the environment as well as to the parties in dispute about it. Carolyn Blackford and Hirini Matunga address issues of justice in bicultural environmental mediation. Using the example of the Maori of New Zealand, they point out that not all persons will approach the mediation process with the same set of *a priori* assumptions and advise mediators to be sensitive to cultural differences of parties in the dispute.

In Chapter 14 Clare Ryan demonstrates the utility of "regulatory negotiation," a practice used increasingly by the Environmental Protection Agency. This is followed by three case studies which examine reasons for and criteria for evaluating the success or failure of mediation.

J. Lynn Wood and Mary E. Guy, in Chapter 15, describe methods that local governments can use to achieve consensus on initiatives with a potential for adverse environmental effects and then move forward into implementation of agreed upon activities. Dennis Baird, Ralph Maughan, and Douglas Nilson offer Chapter 16, with reasons for the failure of a mediation effort which attempted to deal with wilderness issues in Idaho. They propose suggestions for mediation research. Chapter 17, by Mollie Mangerich and Larry S. Luton, describes a mediated environmental dispute in the state of Washington between Kentucky bluegrass seed producers who practiced open field burning and various stakeholders in nearby urban areas.

A final chapter, by J. Walton Blackburn, examines the challenges and issues of research and theory development and suggests future directions for the theory and practice of environmental mediation.

Chapter 2

Mediation and the New Environmental Agenda

Christine M. Reed

Vice President Al Gore, in his challenging new book *Earth in the Balance*, talks about his awakening to the global scale of the environmental crisis. Since 1958, his college professor had been monitoring steadily increasing atmospheric levels of carbon dioxide from the top of the Mauna Loa volcano in Hawaii. Shocked by those trends and their potential to create "global warming," Gore described his new awareness as a spiritual transformation—an awareness of the fundamental connection between human activity and the earth's biosphere (Gore, 1992).

This description is remarkable, because for centuries modern ways of thinking have rejected the idea that humans are part of nature; that the natural environment is affected by human activity and that human economic activity can have unintended social costs. As this chapter will show, however, many scientists and public officials are now calling for a "new environmental policy agenda," one that will focus our attention on the global scale of the environmental crisis and how future economic growth must be based on the principle of sustainable development (Carley and Christie, 1993).

The new environmental agenda provides a powerful rationale for further developing the theory and practice of environmental mediation. This chapter first provides background on some of the events and trends which constitute a new "agenda" or way of perceiving and defining public problems. Second, it describes how public sector mediation, as an alternative to adjudication, is particularly suited to addressing the new environmental agenda.

A NEW ENVIRONMENTAL AGENDA

The study of agenda-setting in the public policy process looks at how and why certain issues attract widespread public attention and result in action by legislative institutions. How problems are initially perceived and defined often determine the shape of policy instruments and programs later on (Kingdon, 1984).

Many scientists and public officials are saying that environmental problems, such as global climate change, acid rain, and the loss of biodiversity, will require new strategies and methods to prevent species from becoming endangered, restore damaged ecosystems, and reduce ecological, as well as human, health risks from pollution. If they are correct, then the public sector should not continue in its traditional, limited, and reactive role of simply adjusting and balancing competing claims for natural resources (Vig and Kraft, 1994).

Sustainable Communities

The new environmental agenda is about "sustainable communities"—defined as maintaining a healthy environment to support long-term community development and managing economic growth in order to protect and restore the natural environment over the long run. The idea of sustainable communities is that the health of human and biotic communities are potentially consistent, rather than conflicting, goals.

Leaders who have engaged in strategic planning for local economic development have realized for some time that they must nurture the creation of small businesses indigenous to their communities. Traditionally, communities have been dependent on a few major employers: manufacturing, agriculture, or "extractive" industries, such as mining and timber. Strategic planning for community economic development requires local teams to rethink their assumptions about economic growth and to recognize the importance of sustaining a sense of themselves as a people with common traditions and values (Luke et al., 1988).

Diversifying the local economy potentially sustains both human and biotic communities. As scientists become more familiar with ecology, they are learning about the long-term impacts on "bioregions" (areas demarcated by natural rather than political boundaries) of large-scale economic activities. Strategies to diversify the local economic base are therefore consistent with "contextual management"—thinking about the cumulative effects of individual economic actions on the larger system (Norton, 1991).

The larger ecosystem could be as small as the immediate surroundings or it could be global in scale. What is significant about the concept of a physical or natural "system" is that it is composed of interdependent habitats and individual organisms. Human communities are also part of the "Great Economy" or larger web of life (Daly and Cobb, 1989). While local strategies to diversify and encourage smaller-scale economic activities are often initiated in order to sustain the human community, they are also less environmentally destructive.

The larger biotic community survives, impervious to changes or activities within smaller habitats or communities, unless those activities represent a trend among their peers, like cells overmultiplying in a malignant tumor. Then the larger system will be affected, perhaps even destroyed, by the activities of its parts (Norton, 1991). Although many communities are in the process of adapting to a post-industrial, service and information economic base, others are still dependent on farming, fishing, timber, mining, and other large-scale "extractive" industries which are very damaging to the environment.

Both the long-term viability of the human community and the larger web of life in which it is embedded are threatened by these economic patterns. William Aiken distinguishes between economic efficiency and *ecological efficiency*: minimizing instability or maximizing the long-term sustainability of the environment (Aiken, 1984).

The fate of Missoula, Montana is an example of what can happen when citizens fail to recognize the larger biotic community within which they are situated. Although a large timber company provided residents with high-paying jobs in the short term, it was soon forced to move to another state, once the most profitable trees had been harvested. The forests on the surrounding mountainsides have been clear-cut, and Missoula is now left without a stable economic base (Egan, 1993b).

The way problems are perceived and issues are defined affects the strategies that are developed to address them. Concern about sustainable development at the local level is the result of alarming new trends in global pollution and the loss of biodiversity. This new environmental agenda calls for strategies to prevent, restore and reduce the aggregate effects of economic activity before they have exceeded local thresholds.

As a later section of this chapter will show, mediation is directly affected by these changes in the environmental agenda. Mediators will be needed to help local participants recognize their *common* interests in a long-term, sustainable relationship with the environment (Amy, 1987). As the following data suggest, this need is an urgent one.

Emerging Issues and Trends

The new environmental agenda "goes far beyond our preoccupations of the past two decades with national regulation of specific types of pollution, or preservation of individual species and landscapes" (Vig and Kraft, 1994:385). Among the priority problems also identified by the National Commission on the Environment are eliminating pollution at its sources and targeting the underlying, principal cause of species extinctions—the destruction of habitat (National Commission, 1993).

Preventing versus regulating pollution. The generation and use of energy are responsible for a large portion of pollution. The extraction, transportation, and combustion of fossil fuels are responsible for global climate change (from carbon dioxide emissions) and "acid rain," as well as oil spills and toxic wastes. Energy consumption is projected to increase 75 percent above 1990 levels unless measures to improve energy efficiency are adopted by industry and consumers (National Commission, 1993).

Until recently, the negative effects of pollution were thought to be localized and outweighed by the economic benefits of agricultural and industrial development. Regulation "at the end of the pipe" made sense from both economic and public health perspectives. Understanding of pollution is now more sophisticated, however, and the notion of "sinks" or final resting places for effluents is considered simplistic and misleading—matter does not disappear (National Commission, 1993).

A 1992 report by the United Nations Environmental Programme states that "pollutants emitted into the atmosphere do not necessarily remain confined to the area near the source of emission or local environment. They can be transported over long distances, cross frontiers, and create regional and global environmental problems. Acid deposition . . . in extensive areas of North America and Europe is about 10 times more acidic than normal" (Tolba, 1992:6-7).

Greenhouse gases have increased in the atmosphere, primarily due to the combustion of fossil fuels and from the destruction of forests where trees absorb carbon dioxide from the air. Atmospheric concentrations have been increasing steadily, producing the potential for global climate change—a distortion of the natural greenhouse effect which traps enough infrared radiation from the sun to keep climates temperate.

Grim scenarios of global climate change from excessive amounts of carbon dioxide in the atmosphere include weather changes that could seriously disrupt agricultural economies around the world. In addition, small temperature changes could cause large water resource problems—flooding of coastal cities and drought in semi-arid regions (Tolba, 1992).

While scientists, farmers, ranchers and others disagree about the seriousness of global warming, the potential effects of carbon dioxide emissions are sobering to think about. Once the ecological and human costs of industrial activity are evident, it becomes more difficult to rationalize economic activity as the private choices of autonomous actors. Rational self-interest *does* affect natural processes, even if private choices do not cause direct harm to individuals.

One energy-saving idea that is gathering support among scientists and economists is that of "social cost" or "full-cost pricing" of energy usage. Energy consumption is rising at a rate higher than what is in society's best interests, because the price of fossil fuels does not reflect the environmental costs society must pay for their use (National Commission, 1993).

The National Commission on the Environment has identified other examples of preventive strategies currently under way at the U.S. Environmental Protection Agency (EPA). The first is an integrated approach toward a single region, the Great Lakes. The second is the possibility of granting each facility a single, integrated permit for all types of pollution. The permit would be based on negotiations that would allow the business owner flexibility in methods used to reduce emissions but set firm performance outcomes (National Commission, 1993).

A third strategy is "comparative risk assessment," in which EPA scientists have discussed prioritizing policies based on the severity of the ecological risk. Presently, the areas that scientists rate as most important, such as drinking water quality and the loss of biodiversity, are low priority items in the EPA budget, because of widespread public attention to hazardous wastes and oil spills which threaten *human* health and aesthetics (Vig and Kraft, 1994).

Protecting human and nonhuman habitats. The idea of internalizing environmental costs is also part of the new environmental agenda: protecting habitats for humans and other species. For almost one hundred years, the federal government has subsidized grazing, mining, logging and irrigation of natural resources on public lands. Despite opposition from organized interest groups, the Clinton administration proposed to let the cost of harvesting natural resources on public lands float to their price on the open market. This policy alone would slow the pace of wilderness destruction.

More than 90 percent of the original forests are gone; 99 percent of the tall-grass prairies are also gone; and less than 6 percent of the original 215 million acres of wetlands remain in the coterminous United States (National Commission, 1993). This staggering loss of wilderness habitat is one of the main reasons why the U.S. Fish and Wildlife Service (FWS) has listed hundreds of animal and plant species as endangered or threatened with extinction.

The administration of the Endangered Species Act is an example of what happens when the government is in a reactive rather than a proactive or preventive mode. This program has suffered from a great deal of negative exposure in the media, because of highly publicized court cases halting development on land designated as critical habitat of endangered or threatened species. The spotted owl controversy in the Pacific Northwest is only one such recent case.

A species has to be endangered or threatened (most often by human actions) before the Fish and Wildlife Service (FWS) can step in to negotiate modifications of development plans. Its authority to act is further constrained by administrative law requirements that make the listing of an endangered or threatened species a long and cumbersome process. Implementation of the law within the Department of the Interior has been further influenced by the agency's own conflicting missions—to promote the highest economic use of public land and to preserve the aesthetic, recreational, and historical values of those lands (Tobin, 1990).

The federal government's limited, and largely reactive, role puts it on a collision course with private developers. When the FWS designates an area as a critical habitat for endangered or threatened species, future economic development is thereafter subject to federal restrictions. Economics and ecology are reduced by the legal process to competing preferences, or rights to property versus rights to preserve and enjoy the heritage of wilderness and wild animals. A less adversarial and more holistic perspective would concern itself with sustaining human *and* biotic communities.

Public Officials as Mediators

If the Clinton-Gore mediation team had been able to intervene in the spotted owl controversy much earlier in the chronology of events leading to litigation, their efforts might have been an excellent case study in how to use mediation to recover a sense of the interconnectedness between communities and the land. Unfortunately, by the time of the 1992 election, the issue had bogged down in the court system, and both the timber industry and environmental advocacy groups were locked into firm positions.

The Clinton administration proposed a solution to the spotted owl controversy in June of 1993 that was based on the principle of sustainability. The proposal allowed logging on federal lands to resume in certain areas; it established old growth forest reserves and no-logging buffer zones to protect key watersheds containing salmon and other endangered species; and it set aside funds to help communities develop new strategies for diversifying their economic base (Egan, 1993a).

The ultimate fate of this proposal has yet to be determined; both the timber industry and many environmental groups have expressed their opposition and distrust. The timber industry argues that restricting logging to certain areas of the national forest will cripple the local economy.

Environmental groups, arguing from within the framework of the Endangered Species Act, say that various endangered species have a stronger legal claim. They point out that the Clinton-Gore Plan ("Option 9") will literally cut the larger system out from under the remaining old growth reserves by permitting the timber industry to harvest large tracts around them.

Each side now perceives that the proposed settlement has served the interests of the other side. The point, however, is that communities in the region cannot afford to rely so heavily on a single, dominant export base. Local jobs in the timber and fishing industries continue to be lost because of economic restructuring and because of intensive "harvesting" of forests and streams, although unemployment is often blamed on the Endangered Species Act.

Those who are concerned with environmental impacts have questioned the legitimacy of the Clinton-Gore plan. The answer, however, is not to return to court. A recent study of alternative dispute resolution techniques used by the U.S. Forest Service to develop local forest plans concluded that the process strengthened the scientific basis of decisions (Manring, 1993).

Bryan Norton, an environmental ethicist, argues that existing laws regarding biodiversity "seem to be impaled on this distressing dilemma: should preservationists play the game of economic analysis of policy decisions with one hand tied behind their back; or should they stay on the sidelines crying foul as the game of dam-building and habitat destruction goes on without them?" (Norton, 1991:141).

Norton is referring to traditional ways of framing and resolving environmental disputes, such as court battles over endangered species. Federal laws, which balance or adjust the conflicting interests of developers and environmentalists may temporarily, but rarely permanently, halt the destruction of critical habitat. In fact, the National Commission on the Environment noted that the U.S. Fish and Wildlife Service successfully blocked only 19 projects out of a total of 350 "jeopardy opinions," formally objecting to projects on federal lands that would jeopardize endangered or threatened species (National Commission, 1993).

A way to resolve this dilemma is to build into the original negotiations an approach which takes the ecological context into account. For example, the Clinton administration mediated a settlement with the Georgia Pacific Corporation in April of 1993, under which the company agreed to restrict operations on more than 50,000 acres of its own land in order to establish reserves for the Red Cockaded Woodpecker. The Clinton administration agreed not to initiate proceedings under the Endangered Species Act which would have curtailed logging even further (Schneider, 1993).

The public sector has traditionally played a limited role in conflict resolution, ensuring fair access to natural resources on federal lands; trying to balance economic and environmental interests; and adjudicating appeals of agency decisions. The ecological effects of large-scale economic activity are a collective concern, however, requiring a more proactive role for government in addressing environmental issues. The public sector has a critical role to play in environmental mediation, as the previous examples have illustrated.

So far, this chapter has laid out a rationale for environmental mediation based on a "new environmental agenda." This new policy agenda calls for a new government role in addressing such critical issues as global warming, acid rain and the loss of biodiversity. That role is more proactive, involving the public sector in efforts to mitigate, through the mediation process, the ecological effects of human activity.

The next, and last, section of this chapter addresses some of the political barriers to sustainable development as the underlying theme of the new environmental agenda. It concludes, nevertheless, that political conditions presently exist for an expanded public sector role in environmental mediation. I call this expanded role a "communitarian approach to environmental mediation," because the necessary conditions include decentralizing policy decisions to the local level.

ENVIRONMENTAL MEDIATION FOR
SUSTAINABLE COMMUNITIES

The idea of government intervention makes many people nervous, because it implies limits to human freedoms. People seem to feel more secure with a political system which limits the role of government to adjudication of private disputes when the parties cannot reach informal agreement. Such individualism produces paradoxical results, however, because people are part of a larger system, and they ultimately suffer the effects of a limited and restrained public sector (Smith, 1992).

Political Barriers to Sustainable Communities

The political heritage of the United States is based on the idea that citizens are free self-governing individuals who are not bound by religious morals or natural laws, as in premodern history. As autonomous individuals "in a state of nature," citizens will not tolerate a government which tries to impose on them a particular religion or lifestyle.

This political system is based on the idea of a social contract among individuals guaranteeing basic ethical and legal rights, chiefly among them the right to private property. Government's authority is limited, and much of the administrative law system is designed to limit agency power to solve collective problems.

Social critics like Henry David Thoreau, who believed that nature teaches values and wisdom not found in commercial society, have typically been considered to be out of step with mainstream political values. The "pastoral," as opposed to the "progressive," vision of American society has seemed undemocratic, because it argues against an instrumental concept of nature—as a source of minerals, water, timber and other raw materials to fuel the agricultural and industrial economy (Taylor, 1992).

The pastoral vision of society appears, at first glance, to be a simple, nostalgic view of the ideal society, consisting of communal authority historically found in small villages and towns. The recent interest in "communitarian" theory, however, suggests that this vision is still very much with us. The call for a renewal of community, as opposed to the more legalistic society, reflects the understanding that, while some communities were once highly parochial, they nevertheless provided people with basic securities in a social and cultural matrix (Daly and Cobb, 1989).

Modern economies (both capitalist *and* socialist) have encouraged people to pursue their subjective preferences, free of moral criticism. Benjamin Barber, another communitarian theorist, argues that individual rights have been won by the ruthless severing of ties and the uprooting of human nature from its foundations in nature, history, and a sense of the divine in the universe (Barber, 1989).

A Communitarian Approach to Mediation

A number of factors point toward an expanded role for environmental mediation. The new environmental agenda calls for a more proactive and cooperative relationship between government and the private sector. The Administrative Dispute Resolution Act has put more emphasis than traditional administrative law on mediation between federal agencies and environmental groups. Finally, the political climate seems ripe for a return to roots in community.

The communitarian critique of liberalism is more than an academic debate. The public mood seems to be one of weariness with the constant struggle for economic survival, especially in the face of persistent recession and evidence that community seems to be breaking down around them. Public opinion polls show a shift in popular attitudes and a spread of "post-modern" values.

Robert Paehelke believes that these new values constitute the essential core of an environmental perspective. Among these new values is "a belief that human societies ought to be reestablished on a more sustainable technical and physical basis" (Paehelke, 1989). Other public opinion analysts concur with this interpretation (Olsen et al., 1992).

Many small, rural communities in Nebraska, for example, are working together to save their family farms and to practice sustainable agriculture. Along the eastern seaboard, town hall meetings are being convened to address the prospects of economic ruin from overfishing. On the west coast, community-based initiatives to enroll public and private properties in conservation reserves are aimed at mitigating the extinction of plant and animal species.

There is a danger, of course, that people will retreat into private, sectarian groups instead of engaging in an open and inclusive public dialogue. For example, local opposition to plans anticipating the long-term social and environmental costs of development in a region may stem from resentment against perceived threats to individual and family economic survival. These fears, though understandable, are a barrier to public dialogue.

The Nebraska START Economic Development program has several features resembling a "consensus process" used by environmental mediators (Crowfoot and Wondolleck, 1990). The emphasis of START is on helping local planning teams to create a shared vision of themselves as communities and to reframe strategic issues from narrow, instrumental questions about how to attract new industries to more fundamental concerns about whether new industries would actually benefit the community as a whole.

From the point at which members of a steering committee begin to realize that they have been entrusting local economic development decisions to the private sector (and usually to a small group of individuals), they are ready to develop a *community* economic strategic plan. The process becomes a difficult and painful effort to reconstitute the members of the steering committee as a civic community (Reed and Reed, 1987:521-530).

Douglas Amy, in his book *The Politics of Environmental Mediation*, points out that a communitarian vision of politics often underlies nonadversarial approaches, like mediation. Historically, this vision flourished in colonial religious communities, such as the Quakers. Like the "pastoral vision" described earlier, the communitarian ideal has meant physical, social, and political isolation from the surrounding competitive society (Amy, 1987).

Mediation, however, is far from a utopian or isolationist vision. The process of working toward a shared vision can be very difficult for the participants and mediator alike. It is much simpler for each individual to pursue his or her self-interest, at least in the short run. The belief that individual actions are isolated decisions in a free market is a powerful rationale for avoiding participation in a town hall meeting or public arena.

Undoubtedly, there will be environmental disputes taking the win-lose form of interest group bargaining and compromise. Nevertheless, methods are now available to reframe many conflicts in the ways suggested in this chapter. The key to their successful use is a public sense that such methods as negotiated rule-making and alternative dispute resolution do not unfairly advantage powerful interest groups.

SUMMARY AND CONCLUSIONS

The difficulty with using the courts to resolve environmental disputes is that the parties are forced by the nature of the adversarial process to fight for their side as the morally correct position. There may, in fact, be a certain number and type of disputes requiring adjudication. In the environmental arena, however, the moral impact of a decision more often stems from what is best for the community as a whole, including the surrounding ecosystem.

Knowledge about which human activities are consistent with protecting biodiversity and preventing the effects of pollution will vary from one bioregion to another and will involve a search for a viable conception of the good life (Norton, 1991). Such a contextual analysis of environmental problems can only be performed effectively at the community level. Once an issue is in the court system, the scope of the conflict has already expanded beyond the point at which mediation is a viable alternative.

The experience of the U.S. Forest Service with mediation of local forest plans suggests that when decision making is decentralized and when bureaucratic rules and regulations are suspended, a public space is created, enabling participants to choose what is best for the community as a whole.

Forest Service managers discovered that what they once thought were neutral, scientific management practices in fact "represent[ed] value-driven trade-offs between competing uses of the same resource" (Manring, 1993:354). Mediation, in their experience, was more than a process of informal bargaining and compromise. It was a method for reframing the issues in ways that recognized and respected the perspective of the local community.

Communitarian approaches to conflict resolution, though superior to litigation, depend on public institutions which were designed to discover and create a common good (Mansbridge, 1990). Institutional norms ensure that mediation can occur in a fundamentally democratic way—among equals. Environmental mediation, especially when the objective is sustainable communities, holds great promise as a vehicle for renewed public dialogue about our common fate on the planet Earth.

Chapter 3

Environmental Mediation:
What Do We Know and How Do We Know It?

Rosemary O'Leary

The purpose of this chapter is to assess the major themes in the literature concerning environmental mediation. The term *environmental mediation*, as used in this chapter, is defined quite broadly to incorporate environmental dispute resolution generally. Environmental dispute resolution means the variety of approaches that allow parties to meet face to face to reach a mutually acceptable resolution of the issues in a dispute or potentially controversial situation (Bingham, 1986). It is often viewed as intervention between conflicting parties or viewpoints to promote reconciliation, settlement, compromise, or understanding in the environmental arena (McCrory, 1981). This includes mere assistance from a neutral third party to the negotiation process (Bingham et al., 1987). Such assistance can be directed toward settling disputes arising out of past events or can be directed toward establishing rules to govern future conduct, such as in the case of regulatory negotiation (Eisenberg, 1976).

Two questions are raised concerning the environmental mediation literature. First, what do we think we know about environmental mediation? Second, how do we know what we know? That is, are there any *empirical* foundations to what we know? *Empirical* is defined as follows: "It must rely on perceptions, experience, and observations. Perception is a fundamental tenet of the scientific approach, and it is achieved through our senses. . . . Knowledge is held to be a product of one's experiences, as facets of the physical, biological, and social world play upon the senses. . . . [It is based on the assumption that] pure reason alone is [in]sufficient to produce verifiable knowledge" (Nachmias and Nachmias, 1987:9-10). Hence, the primary concern is whether there is evidence-based research to support the claims for environmental mediation in the literature surveyed here.

This chapter concludes that, despite the plethora of literature touting the advantages of environmental mediation (and, at times, the disadvantages), the empirical foundations for most of the conclusions are quite weak. While there are some strong conceptual works, few scholars have studied environmental mediation through one or more of the standard empirical methods: theoretically informed case studies, comparative case analyses, surveys, interviews, and statistical analyses of quantitative data. Given the paucity of empirically based research, it must be concluded that much of our "knowledge" concerning environmental mediation is based primarily on thoughtful speculation or wisdom, with few data (broadly defined) to support it.

A few caveats are in order. First, the literature cited here is not the only scholarly discourse on the subject. (A supplementary bibliography of recommended readings is included at the end of this chapter for interested readers.) I have selected what I consider to be only those works that address some of the most fundamental issues in environmental mediation today. These include the key elements of environmental disputes, the supposed success of environmental mediation, and factors that contribute to the success or failure of mediation efforts in the environmental arena.

Second, surveying methods of inquiry in the literature proved to be an immense challenge with imprecise results. In many cases, the authors did not articulate in their works what their methods of inquiry or sources of data were. In such instances, there was no choice but to infer methodology from the context of the work.

Third, not all findings presented here are created equal. They were taken directly from the literature, as presented by the authors. Some address very specific and narrowly defined areas of environmental mediation; others are broader in nature. Differences in wording and coverage of the findings reflect the different approaches to this type of research found in the literature.

Fourth, by assessing the empirical nature of the following works, it is not intended to imply that empiricism is "good" while other types of research are "bad." The intention is not to judge but rather to map the collective observations and claims of authors in the field. The hope is that, by assessing the evidence concerning environmental mediation, both gaps in the literature and future opportunities for research will become evident.

The following are the major findings in the literature concerning environmental mediation. They have been divided into several broad themes, including findings concerning the parties, motivation to negotiate, the role of government officials, goals, timing, the importance of issues, the role of morals and values, the role of mediators and facilitators, power, implementation, education, structure and process, and high-tech alternatives.

THE KEY ELEMENTS OF ENVIRONMENTAL DISPUTES

Most of the literature on environmental mediation maintains (without citing empirical evidence) that there are characteristics of environmental disputes that add to the complexity of environmental mediation. These characteristics include: multiple forums for decision making; inter-organizational, as opposed to interpersonal, conflicts; multiple parties; multiple issues; technical complexity and scientific uncertainty; unequal power and resources; and public/political arenas for problem solving. McCarthy and Shorett (1984), without citing much empirical evidence but impliedly basing their conclusions on their experiences as mediators, point out that a crucial feature of environmental disputes is that they typically involve decisions concerning fundamental and irreversible alterations in the physical environment. Smith, in a work edited by Sandole and Sandole-Staroste (1987), makes similar statements without citing empirical evidence but implying that the conclusions are based on the author's experience with the U.S. Geological Survey. Environmental disputes also are often characterized by one side controlling the technical data, writes Riesel (1985), citing two case studies.

Without citing any empirical evidence, Susskind (1978) makes five major claims concerning environmental disputes: First, in most environmental disputes, a few individuals or groups are in the position of paying a high cost so that others can win modest gains. Second, environmental disputes tend to pit those who stand to gain short-term economic advantages against others who fear long-term environmental losses. Third, in most environmental disputes, the supposed benefits are easier to describe than the alleged costs. Fourth, in most environmental disputes, it is difficult to let the individuals most affected by a decision have the greatest say because of expansive boundaries, externalities, or spillovers. Fifth, groups that stand to lose if an environmental project proceeds find it easier to organize than those that have something to gain (with the exception of generations yet unborn).

Also without citing any empirical evidence but impliedly basing this conclusion on "wisdom" gleaned from experience with the U.S. Geological Survey, Smith (1987), in the work by Sandole and Sandole-Staroste, claims that mediation seems to be particularly relevant to the 60 to 70 percent of environmental cases that appear to be caused simply by misinformation. This statement is seemingly confirmed by Carpenter and Kennedy (1985), who maintain that lack of necessary information encourages conflict in the environmental arena. Carpenter and Kennedy's conclusion is based on their experiences as environmental mediators.

While not all the claims in the environmental mediation literature concerning the key elements of environmental disputes are presented without empirical evidence, when such evidence is presented, it is sketchy at best. For example, basing his findings on six case studies, Talbot (1983) concluded that an estimated 90 percent of environmental cases in which mediators are involved never reach an agreement. A more convincing study with a broader empirical base was done by Harter (1982), who, after examining sixty case studies proposed for negotiation, concluded that only six were in fact negotiable.

The primary weaknesses of these conclusions are that they come primarily from insider accounts and nontheoretically informed case studies. Further, the reader is seemingly asked by the authors to "trust me" without ample evidence being proffered for the authors' assertions. Moreover, few of these works are comparative in nature. For example, as Blackburn (1988) points out, few studies compare environmental mediations with litigation. In sum, there are few studies that demonstrate conclusively the common elements of environmental mediations.

THE SUPPOSED SUCCESS OF ENVIRONMENTAL MEDIATION

Claims concerning the supposed success of environmental mediation abound. Again, what is interesting about the literature is that these "findings" as presented are seemingly based on little, if any, empirical evidence. Examples of the top claims concerning environmental mediation and the "evidence" upon which they are based include the following:

- Mediation has played a significant role in resolving environmental disputes [O'Connor, 1978 (based on a survey of the opinions of mediators)];
- Most environmental mediation has occurred in the context of "major" disputes [O'Connor, 1978 (based on a survey of the opinions of mediators)];
- Mediation is a "compelling alternative" to the use of courts or the legislative process [O'Connor, 1978 (based on a survey of the opinions of mediators)];
- For environmental conflicts, mediation can achieve more expeditious and lasting processing than ordinary litigation [Talbot, 1983 (based on six case studies)];
- Environmental mediation is more likely than the courts to move parties away from purely competitive bargaining toward consideration of a wider range of positions and options than they were willing to consider [Richman, in Sandole and Sandole-Staroste, eds., 1987 (based on a case study of the Corps of Engineers and general mediation theory)];
- Environmental mediation of nonconformance penalties under the Clean Air Act and pesticide emergency exemptions under the Federal Insecticide, Fungicide and Rodenticide Act of the EPA have yielded the "meaningful participation of all those known to have a stake in the outcome" [Croce, 1985 (no empirical evidence cited; based primarily on previous comments of Susskind and Ruckelshaus)];
- The give and take of environmental negotiation provides "an opportunity to explore the rationale and needs of the participants which often leads to an approach satisfactory to all" [Croce, 1985 (no empirical evidence cited; based primarily on previous comments of Susskind and Ruckelshaus)];
- Perhaps the single most important outcome of environmental negotiations is that the participants develop a greater understanding of the interests of the other parties [Schneider and Tohn, 1985 (based on case studies of two EPA negotiated rulemakings in which the authors participated)];
- Most environmental mediations have been initiated by individuals who have hoped to serve as mediators [O'Connor, 1978 (based on a survey of the opinions of mediators)];

- The regulatory-negotiation process of the EPA "seems to be meeting the expectations of producing more balanced rules in a less adversarial fashion, reducing the likelihood of costly litigation" [Croce, 1985 (no empirical evidence cited; based primarily on previous comments of Susskind and Ruckelshaus)];
- The potential advantages of environmental mediation include (1) the possibility that it may facilitate more direct and meaningful participation in the regulatory process by interested parties; (2) the possibility that it may enhance the efficiency of the regulatory process, reducing delays and encouraging timely resolution of contentious issues; and (3) the possibility that it will yield more enduring and satisfying resolutions of contentious issues [Amy, 1983a (thought piece based on a case study of Portage Island, Washington, and secondary sources)].

Not all the conclusions concerning the success of environmental mediation are positive, however. Some authors find reason for pause, or at least skepticism. Here is a sampling of those findings:

- It is still too soon to say that the negotiation of environmental rulemaking significantly reduces the likelihood of litigation [Schneider and Tohn, 1985 (based on case studies of two EPA negotiated rulemakings in which the authors participated)];
- The dangers of environmental negotiated rulemaking include preexisting centers of power, self-regulation by powerful minorities, problems defining and identifying affected interests, lack of accountability of advocacy groups, circumvention of national policy because of decentralization, time and money [Rodwin, 1982 (no empirical evidence cited; based on logic and conceptual thinking)];
- The potential disadvantages of environmental mediation include (1) the possibility that the congenial atmosphere created by mediators serves to disarm and co-opt environmentalists; (2) the possibility that superior political and economic resources create imbalances of power that allow pro-development interests to extract unfair concessions from environmentalists at the bargaining table; and (3) the possibility that the mediation process itself tends to redefine environmental issues in a way that favors pro-development interests [Amy, 1983b (thought piece based on interviews, reports, and other secondary sources); see also Amy, 1987].

Weaknesses of these conclusions are the value judgments and measurement difficulties inherent in attempting to ascertain "success" or "failure." Further, most of the conclusions presented lack precision. For example, few authors define what they mean by "significant role," "major disputes," "compelling alternative," "lasting results," "meaningful participation," "satisfactory results," "greater understanding," "less adversarial," "efficiency," "timely resolution," "enduring and satisfying resolution," and "create imbalances." At best we have in the environmental mediation literature a handful of examples that are built on a very thin empirical base and are not generalizable.

WHAT CONTRIBUTES TO THE SUCCESS AND
FAILURE OF ENVIRONMENTAL MEDIATION?

The literature is replete with wisdom concerning what works and what doesn't work in the field of environmental mediation. Generally, it is maintained by O'Connor (1978), who surveyed the opinions of mediators, that certain ingredients contribute to successful environmental mediation (such as the desire to resolve differences, commitment, a neutral third party, understanding of technical issues, compromises, and written agreements). Susskind (1985), basing his conclusions on three mediated negotiations of the EPA, OSHA, and the Federal Aeronautics Administration, maintains that there are five common ingredients to successful mediated negotiations (including environmental regulatory negotiation): (1) participation by representatives of key stakeholding interests who are able and willing to commit their membership; (2) joint fact-finding; (3) face-to-face negotiation, typically aided by a nonpartisan mediator or facilitator; (4) a focus on inventing the best possible ways of dealing with differences; and (5) the preparation of a written agreement that all parties agree to help implement.

Schneider and Tohn (1985) concluded from examining two EPA negotiated rulemakings that written agreements are important to reaching consensus. After examining 81 "failed" environmental mediations, Buckle and Thomas-Buckle (1986) concluded that while mediators of "failed" environmental negotiations generally felt that the lack of a written agreement was a sign of failure, participants and observers reported an appreciation of the process and the education derived from the process.

Most authors agree with the commonsensical conclusion that key parties to an environmental controversy must participate in mediations for them to be successful. Nash and Susskind (1987) make this observation based on case studies of municipal solid waste incineration. At the same time, Susskind, McMahon, and Rolley (1987) make the same observation without citing any empirical evidence. A similar conclusion is made by Gusman (1983), without offering any empirical evidence, who wrote that interested parties must be involved in the negotiator selection process to the maximum extent that is practical.

Structure and Process

In commenting on the importance of the structure of environmental mediations and the process utilized, many claims are made. Dotson (1983), basing his conclusions on case studies of townhouse, housing, and shopping center disputes, maintains that the structuring of negotiations is a vital precondition for successful mediations. Carpenter and Kennedy (1985) maintain, based on their experiences as environmental mediators, that the first principle of managing environmental conflict is that "to find a good solution, you have to understand the problem," while the second principle of managing environmental conflict is that "planning a strategy can help you reach a better solution."

Similarly, the same authors (again based on their experiences as environmental mediators) maintain that the parties to a dispute must be involved in designing the process and developing the solution because ownership in the process leads to problem-solving. Basing his agreement on an examination of sixty case studies, Harter (1982) writes that in order to facilitate the process, the parties should establish a set of ground rules to guide the negotiations. Citing two case studies, Riesel (1985) agrees.

The use of process to differentiate between interests and positions is a major theme in the environmental mediation literature. It is interesting to note, however, that the same claim is made whether there is empirical evidence to back it up or not. Priscoli (1987), for example, writes that process can make a difference in separating people from problems and interests from positions, based on an examination of case studies of wetland fill and hydrocarbon exploration. Citing little empirical evidence, Fisher and Ury (1981) write that underlying interests, rather than prior positions, provide a basis for seeing new options and possible settlements. Their conclusions are based primarily on their own experiences, theory, and common sense. Dotson (1983) comes to a similar conclusion based on his case studies of townhouse, housing, and shopping center disputes. Putting it another way, Bingham (1986), in an impressive examination of 161 case studies of environmental mediation, maintains that the consensus-building process appears to be important in terms of whether parties are able to identify the basic interests that underlie one another's specific positions in relation to the perceived issues of the conflict. Finally, a common "truism" found throughout the environmental mediation literature is that lasting solutions are based on interests rather than positions [see, e.g., Carpenter and Kennedy, 1985 (based on experiences as environmental mediators) and Riesel, 1985 (citing two case studies)].

The Parties

There is a paucity of empirical data concerning who actually has participated in environmental mediations. The best data come from an examination of 161 cases of environmental mediation, in which one author found that 82 percent of the disputes involved units of government, while 35 percent involved environmental groups and 34 percent involved private corporations. In only 21 percent of the case studies were environmental groups and private companies pitted against each other (Bingham, 1986).

The literature is conflicting about the importance of limiting the number of parties that participate in an environmental mediation. Rocking the boat is Bingham (1986), who concluded that the likelihood of an agreement in an environmental mediation is *not* clearly affected by the number of parties involved. The vast majority of the literature (which is based on far less empirical evidence), however, concludes otherwise. Major findings, for example, include the following: The number of people involved in environmental mediation must be limited. Limiting the size of an audience and extending specific invitations may increase the likelihood that the desired people will participate [Nash and Susskind, 1987 (based on case studies of municipal solid waste incineration)]. There is a rough practical limit on the numbers of participants to around 15 parties [Harter, 1982 (based on sixty case studies); McCarthy and Shorett, 1984 (little empirical evidence cited, but based on authors' experiences as environmental mediators); and Priscoli, 1987 (based on case studies of wetland fill and hydrocarbon exploration)]. The number of clearly identifiable parties with authority to bind others must be limited in number [Marcus, Nadel, and Merrikin, 1984 (based on case studies and legal analyses concerning the Nuclear Regulatory Commission)].

Most authors agree that the parties substantially affected by the negotiations must be included in the negotiations. See, for example, Gusman and Harter, 1986 (based on case studies of hazardous waste siting, site cleanup, and regulatory negotiation); Dotson, 1983 (based on case studies of townhouse, housing, and shopping center disputes); and McCarthy and Shorett, 1984 (little empirical evidence cited, but based on authors' experiences as environmental mediators).

Also a given by most authors is the importance of constituencies. Riesel (1985), for example, writes that the parties must be truly representative of their constituencies and be able to deliver when a deal is struck (two cases studies cited). Dotson (1983) writes that constituents must be kept apprised of the progress of mediation. Failure to check back with constituents can be fatal (based on case studies of townhouse, housing, and shopping center disputes). Susskind, McMahon, and Rolley (1987) make the same claim but cite no empirical evidence.

Finally, Carpenter and Kennedy (1985) maintain that their experiences as environmental mediators cause them to conclude that human relations are as important as technical data. At the same time, however, the same authors conclude that the parties must agree on basic data.

Motivation

A pivotal finding in the literature is that without incentives to negotiate, the conflicting parties often believe they will achieve more of what they want from staying embroiled in the conflict and not reaching consensus [Bingham, 1986 (based on 161 case studies of environmental mediation)]. Hence, it is necessary for all parties to have strong motivations to participate in the mediations. Put another way, negotiated rulemaking is unlikely to succeed unless all parties, including government agencies, are motivated throughout the negotiations by a perception that a negotiated rule would be preferable to a rule developed under traditional processes [Perritt, 1986b (based on four rulemaking negotiations, including two for the EPA)].

Overall incentives to participate in environmental mediation include mitigation of adverse impacts, compensation for actual damages, rewards for assuming risks, and allowing public access to decision making. While Sorensen, Soderstrom, and Carnes (1984) cite no empirical evidence for this conclusion, the authors call for trial of their conclusions through empirical tests and evaluation.

Finally, the most serious incentive (at least for not-for-profit environmental groups) *not* to participate in an environmental mediation, according to Doniger (1987), is lack of money. This conclusion was based on the author's participation in two EPA negotiated rulemakings.

The Role of Government Officials

There is an interesting debate in the environmental mediation literature centering around whether government officials and agencies should be involved in such mediations and the pros and cons of their involvement. Perritt (1986b), basing his observations on an examination of four rulemaking negotiations, including two for the EPA, maintains that a government agency sponsoring a negotiated rulemaking should take part in the negotiations. Further, Perritt writes, government agencies should recognize that negotiations can be useful at several stages of rulemaking proceedings. Taking a stronger stance are Forester and Stitzel (1989), who maintain that activist mediation by government planners is a viable, practical, and ethically desirable strategy. It is interesting to note that these conclusions are not based on empirical evidence but on theory as well as the results of a training simulation.

Harter (1982) maintains that it may be more appropriate for government officials to participate in negotiated rulemaking than previously thought because they have realized a diminution of power from their former status as "sovereign decisionmaker[s]," they might be able to conserve resources, and they might be able to save time. Further, if agreement is reached among the parties without government interaction, the parties may not have any indication of what may be acceptable to the agency. Harter's conclusions are based on an impressive examination of sixty case studies.

Pluses of government participation are many. Participation by government officials can play a vital role in legitimating the negotiation process for other participants (Dotson,1983) (based on case studies of townhouse, housing, and shopping center disputes). Wondolleck (1985) reached the same conclusion. He examined case studies of national forest planning and found that the most valuable impacts a government official can have involved not so much determining a specific outcome but in affecting who is involved; how issues are framed; what information is utilized; how alternatives are developed, analyzed and evaluated; how trade-offs are made; and how implementation and monitoring are carried out.

Several authors, however, see significant problems with the participation of government officials in environmental mediations. First, not all circumstances are appropriate for government officials to participate, especially when they may be reluctant to give away power (Dotson, 1983). Tied in with this, there is concern about whether government mediators can be held sufficiently accountable to the interests of the public at large [Susskind and Ozawa, 1983 (based on three case studies, two of them dealing in part with environmental mediation)].

Citing little empirical evidence but touting their experiences as environmental mediators, McCarthy and Shorett (1984) maintain that government officials are sometimes skeptical or even hostile to environmental mediation on the grounds that the public interest is not necessarily represented in a negotiated settlement. Offering greater empirical evidence in a study of nine cases of environmental conflicts under the National Environmental Policy Act (NEPA), Sachs (1982) outlines obstacles to the use of environmental mediation by federal government agencies: the agencies were operating under formal, often mandated procedures; federal officials feared that use of dispute resolution techniques would violate the Administrative Procedure Act; the agencies were themselves partisan or feared the appearance of partisanship if they were to sponsor mediations; agency officials either did not understand the dispute resolution process or had false information about the process; government officials perceived the process as encompassing more work, less control, legal challenges, and high risks; government attorneys feared that their court cases would be weakened; there was a lack of money; there was no precedent or case history; there was fear of departing from the status quo; there was a lack of support from the highest echelons of the agency; there was difficulty working across jurisdictional boundaries; and agency-wide interim reporting requirements would reveal agency positions to other participants in the mediation process.

Richard Mays, Senior Enforcement Counsel, Office of Enforcement and Compliance, U.S. Environmental Protection Agency, similarly maintains (based on his experience in the agency) that alternative dispute resolution (ADR) techniques generally have met resistance in the enforcement arm of the EPA because of the lack of management commitment, the view that ADR techniques are insufficiently aggressive ways to deal with polluters, the difficulty in identifying proper subjects for binding forms of ADR, and budgetary constraints (Bingham et al., 1987).

But all is not lost. One author concluded that many of the problems with government officials can be countered by consciousness raising through training. A survey of government officials who participated in environmental mediation workshops indicates that after the training, participants perceived a greater understanding of conflict situations, altered how they interacted with their constituent groups, were more sensitive to how and what data they applied to decision making, and were more aware of what alternatives they considered [Wondolleck, 1988a (based on a survey of 214 participants in the U.S. Forest Service workshops with a 72 percent response rate)].

Finally, one author maintains that environmental mediation can be particularly useful in disputes between and among government agencies (i.e., in intergovernmental relations) because the parties hold some interests in common [Dotson, in Sandole and Sandole-Staroste, eds., 1987]. The author cites no empirical evidence but bases his conclusions on insights gleaned from his experiences at the Institute for Environmental Negotiation.

Goals

The environmental mediation literature generally has little to say about the importance of goals. The main study that emerges on the topic is that done by Nash and Susskind (1987). Basing their view on case studies of municipal solid waste incineration, the authors conclude that the goals of environmental mediation must be well defined. Further, they maintain that similar goals must be shared by participants. Finally, Nash and Susskind posit that if advocates with divergent goals are allowed to participate in an environmental mediation, barriers to consensus building may arise. The use of experts whose opinions and goals are rigid and widely divergent may foster public mistrust and confusion.

Timing

There are mixed opinions in the environmental mediation literature concerning the timing of a mediation effort. Citing no empirical evidence for their conclusion, Susskind, McMahon, and Rolley (1987) maintain that mediation can work either in the early or late stages of conflict. Gusman and Harter (1986), examining case studies of hazardous waste siting, site cleanup and regulatory negotiation, and Priscoli (1987), examining case studies of wetland fill and hydrocarbon exploration, conclude that the pressure of a deadline must be present before the parties will be ready to sit down at the table. Contradicting these findings is Bingham's 1986 analysis of 161 case studies of environmental mediation. She found that the likelihood of an agreement in an environmental mediation is *not* clearly affected by the pressure of a deadline.

Most authors, however, agree that the issues must be "ripe," readily apparent, and that the parties must be ready to address them [Harter, 1982 (based on sixty case studies); McCarthy and Shorett, 1984 (little empirical evidence cited, but based on authors' experiences as environmental mediators); Gusman and Harter, 1986 (based on case studies of hazardous waste siting, site cleanup, and regulatory negotiation); and Priscoli, 1987 (based on case studies of wetland fill and hydrocarbon exploration)]. Marcus, Nadel, and Merrikin (1984), however, strongly maintain that only through a case-by-case examination can it be determined whether a specific dispute—as opposed to general issue categories—is appropriate for regulatory negotiation. Their conclusions are based on case studies and legal analyses concerning the Nuclear Regulatory Commission.

Issues

"Ripeness" is not the only important facet of environmental mediation issues. The content of issues, as well as the number of issues, has been the subject of much debate in the literature. Bingham, for example, based on her study of 161 cases, concluded that the likelihood of an agreement in an environmental mediation is *not* clearly affected by the content of the issues themselves. Seemingly contradicting these findings is the work of Marcus, Nadel, and Merrikin (1984), based on case studies and legal analyses concerning the Nuclear Regulatory Commission. Those authors concluded that issues for which the potential benefits of negotiation are the greatest are also likely to be issues for which negotiation is least feasible. Second, they concluded that issues that rank highest with respect to the potential benefits of regulatory negotiation rank lowest with respect to feasibility and vice versa. Finally, the authors concluded that specific categories of issues for which the potential benefits of negotiation would be the greatest are waste management, environmental protection, and emergency response because of the contentiousness, cost, and time involved.

There seems to be consensus in the literature concerning the importance of multiple issues in environmental mediations. Multiple issues surfacing simultaneously can be helpful in giving each party some of what it wants, according to Gusman and Harter (1986), who analyzed case studies of hazardous waste siting, site cleanup, and regulatory negotiation. Moreover, successful negotiations are unlikely when there is only a single item that is subject to dispute, since parties must be able to prioritize issues and trade off positions [Marcus, Nadel, and Merrikin, 1984 (based on case studies and legal analyses concerning the Nuclear Regulatory Commission)].

Finally, Doniger (1987) maintains that there is a limited range of environmental topics and issues appropriate for negotiation. Therefore, there is a risk that environmental negotiation will be promoted simply for its own sake. The author bases his conclusions on his participation in two EPA negotiated rulemakings.

Morals and Values

The topic of morals and values is an important one in the environmental mediation literature. Most authors agree with Gusman and Harter (1986) and

Susskind, McMahon, and Rolley (1987) that disputes involving moral judgments like right and wrong are rarely mediable. It is interesting to note that Gusman and Harter base their conclusions on case studies of hazardous waste siting, site cleanup, and regulatory negotiation, while Susskind, McMahon, and Rolley fail to cite any empirical evidence. Tied in with this, another popular conclusion in the literature is that agreement is unlikely if parties must compromise fundamental values. [See, for example, Harter, 1982 (based on sixty case studies) and Priscoli, 1987 (based on case studies of wetland fill and hydrocarbon exploration)].

Citizens' values also are important in environmental mediation efforts. Accordingly, Beatty (1991) maintains that survey research can be a useful tool in identifying citizens' values (based on a case study of air pollution in Colorado Springs).

The Role of Mediators and Facilitators

A mediator or a facilitator can be significantly helpful in resolving complex, multiparty issues, according to Gusman and Harter's (1986) analysis of case studies of hazardous waste siting, site cleanup, and regulatory negotiation. But what, exactly, are appropriate roles for the environmental mediator or the environmental facilitator? The literature is rich with suggestions.

First, a neutral mediator or facilitator can be useful in identifying interested parties and determining whether they are willing to negotiate in good faith. In fact, many authors maintain that such action is a key factor in promoting a harmonious process. [See, for example, Harter, 1982 (based on sixty case studies); Riesel, 1985 (two cases studies cited); and Croce, 1985 (no empirical evidence cited; the author bases his conclusions on previous comments of Susskind and Ruckelshaus)].

Second, mediators should do dispute assessments. According to Bingham's (1986) study of 161 case studies of environmental mediation, success in environmental mediation is increased by mediators doing a dispute assessment prior to any mediation in order to help the parties decide whether to participate and whether the particular dispute is amenable to mediation. Riesel (1985) agreed and wrote that an environmental mediator must often do a considerable amount of pre-negotiation leg-work (two cases studies cited).

Third, mediators should lay out the costs and benefits of mediation for the parties. According to Riesel (1985), an environmental mediator must help the parties recognize some of the real costs they face if the matter is not resolved through negotiation. Again, Riesel bases his conclusions on two case studies.

Fourth, a mediator/facilitator can help participants prepare for negotiations by clarifying values [Dotson, 1983 (based on case studies of townhouse, housing, and shopping center disputes)].

Fifth, a major job of the environmental mediator is to deal with the usual inequality of information among parties and, in effect, the inequality of power among parties [Riesel, 1985 (two cases studies cited)].

Sixth, an environmental mediator should help build trust among the parties. The long-term success of mediation depends in large part on the extent to which others are willing to trust a broker and refer cases for mediation, according to Dotson (1983), who based his conclusions on case studies of townhouse, housing, and shopping center disputes. Tied in with this, Riesel (1985) maintains that the skilled environmental mediator will encourage the parties to make intermediate concessions that will assist in the building of trust.

What *shouldn't* an environmental mediator, facilitator, or negotiator do? Without citing any empirical evidence, Susskind, McMahon and Rolley (1987) argue that a mediator should not be passive, since a passive mediator can hinder successful negotiation. In addition, Priscoli (1987) maintains that the mediator or negotiator must not lose his or her semblance of neutrality. Facilitators must be perceived as neutral parties to a conflict in order to be successful. Priscoli bases his conclusions on case studies of wetland fill and hydrocarbon exploration.

Other findings concerning the role of environmental mediators and facilitators are more diffuse. Perritt (1986), for example, maintains that a government agency sponsoring a negotiated rulemaking proceeding should select a person skilled in techniques of dispute resolution to assist the negotiating group in reaching an agreement. That agency, the mediator or facilitator, and (where appropriate) other participants should be prepared to address disagreements within a particular constituency. Perritt based his conclusions on four rulemaking negotiations, including two for the EPA.

Schneider and Tohn (1985) maintain that when working with large committees, a team of mediators, rather than a single person, is more effective. They base their conclusions on case studies of two EPA negotiated rulemakings in which they participated. The authors maintain that having a team of specialists (e.g., economists and statisticians) as members of a mediation team helps address issues that demand technical expertise.

What kind of preparation is best for environmental mediators or facilitators? There are two schools of thought concerning training: the process/procedure school and the substance school. Most authors make the commonsensical claim that a combination of substantive and process skills is probably the ideal. (See, e.g., Dotson, in Sandole and Sandole-Staroste, eds., 1987. Dotson does not cite any empirical evidence but bases his insights based on his experience at the Institute for Environmental Negotiation.)

Power

The importance of power differentials is widely discussed. Most authors agree that if power is unequal, the parties will not negotiate. Parties must perceive interdependence and be constrained from acting unilaterally. At the same time, each of the parties must have sufficient power to exercise some sanction over the ability of other parties to take unilateral action. [See, e.g., Harter, 1982 (based on sixty studies); McCarthy and Shorett, 1984 (little empirical evidence cited, but based on authors' experiences as environmental mediators); Gusman and Harter, 1986 (based on studies of hazardous waste siting, site cleanup, and regulatory negotiation); and Priscoli, 1987 (based on studies of wetland fill and hydrocarbon exploration).]

Implementation

The importance of implementation considerations permeates the environmental mediation literature. Some means of implementing the final agreement must be available and acceptable to the parties, according to Priscoli's (1987) analysis of case studies of wetland fill and hydrocarbon exploration. Further, the parties will be unlikely to negotiate seriously if the ultimate agreement is not likely to be implemented, according to Marcus, Nadel, and Merrikin (1984), who based their conclusions on case studies and legal analyses concerning the Nuclear Regulatory Commission. Finally, and perhaps most importantly, the factor most clearly associated with environmental agreements being reached is whether the people with the authority to implement the decision participated directly in the mediation process, according to Bingham's (1986) analysis of 161 case studies of environmental mediation.

High-Tech Alternatives

A final theme in the environmental mediation literature concerns the use of computers. Computer modeling of the diverse interests of parties may provide negotiators with a sense of reality about the relative outcomes of different options, according to Nyhart (1983), based on a case study of the Law of the Sea negotiations. A computer mediator used in a telephone conferencing setting may limit polarization because individuals are drawn into a dialogue early in a dispute, according to Stodolsky (1980). In one experiment, the computer selected speakers in the order in which they requested to speak. In another setting, the computer resolved conflicting requests to speak in favor of the person who had thus far spoken the least. Mediation participants also were able to indicate anonymously when they felt a speaker was in error, which eliminated group pressure as an impediment to reaching consensus.

SUMMARY AND CONCLUSIONS

This chapter has provided an overview of some of the major conclusions found in the environmental mediation literature. How do we know what we know? We know what we know primarily through atheoretical case studies, "wisdom" derived from the experiences of environmental mediators, and conceptual thinking. There is little rigorous empirical evidence to back up much of the claims just presented. While case studies, insider accounts, and conceptual thinking are necessary prerequisites of sustainable research in this area, they are not sufficient. We need survey research and additional comparative case studies that examine not just the spectacular cases but also the less-spectacular, less-successful cases of environmental mediation. Moreover, we need additional studies of what interventions are more likely to be successful than others under what conditions, as well as long-range longitudinal studies of the outcomes of environmental mediation efforts, to see if such agreements really last. Most important, we need an adequate theoretical base from which researchers can predict effects, test them, and ascertain, in a more systematic and rigorous fashion, the impact of environmental mediation.

OTHER RECOMMENDED READINGS

(See bibliography for complete citations.)

Bacharach and Lawler, "Power Dependence and Power Paradoxes in Bargaining," 1986
Bacow and Wheeler, *Environmental Dispute Resolution*, 1987
Baldwin, *Environmental Planning and Management*, 1985
Bankert, Flint, Editors, *Environmental Dispute Resolution in the Great Lakes Region: A Critical Appraisal*, 1988
Bazerman, "Negotiator Judgment," 1983
Brunet, "The Costs of Environmental Alternative Dispute Resolution," 1988
Burton, "Ethical Discontinuities in Public-Private Sector Negotiation," 1990
Carpenter and Kennedy, *Managing Public Disputes*, 1988
Colosi, "Negotiating in the Public and Private Sectors," 1983
Cormick, "The 'Theory' and Practice of Environmental Mediation," 1980
Cormick, "Strategic Issues in Structuring Multi-Party Public Policy Negotiations," 1989
Coulson, "Must Mediated Settlements Be Fair?" 1988
Crable, "ADR: A Solution to Environmental Disputes," 1993
Druckman, Editor, *Negotiations*, 1977
Druckman, Brome, and Korper, "Value Differences and Conflict Resolution," 1988
Dryzek and Hunter, "Environmental Mediation for International Problems," 1987
Fiorino, "Regulatory Negotiation as a Policy Process," 1988
Fisher, "Beyond Yes," 1985
Fisher, "Negotiating Power," 1983
Fisher, "The Structure of Negotiation: An Alternative Model," 1986

Fisher, "Third Party Consultation as a Method of Intergroup Conflict Resolution," 1983

Fisher and Brown, *Getting Together: Building a Relationship That Gets to Yes*, 1988

Fisher and Davis, "Six Basic Interpersonal Skills for a Negotiator's Repertoire," 1987

Fisher and Keashly, "Third Party Interventions in Intergroup Conflict: Consultation is *Not* Mediation," 1988

Forester, "Envisioning the Politics of Public-Sector Dispute Resolution," 1992

Frankena, *Environmental Mediation: A Bibliography*, 1988

Frankena and Frankena, *Citizen Participation in Environmental Affairs, 1970-1986: A Bibliography*, 1988

Fuller, "Mediation—Its Forms and Functions," 1971

Gaffney and Loeffler, "State-Sponsored Environmental Mediation: The Alaska Forest Practices Act," 1991

Galanter, "Reading the Landscape of Disputes: What We Know and Don't Know (And Think We Know) About Our Allegedly Contentious and Litigious Society," 1983

Gellhorne, Dunlop, Edwards and Kuhl, "Alternative Means of Dispute Resolution in Government: A Sense of Perspective," 1987

Goldberg, Green, and Sander, *Dispute Resolution*, 1985

Greenhalgh, "The Case Against Winning in Negotiations," 1987a

Greenhalgh, "Relationships in Negotiations," 1987b

Gunton and Flynn, "Resolving Environmental Conflicts: The Role of Mediation and Negotiation," 1992

Halbert and Lee, "The Timber, Fish and Wildlife Agreement: Implementing Alternative Dispute Resolution in Washington State," 1990

Harter, "Negotiated Rulemaking: An Overview," 1987

Harter, "Points on a Continuum: Dispute Resolution Procedures and the Administrative Process," 1987

Harter, Thomas, McMurray, Fleming, and Millhauser, "Institutionalizing Alternative Dispute Resolution: Where Does the Government Go From Here?" 1987

Hensler, "Science in the Court: Is There a Role for Alternative Dispute Resolution?" 1991

Hettwer, "Ethical Factors in Environmental Negotiation," 1991

Hill, "Negotiating Superfund Mixed Funding Settlements," 1991

Hoard and Lyons, "Negotiating with Environmental Regulatory Agencies: Working Towards Harmony," 1989

Holznagle, "Negotiation and Mediation: The Newest Approach to Hazardous Waste Facility Siting," 1986

Jacobs, "The Concept of Adversary Participation," 1988a

Jacobs, *Predicting the Utility of Environmental Mediation: Natural Resource* and *Conflict Typologies as a Guide to Environmental Conflict Assessment, 1988b*

Johnson, "Negotiating Environmental and Development Disputes," 1986

Kartez, "Planning for Cooperation in Environmental Dilemmas," 1991

Kolb, "Corporate Ombudsman and Organization Conflict Resolution," 1987

Kubasek, "Environmental Mediation," 1988

Lake, Editor, *Resolving Locational Conflict*, 1987

Landis-Stamp, "The Mediation of Environmental Conflicts," 1991

Langbein and Kerwin, "Implementation, Negotiation and Compliance in Environmental and Safety Regulation," 1985

Lax and Sebenius, "Interests: The Measure of Negotiation," 1986a

Lax and Sebenius, "Three Ethical Issues in Negotiation," 1986b

Lentz, "The Labor Model for Mediation and Its Application to the Resolution of Environmental Disputes," 1986

Levinson, "Environmental Dispute Resolution and Policy Making," 1988

Liepmann, "Confidentiality in Environmental Mediation: Should Third Parties Have Access to the Process?" 1986

Lobel, "Addressing Environmental Disputes with Labor Mediation Skills," 1992

Lyden, Twight, and Tuchmann, "Citizen Participation in Long-Range Planning: The RPA Experience," 1990

MacDonnell, "Environmental Dispute Resolution: An Overview," 1988

Macklin, "Promoting Settlement, Foregoing the Facts," 1986

Mank, "The Two-Headed Dragon of Siting and Cleaning Up Hazardous Waste Dumps: Can Economic Incentives or Mediation Slay the Monster?" 1991

Manring, West, and Bidol, "Social Impact Assessment and Environmental Conflict Management: Potential for Integration and Application," 1990

Mays, "Alternative Dispute Resolution and Environmental Enforcement: A Noble Experiment or a Lost Cause?" 1988

Mays, "The Need for Innovative Environmental Enforcement," 1986

Meyers, "Old-Growth Forests, the Owl, and Yew: Environmental Ethics Versus Traditional Dispute Resolution under the Endangered Species Act and Other Public Lands and Resources Laws," 1990

Miller, *Fundamentals of Negotiation: A Guide for Environmental Professionals*, 1989

Miller and Sarat, "Grievances, Claims, and Disputes: Assessing the Adversary Culture," 1980

Mills, *Conflict Resolution and Public Policy*, 1990

Mintz, "Agencies, Congress and Regulatory Enforcement: A Review of EPA's Hazardous Waste Enforcement Effort, 1970-1987," 1988

Moore, *The Mediation Process: Practical Strategies for Resolving Conflict*, 1986

Mosher, "EPA, Looking for Better Way to Settle Rules Disputes, Tries Some Mediation," 1983

Murray, "Understanding Competing Theories of Negotiation," 1986

Nader, "Disputing Without the Force of Law," 1979

Nakamura, Church, and Cooper, "Environmental Dispute Resolution and Hazardous Waste Cleanups: A Cautionary Tale of Policy Implementation," 1991

Nyhart and Dauer, "A Preliminary Analysis of the Uses of Scientific Models in Dispute Prevention, Management and Resolution," 1986

Olpin, Doniger, Crohn, Schatzow, Calvani, and Eisner, "Applying Alternative Dispute Resolution to Rulemaking," 1987

Olson, "The Quiet Shift of Power: Office of Management and Budget Supervision of Environmental Protection Agency Rulemaking Under Executive Order 12291," 1984

Painter, "The Future of Environmental Dispute Resolution," 1988

Perritt, "Negotiated Rulemaking Before Federal Agencies: Evaluation of Recommendations by the Administrative Conference of the United States," 1986 ·

Porter, "Environmental Negotiation: Its Potential and Its Economic Efficiency," 1988

Potapchuk and Carlson, "Using Conflict Analysis to Determine Intervention Techniques," 1987

Pruitt, "Strategic Choice in Negotiation," 1983

Rabe, "The Politics of Environmental Dispute Resolution," 1988

Raiffa, "Mediation of Conflicts," 1983

Riggs and Dorminey, "Federal Agencies' Use of Alterative Means of Dispute Resolution," 1987

Robbins, "Conflict Management and Conflict Resolution Are Not Synonymous Terms," 1978

Ross, "Situational Factors and Alternative Dispute Resolution," 1988

Ross and Saunders, Editors, *Growing Demands on a Shrinking Heritage*, 1992

Rubin and Sander, "When Should We Use Agents? Direct vs. Representative Negotiation," 1988

Rubino, *Mediation and Negotiation for Planning, Land Use Management, and Environmental Protection: An Annotated Bibliography of Materials, 1980-1989*, 1990

Saunders, "We Need a Larger Theory of Negotiation: The Importance of Pre-Negotiating Phases," 1985

Singer, "Arbitration Journal Report: The Use of ADR Methods in Environmental Disputes," 1992

Sjostedt, Editor, *International Environmental Negotiation*, 1993

Stephenson and Pops, "Conflict Resolution Methods and the Policy Process," 1989

Sternberg and Soriano, "Styles of Conflict Resolution," 1984

Sullivan, *Resolving Development Disputes Through Negotiations*, 1984

Touval, "Multilateral Negotiation: An Analytic Approach," 1989

Wald, Coulson, Cormick, Willard, Morrison, and Bruff, "Uses for Alternative Dispute Resolution: Better Ways to Resolve Some Public Sector Controversies," 1987

Zartman, "Common Elements in the Analysis of the Negotiation Process," 1988

Chapter 4

Mediating Environmental Disputes: Borrowing Ideas from a Law and Economics Perspective

Peter R. Maida

More and more, mediation is used to resolve disagreements between people about how the environment is used. Avoiding litigation in environmental conflicts minimizes time and cost and helps community stakeholders in a disagreement achieve interest-based goals. Mediators facilitate communication between disputants and manage negotiations between them. Some suggest mediation is helpful in resolving environmental disputes if the dispute is not complex, if all the parties are represented, if the impact of the agreement is short-term, and so forth.

IDEAS FROM A LAW AND ECONOMICS PERSPECTIVE

Does an inquiry into the economic dynamics of a dispute about the environment add anything to the extant body of knowledge and theory about mediation? (G. Cohen, 1985; Posner, 1972) Painter states, "the old science and the old negotiation strategies will *not* serve the new field of environmental disputes well. The field requires an integrated conceptual base that is as flexible as the environment and unmechanical as human dialogue" (Posner, 1988:146; Crable, 1993).

For the analysis in this chapter, concepts and processes are "borrowed" from the law and economics perspective in the tradition of interdisciplinary inquiry. As we know, many disciplines have contributed to the research, theory, and practice of mediation. One area of thought, relatively unexplored, is the rational-economic explanation of human motivation and behavior. With respect to decision making in the context of disagreements in which laws or rules are relevant, what can a law and economics perspective contribute? Grabbing a limited number of concepts and processes and running with them does not imply that this chapter is a treatise on law and economics. On the contrary, ideas were borrowed for their heuristic value; could they provide more insight than we already have about what happens when we mediate a disagreement in which the court and administrative agencies are likely to become involved?

The relationship between law and economics has been controversial (Polinsky, 1989). Problems in the relationship between the traditionalist approach to legal analysis and the law and economics camp are not the focus here. Our focus is whether the borrowed ideas inform us about the appropriateness of mediation for managing environmental disputes.

To accomplish our goal in this chapter, the following format is used: selected law and economic concepts are discussed; the stages of mediation are defined; an analysis of the mediation of environmental disputes is presented using some ideas from law and economics; some caveats about using mediation in environmental disputes are addressed; and concluding observations are offered.

Disputes typically involve claims for sole ownership of, sole use of, or indivisibility of resources. In environmental disputes, parties argue over who will use the resource and under what conditions they will be used. A private owner of wetlands may want to fill in an area to build houses and the municipality, state government, or federal agency will not permit the fill-in.

Although not the specific focus of this chapter, some mention of the major role administrative agencies have in environmental dispute resolution is warranted. First, they may, through their rules encourage the use of alternative dispute resolution. Second, administrative rules and environmental legislation provide standards that constrain mediation decisions. The EPA Office of Enforcement and Compliance Monitoring has developed criteria and procedures for agencies if they choose to use ADR.

Public interests and private ownership rights conflict with respect to use of land. If another resource can be substituted, the dispute doesn't exist. What ideas from a law and economics perspective will help us understand disagreement when interests of stakeholders are in conflict? To answer this question, the following will be discussed: rational decision making; uncertainty and risk; strategic behavior; transaction costs; and agreements.

ECONOMIC PRINCIPLES AND ECONOMIC ANALYSIS

Rational Decision Making

One way to understand decision making in disagreements is to think of decisions as the result of a rational process whereby, as much as possible, we weigh a number of potential choices and choose one to act on after some deliberation. Three principles explain rational choice in resolving problems when what we want outpaces what is available. First, there is an inverse relation between price and quantity. Second, all of us try to maximize utility. Third, in a free market, resources seek their most valuable use. Let's take these ideas and elaborate on them.

We generally determine the value placed on benefits and costs when we are making a decision about how to act. These values do not vary according to changes in public policy and thus are considered fairly stable. Utility maximization is a way of describing how we act, with some thought given to whether the benefit of acting exceeds the costs. In communities, the unequal distribution of resources or assets among citizens is evidence that most people behave efficiently and not necessarily fairly. We will generally choose the "bundle" of goods that maximizes satisfaction. In this perspective, very narrow economic parameters explain changes in choice.

In our formal contractual relationships with others, we may prefer an efficient over an equitable resolution if a disagreement occurs because of the difficulty in deciding how to distribute scarce resources to achieve equity. We have come to rely on the application of legal rules for the equitable distribution of resources. However, legal rules often sacrifice efficiency to accomplish equity. Legal rules, ideally, should provide incentives for conforming behavior and allocate risk evenly. Do legal rules create incentives for efficient behavior? Whether we behave more fairly than efficiently depends upon whether the legal rules allocate risks evenly or shift risks to third parties not involved in the disagreement. The extent that legal rules do not allocate or shift risk is related to how fairly or efficiently we behave.

Uncertainty and Risk

In a disagreement about use of environmental resources, our decision making is a balancing act; the risk that an action will produce a particular output is balanced with the uncertainty of producing that output. Some of us are risk neutral and rank the prospects of a particular outcome in the exact order of what would be expected if all extraneous values were equal. Risk averse decision makers, on the other hand, discount an expected outcome of higher value (that is worth more to them) and trade it for an outcome of lower value in order to reduce the risk associated with their choice. Those of us who are risk prone select a higher value outcome although it departs significantly from what would be expected with all extraneous factors being equal.

When the norms governing potential choices are more numerous, the degree of risk associated with decision making increases because the number of extraneous variables increases. Risk can be reduced in four ways: party-to-party transfers; risk spreading or pooling; changing by one of the parties the amount of risk associated with a particular outcome; decreasing the number of extraneous variables. If we know the allocation of risk, or if risk is minimal, we will act more equitably. If we can't evaluate the risk, we behave efficiently. With disputes for which the number of unknowns is great (e.g., availability of resources, future behavior of an adversary, role of the court, and so forth), the tendency is to behave efficiently rather than equitably.

Strategic Behavior

Resolving our disagreements involves thinking about the strategy that reduces risks and costs and increases benefits regardless of whether efficient or equitable. Nonetheless, an interesting hypothesis in much law and economics literature is that given the choice, most people will behave efficiently. I suspect nondraconian motivation prevails here; we just can't be certain of all the extraneous risks involved. Holding out for a fairer agreement rather than an efficient one is a transaction cost of strategic behavior. As we position in a disagreement, the most efficient solution is one that represents some, not all, of our interests. The same can be said of our adversary. In this sense, equity is sacrificed for efficiency. An example helps explain this. Assume you and your adversary have ten interests and each of you is positioning because you want to receive all ten. Less than twenty interests can be delivered in any possible solution to the conflict. If either of you has all ten interests met, the other may not have any interests met. Is this an equitable solution? A legal rule may prescribe a particular distribution of interests. Perhaps litigation produces a result in which one of you wins (has all ten interests met) and the other loses (has no interests met). However, if you negotiate efficiently, each of you may end up with some interests realized, say eight or nine each. The solution is efficient since each of you maximizes your positions.

In a particular environmental dispute (e.g., issuance of particulate airborne matter by a factory), if some disputed behavior is allowed (i.e., each party has some interests met), an efficient solution results. Allowing some pollution in an environmental dispute may be more efficient than prohibiting all pollution. The least-cost solution or the Coase theorem is used in the law and economics perspective to describe how the rational actor increases efficiency by reducing costs. In an environmental dispute, if the complainant could costlessly (zero transaction cost scenario) get together with the polluter and negotiate, an efficient outcome would occur. If there is a conflict between efficiency and income and the legal rule does not distribute income costlessly, there will be a distributional effect. Income is redistributed costlessly (zero transaction costs) according to the least-cost solution. When legal rules redistribute income to make the resolution of a problem equitable, efficiency is sacrificed.

Transaction Costs and the Law

Laws that minimize the impact of transaction costs on efficiency are the preferred rule. Transaction costs include costs associated with inefficient choices.

In the resolution of conflict, if rules increase costs associated with resolution, the most efficient solution is not chosen unless the effect of the rule is minimized. The efficient solution to a conflict is the one in which the pie to be divided has been made larger. In an equitable solution to conflict, the size of the pie doesn't increase, but the division is more equal or fairer. In an equitable rather than an efficient solution to a conflict, each party gets less. Conceivably, the fairness issue is a relative one because if efficiency is maximized in the negotiation, the party receiving "less" in an efficient solution will receive more than in an equitable solution to the conflict.

Litigation, injunctions, damages. In litigation, community stakeholders in a disagreement take strategic positions increasing transaction costs, and thus the potential for an efficient solution is reduced. With injunctions courts must have information to decide which outcome maximizes each parties' interests (i.e., the efficient solution). In an injunction scenario, courts cannot reach efficient solutions to conflict. A damages remedy requires courts to know the actual damages to set liability. Courts can reach efficient outcomes in damage suits if they give an absolute entitlement to the "wronged" party and liability and damages are equal. However, environmental disputes are distinguished by easily assessed damages as well as damages that are difficult to assess because of the unknown future, or damages about which there is disagreement among the experts as to the magnitude of the cost.

Information and the application of law. Any limit on information fuels conflict, thereby increasing transactions costs. According to Carpenter and Kennedy,

> conflict is natural and necessary in a free society. But disputes are increasingly damaging and costly, and the consequences of not finding wise solutions become more and more grave. In the United States, we depend on outmoded methods for resolving disputes. The adversarial approach works in some situations but produces avoidable costs and defective conclusions in others. (1985:161)

Or, according to Phillips and Piazza, "The most important function of any negotiation is to educate the parties about their own and opposing interests. This enables them to take into account the perspectives and needs of all parties to the dispute in considering settlement options" (1983:1237). The educational process facilitates substituting one interest for another.

Agreements

Agreements lay out the results of negotiation. If the agreement is efficient, each party will have maximized the joint benefits net of the joint costs. Violations of the agreement are classified as either efficient or inefficient. An inefficient violation results when the benefit is less than the cost. A reduction in efficiency may even increase equity. But ultimately, both parties may have less after an inefficient violation than they would have if the violation did not occur. Inefficient violations should be deterred, keeping in mind the transaction costs involved. High transaction costs increase the damage of an inefficient violation to the point that it may be necessary to negotiate a new agreement.

Are negotiations in which parties' interests are jointly maximized in an efficient violation always preferred? For example, in spite of a prohibition against polluting, a factory and residents of the community have an agreement about the amount of particulate matter released into the environment. Each party has maximized its interest. Residents now have central air conditioning, and the air is filtered more efficiently. Factories can produce more, pollute more, and save money at the same time. The negative impact on the residents is not as great because they can remain healthier in their homes and the factory is providing the community with more jobs and increased working hours. Each party has maximized its interests even though there is a violation of a prohibition. The next step is to negotiate an efficient solution of the pollution outside the home.

While endorsing mediation of environmental disputes, Painter argues that a refinement of negotiation theory is needed to explain behavior in an environmental context. Does maximizing one's self-interest rule out the possibility of acting in the public good? According to Painter, "it is possible, it seems, to choose to act in the community's interest, it is even rewarding, provided that one doesn't lose sight of one's own interest. . . . Processes that encourage recognition of motivating self-interest *and* a motivation to act for the community's good are called for in the future" (1988:169-170). A law that would deliver more interests to each party would be efficient but not necessarily equitable. Any agreement reached by the parties addresses future behavior. Future behavior regulates the use of the resources. Uncertainty as to unanticipated consequences is diminished by reducing the risk that parties will not be communicating with one another. The argument that environmental disputes are difficult to resolve because of the unknown future is weakened. Perhaps the impact of toxic waste or pollution is hard to foresee. Nevertheless, an aspect of uncertainty about the future is how those who disagree with us are going to behave with respect to a particular issue. Agreements can include provisions for future action, thus reducing one aspect of uncertainty.

Summary

We resolve our conflicts rationally, maximizing utility and seeking the most valuable use of the disputed resource. A rational approach is the most efficient one. An efficient resolution of conflict is the maximizing of benefits minus costs. In the face of uncertainty, maximization is difficult and demands risk-taking by the disputants. The comfort level of disputants varies in the face of uncertainty and risk. Regulatory agencies and the court may intervene to increase certainty and reduce risk, thereby creating incentives for dispute resolution. Incentives are not always efficient, and resources are not always equitably allocated. Likewise, incentives don't necessarily reduce uncertainty. This is particularly true if incentives are vague or their enforcement is weak. When risk and uncertainty are reduced and the parties are free to negotiate a resolution of their conflict, an optimal situation occurs.

MEDIATION

Mediation consists of third party impartial assistance for disputants in resolving a disagreement (Gunton and Flynn, 1992; Rennie, 1989). Typically, mediation consists of several distinct steps. Determining whether mediation is appropriate in a particular dispute is the first. Through interviews, data collection, and so forth, we assess the appropriateness of mediation in managing the particular dispute. If it is appropriate to proceed, we would convene the group of stakeholders in the disagreement to inform them of the rules of mediation, such as confidentiality (Liepmann, 1986). Or the parties can develop mutually acceptable rules in an orientation session. With environmental disputes, this may also include stipulations as to what issues the stakeholders will mediate. In the next, the fact finding step, we gather information about the disagreement. Sharing and exchanging information by the parties characterizes this step. Fact-finding is a cooperative effort rather than an opportunity for the parties to withhold important information from one another. Issues to be addressed in the mediation are gleaned from the facts of the disagreement.

Disputants next are encouraged to develop options that could be considered possible solutions to their disagreement. Options should reflect the interests of the parties. Next comes the negotiation between the stakeholders. At this time, relevant power discrepancies between parties should have been resolved so that negotiations occur on a level playing field. That is, one party is not negotiating from a significantly stronger position than the other. As negotiations proceed, an agreement takes shape.

Agreements contain specific details of each party's obligations in the future. Agreements lay out in positive terms future behavior for each party. Future problems are addressed in agreements insofar as they are predictable. Many agreements contain a clause that encourages disputants to return to mediation if an unforeseen problem cannot be mutually resolved. Also, the mediation clause encourages a return to mediation if conditions in the agreement are not met.

Next is the implementation of the agreement. Mediation agreements typically stipulate conditions for implementation. Here, testing of the agreement occurs. Adjustments to the plan will be made, when necessary, by the parties or by returning to mediation. Finally, the efforts to resolve the disagreement are viewed in retrospect. The parties, along with stakeholders, assess how successful the mediation was in generating solutions to the disagreement.

Mediation and Environmental Disputes

Environmental disputes reflect differences in opinion about resource use. Proposed uses often are contradictory (e.g., save a resource for wilderness development or strip mine the area). Not only does resource use involve highly complex scientific documentation, it also is characterized by a great deal of uncertainty. In addition, "an action that benefits some may harm others. For example, a sand and gravel operation benefits the landowner, the operator, and the users of the material; but the noise, dust, traffic and other undesirable effects may harm adjacent property owners. A waste disposal site benefits those generating the waste, but is likely to be resisted by neighboring property owners" (MacDonnell, 1988:7).

In an article that has now become a classic, Bingham and Haygood chronicle the use of dispute resolution from the years 1974 to 1984 in air quality, land use, natural resource management and public land use, water resources, energy, and toxic substance disputes (Bingham and Haygood, 1986). According to the authors,

> there are several characteristics of environmental disputes that make mediation particularly appropriate. In many environmental disputes, the parties have no prior negotiating relationship; the disputes tend to be interorganizational rather than interpersonal; they involve multiple parties with wide disparities in power and resources; there may be technical issues involving data interpretation and scientific uncertainty; and the disputes may involve issues affecting the broader public interest. (Bingham and Haygood 1986:4)

Mediation: An Economic Perspective

What is the interface between mediating environmental disputes and ideas borrowed from a law and economics perspective? Each step in mediation has economic consequences. Previously, we selected and discussed some important concepts and processes because of their potential utility in understanding the economic dimensions of decision making in environmental disputes.

Determining appropriateness. To assess whether the disagreement is appropriate to mediate, we would ask questions such as:

1. Is the degree of uncertainty so great that even the most risk-positive individual would not negotiate in a utility maximizing fashion?

2. Are externalities such as administrative rules and procedures that provide incentives and strive for equity going to increase transaction costs to prohibit an economically efficient resolution of the conflict?

3. Is it possible to translate the unknown future into present certainty through an agreement about how to negotiate over problems in the future?

These and other questions comprise the groundwork necessary for the mediator to determine if it makes any sense to use mediation.

Mediators can also design an overall dispute resolution strategy (Carpenter and Kennedy, 1988; Watson and Danielson, 1982). In designing a strategy, some considerations are (a) defining the problem; (b) identifying external constraints; (c) establishing a conflict management goal including exchanging information and identifying issues and interests; (d) selecting a meeting structure; (e) identifying process steps; (f) determining who should participate; (g) defining other roles; (h) considering other process issues (Carpenter and Kennedy, 1988). Additionally, each of these steps can be rethought as to how they increase certainty and reduce risk, how they might influence stakeholders to negotiate for the efficient and not equitable solution, and so forth.

Orientation. If mediation is appropriate and the parties are willing, or mediation is mandated, the next step is to review the mediation rules. Mediators use rules to insure an orderly process. In environmental disputes, rules reduce uncertainty and risk as they relate to party behavior and potential outcome. Disputants may stipulate that they will not consider the unknown future or the concerns of a marginal interest group, thereby reducing uncertainty and risk. Transaction costs are reduced by such stipulations, and a resolution of conflict that maximizes utility is possible. If the mediator has misjudged the relevance of uncertainty (or any other variable, for that matter) and the rules are inappropriate, the mediation will be difficult.

Fact finding. Fact finding creates an optimal situation for maximizing utility. In this cooperative effort, information is shared. Prior to information sharing, risk includes the possibility that your opponent in the conflict has information that will be used to your detriment when he or she independently resolves the conflict with the objective goal of winning. Likewise, your opponent has this same fear. Sharing information reduces risk for both parties. Risk is not totally eliminated since the future is still unknown. However, even that risk can be reduced by agreeing to behave in a predictable way in the future. Fact finding also reduces transaction costs. If each party is forthcoming with information crucial to the resolution of the disagreement, and if the mediator has conducted fact finding thoroughly, a resolution of conflict maximizes benefits for each party.

Developing options. Here, stakeholders have an opportunity to propose a number of solutions to their disagreement. From an economic perspective, each solution may differ in the degree to which utility is maximized. Disputants can hear their opponent's options and have an opportunity, before negotiating, to evaluate them. Having an opportunity to evaluate an opponent's options helps a stakeholder in four ways: (a) uncertainty is reduced; (b) possible transaction costs are assessed; (c) options that may have never occurred to a party are presented; and (d) unknown and possibly common interests are revealed.

Public interest dispute litigation rarely resolves underlying issues based on the interests of the stakeholders in the dispute (*Mediation Quarterly*, Volume 20, Summer, 1988). According to Phillips and Piazza, "in some cases a litigant wants to secure a declaration of 'good law'. In others, a premium is placed on having an external agency make the decision. Frequently, accepting a negotiated resolution is perceived as weakening the future bargaining credibility of a party. In other cases a vindication of fundamental values is sought" (Phillips and Piazza, 1983:1236).

Option development is crucial for locating hazardous waste sites. States have increasingly used face-to-face negotiation assisted by an impartial third party in siting these facilities (Bacow and Milkey, 1982; Susskind, 1985). According to Susskind and Ozawa, "at a minimum, the prototype mediator arranges meetings, assists in the exchange of information, tenders proposals at the request of one party or another, and assists the parties in developing clearer statements of the interests" (Susskind and Ozawa, 1983:256).

Option building is also motivated by maximum utility, although the margin of error is greater because the range of possibilities before negotiation includes possibilities that have high transaction costs and therefore are inefficient. But option building does provide disputants with a preliminary exercise in testing out utility maximization.

Negotiation. A range of workable options is selected, and stakeholders begin to negotiate. During negotiation, solutions as to how the disagreement will be resolved are refined. In any dispute, including those involving environmental issues, when the conflict is costless (costs imposed by externalities and bad choices are nil), stakeholders negotiate to an equipoise of maximum utility. Hypothetically, a successful mediation is one in which costs have been reduced significantly to allow the parties to negotiate efficiently.

Agreement stage. Costless transactions should produce agreements to which the stakeholders are maximally committed. A common ingredient to mediated agreements, according to Susskind, is the commitment by those involved to implement the agreement (Susskind, 1985). Transaction costs in the resolution of disputes reduce efficiency and maximum utility, thereby reducing commitment. In this scenario, a violation might be necessary to maximize utility. As transaction costs increase, the effectiveness of the agreement is reduced and violations repeatedly occur. Enforcement of agreements by the courts or administrative agencies will not necessarily be effective in preventing violations if the imposed order by the court or agency favors an equitable rather than an efficient result. Parties will still work toward maximization of utility in isolation from one another, thereby increasing transaction costs. In the agreement, parties can decide to reduce uncertainty further by stipulating that for any future disagreements they will return to mediation.

Implementation and follow-up. Implementation and follow-up provide the last two opportunities for parties to maximize utility. During implementation it may be necessary to change the agreement because, as it stands, implementation would be difficult for a number of reasons. Theoretically, only those changes that result in efficient outcomes should be considered. Likewise, during a follow-up analysis, not only will compliance be noted but also adjustments in the agreement may have to be made. Lack of compliance might be a move toward efficiency.

SOME CAVEATS

Critics of mediation often look for certain signs to determine whether using mediation to resolve a disagreement was worth the effort. Mediation, after all, is not a panacea for all of a community's disagreements. For mediation to be worth the effort, it should:

1. result in a negotiated agreement that is acceptable to the parties involved;
2. appear fair to the community;
3. maximize joint gains;
4. take past precedents into consideration;
5. be reached with a minimal expenditure of time and money;
6. improve rather than aggravate the relationships between or among the disputing parties (Fisher, 1979);
7. result in an efficient settlement.

Whether the outcome was worth it is determined by:

1. restrictions on the flexibility of the mediation process that render it less efficient, thereby reducing maximization of utility;
2. the efficiency of the settlement;
3. the incentives that exist for maximizing utility;
4. the allocation of risk;
5. the extent of stakeholder representation;
6. the link between mediation and formal legislative, judicial, and administrative processes;
7. the incentives to bring all parties to the table;
8. community familiarity with mediation;
9. mediator competence.

Some would criticize mediation because its results may be inconsistent with substantive law. Stakeholders may create disputes to mediate the penalty. Even though this could be described as an efficient act, critics argue that it decreases the effectiveness of EPA enforcement efforts and undermines compliance programs.

Sometimes, stakeholders' positions are so far apart mediation will not help. For example, Folk-Williams describes problems with resolving the interests of Native American, and non-Native Americans; users and nonusers; and, public, private, and government agencies in the use of water (Folk-Williams, 1988). Incentives are often not powerful enough. If an interest group has no prospect for specific gains, it will not come to the negotiating table. Similarly, Folk-Williams discusses what he considers the most important factor in producing a final negotiated agreement:

deadlines. In economic terms, "a deadline is a point in time after which the potential costs and benefits to the parties will change markedly" (Folk-Williams, 1988:94).

SUMMARY AND CONCLUSIONS

The analysis in this chapter suggests a burgeoning theoretical explanation of disputants' choices based on several economic processes. At first blush, using concepts and processes from a law and economics perspective provides another, yet different, explanation of what happens in the mediation of environmental disputes. We have yet another way to think about the dynamics, in terms of the economic aspects of conflict resolution in community disagreements over use of the environment. Managing conflict, mediators help reduce uncertainty. Reduced risk for both risk averse and risk positive disputants reduces transaction costs. Conflict resolution, the goal of mediation, maximizes utility and leads to an efficient solution.

These and similar ideas will help us comprehend what impact our choices of strategies have on disputant decisionmaking. Also, we read a great deal about allowing stakeholders to express their interests; the mediated agreement is the parties' agreement, not the mediator's. Will stakeholders, if allowed to play a more active role, always choose the most efficient outcome? Such a possibility raises issues with regard to mediator impartiality and the ethical implications for mediators if they think stakeholders are agreeing to something that is not equitable.

In these instances, does the mediator decide that a particular disagreement should be litigated in the face of the belief that the court cannot achieve redistribution of risk and still be efficient? Perhaps mediators should promote efficiency, understanding that maximization of utility is inherently relatively fair. Some think the goal of negotiation between stakeholders is always efficiency, if not equity. Could the court have another purpose with respect to resolving environmental disputes, and what would that be?

Important empirical questions also flow from the analysis in this chapter. Legal as well as social and behavioral science researchers should help mediators understand the economic dynamics and implications of decision making by stakeholders in an environmental mediation. All those interested in the subject of mediating disputes involving disagreements about land use and the environment will not want for literature. What is lacking is a scholarly analysis of the dynamics of decision making in these kinds of disputes. Particularly lacking is research literature using a law and economics approach to explain decision making in disagreements about the environment. Further work on the conditions under which stakeholders make efficient decisions rather than equitable ones would be useful.

Chapter 5

Training Environmental Mediators:
A Community-Based Approach

John C. Allen

Environmental conflicts frequently develop, take form, and are resolved at the community level. Often, these communities are rural and geographically isolated. These locations, whether urban or rural, usually have their own culture and ways of developing leadership and of resolving conflict. Kenneth Wilkinson presents an argument that "community" is "an interactional field" providing for "both turbulence and cohesion, of order and disarray, of self-seeking and community-oriented interaction" (Wilkinson, 1991:7). Using this theoretical perspective, environmental mediation is a community phenomenon.

The training described here has as its primary premise that most environmental mediation will take place in a community setting, often rural. Therefore mediators must have an understanding of the differences between rural and urban value structures, organizational dynamics, and problem solving approaches. The following sections present a format for mediator training and substantive background useful for mediators in designing and managing mediation efforts.

CLASSROOM TRAINING: THE BEGINNING OF A PROCESS

The training for environmental mediators discussed in this section is an intensive two-day training session. The program begins on day one with an overview of the dynamics of community problem solving and how to develop a community profile. A small group exercise follows which provides practice in developing a community profile.

The development of a community profile is the foundation for understanding mediation in and among communities when facing conflict. A scenario is used based on a real-life community. Participants are then asked to conduct an assessment of the community or communities involved in the conflict.

Following the development of a community profile, participants are given the fundamentals for evaluating the various stages that community conflict generally goes through (Allen, 1992). The next phase of preparing for mediation is identifying the types of environmental conflict. These types of conflict can be clustered into "values" or "resource" areas.

The second day of training focuses on working in a group environment (often up to thirty individuals participate in environmental mediation) and developing a "game plan," or the mediation strategies the mediator or mediators decide upon. Role playing takes up the afternoon, with one participant randomly identified as the mediator and the other thirty participants playing the roles of active players in the conflict.

The close of the day focuses on "trouble shooting." This involves identifying where the problems are and what resources are available to facilitate the resolution of the disagreement. Finally, the day ends with a short session on how to manage stress in a community conflict situation.

It is important to note that all of the mediators participate in an actual mediation under supervision before they go on to mediate a dispute on their own. Preparation is the key to a successful environmental mediation.

BACKGROUND: THE ROLE OF THE MEDIATOR

The role of a mediator in a community or regional dispute goes beyond simply facilitating dialogue between disputing factions. A mediator must help select the key players from the community or region who will participate in the actual mediation. A mediator must identify the type of conflict that is occurring and the stage which the conflict has reached. Without these skills, it will be difficult, if not impossible, to develop a mediation process with thirty key community individuals and achieve what they perceive as a successful outcome.

The first step in preparing for mediation is the development of a community or regional profile. An understanding of the setting (i.e., a neighborhood, community, or region) is necessary before undertaking the preparation to conduct environmental mediation in a community environment.

INTERACTIONAL FIELD THEORY

To conduct mediation in a community environment, "interactional field theory" provides a theoretical background. Kaufman identified three elements of the community: a locality, a local society, and a process of locality oriented collective actions (Kaufman, 1959). Wilkinson continued development of interactional field theory and identified the third focus as a "community field" (Wilkinson, 1970).

The community provides a field of interaction for the manifestation of collective involvement and the social definition of the self. We examine here how interactional field theory provides a background for understanding the mediation of environmental disputes within a community framework.

Research supporting the community as a field of interaction which provides an arena for collective action has identified the notion of "strong ties" and "weak ties" among community residents (Granovetter, 1973). Understanding the strength of ties among individuals internal to the community and external to the community is important in facilitating environmental disputes. Those communities with strong internal ties but weak external ties are more likely to resist at a community level those resolutions developed involving both local residents and external interests. On the other hand, communities with many strong ties external to their community will be more likely to accept resolutions developed with outside players (external to the community).

Many environmental disputes take place in rural settings with residents who live in an interactional field with many strong internal ties but weak external ties. Because of this community form, identifying leaders within the community is important. They can represent differing groups within both the community, and the region which are linked through local ties. Representation in the mediation group by all, or a majority of, linked groups makes community support for the resolution more likely. Therefore, by thinking of the community or region as an interactional field and identifying those participants and their linkages to one another, players in the mediation process who correlate with the current community organizational form can be selected.

PREPARATION FOR WORKING IN
A COMMUNITY ENVIRONMENT

The mediators must gain an understanding of the community or region in which they are working. Developing a community profile is often viewed as time consuming and useless. Yet without a clear knowledge of the setting in which the mediation is to take place, cultural anomalies of the area can make resolving the conflict almost impossible. Therefore, mediators must begin the preparation of a mediation session with a community profile.

A community or regional profile has multiple uses for the mediator: to acclimate to the area; to sensitize to any particular cultural barriers; and to alert to any historical occurrences which may influence the mediation sessions.

A community profile should include several basic components: (1) current population; (2) basic industry; (3) distance from an urban area; (4) ethnic culture (i.e., German, Native American, French, etc.); (5) a brief overview of local history and any *major* historical events; (6) the identification of at least three formal local leaders (i.e., elected officials); (7) the identification of at least three informal local leaders (i.e., non-elected) and; (8) the identification of at least one individual in the community or area who could block a mediation success if he or she were excluded in developing a community profile. Another consideration is the identification of the power structure and the roles that different institutions play in the community. For example, the local school provides education but is also the repository of local historical artifacts.

The first three segments of the community profile are straightforward and can be gathered with little effort by simply contacting the local library or state population center. Finding information on ethnic culture may take a little more effort. Yet as Manik (1992) indicates, "social learning" is very much how constituents view environmental problems. Therefore, the cultural differences between groups must be identified and brought to bear on the resolution process.

The theoretical literature on communities and the adoption and diffusion of technology provide insight into the importance of understanding cultural differences in a mediation process. As Hassinger and Pinkerton explain, "the discussion of primary groups and informal networks shows the intricacies of interpersonal exchanges, the process of information dissemination and validation" (Hassinger and Pinkerton, 1986:149).

Information validation is an important component within the mediation process and can be facilitated or discouraged by the cultural heritage of a community or region. Gaining an understanding of the local validation process is important. Without understanding how locals validate information, the "wrong" people may be asked to be part of the mediation team, decreasing the possibility of acceptance of any resolution within the community. By selecting culturally acceptable leaders to participate in the process, validation may be facilitated.

The importance of validating the resolution of the conflict within the community cannot be overlooked. Therefore, selecting formal and informal leaders who represent different factions or groups is paramount. To identify local elected officials who are seen by the community as representing their interests, it is possible simply to ask local residents. The informal leaders, on the other hand, may be more difficult to identify but may be the most important component of the mediation effort. Informal leaders within the community or region can be identified by asking "key informants" in the community to identify the primary leaders in the community. Floyd Hunter (1980) advocated using a reputational method to identify formal and informal power leaders in a community. By identifying key informants—those local individuals who have a great deal of knowledge about the community or region—and having them identify the power leaders, the mediator can begin the process of leader identification. It is important to take the list of power leaders provided by the key informants to other key informants, hopefully from another socio-economic class, and ask them to duplicate the effort. After several attempts, a list of leaders will develop. These will include formal and informal leaders and will provide the basis for the mediation effort.

IDENTIFYING THE FORMS OF
ENVIRONMENTAL CONFLICT

Conflict is often viewed as being singular. That is, conflict is conflict is conflict. Previous research on disagreements has not supported that notion (Burgess, 1988). Conflict can be viewed in terms of "dissensus" or "consensus" (North Central Regional Center for Rural Development, 1979). To identify the form of conflict, it is important to pinpoint clearly the actual root of the problem.

Dissensus in conflict can be identified by listening to the parties involved. When dissensus is the base of conflict, the factions do not agree as to what is valued among the options facing them. The disputing parties use phrases such as *right or wrong* or terms such as *moral* or *immoral*.

Consensus in conflict can be identified because the major players in the disagreement view only one solution. The conflict is viewed as a win/lose situation where if one side gets the resource the other side does not. All sides are in agreement as to what is valued and the problem is basically a win-lose dichotomy. Members of the disagreeing groups use phrases such as *win it all* or *lose it all*.

Why is understanding the basis of the conflict important? An example will clarify: For an individual preparing to mediate a dispute, it is important to know in which way to guide the process.

In consensus conflicts, which can simply be identified as resource conflicts, disagreement exists over who gets the physical resource. This resource can be physical or human. Often residents of communities will all identify health as their primary value. They may view maintenance of a hospital as very important for their community. Yet the hospital is a physical structure with human resources, and competing communities will view the possibility of a single hospital for several communities as a win-lose situation. They disagree over where the resource should be located. These physical resources are seen as important for the economic and social maintenance of the community. The status of the community and its residents is viewed as part of the conflict.

This type of disagreement often calls for redefining the community boundaries. This is a very social process. Communities take one to two hundred years to develop social boundaries, and redefining these boundaries is a slow process. The mediator, while facilitating the selection of the mediation group, can encourage the selection of leaders outside the current community interactional field or territory. The mediation group will then encompass a larger interactional field or community. As the mediation group members attempt to resolve the current environmental dispute they see themselves, and their constituents see them, as being part of a larger interactional field or community. In this way new social relationships develop. These new relationships, or interaction patterns, provide a foundation for resolving the current dispute and begin the process of redefining community boundaries. Future resource conflicts will be easier to resolve because of the increased scope of the interactional field.

If dissensus is the basis for the conflict, a different strategy may be necessary. Dissensus, a value disagreement revolving around a particular issue or set of issues, needs to be discussed in the realm of personal and community values. The mediator must probe areas of agreement and disagreement concerning values as the participants discuss the cause of the dispute and any possible resolution. Negotiation over the way to retain values for all sides provides a forum for success in environmental mediation.

IDENTIFYING THE STAGE OF
THE ENVIRONMENTAL DISPUTE

Conflict can be viewed as moving through stages on a continuum. Understanding the stages of environmental conflict is important for the strategic planning of a mediation. When to agree to conduct a mediation is often guided by the actual stage of the disagreement. Conflict moves through three stages of disagreement. These stages include (1) build-up stage; (2) high conflict stage; and (3) post or new build-up stage.

The first stage of disagreement in a conflict is the build-up stage. During this stage, the members of communities move from discussing a broad range of local concerns, from the local basketball or football teams to the weather. Conversation then becomes focused on one or two issues. Factions which are easily identifiable to local residents have not developed during this stage. Vocal formal community leaders and informal leaders begin to identify supporters for a position on the issues being brought to the community level.

As community leaders, both formal and informal, gain supporters for issues being discussed, one issue often surfaces as the primary focus of discussion. The movement from a build-up stage to one of high conflict can be very rapid (a few days) or a slow, smoldering process that takes years. Often a primary factor in the speed of movement toward high conflict is the pressure exerted on community residents by external forces. The high conflict stage is one in which clear factions have developed. Community residents can readily identify supporters on one side or the other of the issue.

When the environmental conflict reaches a high conflict stage, the sides no longer interact in informal settings. Even how an individual interacts with other community residents is dictated by the conflict. Communication channels become formal. Public meetings, whether organized for the issue or not, become forums for emotional tirades and personal attacks on members of the other factions. Once formal interaction patterns develop, disagreeing members no longer feel a need to focus on the specifics of a problem. Personal attacks become the norm and historical differences are brought to the forefront of the argument. Dynamics of communities, especially rural communities, play an important part in how conflict is managed at a community level.

Homogeneity of population, low turnover of population, and often geographic isolation create certain dynamics in communities that can seriously impact successful mediation. When a population is fairly homogeneous (i.e., a large portion of the community members are a specific religion, ethnicity, cultural background, or type of employment). People have a great deal of personal information about one another. They interact in the same circles, school activities, religious activities, recreational activities, and work activities. Geographic isolation also encourages frequent interaction at individual, family, and community levels.

During the high conflict stage, these ecological factors provide an environment ripe for personal attacks. It is not uncommon during an environmental mediation to find letters to the editor which attack the morals of the disagreeing factions. These will often be followed up by formal presentations at public forums using examples of personal history, such as "your mother was promiscuous when she was a sophomore in high school. That is why you are the way you are and that's why other community members shouldn't follow you. You are immoral and it is a family trait." Often during the high conflict stage local newspapers will add an additional page or two for the multitude of letters to the editor. The traditional informal way of interacting in the community has broken down and communication is strictly within factions or through formal channels.

The post or new build-up stage often follows the high conflict stage if no resolution is reached. The amount of emotional energy required to maintain a conflict at the high conflict stage soon takes its toll, and parties involved in the dispute withdraw from the conflict. This stage can be identified by observing conversations within the community. A high level of sensitivity toward any subject is exhibited. Community members are hesitant to speak openly about traditionally mundane subjects. A fear develops that any stress placed on the interaction of the community members will result in a return to the high conflict stage. If no resolution is reached during the development of the conflict, the post or new build-up stage provides the foundation for the next conflict in the community. A cycle of continual disagreement develops.

IDENTIFICATION OF KEY PLAYERS
TO PARTICIPATE IN MEDIATION

To implement an environmental mediation, I suggest that about thirty individuals be selected from within the community and any external organizations involved in the dispute. The process of mediation takes place in a field of interaction identified as a community or region, including a variety of individuals who have formal and informal positions. These individuals represent their constituents in the "subculture" which emerges from interaction in small groups and communities (Fine and Kleinman, 1979). Those individuals who represent these different "subcultures" within a community must be made part of the mediation team. For a mediated resolution to be successful, various groups in the community must support it.

One way in which the members of the mediation group can be selected is to identify institutional groups within the community. They include (1) economic (local businesses); (2) religious; (3) educational; (4) legal/political; and (5) family. Local residents can be relied upon to help identify formal and informal leaders in the community. The mediator must also help search for groups that may not be represented. Lake (1980) encourages those who are participating in environmental mediation to make sure they have support for the process from those of lower socioeconomic classes within the community or region. These representatives will be required to go back to the groups they represent with ideas and for feedback, which can then be brought back to the mediation team and discussed. In this way, the total community becomes involved in the mediation, reducing the probability that the resolution will be sabotaged by any particular group or faction.

WORKING WITH THIRTY
POTENTIALLY HOSTILE PEOPLE

Once the preparation for mediation is completed, the type of conflict is identified, and the stage of the conflict and the mediation participants are identified and have agreed to participate, the actual mediation begins. The first session of the mediation should focus on the ground rules of mediation. These should include the role of the mediator. In mediation, the mediator has no legal authority and the role is to facilitate communication between the disputing parties. Confidentiality must be discussed. In the mediation that I conduct, I ask that all members of the mediation team sign a waiver. The waiver includes statements whereby the mediation participants waive the right to use information gained in the mediation in litigation.

The mediation sessions are generally "closed door," which means that how the team wants to work with the media must be discussed. One technique that has been successful in highly public disputes is to have the mediation participants take the last few minutes of each mediation session to draft a short press release that states the general issues being discussed. In this way, the media get some information; but the closed sessions allow the participants to disclose freely their values, positions, and desires.

Working with a group of thirty individuals who represent a variety of value systems, socioeconomic groups, and belief systems as to the import of the environment or the issues in dispute is at first intimidating. Some techniques can help the mediator keep the communication channels open between the participants. A mediator can "weight the room" by standing near the person who is attempting to speak to "support" the person talking. This supports the right to be heard. Hand signals can also be used. A horseshoe setting has been helpful for me, enabling me to move between the factions. By simply raising a hand, the mediator can cue the speakers that their turn to speak is up. In this way, the mediator educates the group in the mediation process without undermining their self-confidence or devaluing their personal beliefs.

A FOUR-STAGE MEDIATION PROCESS

Using a straightforward process that is supported by a long preparation period, it is possible to survive the ordeal of large group environmental mediation. The Institute of Cultural Affairs in Seattle, Washington has developed a method which works well in environmental mediation. The method facilitates "a structure of effective communication that provides for meaningful dialogue, broadens perspectives, results in clear ideas and conclusions and allows for the entire group to participate" (Institute of Cultural Affairs, 1990). The process has four stages: (1) objective; (2) reflective; (3) interpretive; and (4) decisional.

This model begins with getting the facts. The objective step allows each faction to define the facts as they know them. Breaking the large group into subgroups facilitates identification of "the facts," or problems, as seen by the different factions. When the subgroups return to the mediation table they present their "facts." Each group is expected to present the facts without discussion except for clarification of definitions.

The reflective step requires facilitating participants' discussion of their emotions, feelings, and associations pertaining to the topic. During this phase, the mediator(s) must allow "venting" by the participants. As mentioned, during the high conflict stage individuals within the community generate a great deal of emotional energy while failing to interact face-to-face with other residents. This venting process enables everyone in the group to learn about the emotional aspects of the disagreement. This levels the playing field and "we are all human" becomes part of the perceptions of all the other participants.

The interpretive stage occurs when the issues or problems are divided into similar areas. By moving through the listed problems and grouping by similar area, the mediation participants can then begin prioritizing the subissues. Numerical values are placed on the areas and meaning is placed on each of the subareas. The priority of the items to be discussed is then established.

The last phase of mediation is the decisional stage. Each subissue is addressed within the priority scheme identified and voted on by the mediation group. To gain consensus in a group of thirty individuals with differing views, straw votes are taken periodically. A final vote is taken on each decision made, and the group agrees to the decision or resolution. Consensus is reached as multiple straw votes are taken and positions of the mediation participants change. The voting process also identifies subareas in which consensus cannot be reached, and the group moves on to other subareas. Many mediators, especially those who have worked in family mediation or mediation between farmers and banks, have not traditionally supported taking a vote. The position has been that voting forces individuals into choices. In a large group mediation at the community level, individuals are playing two roles. The first is that of a member of a community. The second is that of a representative of a group within the community or region, or external organization or group. For the community to support the resolution, majority consensus must be reached.

As the mediation team works through each subissue of the dispute, decisions are made. These decisions are recorded and approved by everyone in the mediation group. At the conclusion of the mediation, a complete list of decisions is printed and each member of the mediation signs the list. The mediation participants as a group then publicly present their decisions to those public officials who have the authority to enforce the resolutions.

MENTORING: A TEAM APPROACH TO MEDIATION

Mediation is a learned skill and an art. The skills needed include the ability to prepare thoroughly for a mediation. Many individuals who have the desire to play the role of mediator are "process oriented." They believe in the value of social interaction. Yet social interaction is only one segment of mediation. Preparing to mediate often takes longer than doing an actual mediation. Therefore, patience on the front end of mediation is a virtue.

Personality characteristics are risky to identify, but several seem to be important for successful mediators. A mediator must develop the skill to remain objective and absorb the frustrations of the participants. The mediator is often viewed as the focal point of discussion. Participants may feel safe looking at and talking directly to the mediator rather than other participants with whom they have had confrontations. The mediator is often the "flow through" mechanism for a mediation. The mediator must be able to absorb psychologically the dislike from all sides in a dispute and reflect back positively to the group. In the beginning of mediation, the mediator is often viewed by the participants as supporting one side or the other. Balancing the need for open interaction, the need to control outbursts, and the need to show progress at the end of each mediation session requires strong interpersonal and organizational skills.

Team or co-mediation is one way to overcome a mediator's lack of particular skills or personality traits. Two mediators can debrief one another. One can identify points of the discussion for further probing while the other is facilitating the process. I believe that straw votes are necessary. The art of mediation is being able to identify the right moment to call for a straw vote and bring to closure the particular point of discussion. Overall, co-mediation can be an asset to any mediator, and I advise working in teams.

CONCLUSIONS

The process of environmental mediation is difficult and has many potential barriers to success. By conducting environmental mediation as a community process, many of the problems in developing consensus and supporting resolutions can be averted. Preparation is the key to any mediation process. The preparation includes developing a community profile and identifying the type of conflict, the stage the dispute is in, and the key players who must be part of the resolution process.

Once preparation for mediation is complete, the process begins. The mediator should realize that the participants in mediation will often suggest resolution strategies which are not legal. The mediator should plan to bring in experts to evaluate potential proposals as to their legality. This in no way diminishes the power of the mediation group but does save the group from the embarrassment of presenting the community with a resolution that is illegal and cannot be implemented.

Community-based mediation utilizes knowledge of the community and the groups which reside within its interactional field. As mediators begin to conduct mediation as a community process versus an individual or small group process, success becomes much more probable. Yet success at the mediation table is not the only benefit from mediating from a community viewpoint. Education also takes place. The mediation process, if viewed as experiential learning, provides a mechanism for community residents to learn the process of mediation and to carry the process over into other arenas of their lives. Many communities that I have worked with in mediation have continued to maintain their conflict resolution teams and have become involved in resolving conflict beyond environmental disputes.

Environmental mediation from a community-based approach is different from a simple legal approach to problem resolution. In litigation the current law dictates the decisions to be made. Mediation facilitates community and regional consensus leading to long-term resolution of conflict, and it also provides an educational component which can be carried over into multiple aspects of living in an interactional field.

Chapter 6

Midwest Energy Utilities

James B. Dworkin and G. Logan Jordan

This case illustrates the conflict that can arise over business decisions that affect the environment, and it may be conducted as a role playing exercise to emphasize the competitive nature of the dispute. Decisions impacting the environment involve the interests of a broad range of stakeholders and have been among the most legally challenged corporate and governmental decisions. Since lengthy litigation results in substantial monetary costs and time delays, an approach that generates the minimum challenge can significantly reduce implementation difficulties.

In this example, an electric utility is considering several alternatives in its planning for compliance with future air pollution standards. The utility, utility regulators, environmental regulators, environmental activists, and local community leaders all express opinions about various options available to the utility in attempting to comply with the Clean Air Act Amendments of 1990. Since negotiation among such divergent interests is often difficult, a mediator can contribute to a solution by assisting the negotiation process.

Midwest Energy Utilities (MEU) must choose a plan for complying with future pollution emission standards. The low sulfur coal that currently fuels MEU's plants produces too much air pollution. In order to reduce emissions, MEU can install scrubbers at its plants, switch to high-sulfur coal, switch to natural gas, switch to a blend of high-sulfur coal and natural gas, or purchase emission credits. Any of these options could allow the utility to comply with the Clean Air Act, but each option is valued differently by the various stakeholder groups.

Several major stakeholders have been identified as having an interest in MEU's decision. Environmentalists believe that MEU must produce fewer emissions so that the air is cleaner. Community leaders balance their desire for cleaner air with their desire to maintain high employment levels at MEU. The State Utility Regulatory Commission regulates the rates that utilities charge and is concerned that increased costs at MEU will necessitate increased consumer rates. The State Environmental Protection Agency is committed to reducing air pollution, even if it requires substantial capital investment. MEU must move toward compliance with the demands of the Clean Air Act Amendments of 1990 while meeting the performance expectation of stockholders and considering the interests of other stakeholders.

The organization of this case promotes interaction among persons playing the roles of the various stakeholders. There are six roles representing the five major stakeholders and the mediator: David Sparks is the President of MEU. Susie Green is a member of the executive committee of Blue Skies, a local environmental organization. Bob Brown, Teresa Jones, and Tim Powers comprise a select committee appointed by the Mayor of Ruraltown to represent Ruraltown's interests. John Derby chairs the Utility Rate Commission board. Cindy Shines is the chairperson of the state EPA. The roles are described in greater detail in Appendix D. Supplementary roles, such as members of the media and smaller community interest groups can be added. By "role playing" the parts of these stakeholders and representing their apparently incompatible interests, the reader should recognize the conflicts about MEU's choice of alternatives.

ENVIRONMENTAL MEDIATION

Environmental mediation is growing in popularity as a technique for resolving environmental conflicts faced by organizations. Organizations involved in conflicts are attracted to mediation as a means of avoiding litigation and its associated costs and delays. This method for resolving conflicts has been applied in cases involving conflict over a proposed hydroelectric plant, a location for garbage disposal, and a proposed interstate highway extension.

Mediation is the intervention of an outside party providing procedural help to two or more disputing parties. Unlike judges or arbitrators, the mediator does not have settlement authority. Instead of advocating a particular settlement, the mediator ensures that a fair and efficient process is followed by the parties as they mutually settle their own disputes. Since the mediator's authority is granted by the participants in the dispute, the mediator must be acceptable to all of the contending groups. This requires that the mediator be seen as impartial and neutral by the participants. When the number of disputing parties is large, gaining the acceptance of the mediation process and a specific mediator becomes more difficult. However, acceptance is critical if the mediation process is expected to produce negotiated decisions and reduce future litigation over those decisions.

Mediation is not appropriate for the resolution of all disputes. Experienced mediators and researchers have found a number of dispute characteristics that are associated with mediation success. Some conditions under which mediation can be an appropriate tool are presented in Appendix C.

Environmental disagreements usually involve a range of issues and are viewed with interest by a wide range of stakeholders, including those with financial interests, various governmental units, environmental groups, and local residents. Multiple groups become involved in the conflict, with each supporting its own interests. These disputing parties substantially differ on their values toward development and the environment, which makes simple solutions difficult to identify. These groups are somewhat interdependent, as any single group holds some capacity to erect barriers or obstacles to other groups' plans.

While these conflicts often are initially viewed as zero-sum disputes, in which one group's gain is seen as another group's loss, they are typically nonzero-sum disputes. Solutions may exist that are positive for all of the disputing parties. In this case, it is not so much a matter of one party winning at the other party's or parties' expense, but rather it is the groups' provision of concessions that enables agreement upon a solution. This interdependence of groups and the possibility of a win-win solution provides the impetus for negotiated solutions. The possible escalation of conflict and the widely divergent values of the disputing groups often make mediation of the negotiation process desirable or necessary.

This case explores the environmental mediation process as it applies to MEU's decisions.

THE SITUATION

Midwest Energy Utilities (MEU) is a major electric utility serving over 1,000,000 homes, farms, and businesses throughout Illinois. Although its headquarters is in Bigcity, Illinois, its largest generation facility is located one hundred miles south in Ruraltown, Illinois. The Ruraltown facility is expansive and is the oldest and largest in the 15-unit MEU system. The facility consists of six units and generates a third of MEU's electricity. One unit was developed in the late 1940s, three in the mid-1950s, and the other two in the late 1960s. MEU's customer base is approximately 85 percent residential and 15 percent industrial, with a service area that spans over 25,000 square miles. The industrial customer base is diversified among a dozen major industry groups.

MEU's financial standing has had some setbacks in recent years. In 1985 and 1986, MEU wrote off the costs of an abandoned nuclear project. This write-off of the plant's costs resulted in an accumulated deficit that was eliminated through subsequent rate increases. During the past two years, MEU was involved in litigation concerning the charge to operating expenses that allowed the utility to collect a higher rate for the purpose of resolving issues relating to the nuclear plant and establishing a basis for financial recovery. The 1991 financial statements for MEU recorded a loss contingency of $135 million due to an unfavorable ruling requiring the utility to reimburse customers who were overcharged.

Earnings per share (EPS) of common stock were $.50 in 1991, as compared to $3.40 in 1990. This was due to the litigation contingency, a reduction in retail rates, and increased depreciation expenses reflecting additional plant and other operation and maintenance expenses incurred in connection with a March 1991 freak ice and wind storm. This decline in EPS has led to talks among shareholders about management's ability to lead them through tough times. In addition to the financial performance, shareholders are very worried about the current dynamics of the industry. With the recent trends of mergers, acquisitions, and takeovers, MEU could be vulnerable to a hostile takeover.

MEU emits a substantial amount of pollutants into the atmosphere by utilizing medium to high-sulfur coal mined in locations near its power plants. This utility, like several others in the United States, has been greatly impacted by Title IV of the Clean Air Act (CAA) Amendments of 1990 (See Appendix A). Title IV addresses the need to control the sulfur-dioxide emissions generated by power plants. To comply with the new legislation, MEU faces many critical decisions that will affect not only the company's profits but the air quality and economic livelihood in several communities throughout the state. However, due to the size of the facility in Ruraltown, this small community faces perhaps the greatest potential impact.

During the next ten years, the entire energy industry will face one of its greatest challenges: determining how to comply with the 1990 amendments of the Clean Air Act and how to take advantage of the business opportunities that will accompany these changes. By January 1, 1995, MEU will be required to reduce its sulfur dioxide (SO_2) emissions by 40 percent due to the limited amount of emission allowances they will be given. By January 1, 2000, issued allowances would require SO_2 to be reduced another 36 percent. After that date, MEU's SO_2 emission allowances are limited to 150,000 tons per year, regardless of any increases in generation. A unique challenge for MEU evolving from these requirements is to decide whether to select plants to be renovated or purchase emission allowances to comply with the standards. According to the CAA, MEU will have the flexibility to comply by emitting an overall level of pollutants of 150,000 tons per year from all the utility's facilities or by purchasing some allowances to exceed that target. Therefore, MEU would be able to over comply with some plants to allow the remaining facilities to emit additional pollutants into the air.

THE DILEMMA

Midwest Energy faces many issues. MEU estimates that the total cost of complete compliance during the years 1992-2000 would be about $1.3 billion. Phase I requires MEU either to reduce SO_2 emissions by 40 percent from 550,000 to 334,000 tons by January 1, 1995 or purchase sufficient allowances to offset any excess. MEU will have to reduce emissions by an additional 36 percent (or hold additional allowances) by January 1, 2000 in order to meet the system-wide cap of 150,000 tons by that date. Failure to meet compliance dates will result in administrative fines of $2000 per ton over the limit as well as potential criminal and civil penalties.

Midwest Energy has also recently made several public statements concerning their commitment to the environment. The president of MEU, David Sparks, believes that there will be a great deal of discussion regarding MEU's recently published "Environmental Charter" (Appendix B) and fears that organizations may doubt the firm's commitment to environmental clean-up if it is perceived that the wrong option is being pursued.

Sparks has also been working closely with the state rate commission and thinks that with the litigation surrounding the previous rate increases it would be very difficult to persuade the commission to approve any additional rate increases for environmental concerns. Due in part to the fluctuation in recent growth and earnings, MEU has not been able to spend the money needed to purchase the appropriate technology to meet future environmental standards. There have also been concerns expressed about the rate of borrowing or stock offerings. Thus, obtaining rate increases from the commission is crucial for MEU to complete the capital investments economically required to comply with the EPA.

Rate commissions, by their nature, focus on the "least cost" approach to compliance. Thus, it will be necessary for MEU to make the case that the compliance plan submitted is the least cost approach. When this occurs, generally rate increases are approved. However, rate commissions monitor acceptable costs based on a rate of return target for the utility. It is not impossible for a commission to approve a cost plan but reduce the target rate of return so that a rate increase is not necessary. Currently, MEU's target rate of return is near the national average for utilities.

In addition, Midwest Energy faces an interesting dilemma. While the costs and benefits of each strategy can be calculated and a financial decision (within an appropriate financial range based on risk) can be reached, MEU must face other concerns. Not every group weighs the costs and benefits of each alternative equally and a consensus may be hard to reach. Further, the political environment concerning these decisions is becoming highly charged. MEU will need to approach these discussions with great skill if it is to implement a solution with a minimum degree of disruption.

Although all of the options could potentially be acceptable for MEU, each one creates unique ramifications for all the stakeholders impacted by MEU's choice. This stakeholder group includes the communities whose utilities are supplied by MEU; the high-sulfur coal suppliers for MEU; the miners of high-sulfur coal and their union; suppliers of alternative fuel sources; the state environmental regulatory agency; the state rate commission; environmental action groups in the state; the citizens of Ruraltown and other communities in which MEU has plants; and, of course, Midwest Energy Utilities stockholders.

COMPLIANCE OPTIONS

Install Flue Gas Desulfurization (fgd) Units

These units, commonly called scrubbers, would enable MEU to continue its use of high-sulfur coal. Although scrubbers eliminate the concern of burning medium to high-sulfur coal, the installation process can take up to five years. The cost for installation of this equipment across the entire MEU system would approach $1.3 billion. This would require a rate increase of over 30 percent to MEU's customers. The cost of flue gas desulfurization units for an average size generating unit would result in approximately $167 million of one-time capital charges and an additional $7 million of annual maintenance charges per year.

Replace High-sulfur Coal with Low-sulfur Coal

Utilizing low-sulfur coal eliminates the need for scrubbers, but creates other concerns. MEU is uncertain about the equipment changes required to convert the current plants to low-sulfur coal burning facilities. Thus, a testing program would need to be conducted, and substantial capital outlays might be necessary to make the conversion. Additionally, the local coal reserves provide only medium to high-sulfur coal, therefore requiring a change in coal suppliers. As demand for low-sulfur coal increases, the price of this coal could possibly increase as well. Secondary costs, such as MEU's transportation expenses, will rise due to the distant locations of the low-sulfur coal mines (Western states and Southern Appalachian Mountains).

The impact of such a move to the local coal suppliers is of grave concern to the Ruraltown community and to state government. As the need for medium to high-sulfur coal diminishes, employment levels at the local coal mines will be reduced. MEU knows that any decision to reduce the utilization of high-sulfur coal will be fought by both the corporate coal lobbyists and the coal miners' union within the state. These groups are very powerful in the state house and will resist the loss of jobs that would accompany a move to low-sulfur coal.

Utilize Natural Gas as the Only Energy Source

Although natural gas is the cleanest energy source, there are many costs associated with this environmental benefit. Gas is purchased as a commodity, thus creating a potential for price instability. Coal is often purchased on long-term contracts that provide the ability to stabilize prices. Gas, on the other hand, is usually purchased at spot prices, creating an element of price instability. There has been a recent trend toward longer term gas contracts, but the trend is not firmly established. Since a dominant cost in utility generation is the cost of fuel, the use of gas could create an instability in utility rates for the consumer. Also, during the winter months, gas is in high demand for home heating, and suppliers will never agree to a contract without a clause giving them the ability to interrupt the level of supply provided to corporate accounts during this period. Further, the sheer volume of gas required for an electric generation facility may be prohibitive. For example, a utility in a neighboring state discovered that the conversion of three units of a generation facility to natural gas would make that single generating facility the sixth largest customer of the state's gas utilities. The risk of attempting to secure such large quantities of gas is substantial.

Although the current price of natural gas is substantially lower than it was in the 1970s, the cost difference relative to coal is relatively unattractive. The current delivered price of gas to utilities approximates $2.20 per million BTU, while coal has a delivered price of $1.20 per million BTU.

Blend the High-sulfur Coal with Natural Gas

Natural gas does create feasible alternatives for utilities through the possibility of blending this resource with current coal resources. Many nonutility generators (corporations that generate their own electric power for factory use) have moved to this alternative. Using existing turbine generators, MEU could modify its coal-fired boilers, allowing for the blending of coal and natural gas. MEU could potentially utilize this blend at a substantially lower capital cost than that incurred by installing scrubbers; but research would first need to be conducted, a move that would take both time and money. It is estimated a test burn would cost $500,000 and take 18 months. Utilizing these facilities would also be an excellent strategy if MEU ultimately elects to convert to burning only natural gas.

Purchase Emission Credits

The Clean Air Act Amendments seek to set the maximum annual level of national sulfur dioxide emissions at 8.9 million tons by the year 2000. An emission rate of

1.2 pounds per million BTU would result in a total emission level of 8.9 million tons. Emission allowances are the EPA's mechanism for phasing in this level. There are two phases defined in the CAA. During Phase I, which is the period from January 1, 1995 through December 31, 1999, the CAA allots each company enough allowances for its Phase I affected generating units to emit SO_2 at a rate of 2.5 pounds per million BTU of fuel consumed. During Phase II, which begins January 1, 2000 and continues indefinitely, each generating unit can emit SO_2 at a rate of 1.2 pounds per million BTU. During each phase, the number of emission allowances is calculated by multiplying the allowable emission rate by the average annual fuel consumption during the baseline period, 1985-1987. The utilities that do better than exceed the standards of the CAA Amendments are able to sell emission credits to utilities who wish to buy emission allowances. The basic concept would be that units with low compliance costs could sell credits to those units with high compliance costs. When viewed nationwide, this arrangement would still achieve the overall requirements set forth by the Amendments.

This alternative would allow MEU to continue to generate power with high-sulfur coal with no additional capital investments to the power plants. The firm would buy emission allowances on the open market to cover the emissions generated in excess of the CAA benchmark.

Despite the benefits of this option, there are some risks. The price of the credits will be sold as a commodity on the open market and could be quite volatile in the future. Also, although the cost of the credits would be substantially less than the investment in other alternatives, there would continue to be a cost in terms of the air quality of the local community. The national ambient air standards require that certain levels be met in order to protect the health and environment of a local community. However, the purchase of emission allowances implies that the environment will contain more pollutants than it would if the generation unit was in compliance outright, without allowances. In addition to the local community's concerns, eastern states concerned about acid rain are beginning to lobby against the ability of western states to purchase these credits. New York has filed a lawsuit against the EPA on this topic. New York feels that air is a public good and that abuse from Midwest states will create irrevocable damage to the air in the Northeast. This suit serves as a reminder of the sensitive and temporal nature of many public policy edicts.

MAJOR STAKEHOLDERS

Environmentalists

Blue Skies, an active national environmental group, was created during the 1980s to prevent excessive amounts of pollution and dumping by large companies in the United States. The local chapter of Blue Skies has recently turned its attention to the amount of pollutants emitted by MEU. The smoke and smell have prompted the leaders of Blue Skies to petition Ruraltown representatives to take action. The passage of the Clean Air Act led to celebration and relief by Blue Skies representatives in anticipation that this problem would finally be taken care of by governmental intervention.

Recently, Blue Skies' celebration has turned to outrage with the speculation that MEU will not be upgrading its facilities to meet legislation but rather using funds to purchase emission credits. The community faces the possibility of the continuation of pollution and higher utility rates. The cost of purchasing the credits could raise rates because of the uncertainty and potential increased cost of purchasing the credits. In essence, customers of the purchasing utility may pay higher rates without obtaining cleaner air.

Blue Skies leaders have continued to argue that in the long run it would be more beneficial for MEU to improve its facilities rather than buy emission credits to meet the current regulation. One argument used by Blue Skies is that the only clear direction in the law is for cleaner air and that the firm should take action now to bring each individual unit into compliance without using emission allowances.

Community

The community of Ruraltown finds the CAA as a bittersweet piece of legislation. Although several residents are relieved to see pollution controlled, the reaction to this change could be lost jobs and a severe impact on the local economy. One of MEU's largest power plants is located in Ruraltown. There appears to be a growing division between the residents of Ruraltown given some of the alternatives MEU faces.

One compliance alternative involves closing a portion of the MEU power plant. By shutting down some of the boilers at the power plant, MEU would be able to comply with the CAA standards. MEU would continue to burn high-sulfur coal in the plants but generate more power from other locations. This could mean the layoff of 200 people in the area. With a population of 5,000, Ruraltown views this alternative as a huge set-back in the community's employment level. However, several members of the community are in favor of this alternative as they view polluted air as having a higher cost to the community than lost jobs.

Another compliance alternative is to utilize low-sulfur coal in the power plants. Employees of the power plant view this as a viable option as the employment levels at the plant would remain stable and the community would gain the benefit of cleaner air. However, this raises a grave concern with the local producers and miners of high-sulfur coal. Some 500 individuals are employed directly in coal mining. MEU has no sources of low-sulfur coal locally and would have to begin transporting low-sulfur coal from a location outside the area. Currently producers and miners of high-sulfur coal in the area have banded together to push for state legislation designed to compel utilities to burn locally mined coal. Utilizing low-sulfur coal could force several mining companies in the area out of business and directly impact Ruraltown's economy.

Another alternative is to purchase emission credits. As previously mentioned, utilities that do better than exceed the standards of the CAA Amendments are able to sell emission credits to utilities who wish to buy the right to pollute. Credits would be denominated in tons of emission. By purchasing credits, MEU will be able to continue to generate power with high-sulfur coal with no additional capital investments to the power plants. The price of the credits will be determined as a commodity on the open market and, despite the development of a futures market, could be quite volatile in the future. Although employees of the plant and the local miners would find job security, they realize the impact to the community due to the higher pollution levels. Other members of the community, especially local farmers, believe this alternative would be detrimental to the area in the long run.

State Utility Regulatory Commission

The public utility regulatory commission is involved in determining the appropriate rate of return for utilities in the state. In setting the utility rates that will meet the desired return, the commission usually reviews the operations, planning, scheduling, structure, and performance of a utility to ascertain what would constitute a reasonable rate of return.

The passage of the CAA has brought much pressure for the state's rate commission to develop special cost recovery programs for the utilities. Most utilities have chosen to handle these costs as any other capital or plant improvements. The Illinois Commission has expressed concerns about the added costs associated with complying with the CAA. These concerns range from the added costs to customers, financial requirements for updating equipment, appropriate technology, and the financial status of utilities.

The Commission has little interface with the state's air quality offices, which will be setting the standards for pollution reduction investments by the nation's utilities. To understand the technology needed to comply with the current regulation, the Commission relies heavily on the technical expertise of the utilities, supplemented on some occasions with experts from the Commission's staff or outside consultants.

John Derby, chairman of the state's rate commission, is noted for his tough nosed, tenacious approach in dealing with the utilities. Thus, any request for rate increases will be met with rigorous investigation and examination.

Illinois Environmental Protection Agency

The state EPA is committed to reducing air pollution within the state. The EPA believes that the capital investment required to meet such a goal is more than worth the cost in the long run. The EPA is working with local communities within the state in order to create awareness of the long run benefits of cleaner and healthier air. The young commissioner of the state EPA, Cindy Shines, is seeking to be a leader in the aggressive protection of the state's environment.

COUNTDOWN TO A DECISION

David Sparks knows that MEU must formulate its pollution compliance plan soon, as the government will shortly begin implementing the new air standards. Regardless of the ultimate plan chosen, David and the management of MEU definitely want to avoid any legal challenges to their plan. A legal challenge would be expensive to fight and could result in substantial delays in implementing the plan. With lengthy delays, it is possible that MEU could find itself out of compliance with the Clean Air Act. Avoiding any substantial legal challenge is therefore imperative.

Rumors that MEU had made several preliminary decisions regarding compliance alternatives sparked a series of editorials and letters to the editor in the local newspaper. In the hope of creating a more orderly forum for discussion, the citizens' council of Ruraltown recently hosted a public town hall hearing in the local gymnasium, at which representatives of the major constituencies made short presentations of their agendas. The meeting was tense, and it appeared that the environmentalists would consider litigation against MEU if the chosen strategy did not reduce pollution emissions. While the community leaders didn't threaten litigation, it was apparent that they would be very disappointed if MEU pursued an option that either reduced employment or didn't reduce emissions. During the meeting, several members of the environmental group mentioned the work of the National Environmental Mediation Group and suggested that a mediator might be useful. The other disputing parties seemed to agree that mediation was desirable.

MEU enjoyed a generally favorable perception in the community, and David didn't want to jeopardize this asset. Yet he knew any decision must be acceptable to the governmental regulators and must be financially sound. Knowing that environmental mediation had been attempted and sometimes successful in similar situations, David contacted the National Environmental Mediation Group and requested its assistance. Dr. Sarah Middleton, a member of the NEMG, agreed to mediate MEU's dispute.

A preliminary session between MEU, the environmentalists, the community leaders, the utility regulators, and the environmental regulators would be held in one week. In the face of this upcoming first round, David Sparks called his compliance planning team together to prepare. He knew his team would need to do its homework because all the groups in the process, while having different opinions, would be knowledgeable and well prepared.

Appendix 6A

The Clean Air Act Amendments of 1990

The 1990 CAA Amendments are the third major revision of an environmental law that originated in the Eisenhower administration. The CAA is composed of eleven Titles that delineate environmental policy on matters ranging from hazardous air pollutants to disadvantaged business concerns. Title IV, the acid deposition program, directly impacts the utility industry. The following is a summary of Title IV.

PURPOSE

1. To reduce the adverse effects of acid deposition through reductions in annual sulfur dioxide (SO_2) emissions from 1980 levels by 10 million tons.
2. To encourage energy conservation and utilization of cleaner alternative technologies so as to reduce the levels of pollution.

SO_2 Allowances—Basic Program

Due to the sweeping changes required by Title IV, legislation has been passed to phase in the emission reduction requirements through the year 2000. Currently, utility boilers that serve generators larger than 25 megawatts and have emission rates greater than 2.5 pounds SO_2 per million BTUs of fuel consumed are allocated allowances based on their past fossil fuel consumption. Each emission allowance enables a boiler to emit one ton of sulfur dioxide in a given year. Any new utility units not under construction by November 15, 1990 will not be allocated any such allowances.

Utilities can utilize allowances to cover current levels of SO_2 emissions, bank these allowances for future use, or sell them to others. Beginning in the year 2000, the total number of allowances issued by the EPA will be limited to 8.95 million tons. This will maintain the 10-million-ton SO_2 reduction.

SO₂ Reduction Program

Phase I reductions. Extending from January 1995 to January 2000, generating units located at 110 of the highest emitting power plants must reduce their SO_2 emissions to 2.5 pounds per million British thermal units (BTUs) based on the 1985-1987 baseline. These units are commonly referred to as Phase I affected units.

Phase II reductions. Beginning January 1, 2000, all existing units whose energy output is greater than 25 megawatts will be allocated allowances equivalent to a reduction of their SO_2 emission to a level equivalent to 1.2 pounds per million BTUs based on the 1985-1987 baseline.

Penalties for Noncompliance

Sources whose emissions exceed allowances will be required to pay $2,000 per excess ton and will be required to offset excess tons the following year or year(s).

Allowance Sales/Auctions

Direct sales. The EPA intends to create a reserve of allowances available for sale to interested buyers. Purchasers can acquire allowances through a direct sale with the EPA.

Auctions. Utilities that have less pollution than allowed under EPA rules are able to trade their unused allowances through an open auction. (Note: The first auction was held at the Chicago Board of Trade in March 1993. One credit, allowing emission of up to one ton of sulfur dioxide, sold at an average price of $156.)

Appendix 6B

Environmental Charter

1. Incorporate environmental considerations into the planning process.
2. Consider and compare the environmental consequences of choosing certain suppliers and contractors when purchasing supplies or services.
3. Periodically conduct formal reviews of activities to assure compliance with environmental regulations and report the results to the board of directors.

4. Educate all companies on the importance of their corporate conduct in protecting the environment, as well as their own health and safety.

5. Make environmental responsibility and innovation a guideline for measuring performance.

6. Inform corporations, customers, and the community about emissions, waste products, and MEU energy activities that may affect their health and safety.

7. Seek and implement cost-effective technologies and practices to minimize emissions and reduce or safely dispose of waste products in our operations.

8. Pursue methods to prevent pollution and conserve raw materials, including recycling waste and promoting the efficient use of energy by our customers through all cost-effective means.

9. Promote sound environmental practices within our industry, including the sharing of experience with others and the continued support of research and development in environmental improvement.

10. Develop and maintain open and constructive relationships with environmental groups, regulatory agencies, public officials, business and residential customers, employees, and concerned citizens.

Appendix 6C

Conditions for Mediation Success

1. The parties are somewhat interdependent or at least there is a capacity for mutual influence.

2. There are actual or perceived incompatible interests that are difficult to reconcile.

3. The parties have actual or perceived differences in values.

4. There are multiple issues of conflict, and disagreements about the order in which they should be addressed.

5. Communication between the parties is poor in quality or quantity.

6. There is no current or historical negotiation procedure between the parties that is appropriate for the current issue.

7. Misperceptions or stereotypes hinder productive exchanges.

8. Intense emotions or negative behaviors interfere with the settlement process.

9. Some deadline exists.

Source: Moore, 1986.

Appendix 6D

Participant Role Descriptions

PRESIDENT OF MEU ROLE (CONFIDENTIAL)

David Sparks, President of MEU, thinks that the CAA is another piece of bureaucratic legislation that makes it difficult for businesses across America to achieve success and compete globally. Last year, MEU designed an environmental charter to assure environmental groups that the utility was willing to work with everyone to insure prosperity for all sides. While Mr. Sparks helped create this document, he feels strongly that the current output of pollutants by MEU is a reasonable amount and will harm no one.

Despite Mr. Sparks' personal beliefs about the CAA, he is now faced with the question of how to meet the requirements. Phase I requires MEU to control sulfur dioxide (SO_2) emissions or hold allowances and install monitoring equipment at four of its plant locations. Although unknown to the general public, the most popular alternative at MEU, and the one with the least out-of-pocket cost, is to comply with the Phase I requirements by phasing out one generating unit at Ruraltown and to switch to a medium sulfur coal at the other Ruraltown units. Emissions in excess of the CAA dictates of roughly 50,000 tons per year would be covered by allowances. MEU would then install flue gas conditioners and upgrading precipitators at the other three generating sites. Total Phase I compliance costs across all sites are expected to be $335 million, excluding allowances. MEU intends to purchase the medium-sulfur coal for Phase I compliance from upstate mines because of the political consequences of switching to out-of-state coal suppliers. Given the power of the unionized miners in the state, any switch to out-of-state low-sulfur coal would create several problems due to the nonunion workers employed in those mines.

The impact of this strategy for the community is not inconsequential. While the phase out of one generating unit will likely cost approximately 50 jobs, the shifting of coal purchases upstate will probably lead to some 300 layoffs of miners and other support personnel.

Sparks realizes that the labor issues will be only part of the problem if MEU chooses to convert to a lower sulfur coal. MEU is not certain that the current boilers can effectively burn the lower sulfur coal and a large test burn would need to be conducted. Apart from the cost of the test burn program, this option could require a capital investment of over $75 million if major modifications need to be made to the boilers.

MEU's tentative plan for Phase II is to purchase emission credits to meet CAA requirements. While MEU knows that this will not be a popular decision among environmental and some community groups, the feeling is that further investment at that time will severely constrain operating ability and flexibility. With the purchase of credits, MEU will have the time and energy to restructure the organization and its financial position. At that point, MEU would be in a position to afford the huge capital investment for scrubbers. David Sparks also feels that by delaying capital investments, the pressure from environmental groups will force the state rate commission to allow MEU to pass the increases onto the community. MEU must consider the potential of takeovers as well. Would excess funds make MEU a viable target? On the contrary, complying with CAA standards by investing heavily in new capital equipment could make MEU equally attractive. MEU must file its Phase II compliance plan by January 1, 1996.

In summary, your role is to serve as the management team for Midwest Energy Utilities. In addition to making managerial decisions about the direction your firm will take with regard to CAA compliance, in this role you will be involved in negotiations with several constituency groups, speak at community meetings, and respond to the press.

ENVIRONMENTALISTS' ROLE (CONFIDENTIAL)

Susie Green has been active in Blue Skies for several years. She has committed her life to the safety of the community and the environment. Susie has recently moved to Ruraltown and was outraged at the level of pollutants emitted by MEU. After reading the company's environmental charter (Appendix B), Susie felt that the document was only hollow lip service by a company trying to cover up its true beliefs. In accordance with the Blue Skies philosophy, Susie advocates that no amount of investment is too high if it will serve to preserve the community and the environment.

In an attempt to rally local support, Susie has been lecturing to community leaders and local citizens about the dangers to the human body of long-term exposure to pollutants in the environment. A petition she has circulated states that the citizens of Ruraltown disapprove of the excessive amount of pollution currently emitted by MEU and the purchase of emission credits as a solution to the problem in the future. During her short time in Ruraltown, Susie has collected 800 signatures opposing the purchase of emission credits. With this petition Susie hopes to prove to MEU that the community will not accept irresponsible behavior at any cost. She hopes to present the petition to MEU soon but would like to get some more publicity prior to taking this action.

Many local citizens are impressed with Susie's ambition and desire to have an environmentally clean community. Susie has found one strong ally in the local farmers, who feel that diminished crop yields over the past few years may be due in part to the sulfur emissions from the plant.

Still, others in the community would like some additional alternatives from which to choose. While Susie knows that her suggestions will be opposed by some of the local coal miners and plant workers, she is preparing to persuade MEU that reducing pollutants by switching to low-sulfur coals or natural gas is a much more responsible action. These alternative fuels burn more efficiently and emit fewer pollutants. The use of these energy sources would clean up the environment and help meet the standards set by the CAA.

In summary, your role is to serve on the executive committee of Blue Skies. In addition to making decisions about how your organization will support clean air and the CAA, you will be involved in negotiations with other constituency groups and MEU, speak at community meetings, and respond to the press.

COMMUNITY LEADERS' ROLES (CONFIDENTIAL)

The CAA has raised serious divisions within the community that have yet to be resolved. Community residents have attempted several times to band together to lobby against MEU. However, as the options are reviewed, residents segregate into groups favoring those solutions that best suit their individual needs. Many community members are concerned about MEU's final decision. With no consensus held by the community, some residents believe they are powerless against MEU.

Three residents from Ruraltown have been selected to attempt to help resolve the issues facing the community. Bob Brown represents all of the employees at the power plant who could lose their jobs from the closing of a portion of the plant. Mr. Brown would like to see MEU invest in scrubbers to meet current regulation. He feels that it would be irresponsible for MEU to meet the standards set by the CAA by shutting down any facilities. The investment in scrubbers would not only reduce pollutants but save jobs and keep morale high among all workers.

Teresa Jones represents the members of the community who are worried about emission levels into their neighborhoods. Teresa has been working with Susie Green to create an awareness among all local citizens about the effects of pollution. While Teresa admires Susie's ambitious nature, she is concerned that Susie will stop at nothing to create a cleaner environment. Teresa feels that consideration of the balance between environmental cleanup and the number of jobs lost is of crucial concern.

Tim Powers was selected to represent the local miners. Tim is outraged by the talk of shipping in low-sulfur coal from other states. Tim knows that a switch to low-sulfur coal will mean a major reduction in the number of coal miners in the local area. He has vowed not to let this happen.

This group is committed to finding a unified solution that it plans to present to MEU. In an attempt to reach a consensus, the three representatives (Bob, Teresa, and Tim) have met previously to define their position. They agreed that the best approach to take would be that of installing scrubbers. This would allow MEU to meet the CAA requirements, maintain the current level of employment of coal miners and MEU jobs, and clean up the environment. This solution will require the lobbying of MEU and the state rate commission to help with the added costs.

In summary, your role is to serve on a select committee appointed by the Mayor's office in Ruraltown. You were chosen to help select the optimal position the city of Ruraltown can take regarding this issue. In addition to representing the city's position, you will be involved in negotiations with other constituency groups and MEU, speak at town hall meetings, and respond to the press.

RATE COMMISSION'S ROLE (CONFIDENTIAL)

Mr. John Derby is the chairman of the rate commission. While Mr. Derby is concerned about the economic competitiveness of his state's utilities, he has staked the success of his tenure as rate commission chairman on the plight of the disadvantaged in paying for the cost of their utilities. As such, he is most concerned about the poor and elderly in his state who, because of fixed incomes, would bear the brunt of any substantial rate increases. He also feels that too often in the past the public has been asked to bail out utilities strapped by poor managerial decisions. The citizens of Ruraltown and the surrounding communities have been very impressed with Mr. Derby's commitment and understanding of their pleas for lower rates. Mr. Derby's strong and highly visible commitment to the public has led some citizens to suggest that he should run for governor in the upcoming race.

Mr. Derby would like to see MEU focus more on better planning and management of its activities and less on filing for rate increases. By keeping operating costs down, Derby feels MEU's daily operations will become more efficient and less costly. This efficiency would allow MEU to pay for at least a portion of its necessary investments. Since utilities are a natural monopoly, Mr. Derby feels that MEU owes it to the customer base to have efficient operations and low rates.

In summary, your role is to serve on the rate commission board and represent its interests and interests of utility customers. Since your appointment, the commission has had a higher profile and tends to be supportive of your positions. In addition to representing the rate commission, you will be involved in negotiations with other constituency groups and MEU, speak at town hall meetings, and respond to the press.

STATE ENVIRONMENTAL PROTECTION
AGENCY'S ROLE (CONFIDENTIAL)

Cindy Shines is the director of the Illinois EPA. She believes very strongly that the state must comply with the CAA standards through lower emission rates rather than purchasing credits. She is very concerned that utilities will favor credits due to the capital investment required to install scrubbers or convert to utilizing low-sulfur coal. Cindy feels the national EPA is not being farsighted by only concerning itself with the overall emission levels of the country. The national EPA is concerned with compliance in all states but is not particularly worried about the possibility of exceeding the emission level compliance in any particular locality.

Cindy realizes that her power to force greater compliance is limited, but her agency has other ways to bring pressure to bear on MEU. Both ash dumping and water quality issues can be addressed with MEU, and if Cindy fails to get what she wants in air quality it would not be too difficult to apply pressure in these other areas.

Cindy realizes that she will have a very tough sell with the local coal miners' union if it doesn't support the compliance procedures that utilize high-sulfur coal. She believes she can achieve a win-win solution by supporting the installation of the flue gas desulfurization units at the power plants.

Cindy is young and aggressive and has been noticed on the national scene. There is some discussion of how long Illinois will be able to hold onto this rising star before she will be called to Washington to address national issues.

In summary, your role is to serve on the state EPA staff. In large measure, you take your cues from the chairperson of the State EPA, Cindy Shines. Since Cindy's appointment, the commission has had a higher profile and the entire agency is very proud of her. As a member of the agency, you must represent the agency's position regarding this issue. In addition, you will be involved in negotiations with other constituency groups and MEU, speak at town hall meetings, and respond to the press.

MEDIATOR'S ROLE (CONFIDENTIAL)

Sarah Middleton, Ph.D., is employed on a full-time basis by the National Environmental Mediation Group. She primarily mediates issues affecting public policy but has served in a wide variety of disputes, ranging from labor-management conflicts, to neighborhood disputes, to sexual harassment claims. Over the past few years, Dr. Middleton has mediated several environmental disputes. Her generally successful performance has given her a more visible position in the field, which she credits for her selection as the mediator for the MEU dispute.

Dr. Middleton recognizes that the management of Midwest Energy Utilities must come to some decision to assure compliance with the Clean Air Act. She also recognizes that environmentalists, community leaders, state utility regulators, and environmental regulators all have an interest in the choice of a compliance strategy and that their interests are occasionally in conflict. While there is little history of conflict among the disputing parties in this case, from her past experience Dr. Middleton is aware that such deeply held and divergent values can quickly lead to an escalation of conflict in the negotiation process. As conflict levels increase, the likelihood of efficiently negotiating a quick settlement deteriorates.

As a mediator, Dr. Middleton seeks only to manage the process, not the outcome. She must avoid the appearance of favoring any solution or any of the disputants and does not want to antagonize any party. In cases such as this one, she is obligated to ensure that all of the various parties are fairly represented in the negotiations. While she prefers to let the disputing parties negotiate, the responsibility to manage the process efficiently requires her to intervene at times.

In summary, your role is to serve as the mediator for this negotiation. As the mediator, your role is to manage efficiently the negotiation process. Don't appear to favor any solution offered by any of the disputing parties. The parties must negotiate a mutually acceptable solution. You may also be asked to participate in town hall meetings and must be prepared to respond to the press.

Appendix 6E

Teaching Note Problem and Role Descriptions

This case illustrates the conflict that can arise over business decisions that affect the environment. It may be conducted as a role playing exercise to emphasize the competitive nature of the dispute. Eight roles have been developed, representing MEU, the major stakeholders, and the mediator. Developed roles are David Sparks, President of MEU; Susie Green, representing a local environmental organization; Bob Brown, Teresa Jones, and Tim Powers, representing the community's interests; John Derby, of the Utility Rate Commission board; Cindy Shines of Illinois EPA, and Sarah Middleton, the mediator. These roles are described in detail in Appendix D. Supplementary roles, such as members of the media, coal miners, citizens' utilities boards, etc., may be added. If the number of roles needs to be reduced, the three representatives of the community's interests can be combined into one role.

Decisions impacting the environment involve a broad range of stakeholders and have been among the most legally challenged corporate and governmental decisions. A negotiation approach seems likely to produce an alternative that generates the minimum legal challenge. In this case, an electric utility (Midwest Energy Utilities, or MEU) is considering several alternatives in its planning for compliance with future air pollution standards. The utility and a variety of stakeholders (utility regulators, environmental regulators, environmental activists, and local community leaders) exhibit conflicting views of the alternatives. Since negotiation among such divergent interests is often difficult, a mediator can contribute to a solution by assisting the negotiation process. By roleplaying the parts of these stakeholders, the conflict and the value of mediation should become apparent.

The current fuel, low-sulfur coal, produces too much air pollution. There are five alternatives under consideration. MEU can install scrubbers at its plants, switch to high-sulfur coal, switch to natural gas, switch to a blend of high-sulfur coal and natural gas, or purchase emission credits. Any of these options is expected to reduce emissions and is potentially acceptable, but each option differentially affects various stakeholder groups.

The environmentalists and the Illinois EPA want MEU to reduce emissions and other pollution. Community leaders, balancing their desire for cleaner air with their desire to retain jobs, want scrubbers installed. The State Utility Regulatory Commission seeks to hold costs down. MEU must comply with the regulations while meeting company performance expectations. Unknown to the other parties, MEU management's initial preferred alternative is the least expensive. It is to close one generating unit at Ruraltown, switch to medium sulfur coal at the other Ruraltown units, and to purchase emission credits to make up the difference.

PREVIOUS EXPERIENCE

From our experience, you can expect several situations to evolve as you run this case:

1. Coalition building is a frequently engaged in activity of the role players.

2. When the press has been included as a role, the interactions have become more politicized.

3. The disputing parties often rely on the press for information, which can lead to an escalation of the conflict. Thus the inclusion of a press role increases outside pressures and the decision complexity.

4. Role players may fabricate data to support their positions, especially when they do not fully understand the quantitative data. This situation is exacerbated if the mediator takes a passive role.

5. Without extensive process control by the mediator, interactions between disputing parties have lasted for 90 minutes.

6. You need to be prepared for some participants to be angry at their classmates at the end of the role play.

DIRECTIONS FOR ADMINISTERING THE CASE

While the instructor might devise a schedule that best fits his or her particular class requirements and resources, a plan similar to the following can be used.

1. Prior to the class meeting, the participants read the case study materials, excluding the confidential role descriptions. Note that there is some information presented in individual role descriptions that is not available to the other parties. It is assumed that the participants have developed some background in negotiation prior to this exercise.

2. Depending upon the number of participants, the participants are assigned roles or are placed into teams representing the roles. Additional or fewer roles can be used as described above. At least four to five participants in a team for each role can help ensure that the interests of that role are well represented. The participants are given time for each of them to read only their role. Time is also provided for preparation for the negotiation. In our experience, we allotted 30 to 45 minutes for participants to read their roles, organize and choose a spokesperson, and prepare their arguments. This step could also be profitably completed outside class.

3. The participants play their roles and attempt to formulate a plan for MEU that is acceptable to their interests. The instructor might allow the negotiation to proceed initially without a mediator. Doing so allows the mediator's presence in the negotiation process to be assessed and discussed. Several rounds of negotiation could be allowed.

4. The participants relinquish their roles and discuss the processes they observed.

It is very difficult to run this case in a single 75-minute class period. We suggest that roles be assigned prior to the first class period and that Step 3 span the two-day event. We have found that from 30 to 40 minutes is necessary to debrief the case. In part, this is due to the range of emotions that accompany the range of experiences from the different teams.

POSTSCRIPT

This case is based on an amalgam of situations in the utility industry. While it represents realistic experiences of the midwestern utility industry as a whole, it does not represent the experiences of any single organization. Based on our understanding of the industry dynamics, the most commonly chosen course of action at this time appears to be the purchase of emission credits.

NOTE

This case was written by Drs. Dworkin and Jordan of the Krannert School of Management at Purdue University as a basis for class discussion rather than to illustrate either effective or ineffective handling of an administrative situation. The authors benefitted from the efforts of Maureen Jefvert and Steve Seneff, graduate students at the Krannert Graduate School of Management. The authors also acknowledge and thank Tony Kaelin and the staff of the System Planning Department of PSI Energy in Indianapolis, Indiana for their expertise and insight during the writing of this case. Midwest Energy Utilities is based on an amalgam of situations in the utility industry and in no way expresses the viewpoint or positions of PSI Energy or its staff.

Chapter 7

The Problems of Designing Environmental Mediation for Small Communities

Kenneth A. Klase

Approximately one third of the U.S. population lives in small communities. These diverse communities have some common environmental concerns. The proper management of environmental services in small communities is a difficult task for local governments charged with this responsibility. Factors such as changing regulations, financial constraints, and technological challenges pose unique problems for individuals with environmental responsibilities in small communities.

This chapter examines small communities as a context for environmental mediation. It explores their nature, their environmental problems, and the challenges they face in meeting regulatory requirements. An environmental mediation effort to resolve the problems of these communities must consider these factors. The implications of small community characteristics and human resources capabilities for resolving environmental problems are analyzed. With this information, an assessment of the capacity of small communities to address their environmental problems is possible.

An effort to build the capacity of small communities to resolve their environmental problems requires a recognition of their unique characteristics and human resource capabilities in the design of the mediation effort. A national effort to mediate their environmental problems is being undertaken by the National Environmental Training Center for Small Communities (NETCSC) sponsored by the Environmental Protection Agency. This chapter reports on the efforts of this organization. It describes the process of preparing for mediation in the context of small communities. It outlines the process by which a mediation effort was designed that accounts for the unique characteristics and human resource capabilities of small communities. It describes an effort to build the capacity of these communities through training targeted to their assessed needs.

DIFFERENT APPROACHES TO
ENVIRONMENTAL MEDIATION

Environmental mediation is typically viewed as a process in which those involved in a dispute are assisted in resolving their differences by a mediator. Mediation is essentially negotiation with a third party to help. It involves intervention of that third party in an ongoing conflictive relationship to help participants settle their differences. The disputing parties jointly resolve their differences on a voluntary basis. The mediator is usually viewed as facilitating the negotiation process by assisting the parties to reach a settlement acceptable to them. The parties must perceive the mediator to be impartial and neutral to the extent that he or she can help the parties make their own decisions without bias. Unlike a judge or arbitrator, a mediator has no authoritative decision-making power. The mediator has no authority to impose a settlement (Blackburn, 1990; Lake, 1980; Moore, 1986).

Environmental mediation is emerging as an alternative to litigation in resolving environmental conflicts because of its strengths in adaptability, flexibility, participation, and informality. As a consensual approach, environmental mediation enhances the feasibility of achieving a widely accepted solution whereas adversarial approaches do not. Nonetheless, environmental mediation has some potential shortcomings. If litigation is not pursued, minority interests may not be protected. Those who are less sophisticated parties or interests to the dispute or who do not participate directly in the mediation effort may not have their concerns or interests represented or protected (Blackburn, 1988). Of course, litigation has its drawbacks as well, due to problems of participation and lack of effectiveness in resolving disputes. Legislative and administrative approaches have also failed to resolve environmental problems (Amy, 1987). Fundamental qualities of American politics may also be obstacles to the employment of environmental approaches on a broader scale. In particular, the American penchant for conflict and adversarial relationships and the demands for wider participation mitigate against a stable and consensual process (Rabe, 1988).

Environmental mediation takes a number of different forms beyond its typical use in local, site specific disputes. For example, regulatory negotiation is one type of mediation used by regulatory agencies to design environmental regulations by first negotiating with interested parties to "potential" disputes. The intention is to avoid litigation in rule-making. It represents the formal institutionalization of mediation within the governmental policy-making processes. Mediation has thus gone from a more ad hoc and sporadic effort, which only occurred when parties to a dispute decided to use this approach, to a more regular and official part of environmental policy-making. This may represent a trend toward actually incorporating mediation into government as a part of the legislative or rule-making process (Amy, 1987; Fiorino, 1988).

Policy dialogue is another approach to environmental mediation that is also prospective and general, rather than local and site specific to a particular dispute. Policy dialogue takes place over basic environmental policy issues on the national level. While environmental mediation usually involves mediation of a specific environmental controversy, it may also address broader issues in which a third party helps a large number of interested parties (or they meet themselves without a formal third party mediator) to develop long-term strategies for environmental policy by sponsoring policy dialogue on environmental issues (Amy, 1987; Rabe, 1988).

These more general and prospective approaches to environmental mediation have similarities to more general aspects of environmental planning and management. The planner's role in the decision-making process often involves taking the role of mediator in order to deal with conflicts associated with the development and implementation of plans. Planners may also need to assume the roles of technician/administrator, mobilizer, or even advocate (Syme, Seligman, and MacPherson, 1989). Environmental management is concerned with assessing and managing environmental risks and mitigating or lessening their impacts (Freudenburg, 1989).

Fiorino (1990) has suggested that this approach should be called "risk-based environmental planning." He notes that the Environmental Protection Agency is utilizing such an approach for shaping its environmental agenda proactively. The EPA is attempting to allocate a portion of its and societal resources on the basis of evidence and professional judgments about relative risks posed by environmental problems. Risk management would dictate that societal resources should be directed toward problems posing the most harm and the greatest opportunity for reducing risks. Risk-based planning takes agency rankings reflecting judgments about relative risks and links conclusions about relative health and economic risks to a set of program initiatives which represent risk reduction strategies. A planning process such as this can tell administrators not only what problems to address but how to go about solving them.

Risk-based planning may offer the potential for improving participation in environmental planning. The current emphasis on hazardous waste and point source air and water problems reflects societal consensus about the appropriate focus of resource and program efforts. Risk-based planning can also help identify needs for improving the infrastructure for program delivery, such as building the capacity of state and local agencies. In Fiorino's view, environmental policymakers need to develop new strategies which will change their approach from management, control, and regulation to technical assistance, public outreach, and education to incorporate risk-based planning perspectives (Fiorino, 1990).

The different approaches to environmental mediation described in this section have indicated that the thrust of environmental mediation in recent years represents a shift in environmental policy implementation from adversarial to consensual processes and from judicial to administrative procedures. These approaches require a certain amount of information and technical education in order for participants to evaluate available options and fully contribute to the resolution of environmental problems (Lake, 1980). The environmental mediation effort of the National Environmental Training Center for Small Communities fits into broader definitions of environmental mediation. NETCSC's environmental mediation in the context of small communities as a whole is definitely not site specific, but more general and prospective in nature. It is consistent with notions of risk-based environmental planning and is really an outgrowth of that process by the Environmental Protection Agency. NETCSC is attempting to mitigate environmental risks through a broad consensual process which involves a large category of individual parties (i.e., small communities) involved in a planned intervention to mitigate environmental risks and resolve small community environmental problems.

The National Environmental Training Center mediates the environmental problems of small communities by building their capacity to resolve their own environmental problems. The Center is endeavoring to build the capacity of small communities by first recognizing their unique characteristics and human resource capabilities as they affect the context for environmental mediation. They have designed a mediation effort consistent with that context that will increase the capacity of small communities to resolve their environmental problems through training targeted to their assessed needs.

SMALL COMMUNITIES AS A CONTEXT
FOR ENVIRONMENTAL MEDIATION

A number of factors affect the potential for environmental mediation in the context of small communities. Not the least of these is the nature of small communities themselves. Second, the environmental problems of these small communities in drinking water, wastewater, and solid waste present unique conflictive situations. Moreover, the new regulatory requirements imposed on small communities heighten the level of conflict. This section explores the factors that make designing a mediation effort for small communities difficult.

The Nature of Small Communities

A small community is often defined in terms of population size, typically some number less than 10,000 individuals. Putting specific numbers on the size of a small community is difficult due to their diversity. Small communities may include very compact localized suburban settlements as well as rural areas containing residences located considerable distances apart.

Although most people in the United States live in metropolitan areas, approximately one third live in and around small communities. Approximately two thirds of local governments of all types are located outside of Census defined Standard Metropolitan Statistical Areas (SMSAs). The average population per municipal government both inside and outside SMSAs is under 8,000, and over 80 percent of municipalities serve under 5,000 people. Thus most local governments serve small numbers of people, and a great many of those governmental units are in nonmetropolitan areas (Honadle, 1983).

Defining the term *small* is not easy, nor is generalizing about rural communities or small towns. Small communities are characterized by great diversity in population, institutions, governments, resources, economy, cultures, and lifestyles. Some are wealthy, while others are poor. They can be located in urban areas or be isolated. The differences among small communities are almost as great as the differences between small rural towns and large urban cities (Honadle, 1983).

Like the difficulty in differentiating between rural and urban, capturing the essence of small communities is also difficult. A small community is a place or location, a set of social institutions (schools, churches, governments, businesses) through which people's needs can be met, and the repository of a shared sense of identity (Flora, Flora, Spears, and Swanson, 1992). Attempts to define "small community" must deal with many variables or dimensions of life, such as geography, climate, history, population, culture, ethnicity and race, institutions, and occupations, as well as the degree to which the community can be characterized as urban or rural. Wide variations in such variables mean that distinctions are often blurred along a continuum encompassing a wide variety of social and economic characteristics. Nonetheless, small community is a broad term of common use which is accepted as having meaning which cannot be defined precisely even though it broadly characterizes a certain type of environment (Carlson, Lassey, and Lassey, 1981; Gilford, Nelson, and Ingram, 1981).

The environment of small rural communities is affected by spatial distinctions and citizen identification with a specific geographic location. These places are characterized by small size and scale, including small governments and small institutions such as schools and health care facilities. They are often served by part-time officials. Their smallness is rooted in sparsity of population, and it is often necessary to aggregate the resources of the population in a wide area to support essential services. Limited resources are frequently a major constraint (Powers and Moe, 1982).

The social context of these communities is often affected by a narrow range of occupations and educational differences, especially in rural communities. There are also significant contrasts in attitudes, values, beliefs, and behavior from those prevalent in large, urban areas. Small communities tend to be somewhat less integrated with the state and national society in many respects. Bureaucracy in government and impersonality in general are likely to be less pronounced in small communities than in large urban areas, and interest groups and formal organizations are fewer in number. In general, the quality of life in small communities in rural areas is often less affluent with regard to material goods and income but is often considered richer with regard to environmental quality. Residents are usually quite satisfied overall with most aspects of their small communities (Carlson et al., 1981).

Residents of small communities often tend to perceive environmental issues somewhat differently than those from more highly urban areas. This is the result of relative differences in exposure to adverse effects of environmental pollution. People from small communities are often less concerned about environmental problems which don't seem to have a direct impact on them (Tremblay and Dunlap, 1978). But there can be little doubt that environmental problems are affecting small communities with increasing severity. The nature of small communities has a direct effect on the types of environmental problems they face and how they deal with these problems. That nature is best described in terms of local government and community characteristics and human resources capabilities (Klase, 1993).

Local Government and Community Characteristics

Local government and community characteristics of small communities are important. Small communities have unique characteristics with significant implications for environmental management. Their major characteristics include local government structure, decision-making process, social factors, economic conditions, and the financing of environmental services.

Local government structure determines the degree to which a small community can act to meet its environmental management needs. That structure is the context in which decision making takes place and in which essential services are provided. In that sense, it determines the nature of the decision-making process and the type and level of services provided. Small communities have local government structures which are generally fragmented and consequently less efficient. The single-purpose governments (i.e., independent boards and authorities) that generally provide environmental services have the advantage of heightening technical expertise and divorcing revenue raising for this purpose from general-purpose governments, but they create their own problems of control and accountability.

The decision-making process in small communities is affected by numerous political and organizational factors. Organizational skills, authority and power, and financial and human resources all play a part in setting the policy agenda for small communities. A number of variables have an impact on the style and pattern of decision making, including urban or rural character of the community, political and governmental structure, community values and norms, the characteristics of community leaders, the values and goals of political and community elites, and outside influences, resulting in less autonomy. Many times, the obstacles to local decision making are administrative in nature. Small communities are often served by part-time officials who are not experienced administrators and planners. As a result, local decision-making processes are often reactive in nature and characterized by crisis management rather than planning. Nonetheless, the severity of environmental problems insures that they are a part of the local policy agenda in spite of forces that would work against it.

Social factors are also important as characteristics which have an impact on environmental management issues. Population characteristics of small communities differ significantly from urban populations. Small communities are composed of populations which contain significant segments which are older and younger than the general population. Educational status is also relatively lower than that of the United States. The populations in small rural communities are often quite homogeneous, and they have fewer minorities. Small communities are frequently isolated and lack integrated social structures. Generally, the social and political attitudes differ from urban populations as well. Being less influenced by outside forces, the population of small communities is often more resistant to change.

Economic conditions are quite adverse for many small communities. They have high unemployment and significant levels of poverty. Declining manufacturing, mining, and agricultural sectors of the economy have decimated the economic base for financing environmental services and infrastructure. The lack of financial resources among small communities means that they have difficulty sustaining existing facilities and services, let alone undertaking needed improvements to address environmental problems. Economic conditions can thus be said to constrain significantly local responses to environmental needs.

A wide range of social, economic, political, and environmental factors influence services provided by small communities. The fragmented structure and inadequate management of local services make it difficult to provide adequate services. The cost, quality, and availability of services depends on the resource base available. That base is usually lacking due to local fiscal stress. Environmental services are particularly subject to high unit costs, increased costs of service delivery, and unfavorable economies of scale. Clearly small communities will have to find even more innovative ways to finance essential environmental services and infrastructure to meet the environmental problems that they face.

Human Resources Capabilities

Professional and nonprofessional human resources affect environmental management in small communities. Such human resources are constantly challenged with problems ranging from financial to technical difficulties associated with environmental services. They also face significant challenges to their ability to perform related to their own human capabilities. Their experience, behavior, attitudes, and working relationships often have direct impacts on environmental management. Sometimes they fail to recognize that significant environmental problems exist. Moreover, the resolution of many of these environmental management problems requires the interaction of various human resources at the local and state levels, which creates even more challenges for those local human resources.

A lack of staff expertise is a significant obstacle to environmental management in small communities. Inadequate financial resources often create this situation since small communities usually cannot afford staff expansion, training, or consultants and frequently must rely on insufficient assistance from federal and state officials or other local governments. Information on environmental programs, management techniques, and innovative ideas and approaches is generally lacking (Magazine, 1977).

While the lack of expertise is in part due to inadequate fiscal resources, it is also due to lack of training opportunities to develop and maintain qualified personnel. The implications of inadequate human resources include under-staffing, poor job performance, overworked personnel, low quality and quantity of service, and inattention to long-range planning (Honadle, 1983).

Some have suggested that rural jurisdictions suffer from an acute crisis in administrative capacity that has created a rural administrative gap (Seroka, 1986). A technical dependence on outside know-how and trained personnel has developed in many instances (Lapping, Daniels, and Keller, 1989).

The local officials who must establish and implement environmental management and policies for small communities are faced with staggering obstacles. The environmental problems that they face are complex and time-consuming. These procedures would tax the abilities of well-trained professionals. Typically as part-time officials, they lack appropriate expertise in the environmental area, have limited administrative capacity to address environmental problems, and may face potential political disincentives as well.

Consulting engineers who plan, design, and implement infrastructure for environmental services are often not attuned to meeting small community needs. They exercise considerable influence over environmental decision making in small communities due to their technical expertise. However, they are used to dealing with conventional systems and often lack knowledge of small systems and alternative technologies useful to small communities. For reasons of risk avoidance and because fees are usually based on a percentage of the project cost (costs for projects using alternative technologies are usually less than traditional approaches), they are often hesitant to consider these approaches. While consulting engineers have considerable technical expertise, they often are not good at communicating with the public. Consulting engineers can only be effective in addressing small community environmental needs with a solid understanding of the economic, social, and political factors in small communities and deal realistically with their financial constraints.

Operation and maintenance personnel have a significant influence on the day-to-day operations of environmental infrastructure facilities. Since many states require operators to be certified, they provide local expertise on environmental management. Shortages of trained personnel and inadequate funding for training make retaining trained O&M personnel difficult.

Regulatory officials need to understand the unique conditions of small communities in establishing and enforcing environmental regulations and how to work with small communities to help them meet mandatory compliance. Conversely, small communities must strive to educate regulatory officials about conditions and special needs of small communities.

The human resources involved in environmental management have specific roles to fulfill which insure that adequate environmental services are provided in small communities. Their characteristics and limitations noted in this section may tend to make the solution to environmental problems in small communities even more difficult to achieve. Provisions for human resource development to overcome these characteristics and limitations present a formidable challenge for small communities.

Human resources are the critical element in environmental management for small communities. Their characteristics and capabilities determine whether environmental problems will be meaningfully addressed and the degree to which adequate environmental services will be provided in small communities. The characteristics of local officials, consulting engineers, operations and maintenance personnel, and regulatory officials have been presented in this section, and their roles in local environmental management have been discussed.

Small Community Environmental Problems and Impacts of Regulatory Requirements

The environmental needs of small community residents for potable water, adequate wastewater treatment, and availability of solid waste disposal are met to varying degrees. The relative lack of local expertise, among both local leaders and service providers, can exacerbate environmental problems. Difficulties in the provision and management of environmental services and financial planning associated with environmental problems often lead to larger economic and legal problems. This makes outside financial, technical, and planning assistance very important for these communities, which often look to a variety of regional, state, and federal entities for solutions to their problems.

Many of the problems of small communities are heightened by some of the characteristics associated with rural areas. The traditional rural economic base has difficulty generating sufficient income and employment as a result of a preponderance of low-wage and unskilled jobs. This contributes to the financial difficulties they face. In addition, the physical distances within and between small communities in rural areas make solving their environmental problems more challenging.

The nature of small communities, as outlined in the previous section, leads to the specific environmental problems small communities face. This section highlights the specific environmental needs of small communities in the areas of drinking water, wastewater treatment, and solid waste disposal and identifies the characteristics which often lead to these environmental problems. The impacts of regulatory requirements are also discussed (Klase, 1993).

Small Community Environmental Problems

Environmental problems relating to drinking water in small communities center on problems of access to potable water as well as on problems of water quality. Part of the solution is to treat wastewater and to maintain water quality. But this is easier said than done. Preventing the contamination of local water supplies requires investments in infrastructure needed to maintain water quality by both private and public organizations. Most rural communities, especially those lacking adequate wastewater treatment facilities and public water systems, have great financial difficulties undertaking these investments due to limited fiscal capacity. They have only received limited assistance from the state and federal governments in recent years. These significant infrastructure problems as well as water quality concerns are some of the major environmental problems related to drinking water which small communities must begin to resolve (Flora et al., 1992).

The environmental problems of small communities relating to wastewater treatment center on the inadequacies of existing infrastructure and on-site systems. Where systems do exist, they frequently are costly to operate and maintain, exceed their designed capacity, and are not geared to meeting the increasingly stringent water quality standards being mandated. Where they do not exist (the most prevalent situation in small communities), the cost to build them appears beyond the financial capability of small communities, and on-site systems now in use are often wholly inadequate or inadequately maintained.

Solid waste collection and disposal is also a significant environmental problem for small communities. Blair (1986) notes that the use of different solid waste disposal methods depends, among other things, on the soil and climate conditions and availability of sites. Disposal in sanitary landfills has the advantage of being low cost relative to other methods. The lower population density relative to urban areas makes these rural areas attractive for locating solid waste disposal sites. Typically, regional landfills have been developed in rural areas and larger communities have charged neighboring towns for use of their facilities. Recent trends have been to develop private landfills and waste disposal operations as a result of the potential profits (Flora et al., 1992).

The amount of solid waste and restrictions on the availability of landfill sites have placed a large burden on existing land sites for disposal. The number of active landfills has dropped dramatically as a result of more stringent requirements and enforcement efforts. Many of these landfills create environmental problems by contaminating local groundwater and making it unfit for drinking. Many local governments are being forced to utilize recycling as the costs of waste collection and disposal have continued to increase and as state regulatory requirements have been enacted and enforced. In the future, local governments will undoubtedly have to rely more on recycling to deal with the increasing costs and restrictions on landfills and the lack of available landfill options.

The Impact of Regulatory Requirements on Small Communities

Since the 1960s, national legislation has been developed on a number of environmental issues affecting small communities. In 1969, the National Environmental Policy Act required environmental impact statements when federal funds were involved in development projects and included policies and goals relating to environmental quality. The establishment of the United States Environmental Protection Agency (EPA) followed in 1970, and Congress initiated a wave of environmental legislation, the effects of which are still being seen today. The legislation includes the Solid Wastes Disposal Act of 1970, the Federal Water Pollution Control Act of 1972, the Safe Drinking Water Act of 1976, and the Clean Water Act of 1977.

The EPA is responsible for the implementation of clean air and water legislation. Its responsibilities involve setting minimum air and water quality standards, monitoring air and water quality, regulating pollution emissions, imposing fines on polluters, and, until recently, making grants to localities for water and wastewater facilities. EPA decisions affect a wide variety of small community activities, especially in rural areas where decisions can affect many aspects of sewage and solid waste disposal and drinking water provision. Although small communities often resent the intrusion of federal and state regulators, local decision makers must legally comply with state and federal environmental regulations which are aimed at enhancing environmental quality while also balancing diverse often conflicting local interests (Lapping et al., 1989). Some of the more recent regulatory requirements strengthen regulations concerning drinking water, wastewater treatment, and solid waste disposal facing small communities (Klase, 1993).

The National Primary Drinking Water Regulation (NPDWR) and the Safe Drinking Water Act (SDWA) limit the amount of contaminants that are allowed to remain in drinking water after treatment. Amendments of the SDWA protect aquifer source well-heads and provide groundwater purity. Monitoring for contaminates is to be carried out on a regular basis. Any violations of maximum contaminant levels will have to be made public within 14 days. The impact of these drinking water regulations on small communities results mainly from the increased costs associated with laboratory testing and compliance with other provisions.

Other regulations concern wastewater pollution. Operators discharging pollutants, including wastewater effluent, must obtain a permit under the National Pollutant Discharge Elimination System (NPDES) of the Clean Water Act. Any discharge must meet minimum EPA standards as well as standards set by individual states which in most cases are more stringent. Any Publicly Operated Treatment Works (POTW) that cannot comply with secondary treatment standards will need to upgrade their system or review existing system processes to comply. Effluents discharged by industries into public sewer systems must be pretreated to standards specified in the NPDES permit.

Since October 1990, Congress has phased out funding for an EPA program, the Wastewater Construction Grant Program. This program provided financial resources to small communities for constructing or upgrading existing wastewater treatment plants. The end of the program has resulted in increased capital and operating cost for small communities. Small communities must now bear significant responsibilities for all aspects of the construction and upgrading as well as the operation and maintenance of wastewater collection and disposal systems (U.S. EPA, 1991a).

Solid waste disposal regulations have also been strengthened, encouraging recycling nationally. Recent increases in the number of small communities mandating recycling resulted from closing existing landfill facilities, the public's attitude about locating new landfills, and the desire to recycle and reduce waste (Massachusetts Bureau of Solid Waste Disposal, 1986). Many legislatures have enacted laws to promote reduction in waste. In addition, the EPA is enforcing more stringent landfill regulations and promoting recycling. Small communities that own or operate a landfill are required to meet many new facility standards, groundwater monitoring requirements, closure and postclosure standards, and performance requirements. If these requirements cannot be met, closure or extraction of the landfill contents may be enforced.

In summary, legislation at both the state and federal levels continues to establish ever tighter requirements relating to drinking water, wastewater, and solid waste. The environmental quality standards and time constraints for compliance which have been imposed place heavy demands on small communities. The environmental problems of small communities are great, and the new regulatory requirements they face impose even greater challenges.

PREPARATION FOR MEDIATION

This chapter shows that small communities have numerous characteristics that affect their capability to respond to environmental needs. These characteristics increase the vulnerability of the small community to new environmental regulations and have a detrimental effect on local environmental service provision. The cost of such services and current situations in small communities frequently prohibit compliance with new regulations.

This chapter has also shown that the people involved often complicate the environmental problems of small communities. They are not a congruent group— they do not fully interact with each other, nor do they cooperate in sharing knowledge between all parties. Improving communication between human resources involved in environmental management in small communities can enhance decision making, take better advantage of expertise, and provide increased service capabilities.

Other characteristics of small communities, such as financial conditions, often limit human resources or time availability. In spite of these limitations, the capabilities of small communities can be increased through capacity building, of which training is a key component. Only training can overcome the negative aspects of the characteristics of small communities and the limitations of the human resources involved in local environmental management.

Building the Capacity of Small Communities

Capacity building as a concept has received some attention in the literature. Usually capacity building addresses specialized management problems that are important to the capacity-builders. Honadle (1986) has described the concept as one that goes beyond survival to empowerment and enhances the capability of local communities to be able to identify and resolve problems. The capacity-building framework which she has devised defines capacity in terms of the ability of the community to anticipate change, make informed decisions about policy, develop programs to implement policies, attract and absorb resources, manage resources, and evaluate performance to guide future action.

Actually doing capacity-building is much more difficult than defining it. There have been numerous attempts to build the capacity of local governments in the United States over the years. These attempts have not always had clear goals or utilized the most effective methods for generating lasting change. What has made some of these efforts successful included tailoring solutions to local needs, alleviating the risks associated with innovation, and providing incentives for recipients of assistance to make desired changes (Honadle, 1986).

Discussing the capacity-building needs of small communities from the framework described above overlooks the obvious fact that local people may not recognize the same needs or attach the same priorities to them. Some conclusions have been drawn about the need for capacity-building in small communities. Small communities have identified a fundamental need for training. Local officials have cited a variety of specific training needs, ranging from technical skills to general orientation to job responsibilities. They have generally emphasized the following: roles and responsibilities; budgeting and financial management; revenue administration; decision-making techniques; planning, management, and leadership skills; and working with consultants (Reid, 1986).

Honadle (1988) has indicated that the federal government does bear a role in capacity-building of this sort for local governments. In her view, the primary role of the federal government in the area of environmental infrastructure and services is to develop and provide information for these small governments. The essential activities that are envisioned for the federal government include (1) monitoring conditions and identifying trends in existing community services and infrastructure, (2) promoting networks for the sharing of information, (3) encouraging the use of new technologies, and (4) serving as a clearinghouse for information. The federal government also has had in the past, and continues to have, a role in the financing of infrastructure and locally provided services in the environmental area; but it more clearly has an institutional role and responsibility to develop and share information for policymakers.

Service organizations clearly have a role to play as change agents. Contributing to the process of change through the provision of training to the human resources involved in environmental management in small communities is an appropriate capacity-building strategy which can contribute to their ability to recognize and deal successfully with local environmental problems and regulatory requirements.

Environmental Training Development for Small Communities

Meeting basic training needs will overcome the negative effects of small community characteristics and their human resource limitations. The activities to accomplish these goals include training, curriculum development, and eventual provision of training addressed to local officials, consulting engineers, operations and maintenance personnel, and regulatory officials—the major human resource groups involved in environmental management for small communities. NETCSC has undertaken these activities as a mediator in the environmental problems of small communities. It seeks to prepare the human resources of small communities to resolve their environmental problems and meet regulatory requirements through capacity-building training.

NETCSC, as a service organization and change agent, has devised a curriculum development process designed to develop training for both instructors and relevant small community human resources. An initial step toward mitigating the negative effects of small community characteristics and their human resource limitations is the accomplishment of individual curriculum development projects which assess the subject matter that small community human resources need to know and other analysis that is needed to guide the development of curricula for them. To this end, NETCSC conducted a national training needs assessment to request information and feed-back in order to target the training needs of specific critical small community human resources. The basic steps in the process were as follows: identify the primary target groups; identify high priority knowledge and skills for each group; survey a national sample from the target groups concerning training needs; and analyze the results to determine priority training needs.

The priority training needs for each of the primary target groups are being utilized for curriculum development for the individual training needs basic to mediating environmental problems of small communities. The curriculum development process is focusing on those who will train the primary target groups as well as the primary target group itself. In this manner, the curriculum development process NETCSC has undertaken exemplifies how training efforts can enhance the environmental mediation process.

One aspect of the curriculum development effort focuses on the basics of environmental system management for local elected and professional officials. This training endeavors to help these officials understand the fundamentals of construction, operation, and management of water, wastewater, and solid waste systems for small communities.

Another aspect of the curriculum development effort focuses on how consulting engineers can work more effectively in small communities. This training helps consulting engineers understand the nature of small communities and their strengths and needs, how to develop good communication and personal relationships, and successful methods for gathering information and educating local leaders and the general public.

Curriculum development efforts for operations and maintenance personnel focus on technical and regulatory knowledge and technical procedures, public relations techniques, and strategies for system troubleshooting. Training to address these targeted needs emphasizes technical knowledge and skills for more effective water, wastewater, and solid waste system operations. This training seeks to enhance the capabilities of operations and maintenance personnel so that they can maximize the capacity of existing facilities and comply with state and federal regulations.

A final area for curriculum development focuses on training regulatory officials to understand small community dynamics, local finance, and management limitations. This training endeavors to help regulatory officials understand the social and economic factors that influence small community decision making and the management of water, wastewater, and solid waste systems. The curriculum focuses on decision making and leadership in small communities, social and political processes in small communities, small community strengths and resources as well as their limitations and economic constraints, successful strategies used by small communities for environmental system management, and how to utilize regulatory agencies for the assistance of small communities.

Future environmental training development for small communities in the areas indicated above will reduce the negative effects of small community characteristics and overcome the human resource limitations noted in earlier sections. This training development process highlights the role of NETCSC in fostering mediating activities that prepare small community participants for mediation of environmental management issues. The National Environmental Training Center has a vital role to play in developing and providing the training described. The focused training effort that it is are providing will help to build the capacity of small communities to recognize and deal successfully with their environmental problems and regulatory requirements and will enhance their capabilities in environmental management.

SUMMARY AND CONCLUSIONS

This chapter has examined environmental mediation in the context of small communities. The activities of the National Environmental Training Center for Small Communities in building the capacity of small communities to resolve their environmental problems were presented in this chapter as an example of a broad, prospective approach to environmental mediation consistent with the recent trend of environmental mediation toward such approaches. The preparation for such environmental mediation activities involved designing a mediation effort which accounted for the unique characteristics and human resource capabilities of small communities. This chapter examined these characteristics and human resource capabilities as a context for environmental mediation.

NETCSC is preparing participants in its programs to resolve their own environmental problems by designing a capacity-building training development approach to environmental mediation for small communities. It is targeting assessed needs as determined by the individuals involved in small community environmental problems: local officials, consulting engineers, operations and maintenance personnel, and regulatory officials. In providing such capacity-building training, NETCSC is overcoming the negative aspects of the characteristics and human resource capabilities of small communities and recognizing the unique context and environmental problems of small communities. Its activities are in the truest sense an intervention, or mediation, to help small communities resolve their own problems.

Chapter 8

Beyond the Limits: Dispute Resolution of Intractable Environmental Conflicts

Guy Burgess and Heidi Burgess

The successful application of environmental mediation and consensus-building techniques is limited by two factors—the intractable nature of many environmental conflicts and the fact that the parties are unlikely to agree voluntarily to a settlement that offers them less than might be obtained by pursuing their interests in legal, political, or other arenas. This frequently results in destructive confrontations in which substantive issues are neglected amid a climate of recrimination and hostility.

A strategy, which we call constructive confrontation, takes the environmental mediation field beyond these limits. It first requires efforts to limit the distracting effects of a series of problems—confused interests, technical disagreements, mis-understandings, questions of procedural fairness, escalation, and polarization—which overlay the core conflict. Next the parties need help in honestly and inexpensively assessing whether or not confrontations, with their associated power contests, offer more desirable alternatives to negotiated agreements. Once the power contests required to pursue these alternatives are completed, then the parties can return to the negotiating table in an effort to fine tune the settlement in ways which prevent potential win/win trade-offs from going unrealized. This chapter develops four key ideas: (1) limitations to environmental mediation; (2) strategies for overcoming the overlying conflict problems; (3) techniques for lowering the costs of power contests needed to assess the parties' alternatives to negotiated agreements; and (4) negotiation in the aftermath of necessary power contests.

The next section presents the limits of environmental mediation which are intractable conflict and power alternatives to negotiation.

THE LIMITS OF ENVIRONMENTAL MEDIATION

Limit I: Intractable Conflict

The ability of environmental mediation, consensus-building, and related techniques to enable the parties to negotiate mutually acceptable resolutions of environmental problems is limited, first by the intractability of most serious
environmental conflicts. These intractable conflicts may involve fundamental
moral conflicts (such as those dividing the deep ecologists and the "fair use"
movement) or high-stakes distributional questions over who gets what. In these
cases the parties are unlikely to be willing to negotiate, since negotiation is usually
seen as a way of forcing them to compromise their basic values. The parties are
also unlikely to respond to defeat or *forced* compromise with acceptance and
submission. Instead, they are likely to attempt to strengthen their resource base
with the goal of reversing their defeat at the earliest possible opportunity.

The key to understanding this limit to successful mediation lies in the distinction between *conflict* and *dispute*. This is an idea that we have adapted slightly
from John Burton's original insight (Burton, 1990). Environmental *conflict* refers
to long-term divisions between groups with different beliefs about the proper
relationship between human society and the natural environment. In addition to
the deep ecology/fair use conflict, other conflicts divide snowmobilers and cross-
country skiers; stream-side and reservoir-based recreation advocates; hunters and
those favoring biodiversity and "watchable wildlife"; solitary wilderness trekkers
and mountain resort patrons; pro- and antigrowth factions; advocates of a "small
is beautiful," low-consumption lifestyle and proponents of the more materialistic
"good life"; and advocates of tight pollution control requirements based upon the
belief that human life is priceless and persons wishing to take a hard look at the
economics of pollution control.

Conflicts between these groups are played out in a seemingly endless series of
incremental *disputes* concerning the enactment of specific policies. While the
resolution of each dispute determines, for the moment and the place, the balance
between competing positions, this policy balance remains a matter of continuing
conflict in which a never-ending series of disputes lead to decisions which move
social policy back and forth between competing positions.

This relationship between conflict and dispute is summarized in Figure 1. Here
social policy changes through time are indicated by the arrow moving up and
down in the center of the figure. When the social arrow is toward the top of the
figure, social policies tend to favor, in this example, water development interests.
An arrow toward the bottom of the figure indicates that the pendulum has swung
toward policies which favor environmental interests. These policy swings result
from (and follow) the settlement of individual disputes and may either affirm or

Figure 1
The Relationship Between Environmental Conflicts and Environmental Disputes

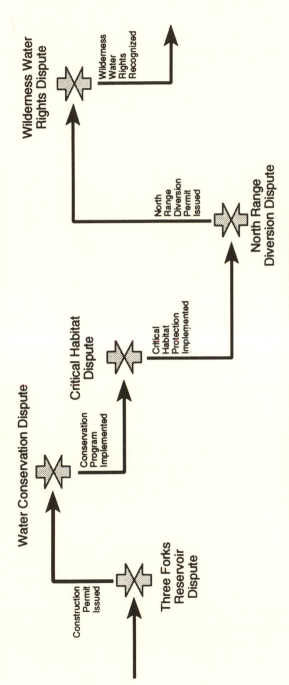

Social Policies More Favorable to **WATER DEVELOPMENT** Interests

Wilderness Water Rights Dispute

Wilderness Water Rights Recognized

North Range Diversion Permit Issued

North Range Diversion Dispute

Critical Habitat Dispute

Critical Habitat Protection Implemented

Conservation Program Implemented

Water Conservation Dispute

Construction Permit Issued

Three Forks Reservoir Dispute

Social Policies More Favorable to **ENVIRONMENTAL** Interests

Environmental Conflict

 = Environmental Dispute

= Social Policy

change existing policies. This example shows the policy shifts following the resolution of five disputes—the Three Forks Reservoir, water conservation, critical habitat, North Range diversion, and wilderness water. The specific arena (e.g., administrative action, litigation, legislation, electoral politics, and economic markets) in which these disputes were resolved is not shown. This long-term process of continuing policy dispute resolution is what we call environmental conflict (grey arrow at the bottom of the page).

Limit II: Power Alternatives to Negotiation

The potential success of environmental mediation and related techniques is also limited by the availability of better alternatives to a negotiated agreement (BATNAs). For a more complete discussion of BATNAs, see Fisher and Ury's, *Getting to Yes* (1991:97-106). While persuading people to participate in an environmental mediation or other problem-solving process is a challenge, getting them to agree on a settlement is an even bigger challenge. If mediation or related processes are carefully facilitated according to the principles outlined elsewhere in this volume as well as in the many other excellent publications in the field, remarkable progress can be made. Participants may even undergo what might be described as a conversion experience in which "evil" stereotypes, distrust, and malevolence toward an opponent are replaced with much more trust, cooperation, and benevolence. These processes can be very successful in pursuing opportunities for mutually beneficial compromise.

What these processes cannot do, however, is alter the basic fact that many of the interests of participating parties are inherently competitive and that often one party's interests can only be satisfied at the expense of another's. In other words, win/win solutions simply do not exist and cannot be created for all disputes.

This situation creates a mirage effect in which participants in environmental problem-solving processes may amicably and sincerely work to achieve the best possible negotiated settlement. However, once the final settlement begins to emerge, participants will be asked by their constituents (if not themselves) if there are other arenas or power contests through which their interests might better be pursued and their opponents confronted. In other words, can they get a better deal by pursuing their interests in other forums? For example, they may be able to appeal directly to the regional administrator of a key government agency, take their opponent to court, lobby Congress to pass legislation which directly advances their interests, use their economic resources to buy what they want, or take their case to the court of public opinion. If *any* of the parties believe that they can get a better deal through *any potentially viable* alternative to a negotiated agreement, then they can be expected to try to do so. The negotiation process will then fail and the mirage of a draft settlement will vanish—just as it appeared to be so tantalizingly close.

Put another way, mediation and negotiation are not techniques for altering the fundamental power relationships within a society, no matter how desirable that might be. The reason is that agreement is voluntary. If people don't like the settlement, they can simply resort to the other powers that are available to them. Occasionally conversion experiences associated with participation in these processes will cause one or more of the parties to redefine their interests in ways which are more charitable to opponents. While often highly desirable, such transitions toward more altruistic and socially responsible positions present a difficult scale-up problem because the conversion experiences of individual participants in the process are not likely to be shared by their constituents. In these cases, the participants are unlikely to be able to bind their constituents to the agreement and their constituents are likely to feel so betrayed that they will simply find new leaders. Thus, one of the most pressing problems for environmental mediators is the development of effective techniques for scaling up conversion experiences to encompass the larger constituency group.

This limit is summarized in Figure 2, which portrays an example of a relatively simple, hypothetical dispute between environmental and water development interests. The leftside of the figure lists alternative strategies through which environmentalists and water developers might seek to advance their interests. Graphically portrayed to the right of each strategy is a black square indicating the expected outcome, from the perspective of water developers, and a grey circle indicating the outcome environmentalists expect. The graph indicates that developers believe that there is very strong public support for water development and that that support will be translated into electoral victories at the federal, state, and local level. However, environmentalists disagree and think that they will be victorious in any electoral power contest.

The figure also shows that environmentalists think they can prevail in a legal challenge based upon the argument that the proposed project would threaten the habitat of several endangered species. Meanwhile, developers are counting on strong support from administrative appeals to political appointees in federal natural resource management agencies. Since both sides believe that they have alternatives that will yield much more favorable outcomes than the draft negotiated agreement, they can be expected to reject the agreement. Even the best environmental mediation and consensus-building processes are unlikely to succeed in such instances. For mediation to work, the expected alternatives to a negotiated agreement for both environmentalists and developers would have to be much closer to the compromise negotiated position. Only in this case can the parties reduce transaction costs and uncertainties without really giving up a great deal. This possibility is explored in greater detail in the next section.

Figure 2
Expected Alternatives to a Negotiated Agreement for Environmentalists and Water Developers,
Non-Negotiable Example

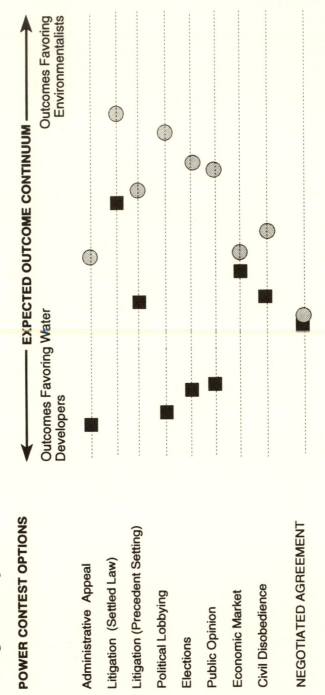

POWER CONTEST OPTIONS

EXPECTED OUTCOME CONTINUUM

Outcomes Favoring Water
Developers

Outcomes Favoring
Environmentalists

Administrative Appeal

Litigation (Settled Law)

Litigation (Precedent Setting)

Political Lobbying

Elections

Public Opinion

Economic Market

Civil Disobedience

NEGOTIATED AGREEMENT

■ = Outcome Expected by Water Developers

⬤ = Outcome Expected by Environmentalists

Note: Substantial Uncertainties Surround Each Expected Outcome

BEYOND THE LIMITS

Mediation, consensus-building, and related techniques cannot be expected to resolve environmental conflicts or persuade people to abandon power contest alternatives to negotiated agreements. Three major areas within the environmental mediation field's understanding of conflict processes and intervention techniques can, however, if used appropriately, significantly reduce the destructiveness associated with many of these conflicts. We refer to this approach as "constructive confrontation." This approach recognizes that, while confrontations with associated power contests are inevitable, the frequent destructiveness of these confrontations is not. The constructive confrontation approach begins with an attempt to limit the destructive effects of what we call the "conflict overlay" problems. These problems, which overlay the conflict's intractable core, include, for example, misunderstandings and the insidious dynamics of escalation and polarization.

The next area of potentially successful intervention represents a substantial departure from commonly applied, alternative, environmental dispute resolution practices. Here steps can be taken to help the parties identify and pursue only those power contest strategies which truly offer better alternatives to negotiation. These efforts can also include steps to reduce the costs and overall destructiveness of power contests. Finally, there are cases in which mediation and negotiation techniques can be used to fine tune the results of the inevitable power contests in ways which realize win/win trade-offs that would otherwise have been missed by power contests alone.

We believe that open acknowledgment of the inevitable and appropriate role of power contests in these conflicts is important. By acknowledging the inherent limits of mediation and consensus-building in altering power relationships, mediators help advance the prestige of the environmental mediation field by reducing the number of instances in which mediation is oversold by people claiming that the field can deliver more than it actually can.

LIMITING CONFLICT OVERLAY PROBLEMS

The first step toward making inevitable environmental confrontations more constructive requires an understanding of the distinction between *core* and *overlay* components of conflict. At the core of the most serious environmental conflicts lie intractable conflicts over fundamental moral issues or high-stakes distributional questions. Overlaying and often obscuring this core conflict are confused interests, misunderstandings, disagreements over technical facts, questions of procedural fairness, escalation, and polarization. These overlay problems can become so severe that the decisions which resolve the conflict's many disputes are based upon overlay problems, not core substantive issues. The environmental dispute resolution field has already developed a number of techniques which, when properly implemented, can go a long way toward limiting the overlay problems. These techniques can be beneficially applied even in situations in which the mutually agreeable resolution of a dispute cannot be expected. Specifically, we believe that efforts could be concentrated in the areas discussed next.

Confused Interests

As Fisher and Ury (1991) have observed, interests reflect the underlying goals and objectives of the parties to a conflict, while positions refer to the specific actions or policies the parties are pursuing in order to achieve those goals. All too often positions become the focus of the conflict and the parties fail to consider the possibility that their *interests* might better be served by pursuing different *positions*. What is less commonly recognized is that the interest clarification steps embodied in "principled negotiation" are still applicable to confrontational situations in which successful negotiation or mediation is unlikely.

Misunderstandings

Misunderstandings arise whenever one or more parties develop an inaccurate image about the interests, positions, or actions of another party. This can arise as a result of unintentional miscommunication, stereotyping, or even deliberate disinformation. It can be combated with a number of effective communication techniques, including, for example, (1) improved speaking skills; (2) sensitivity to likely points of misunderstanding; (3) active listening skills; (4) widely trusted "blue ribbon" committees to investigate and report on the validity of rumors; and (5) advisory committees composed of opinion leaders willing to take the time needed to truly understand a complex issue.

Technical Disagreements

Core issues can also be obscured by 'tis/'tain't conflicts over issues amenable to resolution with generally accepted scientific research methods. What is needed is (1) necessary funding; (2) skilled investigators; (3) a mechanism for insuring the analysis is worthy of the public trust; (4) a credible mechanism for demonstrating this trustworthiness to the public; and (5) an ability to explain results in nontechnical terms.

This approach only applies to technically-resolvable issues. In cases with an irreducible element of risk and uncertainty, moral judgments concerning the acceptable level of risk become part of the core conflict. In this case, strategies for overcoming technical overlay problems need to focus upon providing an informed basis for acceptable risk judgments. These irreducible uncertainties and risk are so painful that it is common for the process to suffer "analysis paralysis," as people engage in a time-consuming and inevitably fruitless search for certainty. The result tends to be *de facto* adoption of the default, business-as-usual alternative, which could easily be among the least desirable.

Perceived Procedural Unfairness

The process must do more than make decisions which are, in fact, fair and wise. The process must also be *perceived* as fair. For example, well-established procedures coming out of the dispute resolution movement and the more general field of public administration provide excellent guidelines for limiting the conflicts of interest which are a major contributor to this problem (Carpenter and Kennedy, 1988).

Escalation and Polarization

At the core of the conflict overlay problem are the processes of escalation and polarization in which one intentional or accidental provocation begets a stronger counterprovocation in an ever-intensifying loop. Escalation tends to produce five key transformations: (1) Focused, unlinked single-issue conflicts tend to become linked with a great many other conflicts, eventually polarizing the society into two hostile camps; (2) isolated issues involving a relatively small number of people become widespread conflicts with almost universal public involvement; (3) more and more resources are committed to the prosecution of the conflict; (4) efforts to persuade opponents of a position's validity or work out mutually beneficial exchanges give way to efforts to force opponents to comply; and (5) efforts to pursue specific substantive objectives give way to the much more vengeful motive of simply hurting an opponent. For a more detailed discussion of escalation processes, see Pruitt and Rubin's *Social Conflict: Escalation, Stalemate, and Settlement* (1986).

Escalation processes can be triggered and driven in a number of ways. The widespread tendency of people to attack personally and impugn the character of their opponents is one common cause. Anger and personal ego involvement can also make it much more difficult to plan and implement measured, rational confrontation strategies. The tendency of the media to focus its coverage on the actions of unrepresentative extremists drives the escalation cycle as well. The extremist who receives media coverage tends to become the basis upon which opposing groups develop stereotypes of each other. Also fueling the escalation spiral is the bargaining-chip syndrome, which can lead the parties to make unreasonable and, therefore, inflammatory demands on the assumption that they will then have something to trade away. The problem is that the escalation spiral may lead to all-out "war" in which the opponent's goal becomes total victory rather than mutually beneficial trade-offs.

There are also those who intentionally initiate an escalation spiral, figuring that escalation is the best way to mobilize supporters. As escalation progresses, the parties frequently note an increase in both the number and level of commitment of their supporters. They frequently fail, however, to note a corresponding (and often greater) increase in the level of support for their opponents.

Escalation is also driven by the fact that people simply enjoy sitting around with their compatriots and complaining about how their opponent is the source of all evil and, of course, they are the source of all virtue. Victory in one dispute is also often accompanied by celebrations which clearly reveal a lack of respect for and often ridicule of an opponent. Not surprisingly, this results in the loss of opportunities for conversion and conciliation while simultaneously inspiring an opponent to try harder the next time.

The choice of power contest or confrontation strategies also has important implications for escalatory processes. Those which place a greater reliance upon forcing power tend to foster resentment and backlash, while those which feature substantial efforts to persuade opponents are more likely to limit escalation. This issue is discussed in more detail below.

Finally, escalation is a true slippery slope—it is easy to slide down and awfully hard to climb out. The dispute resolution literature has, however, developed a number of de-escalation strategies, which can be quite helpful (Carpenter and Kennedy, 1988; Pruitt, 1986; Susskind and Cruikshank, 1987; Ury, 1991). In general, one should respond to provocations not with submission or counterprovocation, but by clarifying misinformation, avoiding the temptation of counterprovocations, making conciliatory gestures, and attempting to persuade opponents that one's position is based upon general principles of societal welfare to which they ought to subscribe.

Figure 3 summarizes the relationship between the conflict core and overlay problems. It shows the effect that existing dispute resolution techniques can have on limiting the size of the overlay, allowing the parties to focus better on the core substantive issues. The top circle presents a picture of a typical environmental conflict prior to successful intervention. Here the conflict core is surrounded by the five principal conflict overlays. The first objective of an intervention strategy which seeks to go beyond the limits of environmental mediation is to minimize these five overlays. The bottom circle depicts the conflict following successful minimization (but not elimination) of all conflict overlays—so that the confrontation can better focus upon the underlying core issues.

Figure 3
Limited and Unlimited Conflict Overlays

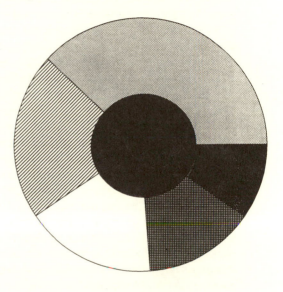

Unlimited Conflict
Overlay

Escalation/Polarization
Technical Disagreements
Misunderstandings
Confused Interests
Procedural Fairness Questions

Core Conflict/Dispute

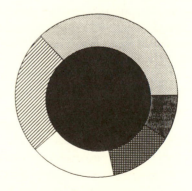

Limited Conflict
Overlay

CONSTRUCTIVE CONFRONTATION STRATEGY SELECTION

Extending the limits of environmental mediation next requires the continued development of interventions which help the parties make more enlightened decisions regarding the selection and implementation of specific power contest or confrontation strategies. This first requires an understanding of the crucial difference between forcing power and persuasive power. Forcing power is the quickest way for the parties to get their opponent to do what they want (assuming that they have the necessary power). Here the key is a credible threat which is so severe opponents feel they have no choice but submission. While this usually includes administrative, legal, or political efforts to mobilize the power of the state, it can also involve economic action, physical resistance, or efforts to foster public condemnation of an opponent. Over the short term, forcing power is the fastest way to produce behavior change in an opponent. However, being forced to do something that one does not want to do inspires substantial resentment and often a backlash effect. While opponents may comply, they are also likely to attempt to build the power base needed to overcome the threat at the earliest possible opportunity. This is frequently accompanied by a clever search for loopholes which will effectively allow opponents to avoid the required behavior after all.

The principal alternative to forcing power is persuasive power in which the parties convert opponents to their point of view. While there can be complete conversion in which an opponent becomes an ally, this is extremely rare and occurs very slowly. Partial conversion is more common and, therefore, more important. Here the parties are at least able to persuade their opponents that their position is not outrageous enough to warrant intense opposition. While persuasion produces much more stable change, it occurs only when positions which serve the best interests of the community as a whole are advocated. This may include, for example, appeals based upon general policy-making principles to which both sides adhere. While a set of universally accepted principles does not exist, the following seem to enjoy broad support:

- Relationships needed to deal with problems in other areas should be maintained.
- The general principles of majority rule with protection of minority rights should be followed.
- Decisions should implement as many win/win trade-offs as possible.
- Transaction costs should be minimized.
- Market mechanisms should be tempered by a social safety net.
- Decisions should be made in a timely manner so that delays leading to an unexamined, default, business-as-usual decision are avoided.

Confrontation strategies which are based upon these principles are likely to be more persuasive than those based upon more transparently selfish criteria. While it would be unrealistic to expect to be able to eliminate the need for forcing power, the backlash effect can be reduced by coupling it with persuasive power wherever possible.

Social Power Hierarchy

The pursuit of more constructive confrontation strategies requires an understanding of the hierarchy of social powers. These powers ultimately determine how the many disputes associated with an environmental conflict will be resolved. In most cases this involves public sector decisions concerning the expenditure of public funds, the management of public lands, and government regulation of the private sector. In other cases it may involve the environmentally related decisions of the private sector. The principal sources of power, ranging from the least to the most powerful, are listed next.

Administrative power. In the public sector the first recourse is to administrative power. Here a party simply appeals to government officials with discretionary jurisdiction over a particular area of concern and asks them to make the desired decision in as persuasive and mutually beneficial a way as possible. One must remember that these officials must constantly look over their shoulders to make sure that their superiors approve sufficiently of their actions to reduce the risk of reprimand and reversal.

If the government official doesn't offer to resolve the dispute in the desired way, the parties can always appeal up the hierarchy to higher-level career bureaucrats, political appointees, and, ultimately, elected government executives—if they think that this will yield a more favorable result. If not, the parties can either appeal to higher levels of the social power hierarchy or accept the administrative decision and return to the bargaining table to see if any win/win trade-offs can be worked out within the broad constraints of the administrative decision (see Negotiated Fine Tuning section below).

Litigation. If the parties believe that uncooperative administrative officials are in violation of applicable statutes, they can challenge administrative decisions in court. In some cases this may be a relatively straightforward process involving settled legal principles. In others, there may be legal uncertainties requiring precedent-setting appeals to the higher courts.

Political power. If the courts decide that the law, as currently written, does not support a particular position, the party's next alternative to consider is to use the political system to persuade legislative bodies to change the law. A first step can be simply to lobby the appropriate legislators at the federal, state, or local level. If parties think that they still don't have enough votes, the next step is electoral politics, in which they can try to elect more representatives who agree with them. In many jurisdictions there is also the option of putting the issue directly to a vote of the people through a referendum process.

Public opinion. If existing public opinion as reflected through political action does not support the parties' position, the next option is to attempt to persuade the public to change their opinions through some sort of educational campaign. If successful, this opinion change can then become a basis for renewed electoral campaigns and lobbying efforts.

Physical resistance. If the above options fail, the only other option involves physical resistance, which may either be violent or nonviolent. This is likely to be a relatively futile task since it requires a direct challenge to both the popular majority and power of the state. It is also likely to foster resentment and backlash.

Private sector decisions. Contests involving private sector decisions, economic markets, and private property provide another source of power which is somewhat separate from the public sector hierarchy discussed above. These contests start with efforts to persuade property owners to change their behavior. In a hypothetical example, environmentalists might ask ranchers not to shoot wolves attacking their livestock. In some cases ranchers may simply comply with the request. In other cases they may insist on being compensated for any livestock losses. If environmentalists have the money and are willing, they can simply pay the ranchers.

If, as is more commonly the case, the environmentalists don't have the money, then they can resort to the public processes in an attempt to deny ranchers the right to shoot the wolves. At this point the confrontation reverts to the public sector power hierarchy discussed above.

Implications

Since transaction costs tend to escalate as one moves up the power hierarchy, one goal is to use the lowest power level likely to be effective. This goal must, however, be balanced with the fact that success at higher levels tends to prevail over success at lower levels. At each level a failure to prevail may be traced to either an inherent powerlessness and general lack of support for a particular position or an inability of the parties to exploit their powers effectively. This suggests that before moving to the next higher level, the parties should make sure that they have the skills and the resources to use the system effectively.

One must also beware of the illusion of invincibility, especially at the earlier stages of a confrontation. Here parties can become convinced that they can't possibly lose and that the confrontation might actually be an enjoyable "blow-out" of the opposition. At this point it is quite easy to be lured into destructive (and possibly defeating) confrontations. Once involved in a destructive confrontation, falling into what Kenneth Boulding called the "sacrifice trap" is easy (Boulding, 1978:206). Here the parties may be unwilling to admit that their confrontation strategy has been ill-advised and that alternative strategies should be pursued. The problem is that such an admission is tantamount to saying that the sacrifices have been meaningless (or worse, destructive). Since nobody wants to do this, people tend to pursue destructive confrontation strategies much longer than they otherwise would.

Bitter-End Syndrome

The biggest problem associated with traditional power contests is what we call the "bitter-end syndrome." Here the parties may mistakenly conclude that they must pursue power contests (alternatives to negotiated agreements) to the bitter end. The fact is that they have to pursue them just long enough for both sides to be able to predict the outcome with a relatively high degree of confidence. In a few "toss-up" or precedent setting cases, this may truly require pursuing the issue to the bitter end. More frequently, however, one can narrow the differences between expected outcomes to the point at which negotiated dispute (not conflict) resolution seems workable. This can be achieved through alternative or "mock" power contests. For example, a well-crafted, objective opinion poll might be able to resolve differences between the two sides over the probable outcome of an electoral power contest to the point at which one party will conclude that elections don't really provide a better alternative to a negotiated agreement. Similarly, a key test vote on a relatively minor matter in a legislative subcommittee may reveal the balance of legislative power and persuade at least one side that this route does not provide a better alternative. The ADR (alternative dispute resolution) field has pioneered the use of mock trials, so-called "rent-a-judge" programs, to predict the outcome of protracted litigation. While this technique has not been widely used in the environmental dispute field, it theoretically offers promise in a number of situations. Frank discussions with government administrators may also be able to help the parties develop more accurate images of the probable results of administrative power contests. Focus groups can be used to gauge potential public response to a new idea, about which the public has yet to develop an informed opinion.

Figure 4 offers an illustration of the theory behind these mock power contests. Here the expected outcome continuum reveals that, following negotiation/mediation, water developers and environmentalists both believe that power contests will yield better results. They then have two alternatives through which better results might be pursued—the bitter-end path and (for want of a better name) the "sweet-end" path. While both paths lead to a convergence of expected outcomes, the sweet-end path is much shorter, less painful, and less expensive. It also leads back to negotiation in which the decision can be fine tuned (see next section). The bitter-end path leads to business-as-usual—unnecessarily destructive power contests. This negotiation loop-back also allows the parties to reduce power contest uncertainties—the risk that they might unexpectedly lose.

In Figure 2 the conclusion of power contests would have the effect of moving

Figure 4
Bitter End and Mock Power Contest Alternatives to Negotiated/Mediated Agreement

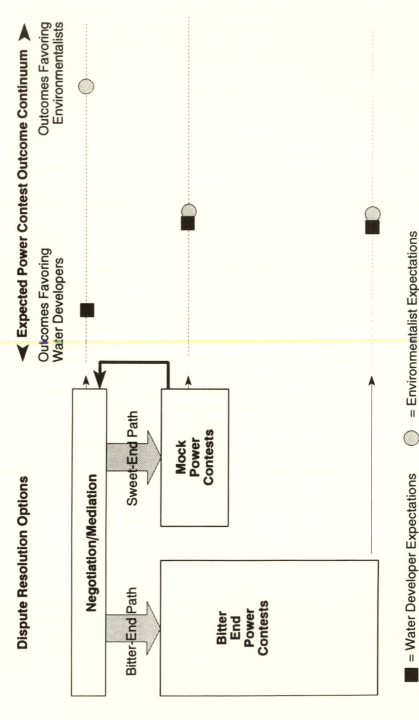

the water developers' boxes and the environmentalists' circles closer together. If the negotiated agreement was then revised to be consistent with the new, more accurate image of each party's alternatives to a negotiated agreement, then negotiation would become quite an attractive alternative.

Thus, the key objective of the power contest component of any constructive confrontation strategy is to help the parties obtain, quickly and at the lowest possible cost, more accurate estimates of their true alternatives to any negotiated agreement. Ideally the parties would use mock contests to determine the *short-term* limits of their power and then use this information as a basis for negotiating the resolution of *current dispute*. Here, the hope is that the parties' differing images of their alternatives to a negotiated agreement will narrow to the point at which negotiated resolution of the dispute is feasible. The parties would, of course, also be expected to continue pursuing *long-term* power-building efforts aimed at more successful prosecution of the conflict in *future* disputes.

Limited Negotiation/Mediation

The final component of constructive confrontation is the negotiation of mutually acceptable solutions to dispute episodes. Here negotiation provides an alternative to the "bitter-end" syndrome. Left to follow their natural course, power contests tend to produce relatively crude results with many unrealized, win/win, trade-off opportunities. This phenomenon is summarized in Figure 5. For ten hypothetical issues associated with a water development dispute, the figure shows which issues would ultimately be decided in favor of environmentalists and which would be decided in favor of water developers. In this example, the water developers won some things that they didn't really care about and, similarly, environmentalists won on some issues that they thought to be relatively unimportant. This situation creates the possibility of negotiating win/win trade-offs in which both sides get more of what they want than they otherwise would. These trade-offs are shown by arrows in the figure. This approach pursues opportunities for mutually acceptable agreements that are dependent on, rather than independent of, power contest alternatives. In the figure these trade-offs are indicated with arrows.

CONCLUSIONS

Serious environmental conflicts tend to consist of highly intractable moral conflicts or high-stakes distributional debates. The result is that, in many instances, negotiation of a mutually acceptable resolution is simply not possible. Environmental mediation and consensus-building are also limited by the fact that nobody is going to agree to a negotiated settlement if they think that better

Figure 5
Negotiated/Mediated Fine Tuning of Power Contest Outcomes

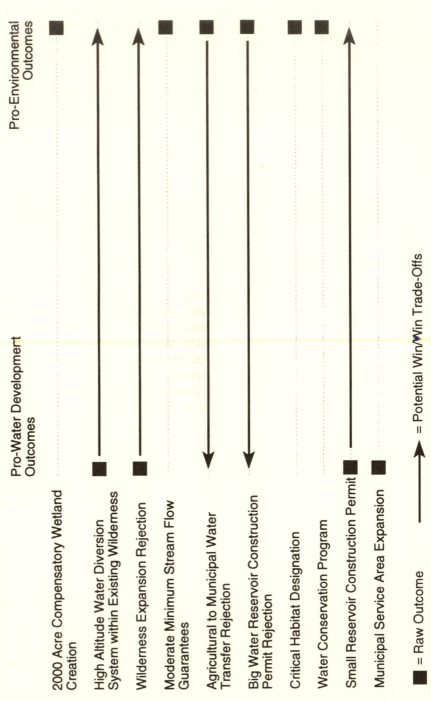

alternatives are available through power contests. Yet steps can still be taken to make these inevitable confrontations more constructive. These steps include, first, reducing the conflict overlay problems associated with confused interests, misunderstandings, technical disagreements, questions of procedural fairness, polarization, and escalation. Second, a number of steps can help the parties select and implement more constructive power contest strategies which limit the bitter-end syndrome. Third, the relatively crude outcomes of inevitable power contests can create important opportunities for the negotiation of mutually desirable win/win trade-offs. These trade-offs would adjust the outcomes of the power contests for the best possible results for all while still recognizing the newly established power relationships.

Chapter 9

Evaluating ADR as an Approach to Citizen Participation in Siting a Low-Level Nuclear Waste Facility

Bruce B. Clary and Regan Hornney

Within the literature on alternative dispute resolution (ADR), two types of studies predominate. The first is descriptive—case studies of the use of ADR in different negotiation settings. The other is prescriptive—arguments for the best technique or questions about the circumstances in which one type of approach is better than another. A critical perspective is less evident: the actual impacts of ADR and in what contexts (e.g., environmental conflicts, labor negotiation or rule-making) it is most effective. Where ADR substitutes for litigation, the most straightforward measure of impact is whether the dispute is resolved successfully and the parties come to agreement. Some research indicates that ADR is effective in this regard. One study reported that in cases in which explicit agreement among the parties was the goal, this outcome was achieved 78 percent of the time (Bingham, 1986).

Despite this evidence, a recent study of ADR found a paucity of attempts to evaluate it formally. Additionally, the concept was applied to a wide variety of disparate activities, from litigation to the provision of recommendations to decision-making bodies, making systematic assessment even more difficult (Nakamura, Church, and Cooper, 1991). This conclusion serves as the starting point for this chapter. How effective is ADR when applied to processes, like advisory panels and citizen participation programs, in which the relatively defined and concrete focus, characteristic of environmental mediation, is often absent?

This study examines the use of ADR in facilitating citizen participation in the siting of a low-level radioactive waste (LLRW) facility in Maine. The case has many of the attributes of those conflicts for which environmental mediation is employed. Foremost, like other controversies related to nuclear energy, is the high level of conflict. Under the federal Low-Level Radioactive Waste Policy (LLRW) Act of 1980, states have to enter into interstate compacts to provide for disposal or to site their own facility. A long and protracted bargaining process has resulted, both among and within states (Burns, 1988; Kearney and Stucker, 1985). Few empirical analyses are available, but existing studies indicate that the legislation produced a difficult problem of negotiation (Hill and Weissert, 1992; McGinnis, 1993).

Federal law requires states to take responsibility for disposal of LLRW generated within their own boundaries. Maine could either contract with an out-of-state disposal facility or construct a disposal facility within the state. Should out-of-state disposal become unavailable, the state would have to find and develop its own environmentally acceptable site.

The state legislature established the Maine Low-Level Radioactive Waste Authority in June, 1987. It was funded by assessments from in-state LLRW generators and required no tax dollars. The seven members of the Authority were responsible for all parts of the process, from siting through operation and eventual closure of the facility.

What is distinctive about the Maine siting process is that ADR was used to facilitate citizen participation. In the summer of 1989, a Citizen Advisory Group (CAG) was formed to provide the Authority with broad-based public input. Unlike most advisory bodies of this type, a formal process of facilitation was employed. A nationally known mediator, Lawrence Susskind, was hired. The approach closely paralleled the description of alternative dispute resolution outlined in his co-authored book, *Breaking the Impasse: Consensual Approaches to Resolving Public Disputes* (Susskind and Cruikshank, 1987). Facilitation can be grouped under a category of mediation which the authors term "assisted negotiation," a process devised to resolve specific problems. It differs in an important respect from the other types they identify, mediation and nonbinding arbitration, since agreements or settlements are not necessarily a product of facilitated processes such as an advisory committee. But the techniques share many common elements: identifying participants, setting agendas, fact finding and deliberation. In any given situation, a mediator/facilitator may use elements from all of them. Consequently, evaluation questions pertinent to more formal approaches, like mediation, can apply to facilitation as well.

RESEARCH DESIGN

This chapter examines the initial phases of facilitation in this application of ADR. These stages, defined by Susskind and Cruikshank (1987) as "Prerequisites for Negotiation" and "Prenegotiation" are essential building blocks of the successful application of ADR. The dimensions include getting the appropriate actors involved; drafting protocols, coming to agreements on how scientific, legal, and other data will be used; choosing preliminary alternatives; and, in the specific case of an advisory group, making recommendations. If problems develop in these initial phases, reaching the "Negotiation" and "Implementation" stages becomes difficult (the next steps as defined by Susskind and Cruikshank).

The early stages of the process are the focus of this analysis for several reasons. First, the end of this period roughly coincided with a change in facilitators. The Citizen Advisory Group (CAG) format was maintained, but the Authority allocated fewer resources, reducing the level of certain activities such as fact finding (less information was available to the CAG members and minutes were not as detailed). Also, the analysis ends at a natural breakpoint in the siting process. The case study extends to identification of specific candidate regions and the volunteering of local sites. At this point, a major shift occurred in the types of citizens involved, from a broad statewide level to a more local orientation, and in the types of siting methodologies employed.

A study of the entire siting process would be preferable to this narrower focus. Ultimately, the most important question is What did ADR contribute to the final siting decisions (to locate a facility or not and if it is built, how should it be constructed and run)? Yet many interim determinations were made by the Authority during initial phases in which the CAG was involved. These policy choices were critical in moving the process forward. In other states, similar decisions ignited major controversies and often stalled the siting process for extended periods.

From a methodological viewpoint, the analysis of the CAG process when Susskind was facilitator allows for the empirical assessment of his model. Several research questions follow:

- How was the model actually applied in the Maine CAG process?
- What were the strengths and weaknesses of the approach in facilitating citizen participation?
- To what extent did Susskind accomplish the objectives of the model?
- What were the results of the process, especially the extent to which the Authority adopted CAG recommendations in its own planning process?

The CAG process produced detailed and diverse sources of information. These data will serve as the basis of analysis. Materials include:

- Detailed minutes of all CAG meetings from June 1989 to January 1992 (each one approximately 25 single-spaced pages in length)
- Video tapes and/or cassettes of all meetings
- Correspondence
- Personal notes from CAG participant/observer, Bruce Clary (chapter coauthor)
- Studies, reports, and other material distributed to the participants
- CAG member survey.

The last item, the CAG survey, will be referenced throughout the analysis. In July 1990 (one year into the process), the facilitator sent a survey to each member.

Sixty members returned the survey for a response rate of 75 percent. Questions focused on the general process and specific reports issued by the Authority. Respondents indicated on a simple yes-no scale whether they were satisfied with the extent to which their group's concerns were being addressed. Additionally, two separate evaluations were done of the facilitator's role. Items dealt with process issues such as the whether agenda items were fully covered in the meetings and groups had equal opportunity to contribute at meetings.

PREREQUISITES FOR NEGOTIATION

Susskind and Cruikshank (1987) identify elements that must be present if facilitation is to be successful. They were all important to the CAG process and include identification of key players, sufficient balance of power, legitimate spokesperson for each group, realistic deadlines, and reframing disputes. These are not static elements but arise as issues throughout the course of a facilitation.

For the purposes of the subsequent analysis, two areas will not be covered: the question of spokesperson legitimacy and deadlines. The reasons for their noninclusion are outlined below.

The "Goals and Ground Rules" stated that spokespersons were to seek input from their constituencies and reflect the interests of those they represented, the basis of "legitimate representation." They were also to serve as a communication link between the CAG and their group. The impact of these procedural elements is difficult to ascertain. The CAG meetings were not the place where problems of representative behavior would be discussed. If the participant was perceived by his or her membership as not sufficiently representing them, an exchange would occur in a group meeting or privately; thus, the information would not be easily accessible. Additionally, the issue of whether a person was a legitimate representative of a group never arose in a meeting.

Deadlines were not a driving force, even though Maine's siting process had to function under a legal timetable stipulated by the federal Low-Level Radioactive Waste Policy Act of 1980 and later amendments (1985). The most important deadline was January 1, 1993, when the existing three commercial disposal sites were scheduled to close and the state would lose access. The pressure was lessened when the Barnwell, South Carolina facility, under specific conditions, decided to accept out-of-state waste through June 1994. This change resulted in deadlines playing a relatively minor role in pushing the CAG forward in its deliberations.

Identification of Key Players

Adequate representation of stakeholder interests in decisionmaking and planning is not a sufficient condition for an effective LLRW process, but certainly a necessary one (i.e., without this element, a successful siting effort will not result). Ample evidence exists on the volatility of LLRW siting if citizens do not think they have adequate opportunities to be heard. For example, opponents to a facility in New York prevented proposed site inspections. Nebraska has been the scene of many confrontations, including vandalism, arrests, law suits, hunger strikes, fights and shootings (see Benford, Moore, and Williams, Jr., 1993).

Unfortunately, a move toward increased citizen participation does not guarantee that a program will be successful in garnering representative input. The question of what interests should be included is complex. Sullivan (1979) posits two broad sets of interests which must be represented: individuals and groups who hold formal positions of power and those potentially affected by the decision. This simple typology becomes rapidly complex when decisions are made about actual participants. An environmental controversy includes, at a minimum, these interests: governmental and regulatory bodies, state and local officials, local residents likely impacted by a proposed action, individuals and groups concerned with broad regional-level effects, and special interest groups such as environmentalists and pro-development associations.

No formula exists for the identification of stakeholders. Some suggestions focus on ethical codes or legal definitions of participants (as in labor negotiations), but little consensus exists on how to identify the participant groups (Bacow and Wheeler, 1984).

Given the multiparty nature of low-level waste controversies, this issue arose at the beginning of the CAG process. The facilitator, rather than trying to develop an *a priori* categorization of potential individual and group participants, proceeded empirically by seeking names and nominations to develop a list of potential participants.

The original CAG membership consisted of 81 members. Participants were divided into six categories: Business (18 percent), Environmental (16 percent), Governmental (17 percent), Individual Members (18 percent), LLRW Generators (23 percent), and Public Interest (7 percent). At a later date, Indian Tribes were added, although they never totalled more than 1 percent.

This distribution in group membership remained relatively stable throughout the life of the CAG. The major change occurred with Individual Members. As specific sites were identified, more community residents became members. In December 1989, 15 Individual Members made up 18 percent of the CAG. The number dropped to a low of 12 (15 percent) in June 1990. A year later, 24 members identified themselves as individuals, comprising almost one quarter (24 percent) of the total membership. The rough parity in members of each of the identified groups and the ability to include new participants as the scope of the siting process changed (from state-wide to regional and then site-specific) is an indicator of the ability of the process to secure participation which was relatively representative.

Sufficient Balance of Power

Balance of power is less critical in an advisory compared to a mediation process. By definition, advice is informational, not the making of the decision itself. Yet if an advisory body is to serve more than a symbolic purpose, there must be recognition (by those receiving the advice) that it has something to say of value. Citizens in advisory roles can be used for co-optation purposes. They can serve to legitimize decisions without much attention given to their concerns. On Arnstein's (1969) widely cited "ladder of citizen participation," advice is ranked at the bottom rung of involvement. Yet an advisory committee is not without power. It possesses information—what its members think about proposed actions and/or decisions. Although not a part of the formal organization, an advisory committee plays a boundary role between an agency and its environment through its information functions. Central to the CAG's power resources was the information it provided to the Authority. It was not just unsolicited advice but often recommendations made at the specific request of the Authority. As an example, the CAG did an exhaustive review of the initial list of site exclusion criteria, recommending many changes. These were reviewed by the Authority's consultants, who originally formulated them, and modifications were made in accordance with the recommendations. Besides this tangible role, the CAG also had a form of "veto power" in that if the members thought their advice was being ignored or downgraded, they could refuse to support the Authority's actions, prompting a crisis of legitimacy for the agency (although this type of event never occurred).

Another axis of power in advisory processes is the more traditional balance among the participants themselves. Since the CAG was advisory and not responsible for the final site decision, this dimension is perhaps less critical. Participants do not have to bargain and negotiate to reach a settlement. There is not the pressure of decision evident in mediation. Nevertheless, CAG participants were sensitive to power balance as measured by what groups and individuals were most vocal in the meetings. Members often raised the issue of domination by antinuclear advocates, arguing that they were controlling the agenda. The extent to which a group can dominate discussions produces a power imbalance. This problem can be partially addressed through representative membership, which the CAG was able to achieve. On the other hand, equal representation is no guarantee that discussion will not be controlled by one faction or another.

The most important dimension of power in an advisory process is whether advice is heeded or not. An advisory committee is powerless if its opinions are ignored (the only power option at this point being a "walkout," the goal to discredit the agency). Whether an agency listens to advice is difficult to estimate. The CAG survey conducted in 1991 indicated a wide-spread perception among the membership that the Authority was responsive. Seventy-five percent said it adequately responded to comments, suggestions, and questions voiced "By you and

your organization." Only 10 percent said "No," with the remainder not responding to the question.

This finding does not mean that disputes were absent between the CAG and the
Authority over whether the former's advice was considered. For example, in
spring of 1990 a volunteer process, whereby landowners could propose their
property as a site, was incorporated into the overall selection procedure. Many
issues related to this question had been discussed in prior CAG meetings. They
included how volunteers would be sought, methods of advertisement, when towns
would be notified that land had been volunteered, and when officially to accept
volunteer applications (for further site studies). Consensus had not yet been sought
from the CAG on any of these questions when the Authority announced the
volunteer process. Many CAG members expressed frustration that the Authority
had proceeded before the group had reached consensus on the question. However,
as evidenced by the survey data, these types of conflicts did not result in the
overall perception on the part of CAG members that they lacked influence in
Authority decision making.

Reframing the Dispute

A major challenge faced by the CAG facilitator was the development of a
collaborative, problem-solving orientation. The deep political divisions over nuclear energy were mirrored in the CAG. Some members of antinuclear groups
were opposed to the building of any waste facility. Behind this position was a
desire to stop the nuclear industry in Maine. For some time, the cutting edge issue
of the antinuclear movement has been radioactive waste. The political strategy is
straightforward: if there are no waste disposal options, then the production of
nuclear energy has to cease (Clary, 1991).

A basic prerequisite of any mediation process is that the participants are open to
resolution of the conflict. In game theory terms, the dispute is a mixed-motive, not
zero-sum game. It is not seen as a win-lose situation, but competing parties are
open to alternatives that reflect compromises. In these cases, groups usually do not
get all they wanted, but neither do they face the prospect of losing everything.

Game theory is useful in understanding the nuclear waste controversy. The
challenge is to move the conflict from the "prisoner's dilemma" of either-or
competition to an assurance game in which trust and collaborative behaviors are
fostered (see Gillroy, 1990). The assurance process has close parallels to the
emphasis in mediation on the importance of moving participants from concern
with maintenance of position to the seeking of mutual interest (Fisher and Ury,
1981).

Research on environmental mediation indicates the importance of participants
being open to alternative solutions which will meet concerns of others involved in

a controversy. When this condition is met, the process can proceed in a way similar to an assurance game. When the groups mutually explore and analyze various options in a problem-solving manner, trust and cooperation can be fostered. Lobel (1992) observed in a ski area controversy that mediation efforts would have been completely undermined if environmentalists argued that development could not occur or project sponsors took the position that environmental protection was not necessary.

In the CAG process, there are examples of the concerns of antinuclear advocates being successfully incorporated into the deliberation process. The facilitator usually would redefine issues in a way that moved the discussion from a conflictual plane, often resulting from ideological differences, to one in which problems were approached proactively. An exchange between a member and the facilitator provides an example of how the "zero-sum" characteristic of an antinuclear position was successfully addressed within the CAG:

> One member said that her intention as a CAG member was not to site a "dump" but to advise the Authority on the safest possible way to dispose of waste, and she believes this is through reducing the volume and production of waste to zero. She wanted to be sure that the CAG could give that advice to the Authority if members wished to. The Facilitator clarified that the Authority had asked its consultant, Stone and Webster, to develop proposed Exclusion Criteria, and had asked the CAG to comment on the consultants' report and process; this could include recommending no site. (Maine Low Level Radioactive Waste Authority, *Summary of Points of Agreement and Disagreement, Citizens Advisory Group Meeting*, November 2, 1989:1)

Despite the examples of "reframing issues," there is no clear evidence that attitudes of most antinuclear advocates changed. Many thought that no facility would be safe, regardless of the precautions. This "sacrosanct" value ("nothing is safe enough") altered little over the course of the facilitation. If the CAG had faced the ultimate question, would it support an Authority proposal to locate an actual facility at a specific site, consensus would have been difficult to achieve.

A particular characteristic of conflicts over nuclear energy is that opponents remain firm in their beliefs, largely unwilling to change them. Psychological research shows that the perceived risk from nuclear energy is much greater than for other, more conventional social and environmental problems (Slovic and Fischhoff, 1983). Individuals may be unwilling to compromise on nuclear issues because of their perception of the high risk nuclear power poses for society. Other studies amply document the highly ideological nature of the antinuclear movement (Ebbin and Kasper, 1974). Persons who hold such strong beliefs may be resolute, viewing negotiation as a betrayal of their values.

PRENEGOTIATION PHASE

The phase consists of four stages: beginning the meeting cycle, ensuring representation of stakeholders, drafting ground rules, and fact finding (Susskind and Cruikshank, 1987). All these dimensions were part of the CAG facilitation. The initial meetings of the CAG were used to accomplish most aspects of the "Prenegotiation Phase," although the process is certainly not linear. As with "Prerequisites to Negotiation," related issues arose throughout the history of the advisory committee. Even at the end, some were still being debated and discussed. Based on the CAG experience, the elements of the "Prenegotiation Phase" are most important at the beginning but must be addressed throughout a facilitation for the process to be effective.

One stage is not considered in the following analysis. The initial steps in the CAG process ("Getting Started") were accomplished relatively easily. Most critical is the decision to proceed, which was made by the Authority and not a specific element of the CAG process itself. Additionally, since the purpose was not a negotiated settlement, there was not significant controversy about whether an advisory group was a good idea or not.

Representation

A frequent question asked about ADR is whether all potential stakeholders are adequately represented. This issue manifests itself in several ways. The process is compromised if the original composition of the group is not seen as reflective of major constituent interests. In an advisory group to a siting process, such as the CAG, the focus changes over time as broader state or regional considerations are replaced by site-specific ones. This shift necessitates constant attention to the makeup of the group. Unless these issues are successfully addressed, splinter groups (outside the context of ADR) may form. The development of such factions immediately brings into question the legitimacy of the ADR.

The CAG was designed to include important stakeholders (see earlier section on Identification of Key Players), but also to maintain a process open to the inclusion of new groups and interests. The section on outreach in the "Goals and Ground Rules" allowed members to invite observers to the sessions. Additionally, anyone could attend the meetings. The section on these observers stipulated that they could ask questions and comment after CAG discussion of an agenda item was concluded. These comments were recorded the same way in the minutes as they were for CAG members. These provisions allowed for broader participation, on a meeting-to-meeting basis, than just the CAG membership itself. They also provided an opportunity for members to hear new opinions and ideas, helping to avoid possible "group-think" (i.e., the CAG only looking to itself for information. Some observers later became regular participants, serving to broaden representation as well).

When specific sites were under consideration, leaders of organizations and agencies in affected areas were invited to join. The issue became important in November, 1990 when 12 candidate regions (approximately 10 by 20 miles in size) were identified in the state-wide screening process. An agenda item was representation of these regions in the siting process. A number of questions emerged: who should represent the candidate regions, how should these individuals be nominated, what balance should exist between elected officials and the general public? During this period, sites were also being volunteered by local landowners. How should residents in these areas be included in the CAG process? Further, a question arose regarding the way to balance new, more localized interests against existing CAG membership which included few individuals from communities named as proposed sites. The composition of the CAG did change in an attempt to include more site-specific interests, especially individual residents. Observers also were likely to come from potentially affected communities.

The experience of the CAG with these representational issues is not exceptional. Whether all affected parties are included is a concern in any ADR in which the focus of activities change so that different individuals and groups are affected as the process moves forward. Representation is not a static concept, something that is only determined at the outset of deliberations. The CAG process proved reasonably effective in meeting the changing representational demands it faced. Its initial ground rules were helpful in producing this flexibility.

Another critical representational issue was maintenance of the membership. The long period of time in which the advisory group functioned, almost four years, made attrition a problem. In the middle years, initial enthusiasm had abated and the focus had not yet shifted toward specific sites. It was a natural point for a downturn in membership.

The first meeting on June 8, 1989 had 41 participants. The number had dropped to 21 in January, 1990 and 11 the following December. The only group of individuals who maintained their original level of attendance were those with environmental affiliations. Many of these persons had strong antinuclear sentiments which served as a strong motivation for them to attend. A lack of motivation, as observed earlier, is a reason for the lower participation rates of general citizenry in ADR.

Because of the declining number of participants, the Authority announced in the October, 1991 meeting that the CAG had "lost balance." It said it was only hearing from the "antinuclear" people. A change in format to increase participation was discussed. Among items suggested were: increasing the length of meetings to allow for more extended discussion of items and findings ways to improve communication between the Authority and the CAG. The issue was never fully resolved and remained controversial throughout the course of the CAG deliberations.

The problems faced by the CAG in maintaining its overall membership and the overrepresentation of strongly motivated groups are problems for environmental mediation in general (Amy, 1987). Environmental groups are very committed and, because of this, participate at a high level. Members who represent organizations with a less defined purpose, such as hospitals, businesses, and universities, tend to participate at a lower rate. Involvement over a long period of time is burdensome for members who participate as individuals since they do not have the option of asking an "alternate" to represent them. The CAG was successful in the identification of a representative set of participants at the outset and able to include new members as the geographic focus of the siting process shifted. It was less effective in maintaining the overall level of participant involvement and, like other examples of ADR, faced domination by some groups due to their high level of motivation and commitment to their agenda.

Development of Protocols and Agenda-Setting

Critical to mediation are the ground rules that define how the process should be structured and proceed. Blackburn (1990) identifies two approaches to environmental mediation which have among their differences the approach to rule-making. The first is relatively formal. The facilitator plays an active and frequently determining role in planning. The second model is relatively open and interactive. The involvement of participants is central in devising ground rules. In most cases, advisory committees will use the latter approach because they usually function informally. The lack of decision-making responsibility also makes the adoption of rules less pressing.

Central to setting CAG ground rules was determination of the appropriate issues for consideration. Some controversies, such as the continued use of nuclear power and the consequent production of waste, could serve to immobilize the group. Blackburn (1988) lists six conditions for successful environmental mediation. One is that disputes should not focus on issues which strongly divide groups along ideological grounds. The disposal of radioactive waste does not meet this criterion. Strong ideological positions are held by nuclear opponents, many of whom were CAG members. The facilitator faced the challenge of developing an agenda which could guide deliberations while avoiding the polarization of the nuclear issue.

The facilitator was relatively successful in balancing these demands. Essential to his success was the thoroughness with which the initial agenda of issues was formulated. In the first meeting on June 8, 1989, the concerns of CAG members were discussed in a brainstorming session. The results of this meeting were significant because they helped to establish the content of the agenda for the next year and a half. Major efforts were made to see that the issues were systematically addressed. Events would intrude, temporarily shifting the CAG's focus, but meeting agendas were shaped to encompass these broader questions. The agenda appears in Table 1.

The concerns were wide-ranging. They included public health and safety, environmental impacts, the technology to build a waste facility, the process of siting, and economics. Health issues were listed most frequently—predictable because of the perception of major societal risks and the limited amount of scientific information available on these questions. Economics was mentioned least, probably a function of the unwillingness of many CAG members to view the siting process in monetary terms.

Concerns of antinuclear advocates were evident in the initial list of CAG issues. The significance of agenda-building was that it forced the participants to look at issues from a broader perspective. A "single issue posture" (a cause of polarized conflict and frequently evident in the radioactive waste debate) was more difficult to maintain when other questions were on the table as well. "Public health and safety" is an illustration. Although many antinuclear advocates thought no safe means of disposal existed, the issue was phrased in terms of questions, not assertions (e.g., "What are the federal/state dose and radiation limits/ranges for each type of Low-Level Radioactive Waste?" "What are the short-term and long-term effects on human health?" "What is safe isolation?"). Handling the controversy in this way brought the antinuclear issues into the deliberative process thus reducing their potential for polarizing the group.

Joint Fact Finding

At the base of many environmental conflicts are disagreements over technical and scientific data. Differences of opinion regularly occur on whether information was collected appropriately, whether it was analyzed using acceptable statistics, and how it should be interpreted. Few mediation efforts do not involve disputes over one or more of these issues. In some instances, conflicts revolve more around adequacy of data than specific alternatives under consideration (Nelkin, 1984).

The "Ground Rules" dealt specifically with data questions in the communication section. Provisions were made for distribution of information to the membership as a whole. Workgroup meetings were established to coordinate the presentation of studies and other relevant data sources. Meetings were held by the Authority and their consultants immediately after CAG sessions to respond to requests for information. CAG members could attend the meetings as observers and ask questions as well as engage in discussion.

In Table 2, the sources of information provided to the CAG are broken down by category and number for the period June 1989 to December 1991. The table shows

Table 1
Initial Agenda of Citizen Advisory Group (CAG) Concerns, June 1989

I. PUBLIC HEALTH AND SAFETY CONCERNS
- No adverse effect on public health or safety.
- Need more information on the public health impact of exposure levels.
- Ensure public health and safety and environmental protection.
- What are the federal/state dose and radiation limits/ranges for each type of waste? What are the short-term and long-term effects?
- Have Authority compare benefits and risks of using/producing radioactive isotopes. Exclude waste with life over 100 years.
- We need safety regulation, guidance, and training for whatever facility siting approaches are adopted.
- How are safety aspects of Siting spelled out? What are the implications for hospitals in treating? What special training might be necessary?
- Assure that plans guarantee good access for emergency vehicles.
- What is "safe" isolation?

II. ENVIRONMENTAL IMPACTS
- What will be the impact of a facility on watersheds?
- What are environmental impacts of a storage facility?
- How can we minimize impacts on wildlife and wildlife habitats and on marine life?
- Ensure that natural resource values of the state are respected, particularly in the unorganized areas.
- Look at impact on the surrounding area at specific sites.

III. FACILITY TECHNOLOGY
- Eyewitness accounts of existing LLRW disposal sites and how they operate. Why are they being phased out?
- What is the best way of handling the "current reality" of waste products already produced? How can we dispose of or store the material we already have?
- Focus on designs that assume leaks, focus on monitoring and remediation.
- Look for best site and best technology so that danger is as low as reasonably achievable (ALARA).
- Must monitor storage containers; eternal vigilance.
- Should we consider only passive technology? What is safest?
- Look at facilities that have failed. Why?
- What are "safe" handling procedures?

IV. SITING PROCESS
- What is the role that 450,000 acres of public land might play in siting?
- Look at inter-generational equity issues regarding risks and benefits.
- If a site is needed, community control is important (e.g., community capability to monitor, inspect, and shut down).
- What is the "territorial jurisdiction" of the State of Maine as related to expanding site possibilities?

V. ECONOMIC
- Look at positive and negative impacts of Low-Level Radioactive Waste disposal on state's economic development.
- Is this disposal system supposed to be self-supporting?
- How to meet the needs of small generators such as hospitals.

Table 2
Informational Adequacy of Citizen Advisory Group (CAG) Process,
July 1990 Membership Survey

Concerns	Percentage Satisfied That Item Addressed [n=60]
Quality/Quantity of Material	92%
Exclusion Criteria	85%
Consultant Data	85%
General Issues	83%
Performance Criteria	77%
Avoidance Criteria	77%
Siting Timetable	68%
Public Information and Education	68%
Volunteer Process Proposal	65%
Proposal on Community Assistance	53%

the breadth of the CAG fact-finding process. Topics range from Maine laws and regulations to health and safety impacts of radioactive waste. The largest category of distributed material related to the siting of a LLRW disposal facility. Twenty-two percent of the total material focused on this topic. Included in the items were consultant reports, sample surveys, correspondence, liability and insurance information, and legal opinions. Approximately 11 percent of the distributed items pertained to health and safety risks associated with LLRW, a reflection of concern for the central question of social risk: "When is something safe enough?"

Fact finding served to develop working relationships among group representatives who had substantially different positions on the disposal question. Data collection efforts, in particular, moved members from less ideological positions to more problem-solving orientations, an important prerequisite of consensus-building. As an example, the facilitator requested that two CAG members with diametrically opposed views (one representing Citizens Against Nuclear Trash and the other a nuclear power plant, Maine Yankee) work together with Authority consultants to develop a database acceptable to the groups.

In general, the CAG was a reasonably effective vehicle for identifying data sources and disseminating this information to the membership. In the meetings, frequent reference was made to specific articles and to other forms of information collected and distributed by the facilitator and by the members themselves. Also, questions from the 1990 CAG membership survey suggested that the process was effective. Members were asked whether they thought the CAG addressed issues of concern to themselves and/or their group. Eighty-three responded "Yes." The quantity and quality of the data provided to the CAG were also assessed. An even higher percentage, 92 percent, said they thought it was adequate. Additionally, a number of informational aspects (e.g., memos, criteria, proposals) were evaluated in terms of whether they reflected issues of concern. The response was uniformly positive. The mean percentage across the eight items was 72 percent. The items and the percentage indicating satisfaction appear in Table 3.

Table 3
Materials Distributed to the CAG, June 1989-December 1991

Category of Material	Percent (n=412)
Siting of a LLRW Disposal Facility	22%
Material Made Available by Others at CAG Meetings	18%
Health and Safety Impacts of LLRW	11%
LLRW Disposal Technologies	8%
CAG Process and Activities	7%
Other Siting Issues	6%
Organizational Position/Goal Statements and Publications	6%
MLLRW Authority Responsibilities and Activities	6%
Federal Laws and Regulations Concerning LLRW	5%
Interstate Compact and Contract Negotiations for Out-of-State Disposal of Maine Waste	5%
Data on LLRW Generated in the State of Maine	5%
State of Maine Laws and Regulations Concerning LLRW	1%
TOTAL MATERIALS DISTRIBUTED	100%

CONCLUSIONS

Despite the many articles written on alternative dispute resolution (ADR), few include systematic assessments of it. Most research is descriptive, describing in case study fashion what occurred during an intervention, or prescriptive, suggesting the best course of action. These studies rarely employ a conceptual framework within which the case can be evaluated. Additionally, ADR is applied to a wide variety of activities, from alternatives to litigation, to the basis of citizen participation in government.

In contrast to much of the research, this chapter attempted to present a conceptually based assessment of an ADR process. The focus was citizen participation in the siting of a low-level radioactive waste facility in Maine. A Citizens Advisory Group (CAG) was set up to advise the Maine Low-Level Radioactive Waste

Authority on matters relating to the process. A nationally known mediator, Lawrence Susskind, was hired to facilitate the process. The approach paralleled a description of alternative dispute resolution, "assisted negotiation," outlined in Susskind's co-authored book, *Breaking the Impasse: Consensual Approaches to Resolving Public Disputes* (Susskind and Cruikshank, 1987). The analysis focuses on the initial phases of facilitation. These stages are defined as "Prerequisites for Negotiation" and "Prenegotiation" and include dimensions such as identifying key players, setting agendas, and reframing issues. If problems develop in these initial phases, it becomes difficult to move to the next stages, "Negotiation" and "Implementation." Discussion focused on the strengths and weaknesses of this approach to the facilitation of citizen participation, whether the objectives of the model were realized, and its impact on decision making.

Overall, the process paralleled closely the model developed by Susskind and Cruikshank. Each step in the process could be clearly identified. Over its four-year history, the CAG moved through the particular stages specifically enumerated by the authors.

Many difficult issues were resolved. Most of the "Prerequisites to Negotiation" stage were evident at the outset, although the process was certainly not linear. Related issues arose throughout the history of the advisory committee. Even at the end, some were still debated, especially the question of representation. Nonetheless, there was a rough parity in the number of members from identified groups. New participants were also included as the scope of the siting process changed (from state-wide to regional and then site-specific). While criticisms were made at different points about the dominance at meetings of antinuclear members, the process was reasonably successful in securing equality of participation.

Balance of power issues continually arise in an advisory group when its only power is that of advice. There is always the possibility that this input will be ignored, making the advisory process largely symbolic, only serving to legitimize the activities of the decision-making body. While questions of this kind arose, the Authority remained generally responsive to citizen input. It modified site evaluation criteria in response to CAG criticisms. A survey of CAG members indicated that three quarters were satisfied with the responsiveness of the Authority to them.

This assessment of the CAG facilitation, while indicating that the process was successful in bringing the attitudes of Maine's citizens to the attention of the state's siting body and producing responsiveness on its part to these concerns, does not answer the most important question: If the siting process had proceeded to the end, the selection of a specific site, would the CAG have supported such a measure? The decision never had to be made because the state formed a waste compact with Texas, allowable under the federal legislation, which permitted the state to ship its waste to an out-of-state site.

This question, however, is not the most appropriate. The goal of CAG was to facilitate the participation of citizens and other parties in the location of a low-level nuclear waste site. It was an effective vehicle for this purpose. A model of ADR was an important contributor to this outcome. The analysis does not answer whether ADR can solve the impasse of how to locate a nuclear waste facility. It does suggest that ADR can make an important contribution to the development of an effective process whereby citizen apprehensions, concerns and opinions are included in the deliberations. This step is an important first one in avoiding "Not in my back yard" (NIMBY) and the resulting gridlock as states seek a process which is politically equitable and scientifically justifiable.

Chapter 10

Negotiating Community Consensus in Preparing Environmental Impact Statements

James R. Richardson

Since the early 1970s, citizens, regulators, environmental advocates, and elected officials have disagreed over the structure and content of environmental impact statements (EIS). These disagreements often result in lengthy disputes over the citizen involvement process itself as well as the methodologies used to assess the environmental impacts and evaluate project alternatives:

> The National Environmental Policy Act (1969) paved the way for the passage of a profound set of environmental laws and regulations designed to enhance air and water quality, protect the public from toxic substances and encourage the reuse and conservation of resources. This landmark legislation also subjected development proposals to public review and gave citizens the right to participate in environmental reviews. (Sullivan, 1984)

> By the end of the decade environmentalists, concerned citizens and organized interest groups had the capability to affect the outcome of decisions about major projects through direct participation and intervention in the environmental review process. (Stewart, 1975)

Since the early 1970s, researchers and practitioners have argued for the need to develop innovative methods to avoid and manage environmental controversies (Aleshire, 1970; Bacow and Wheeler, 1984; Levitt and Kirlin, 1985; Susskind, Richardson, 1978; Hildebrand). More recently, environmental mediators have looked for ways to improve how citizens and project proponents can be involved in face-to-face discussions to make regulatory judgments and assess environmental impacts (Moore, 1986; Richardson, 1991; Susskind and Cruikshank, 1987).

This chapter highlights the negotiation aspects of environmental mediation by focussing on a citizen participation program carried out during the early stages of preparation of an environmental impact statement (EIS). It emphasizes key strategies in the participatory process which framed negotiations between citizens, regulatory agencies, and interest groups. Strategic steps used by the process managers to shape the negotiations included

- Meeting informally with citizens and community leaders prior to any public meetings or regulatory hearings;
- Instituting a program of public education, in addition to managing and facilitating public meetings; and
- Creating a way for citizens to be actively involved in preparation of the EIS after the terms and scope of the study are set.

The strategies reveal how a public participation process can be structured to hold negotiations with the public to reach consensus on how to assess the probable impacts of proposed development. Methods used by the facilitators are described at key points in the case, and the analysis addresses the regulatory context, the history of the proposed project, and the participation and consensus-building process. The chapter recommends methods to involve local citizens and negotiate public consensus in preparing environmental impact statements, which may be useful to environmental planners, citizens, and governmental officials.

The recommendations grow out of a case study of an innovative citizen participation program organized in 1988 to prepare a "Scoping Document" for an environmental impact statement on a disputed project with a long history of conflict in central Arizona. The case study documents how the structure of a participation process provided for facilitated negotiations between federal agencies, the project proponent, and disparate community interests and how these negotiations led to community consensus around the scoping document.

The case describes how trust was built between the facilitators and the local citizens, and it highlights the mediating role that the facilitators played in designing and implementing a process of public negotiations to set the scope of study for the environmental impact statement. The author explains the need for professionals to establish a process of open communication and negotiation in the earliest stages of preparing environmental impact statements and provides strategies that may be used in other situations. This chapter concludes with a review of the key issues and reflects on the lessons learned during the project.

Major recommendations growing out of the Arizona experience are to design participatory processes and public negotiations that

- *Begin early in the project:* The process should start well before public hearings to provide ways for the facilitators to identify who is going to be affected by the project and what are the key issues. It should also provide ample avenues for citizens to express opinions and ask questions early in the process, preferably during the project planning stages.

- *Design a visible and accessible process*: Opportunities for participation and negotiation should be visible and easily accessible to enable participants to gain trust in the process and in the process managers.

- *Create several avenues of dialogue*: There should be several avenues for communication to occur among and between interests, such as informal meetings, private interviews, civic forums, newsletters, focus and interest group meetings, and formal public meetings. A variety of forums should be offered to citizens, regulators, and project proponents to exchange information and discuss points of view.

- *Allow the participants to shape the process*: To create legitimacy, participants should be encouraged to play a major role in shaping the impact study and evaluation methods. The process should provide opportunities for interested parties to collaborate in joint fact finding to guide scientific studies.

- *Focus on the process*: The process managers should institute a program of public education about the project, the regulatory process, and opportunities for participation.

- *Create a safe environment for negotiations*: Clear and simple ground rules should be set for sharing information, exchanging points of view in public meetings, and gaining access to technical information.

THE SETTING

Prescott has always been a place in transition, and mining has been important to the town's economy since gold was discovered in the early 1850s. The mining business grew to include silver and copper, and Prescott provided a business and commercial center for the surrounding rural area. Mining followed a traditional boom and bust cycle in concert with the national and international economic trends, and Prescott's economy diversified to include cattle, railroad maintenance, government administration, finance, and real estate (Garrett, 1978).

By 1910, Prescott grew to a population of about 4,000 people, and growth remained fairly stable for several decades. Between 1940 and 1950, the population increased marginally, but with the end of the World War II the character of Prescott began to change. By 1948 a steady stream of well-educated professionals moved to Prescott because of its attractive living environment. In the 1950s, Prescott was well known for its beauty, small town character, and outstanding quality of life.

Between 1950 and 1960, the population nearly doubled as the town was discovered as a retirement community, and by 1980 the population had increased to 25,000 residents (Prescott Planning and Zoning Department, 1986). Prescott was characterized in national magazines as an idyllic American small town in a utopian physical setting. Its reputation as a health oasis was fueled by articles about the temperate climate and pastoral life style (Windsor, 1985).

Along with the "discovery" of Prescott came a shift in the age composition. By 1980, 29 percent of the residents were over the age of 60 and the median age was over 40 years, whereas the previous decade had been dominated by growth in young adults between the ages of 19 and 34. Debates about development keyed the needs and interests of the younger age groups versus older retirees and recent immigrants. Growth management and environmental quality became major issues as Prescott struggled between the desire to keep things the way they are (or were) and the need to provide jobs and affordable housing.

Although local leaders argued for stringent controls on growth, long-time residents were concerned with the lack of economic development and jobs. Prescott's native residents were frustrated with the inability to find good jobs and were angry with the attitudes of newcomers, who resisted change in the town. Most of Prescott's retirees wanted to preserve the community's natural environment and reputation as a health spa and were prepared to resist any development that threatened the region's qualities as a retirement center.

While long-time residents felt that the leaders were unduly influenced by retirees who discouraged economic development, recent retirees and environmental advocates remained adamant that new development would result in disastrous changes in the quality of life. To long-time residents, mining was a source of economic resurgence and an important part of Prescott's social and economic history; to newly arrived retirees, mining was a potential threat to health, environment quality, and the town's future as a retirement community (Hilgendorf, 1989a). This was the social and economic backdrop in which the Phelps Dodge Corporation proposed a land exchange and copper mine.

REGULATORY CONTEXT

Scoping, the first step in preparing an environmental impact statement, focusses on identifying the substantive issues and range of alternatives that need be addressed in the EIS. Scoping results in a document that identifies the boundaries, time horizons, and analytical methods that will be used in the EIS. In most instances this activity remains the responsibility of a federal agency and a project proponent. However, because of a history of conflict surrounding Phelps Dodge's proposal, there was a stated need to transform the regulatory process.

Regulatory guidance about ways to manage public involvement during scoping for an EIS is limited. In the final regulations implementing the National Environmental Policy Act (NEPA), the Council on Environmental Quality indicated that federal agencies sponsoring an EIS must make every effort to involve the public in preparing and implementing the document, including providing public notice for related hearings, holding public meetings, and making relevant documents available. The regulation also encouraged agencies to hold or sponsor public meetings and solicit appropriate information from the public (*Federal Register*, November 1989).

Although the regulations give guidance about the need to provide public notice and hold public hearings, there is little information about what it means to provide diligent efforts to carry out participation. Since the adoption of the NEPA regulations, planners, regulators, and local citizens have used a variety of ways to create avenues for communication among project participants, avoid disputes, and stimulate dialogue about the focus and content of an EIS (Bleiker and Bleiker, 1981; Creighton, 1980; Denke, et al., 1981; Hollister and Lee, 1979).

THE PROPOSED COPPER BASIN PROJECT

In April 1970, the Phelps Dodge Corporation proposed a land exchange with the Forest Service and the Bureau of Land Management to facilitate the development of an open pit copper mine in the Prescott National Forest. The mine, located approximately eight miles from Prescott, would develop about 800 acres of mining claims. In the proposed land exchange, Phelps Dodge requested the use of 9000 acres of federal lands for ancillary mining facilities in exchange for 2400 acres of land owned by the corporation in the Coconino, Kaibab, and Prescott National Forests (United States Forest Service, 1989).

In 1976, a consultant drafted a 60-page "Environmental Assessment," concluding that there would be little or no significant impact resulting from the proposed land exchange. Local citizens questioned the impartiality and validity of the information, and the Environmental Protection Agency prepared a highly critical review of the document. Eight years later the Phelps Dodge Corporation completed validating the mineral rights and proposed to proceed with the land exchange. The Forest Service tentatively approved the company's request in the face of mounting concern by several citizen groups and the unfavorable EPA review of the original environmental assessment. The citizens organized a town hall meeting to discuss the project and the discriminatory process to date.

The meeting, moderated by one of Arizona's congressmen, attracted more than 800 people. Staged as a panel discussion between representatives of the Forest Service, the Bureau of Land Management, Phelps Dodge, the Citizens for the Preservation of the Prescott Area (CPPA), and city and county officials, the meeting lasted past midnight to allow all the citizens who wanted to ask questions and get answers from the panel to have the chance to do so (*Prescott Courier*, December 13, 1984). The evening consisted of a litany of complaints and accusations about inadequate environmental information, collusion on the part of the Forest service, the reputation of Phelps Dodge in other communities, and the negative effects a copper mine would have on Prescott.

Representatives of the federal agencies were surprised. Never had there been such animosity and such a large turnout for an issue in Prescott. Citizens felt the federal agencies were promoting the project rather than protecting the public interest, and they mistrusted the Forest Service's intentions to require a full EIS. One week after the town hall meeting, the CPPA filed a lawsuit in federal court requesting that the land exchange be designated as a major federal action and that the Forest Service be prohibited from approving a land exchange until an EIS has been prepared (*Prescott Courier*, December 14, 1984). To resolve the CPPA lawsuit, the supervisor of the Prescott National Forest decided to prepare a full EIS that would address environmental impacts of the proposed mine, in addition to evaluating the land exchange (United States Forest Service, 1987).

By March 1988, the Forest Service, Bureau of Land Management, and Phelps Dodge negotiated a Memorandum of Understanding to fund the preparation of the EIS. Phelps Dodge agreed to finance the work and would not play a role in selecting the contractor, setting the scope of work or preparing the EIS. The Memorandum described the process under which the Forest Service would solicit consulting teams and evaluate proposals to prepare the EIS.

In requesting proposals for the EIS, the Forest Service emphasized that the consultant must prepare a comprehensive plan for citizen participation that would detail methods to permit all interested parties to have the opportunity to be informed throughout the process. The Request for Proposal also stressed that public conflict must be avoided (United States Forest Service, Request for Proposals, July 1988). In November 1988 the Forest Service selected a multidisciplinary consulting team consisting of biologists, hydrologists, engineers, economists, and land use planners. An integral part of their proposal was a subcontract with an independent group of facilitation specialists who had outlined a strategic program for citizen participation.

THE SCOPING PROCESS

While the practice of making environmental assessments is shaped in large part by the judgments of the professionals involved, personal or nonobjective considerations have positively affected outcomes of environmental assessments (Susskind and Dunlap, 1981). The facilitation team was not only interested in developing ways for citizens to express their views about the issues but wanted residents to take the lead role in shaping the study process. The history of conflict surrounding the proposed project, and Prescott's conflicting values about the effects of growth, meant that the scope of work would have to be negotiated in a public forum involving all of the affected parties.

The facilitators met at length with the Forest Service to recommend the steps to implement the proposed participatory program. The Forest Service agreed that the team should engage concurrently in three strategic activities: first, to gather and document issues systematically that citizens and concerned organizations felt should be addressed in the EIS; second, to provide a broad and inclusive program of public education about the EIS and proposed land exchange; and third, to create a way for participation to continue after the scoping process was complete (Hilgendorf, 1989b).

Identifying affected parties and understanding their respective interests provides invaluable guidance in structuring negotiations (Fisher and Ury, 1981). Assessing positions and relative levels of power is also a prerequisite to structuring dialogue in public disputes (Susskind and Cruikshank, 1987). The first set of activities centered on gathering written comments from interested parties; interviewing representatives of local, state, federal, and tribal governments; and managing and facilitating public meetings.

To identify key interests and concerned parties in a systematic way, the consultants felt it was important to meet with as many concerned groups and agencies as possible prior to holding scoping meetings. They felt this would encourage active involvement and enable the team to understand differing points of view. It would also encourage citizens to become substantively involved in shaping the EIS by influencing the scope of the technical work.

Providing information to the public and sharing power over decision making are critical to building legitimacy and creating trust between citizens and managers of the participatory process (Cormick, 1980; Johnson, 1993). Creating ways for citizens to gain access to technical information is a primary way to begin to share power over public decisions (Arnstein, 1969).

The second set of strategic activities centered on providing the residents of Prescott with accurate and timely information about the scoping process and the land exchange and mining proposal. The objective was to provide information about what was going to happen in the scoping process together with technical information about the project proposals. The team hoped this approach would result in an informed public debate.

In addition to identifying interests, it is important to focus on solving problems rather than on participant personalities if the negotiations are to seek out options that are mutually beneficial (Fisher and Ury, 1981). It is equally important to build positive working relationships if multiple parties are going to achieve consensus (Fisher and Brown, 1988).

The third strategic activity centered on instituting on-going participation after the scoping process. This effort focussed on creating citizen "monitoring and advisory committees" that would provide on-going review and guidance to the multidisciplinary team preparing the technical studies for the EIS. However, the citizens in Prescott not only mistrusted the federal authorities but had not worked together to solve problems of mutual concern. Establishing monitoring and advisory committees would provide citizens with the opportunity to work together in reviewing and guiding the technical studies of the multidisciplinary consulting team. The suggestion to establish the advisory committees was also aimed at providing oversight during the technical work and raising the level of trust. The facilitators wanted a process which was transparent, open, and legitimate.

Informal Meetings and Citizen Discussions

To initiate the three strategic activities, the facilitators established an independent public presence in Prescott. They opened a local office two months prior to the public meetings and met with the press, made presentations to service organizations, and encouraged informal discussions that were both on and off the record. They were also available to citizens and lay groups to discuss scoping issues and the substance of the EIS. A newsletter was instituted to inform citizens of progress in preparing the EIS and to highlight emerging controversies and important issues. The newsletter, distributed to over 4,000 residences in the city and region, included a description of the EIS process, introduced the backgrounds of the multidisciplinary team, and provided a graphic time-line for the EIS, which highlighted when and how citizens could participate in the process.

In addition to meeting with the local media and making presentations to service organizations, the facilitators interviewed more than 200 individuals and representatives of organizations in the Prescott region. The interviews were intended to provide the public with the opportunity to identify issues that should be addressed in the EIS and to become familiar with the participatory process. The interviews were held in small groups and confidentially with individuals to encourage the participation of citizens who might have been uncomfortable speaking at public meetings (Hilgendorf, 1989a).

Formal Hearings and Public Meetings

In January 1989, three public meetings were scheduled to allow all interested citizens the opportunity to express views and concerns about the scope of work for the EIS. The agenda for the first two meetings encouraged the participants to identify issues of concern. The meetings, which drew over 400 people, were structured to draw out the greatest number and widest variety of comments and ideas. Following a brief description of the proposed project, the facilitators suggested four ground rules to guide the meeting:

- Participants should try to state concerns as issues and questions rather than expressing judgments about the proposed project;
- Participants were asked not to repeat questions and issues previously raised in the meeting, but simply reinforce the issue's importance;

- Participants were asked to be as brief as possible so all that participants could be given the chance to speak; and

- Since written comments could be submitted at any time, citizens were asked to orally summarize prepared text.

During the first two meetings, the two facilitators worked as a team, with one person managing the meeting and the other recording questions and issues on a flip chart. The first part of the meeting was devoted to identifying the major topics that needed to be addressed. For instance, water, air quality, health, archeological resources, and other broad categories were listed as topics that would be covered during the evening. The second part of the meeting focussed on each topic, and the facilitators proceeded through the list until all concerns and issues had been discussed. The format for the meetings allowed the participants to state their concerns, clarify the issues, and reflect on how they should translate the issues into the scope of work for the EIS.

In the first two meetings, the audience was composed of mining proponents and opponents. Representatives of organized groups were present, along with elderly and retired citizens, middle-aged residents, and young people. Environmental activists from local colleges attended, along with representatives of the mining company. In addition to identifying concerns about the physical, social, and economic environment, the issue of the credibility and objectivity of the facilitators was discussed in both meetings. Because of the structure of the meeting, people were able to speak, listen, and see that all concerns were recorded. In both sessions participants stayed after the meeting to discuss the issues among themselves and with members of the facilitation team.

The Final Meeting: Shifting to Public Dialogue and Negotiation

The third meeting was designed to provide a forum for public negotiations and dialogue among the citizens and the multidisciplinary consultants, who would prepare the scientific and technical studies for the EIS. The setting for this meeting was substantially different from the first two meetings. Rather than the traditional format in which people would identify concerns and issues from the floor, this forum provided participants the opportunity to meet in small groups to discuss issues and the study methodology.

A large room was divided into smaller areas, with tables and chairs set for groups of ten to fifteen discussants. Citizens could drop in anytime during the day and participate in as many groups and discussions as they wished. The event was attended by more than 300 citizens and included many who had not been to previous meetings. Each of these groups was led by a facilitator who mediated discussions among the participants and members of the EIS technical and scientific team. The groups were organized around the categories which had been identified in the previous meetings (i.e., air, archaeology, wildlife, vegetation, social and economic effects, and the EIS process itself).

One of the important aspects of this meeting was providing a way for the citizens to meet members of the multidisciplinary technical and scientific consultants. During the day, members of the public were able to learn from the technical experts more about how technical studies for the EIS would be carried out and to make suggestions for the methodologies that were to be used. Many of the questions probed the time horizons, physical boundaries, and methodologies that would be used to collect base-line data and make projections in the EIS. The credibility of the technical team grew as the consultants responded to insightful questions and changed or amended proposed approaches for the studies. By mid-day the process of negotiating a scope of work and discussing methodologies for the study was well underway.

The event not only provided the opportunity to focus on issues of concern but also allowed free-flowing discussion about how scientific studies would be carried out. As a means to sustain participation during the EIS, citizens were invited to serve as members of the monitoring and advisory committees that would meet with the scientific and technical consultants during preparation of the EIS.

Reporting, Feedback, and Reflection

Within two weeks of the last public forum, all of the comments and concerns were summarized in a document that framed the scope of work for the EIS. In addition to this report, each participant received xerox reductions of the flip chart notes taken by the facilitators at the first two meetings. Material from each of the discussion groups in the third forum was summarized in the form of a brief report and was highlighted in the scoping document. This material set the agenda for the volunteer citizen advisory and monitoring committees.

After a month's time period, few additional comments were received, and the consultants produced a final document that summarized key issues and recommended a scope of work for the EIS. The Forest Service reviewed the scope and negotiated the cost of implementing the scientific studies with the multidisciplinary technical consulting team. The Forest Service not only agreed to support the citizen advisory and monitoring groups but welcomed their role in guiding the EIS.

Shortly before the technical work was to proceed, the Phelps Dodge Company decided to put the project on hold because the market for copper and copper products was lagging worldwide. The EIS and the citizens are prepared, however, if the company revives the project.

LESSONS AND RECOMMENDATIONS

The Copper Basin project had a history of conflict in which the decision makers were mistrusted by the people of Prescott. Moreover, the land exchange and mine were proposed near a community with a population increasingly divided in age and attitude toward development and mining. Consequently, few people were initially willing to trust the EIS process and were initially suspicious of the facilitation team despite the requirement for participation in the Forest Service Request for Proposals and the terms of the Memorandum of Understanding.

The facilitators learned that it is important to enter the situation early. It was a tremendous advantage to be able to begin working with citizens in the community well before public hearings and meetings were scheduled. The team was able to identify parties having a stake in the outcome, gain insight into local dynamics, and understand key issues that the study should address. These early meetings also helped the facilitators to establish an identity separate from the regulators and organizations that had a history with the project. The meetings worked to build trust in the facilitation team's ability to manage the process.

Initiating participation early also meant that citizens were able to ask questions and express concerns while the facilitators and the technical and scientific consultants were designing the EIS study process. To enhance credibility and build trust in the process, the facilitators found it essential to be visible and accessible. Early meetings with reporters and appearances on radio, television, and talk shows helped get the word out that the process would be open and accessible. The team's local office contributed to establishing an independent identity and provided a place to meet informally with individuals and small groups.

It is important to create many avenues for public input. The facilitation team designed and edited a newsletter, managed and facilitated public meetings, accepted written testimony, conducted interviews with individuals, and attended small group discussions with local citizens. It is important to provide a range of settings to allow citizens to be as comfortable as possible. These forums included private meetings, confidential discussions, small group discussions, and large group meetings with traditional and untraditional formats.

Members of the public were encouraged to shape the process by making suggestions for new avenues of participation or suggesting other people or organizations that should be contacted. One of the discussion groups in the third public forum focussed on the EIS process itself and was aimed at shaping the next stages for participation.

The format for public meetings was nontraditional to increase the level of communication and to avoid exacerbating the history of conflict in the community. During the first two public meetings, two facilitators were employed to manage the meeting and record the comments in bold print simultaneously in front of the audience. This method of team facilitation enabled the consultants to listen to comments, clarify concerns, and help frame questions to focus the scope of work for the EIS. The ground rules suggested for the public meetings established a clear structure for the meeting and created an atmosphere of "safety" for the participants. The citizens gained trust in the EIS process, and the scoping document accurately reflected their concerns and interests.

The format for the third public meeting provided an avenue for the multidisciplinary team of technical and scientific consultants to meet with the citizens. The meeting was designed to create a bridge to the scientific studies that the EIS would address. The value and legitimacy of the citizen monitoring and advisory committees was established during the day-long open house. These groups were designed to promote the education of the citizens and the scientific team throughout the life of the study. The advisory and monitoring committee groups would become a vehicle to educate both the public and technical experts, particularly about making value judgments and assumptions throughout the course of the study.

Many characteristics of the situation in Prescott are found in other EIS projects: lack of trust, a history of conflict, sharp differences in values and perceptions, technical sophistication, and procedural complexity. The citizen participation process designed to scope the Copper Basin Environmental Impact Statement was aimed at building trust and legitimizing the technical studies. The scoping process was structured to enable the citizens to express value differences clearly, openly, and fairly. It also provided avenues and modes of communication that were socially and culturally acceptable to the local population. The facilitators remained accessible, flexible, informed, and amenable to change. In response, the citizens began to take ownership of the project and were equipped to understand and guide the technical results.

This study leads to six recommendations for creating a public dialogue and negotiating community consensus about environmental impact statements. First, interaction with citizens should start at the earliest possible stages of project planning. Second, the process of participation should be highly visible and easily accessible to all citizens. Third, there should be many avenues and modes for citizens to engage in dialogue and negotiate what is important in an EIS. Fourth, the participants should be empowered to establish the scope of an impact statement. The process should provide opportunities for local citizens to collaborate in finding facts and guiding the technical work. Their participation is critical to the legitimacy of the scoping process and is especially important in a situation of prolonged conflict. Fifth, it is critical to focus attention on the regulatory process by providing education about what is going to happen in the future, when citizens can affect the decisions, and when regulatory actions will occur. Finally, in creating a public dialogue and negotiating consensus, it is essential to set ground rules for exchanging information openly, sharing data, exchanging points of view, and guiding the development of the environmental impact statement.

Chapter 11

Consensus Building to Write Environmentally Responsive Rules for Maine's New Transportation Policy

Sondra Bogdonoff

The writing of Maine's transportation policy represents an innovative approach to broad-based citizen participation in a policy arena (transportation) in which public involvement has traditionally been limited. Through consensus building and shared stakeholder power, environmental concerns were integrated into transportation policy planning. The process offers a alternative to the gridlock and high expense associated with the use of litigation to resolve conflict.

In 1991 the Maine Department of Transportation (MDOT) was mandated by public referendum to write new rules governing transportation policy. It was were charged with creating a new policy that would be multimodal, environmentally responsive, and that would improve public participation. Using negotiated rule making, 58 stakeholders, from environmental, state, and business interests, arrived at rules within the designated one-year period. There was widespread citizen support for the new rules and for the process by which they were written. MDOT is in the process of implementing the rules, which include institutionalization of the process at the regional level.

The rule writing group, the Transportation Policy Advisory Committee (T-PAC), provides a model for consensus building and public participation for state government policy. Beyond effectively completing the task, the process has resulted in a reorganization and cultural change within MDOT. New lines of communication and new alliances have formed within the state, as well as a new perception of shared stewardship of Maine's transportation policy.

NEGOTIATED RULE MAKING

Negotiated rule making brings together an agency and other parties with a significant stake in the new rules to participate in facilitated face-to-face dialogue designed to produce a consensus. The Administrative Conference of the United States has endorsed a model developed by Philip Harter, commonly called Reg-Neg, and has encouraged federal agencies to experiment with the technique (Susskind and McMahon, 1985).

The Environmental Protection Agency, faced with problems of delay, increased cost, and loss of political legitimacy associated with court challenges of more than 80 percent of its rules, has turned to negotiated rule making as an alternative. Other federal agencies have experimented with modified negotiated rule making processes and have met with limited success (Susskind and McMahon, 1985).

Philip Harter, generally considered the "father" of negotiated rule making, has identified eight preconditions critical for success (Harter, 1985). These are summarized by Susskind and McMahon (1985:138-140):

1. People come to the bargaining table only if they believe negotiations will produce an outcome for them that is as good or better than the outcomes that would result from other available methods of pursuing their interests.

2. The acceptability of negotiation is determined by relative power. If the imbalance of power is too great, the less powerful party will seek an alternative context in which to press its claim.

3. Fifteen parties is considered the general practical limit on effective negotiated rule making efforts.

4. The issues must be readily apparent and the parties must be ready to address them.

5. Consensus building will be stymied if deeply held beliefs or values are in conflict. If values are incontrovertible, there is no room for negotiation.

6. There must be two or more issues on the table so that parties can trade across issues or items that they value differently, thereby arriving at a win-win solution.

7. The pressure of a deadline is necessary for successful negotiations.

8. Some method of implementing the final agreement must be available and acceptable to the parties.

BACKGROUND: PRECONDITIONS FOR
NEGOTIATED RULE MAKING

The referendum dictated a specific direction and a set of considerations and time constraints. The referendum campaign raised new issues, identified spokespeople, and, with the referendum's passage, changed the traditional balance of power within the state. More than any other influence, the referendum victory determined the preconditions for success and set the stage for negotiations.

The Referendum—History

Groups in Maine with a concern for the environment and the economy felt excluded from formulating transportation policy and influencing investment decisions. The Natural Resources Council of Maine (NRCM) was the most active of the environmental groups on transportation issues. It was frustrated with the State Legislature and with MDOT's lack of responsiveness. When NRCM was unable to block legislative and agency approval of a proposal to widen the turnpike in the southern part of the state, it made a decision to go to the people with a citizen-initiated public referendum.

NRCM believed it was critical that the referendum address the way in which transportation planning was conducted. The referendum, with new proposed transportation policy, was more complicated and harder to pass than one simply to stop the widening. Maine Audubon, other environmental groups, and alternative transportation advocates joined with NCRM to form the Campaign for Sensible Transportation.

The new policy included in the referendum, named the Sensible Transportation Policy Act, directed the Maine Department of Transportation (MDOT) to cease being a "Department of Highways and Bridges" and to become a multimodal agency concerned with the movement of people and goods by the most efficient, least damaging means possible. It required that alternative modes of transportation demand management techniques be given preference to highway construction and widening. MDOT would be required to take into consideration energy costs, air pollution, land use impacts, and the needs of all citizens, young and old, urban and rural. The Act linked transportation policy to the environment and to the economy. MDOT was directed to write the specific rules to accomplish these goals.

The expensive, hard fought and divisive referendum campaign resulted in the solid defeat of the turnpike widening and a mandate for a new transportation policy. The referendum passed in part because of an effective last-minute campaign that played on the public's discontent with state government and its spending priorities.

The Effect of the Referendum

By taking the transportation issue into the public arena, decisions historically internal to MDOT became open to public influence. MDOT was alerted to a new set of citizen issues and a new era of transportation planning. This changing environment was reflected in federal transportation policy, enacted soon after the passage of the referendum, which strongly reinforced a multimodal approach and provided more flexibility in federal funding. The federal Intermodal Surface Transportation Efficiency Act (ISTEA), combined with the referendum, provided a fundamental departure from the way Maine had done its transportation planning and investing for the last forty years.

The balance of power had shifted. The referendum victory highlighted the erosion of public confidence in the MDOT. At the same time, the victory gave environmentalists the power they believed they needed to get to the negotiating table and be taken seriously by MDOT. Critically, the referendum campaign made everyone aware of their interdependency. Both the MDOT and the environmentalists realized they had to deal with each other to have any chance of moving their own agenda, or the state's, forward.

The referendum served another function: it provided an important "exhaustion" factor. A lot of time, money, and energy had been spent in bitter argument. The campaign had been dehumanizing, turning everyone into "good guys" or "bad guys." Weary of conflict, people were receptive to the alternative negotiation offered.

Decision to Use Negotiated Rule Making

In the week after the referendum victory, NRCM and a delegation of others from the Campaign for Sensible Transportation went to MDOT Commissioner Connors. They proposed that the rules and regulations required by the new Maine law not be written by his Department as charged by the Act and as they traditionally would be. Instead, they asked that Commissioner Connors invite all the parties on both sides of the referendum to participate in the writing through a process of negotiated rule making (Reg-Neg). This seemed a natural extension of the referendum to NRCM in the light of its victory.

MDOT took the suggestion seriously. It contacted Philip Harter, by general agreement the "father" of Reg-Neg, and invited him to Maine. Although that visit didn't take place, a conference call between Harter and MDOT staff helped allay MDOT's fears about losing control of rules it would be responsible for implementing.

Commissioner Connors had been a strong and vocal opponent of the referendum. His consideration and ultimate support of negotiated rule making set a tone of cooperation and conciliation that provided the opening for a new dialogue.

THE RULE WRITING PROCESS

The Department of Transportation advertized for neutral facilitators to guide and mediate the rule writing effort. It ultimately hired the team of Ann Gosline and

Jonathan Reitman, both of whom had alternative dispute resolution practices. Although technically MDOT was the client, the extent of the agency's control remained minimal throughout the negotiations.

The Rule Writing Process—The Beginnings

The facilitating team of Gosline and Reitman started in late February to meet with indispensable key players to formulate an agenda and identify key issues. MDOT had a file of people who had expressed interest in the transportation rules. Ads were placed in state newspapers inviting other participants. Gosline and Reitman limited participation in the rule making process to individuals representing a *group*. They believed a workable total would be about 25 to 30 representatives, in line with Harter's recommendations.

Why people came to the table. Various constituents had different reasons for participating in the negotiations. Morale at MDOT was at a low point. Environmental efforts to intercede in transportation policy in the past had caused long delays and lengthy and expensive legal battles for MDOT. This was combined with severe cutbacks in state support, including nonoptional furlough days. The referendum victory had further weakened MDOT's credibility. It was open to negotiation and it wanted to be involved. MDOT was there to make sure the rules were grounded in reality and were workable.

The business community grudgingly agreed to an open process. It was there to defend itself, protect its interests, and to keep its concern for the economy in the forefront. Business representatives worried that the results of the rules would be to stifle MDOT and that valuable tax dollars would be consumed in endless planning.

The proponents of the referendum believed they had proved they belonged at the negotiating table. Most had little actual experience in consensus building outside their constituencies. This meeting was for them a first real chance to impact state planning.

The Rule Writing Process—First Meetings

The first meeting of the Transportation Policy Advisory Council (T-PAC) was on April 3, 1992. Fifty-eight representatives of various groups were present. Commissioner Connors outlined three requirements. First, the rules needed to be written by September, in time for public hearing before the rules would take effect in December. Second, all parties must be in complete agreement to the rules in their entirety. Third, the rules must be workable in the judgment of MDOT.

The facilitators, Gosline and Reitman, presented their view of the process and an explanation of dispute resolution using negotiated rule making. They provided a list of proposed protocols and ground rules for the group. These included acknowledging wounds from past involvements; being active listeners; welcoming and holding differences without judgment; discussing interests, not just positions; respecting the pace of each member of the group; "Walking a mile in their shoes"; and tolerating imperfection.

Gosline and Reitman brought to the first meeting a plan for a two-tier structure composed of a steering committee and associate members. The whole group would participate in discussions on the rules, but the steering committee would take responsibility for drafting the rule and would have to approve it by consensus. The facilitators had chosen 20 participants who they proposed would form the steering committee for T-PAC.

The balance of representatives on the steering committee was immediately questioned. Proponents of the referendum thought they were outnumbered. After intense debate, the group agreed to add three balance seats. Three individuals, whom the group believed could broadly represent the referendum proponents' point of view, were invited to join the steering committee. The meeting was awkward and tense. People were unfamiliar with the process and concerned about consensus as a model. Basic trust was minimal.

Building an information base. At the second meeting, the group identified the need to develop a common base of knowledge; to level the information playing field. A subcommittee worked with the facilitators to design an information sharing plan for two all day meetings.

The first information session opened with a group exercise conducted, at the request of Gosline and Reitman, by one of the participants. He asked everyone to stand and divide into groups, according to a long list of personal characteristics that had everyone moving from one side of the small room to the other. They divided in various combinations of left- and right-handed persons, people who liked dogs versus cats, middle children versus other standing in one's family, belief in the prospective fortunes of the Red Sox, and so on. Although some T-PAC members said they "just wanted to get out of there" when Reitman announced the exercise, the outcome was light and humorous. For the first time, participants recognized a tentative basis for mutual understanding.

Various constituencies made presentations. MDOT educated the group in the intricacies of the transportation department, federal regulations and the myriad regulatory systems within which MDOT operated. Other group members made presentations that included possible models gleaned from other governmental jurisdictions and examples from other arenas, such as utility regulation. Some people were impatient with this period and saw no immediate relevance of much of the information. In retrospect, participants acknowledged that a common data base served to break down some barriers and to build a larger context for the negotiations.

The Task

Following the information meetings, the facilitators asked members of the steering committee to, in essence, "put their cards on the table." Several groups, including MDOT, business, and environmental groups, wrote vision statements of their goals for transportation. They produced widely divergent papers, in both language and focus. Although this increased the tension in the group, perspectives were brought into the open. All the stated goals were put together in one list arranged under sections of the rules. From there the group worked to agree on a list of goals. The list formed the basis of the work that came afterward and remained an appendix to the final rules.

The facilitators wanted the steering committee to divide into task forces according to different sections of the Act. Each sub group could write a draft and then return to the full group to assemble the final set of rules. The steering committee was resistant to that plan, in part because the referendum proponents felt they would be outnumbered and outvoted if the larger group broke into smaller components.

June was half over and there was no agreement on how to approach the task of rule writing. A breakthrough came with the idea to divide not along functional lines, but according to voluntary "affinity groups" of like-minded people. Over the course of several meetings, the half-dozen affinity groups reduced themselves to just three: the environmental, the business, and the MDOT group. The larger T-PAC group divided along the same lines, although a few people remained unaffiliated, and a few attended meetings of two of the affinity groups.

Attempts to translate the vision goals into specific language led to a frustrating impasse. The facilitators talked to Harter, who had written extensively on Reg-Neg. He suggested the facilitators write a framework draft document for the steering committee. The idea was rejected, largely due to lack of trust that this process would allow various views to be aired fully.

The three affinity groups in the steering committee resolved the issue by deciding to pick negotiators from each group, who (under the guidance of Gosline and Reitman) would do the final drafting. How the drafting would be accomplished was not clear. Finally, the facilitators circulated an outline of the rules, based on the referendum. There was some agreement on the format the rules would take. Following that outline, the environmental negotiators wrote a first draft. MDOT countered with its version. The business negotiators gave input. The versions were put side by side, where they could be compared. Where agreement was close, resolution came quickly. In difficult places, working out an agreement went word by word.

Six months after it began, the full T-PAC group approved the final rules. A press conference was called and a group from T-PAC talked of its process and what it had accomplished. The group described itself as laying the groundwork for the equally important implementation phase.

Role of the Facilitator

The facilitators were available day and night: for 9 P.M. calls, Sunday meetings—anytime anyone wanted to talk. There were times when they took the initiative and went to key players. They met at the negotiators' work places and talked on their turf. Key players had a chance to say things that they wouldn't say at the negotiating table. At times, when someone had taken an extreme position, the facilitators would give them feedback on how others perceived their stance and encourage them to give a little. They carried ideas and alternatives back and forth between constituencies outside the meetings as well as during frequent affinity group caucuses.

The facilitators were a good team, with different skills and personal strengths. They consistently forced leadership back on the group. Only out of the process and the frustration did they think the group could gain a depth of commitment. The facilitators held the vision of success for the group and projected faith that the task could be achieved. Their attitude and encouragement became critical at those times when things were closest to falling apart.

The Structure

The T-PAC group evolved for itself a three-tier pyramid. The 58 representatives from constituent groups formed the T-PAC membership. All decisions were arrived at after discussion in this entire group. The 23-member steering committee, which represented T-PAC members in the rule writing process, was charged with actual consensus authority for the larger group. Two to three members from the three affinity groups within the steering committee formed a drafting group, who with the facilitators did the actual rule writing. Information passed up and down the pyramid as well as between members.

This operational structure was not what the negotiators intended but what T-PAC itself evolved. Because decisions were made and supported by the group, they were effective in moving the process forward.

Analysis of the structure. The pyramid structure allowed a large number of people to be involved in the process. There was a natural progression from the beginning, when the most people were involved and the whole group met monthly, to those few negotiators who, at the end, worked on the draft rules nearly full time. The affinity groups continued to meet on a regular basis throughout the process. Over the final few months, the entire T-PAC group did not meet until the end.

One of the difficulties with the pyramid structure was communication. As the work load and the time commitment increased, keeping the whole group informed and involved became difficult. Some of those people in the larger group felt left out. The facilitators did circulate to the full group several drafts of the rules and asked for feedback at various times during the process. In retrospect, the facilitators thought more deliberate communication would have been helpful, specifically in having the full group endorse the use of a drafting committee. Although the decision evolved naturally and worked, it was never formally sanctioned.

The structure inherently demanded a tremendous personal investment of time, energy, and trust by the drafting group. At the end the drafters were under severe pressure from both their constituencies and each other. They had two equally important jobs to balance. One was to represent and negotiate responsibly for their constituents. Their second job was to inform, educate, and bring along their constituents in the process of consensus building. At times, this later function appeared to be the harder of the two jobs. From the beginning there were uninvolved members of the stakeholder groups who considered it unforgivable to be sitting at the same table with the "enemy." There were moments when some of their constituents were concerned that they were selling out and, on the other side, concerned that they were being unreasonably stubborn and uncompromising.

WHY NEGOTIATED RULE MAKING WORKED

T-PAC was supported by preconditions for success. The referendum set the priorities of the rules and made clear a set of values and goals. These were not negotiable. Within those parameters its effort was further helped along by several conditions. The task was clearly defined, the time frame immediate and concise, and if this group didn't get it done, MDOT would. Everyone, including MDOT, stood to lose if that happened. The participants were clear about their responsibility and the importance of their task. The end result would be law.

The effort was supported at the top by the organizations involved. They gave their representatives the power to negotiate and the time to do the work. MDOT Commissioner Connors monitored T-PAC's progress, but, by tacit agreement, MDOT kept its hands off, not wanting to undermine either its own negotiators or the process itself. In the long term this was important in maintaining the facilitators' credibility. It also allowed the working group to develop its own authority and legitimacy as a rule making body, with the facilitators accountable to T-PAC, not to MDOT alone.

Conference Model for Systems Change

T-PAC's success in many ways reflects the findings of Marvin Weisbord (1992). He has found that when organizations focus on conflict, they fence off access to common ground. Through his studies of whole system change, he has developed a conference model to promote consensus and change. He has identified three critical specifications for success:

1. The whole system must be in the room.
2. There must be the broadest possible database.
3. People must be task-focused and willing to self-manage their work.

Although the facilitators' decision to limit participation to groups eliminated unaffiliated citizen participation, representation was quite broad and all major stakeholders were there. Commissioner Connor's support for the process from the beginning, and the public's interest in the outcome, brought stakeholders to the table and kept them there.

Education was a key ingredient in the process. Through careful listening to each other, it became clear that neither side had really understood or appreciated the other's position. In fact, MDOT's process for approval of major projects, which already required public involvement, was more stringent than the plan environmentalists were pushing. There had been so few projects that no one outside of MDOT was aware of the process the agency used.

Building Trust among Participants and Stimulating Personal Change

T-PAC required risk and leadership by many who had to engage in an unfamiliar process and work with people they only knew as adversaries for a result no one could visualize. To succeed and reach consensus on the transportation rules would have been satisfaction enough, but something more happened. People sat across from former "enemies" and not only gained mutual respect, developed admiration and even affection for one another.

During negotiations, small relational changes happened and people began to see each other as individuals, not just representatives of a particular viewpoint. At a break in the discussions, an environmentalist and a business leader discovered that they shared a common love of gardening. An animated conversation over ways to rid tomato plants of aphids caused a lasting change in their relationship.

This process was not about one star, one leader, but about a group working together. At numerous points one individual came up with the knowledge, trust, or perseverance to move the group forward. Several participants noted "how they never knew where the next good idea would come from."

Their success may also be about the effectiveness of collaborative male and female involvement. The negotiating teams for the affinity groups, and the facilitators as well, included a man and a woman. Participants appreciated the strengths both genders brought to the process. Each identified their partners in the drafting sessions as indispensable. There were times when they relied on each other and times, as one of MDOT's negotiators put it, "when Tom's feet were stuck in concrete, [and] I could say, 'You've got to move, Tom' and of course there were times when I refused to budge and he needed to push me."

The amount of plain work—studying, telephoning, attending meetings, meetings, and more meetings—became another cause for the mutual respect and trust group members ultimately had for each other. Their shared involvement and commitment became a bond between them.

The Media

An editorial in a local paper brought forward a request from the press to attend drafting committee sessions. Some of the group were concerned over how freely they would be able to speak and how the press might undermine delicate negotiations. Their concerns were balanced by others who felt exclusion would raise a red flag and give a negative image of T-PAC. Other T-PAC members, who routinely conduct business in a public arena, felt that open meetings were critical to the success of T-PAC and helped to assuage the fears of others.

The group agreed to open meetings. The length and complexity of the meetings made dull press for most reporters and their interest faded quickly. For the reporters who diligently covered most of the meetings, the process instilled in them the same sense of responsibility and collaboration as in the participants. The reporting was generally both fair and supportive.

IMPLEMENTATION OF THE NEW RULES

The rules were put out for public comment, and Commissioner Connors traveled around the state, explaining the rules and inviting comments. He outlined to the public the basis of the rules and explained that they were not self-executing. Their success relied on the involvement of the public. The new rules divided the state into regional areas, each of which would have an advisory group, modeled on T-PAC. He asked for volunteers to help form the Regional Transportation Advisory Committees (R-TACs) that would "put flesh on the bones of the rules."

Institutionalization of the Process

The new transportation rules themselves reflect the process out of which they came, one of shared power and responsibility. They provide a process and a planning model, not a product. Commissioner Connors calls the rules "a living document." The Regional Transportation Advisory Committees (R-TACs), mandated by T-PAC, institutionalize the T-PAC process at the regional level. The new rules take this system of conflict resolution into a widening circle of community involvement and regional organizations.

The rules call for the division of the state into regional areas, each with its own Regional Transportation Advisory Committee (R-TAC). Members from T-PAC met with the same facilitators in the months following T-PAC to come up with the regional boundaries and the general composition of the R-TACs. Five hundred people responded to Commissioner Connors' request for volunteers. He has appointed the groups, and they met for the first time in December 1993.

The R-TACs are modeled on T-PAC and include a balanced representation of various stakeholders and a commitment to decision making by consensus. The general composition of the groups are five or six municipal members, three or four environmentalists, three or four representatives of alternative modes of transportation, three or four business representatives, and two or three public-at-large members.

The R-TACs will advise the MDOT on transportation issues and goals critical to their region. They will determine multimodal preferences for their region, identify important social, economic, and land use issues within their region, and assist MDOT in developing an early and effective public participation process. Within the parameters of the Sensible Transportation Act and federal guidelines, they will have substantial authority to decide options and goals.

MDOT has hired four new people who were picked for their interpersonal skills and conflict resolution experience. Under initial supervision by one of MDOT's T-PAC negotiators, they will act as liaison between MDOT and the R-TACS. Members of the R-TACs have received conflict resolution training and will have access to facilitators.

The T-PAC, R-TAC process has been attracting national attention. In December 1993, the U.S. Department of Transportation came to Maine to look at the R-TACs as a potential national model.

CHANGE WITHIN MAINE—A RIPPLE EFFECT

As a result of T-PAC, lines of communication between MDOT, the business community, and environmentalists opened up. There is more respect and understanding. Other issues of possible consensus grew out of the process—transportation funding issues, the implementation of the Clean Air Act, and broader environmental priorities.

The key players in T-PAC are the key players in many other circles of interest and concern—economic development, natural resources, and government policy. History is important in this state, where distances are great and the number of people is small. The development of relationships across traditional boundaries has had a ripple effect, carrying a new level of collaboration and communication into other areas of mutual interest.

New Initiatives

Throughout the state there has been growing interest in workshops and speakers on conflict resolution. Although this is a national trend, the success of T-PAC has played a part in providing a concrete example and in educating people in the process.

In December 1993 there was a statewide Conference on Conflict Resolution sponsored by the Maine Consensus Project and attended by more than 300 policy makers. The Maine Association of Dispute Resolution Professionals (MADRP) saw its membership grow in 1992 from three to 50 professionals committed to conflict resolution.

T-PAC drove consensus building into a much wider range of issues. Probably the most direct attempt to duplicate the T-PAC process is the Maine Environmental Priorities Project-Comparative Risk Assessment. The stakeholders' goal is to list environmental threats, rank them as to seriousness, and then develop risk management strategies. The 37-member steering committee is made up of environmentalists, consumers, lobbyists, and municipalities, working within a two year time frame.

In the private sector, New England Telephone is just beginning a collaborative planning process. It is putting together a group of stakeholders to do long-term visioning for the telecommunications industry in Maine.

CHANGE WITHIN THE MAINE
DEPARTMENT OF TRANSPORTATION

Frustration with the current system, the referendum, ISTEA at the federal level, societal changes—in both new visions of transportation, greater public concern for the environment, and new "whole systems" approaches—all were having an effect on MDOT. T-PAC, in both its process and its product, clarified and helped to move change along faster.

MDOT and the Negotiations

MDOT put together a working group of people from different departments within MDOT to act as the planning and reporting committee for the rule making process. They originally interviewed and picked the facilitators. Bringing this group together was already a departure from previous policy. The group had representatives from the Legal Division; Location and Survey; Design; Technical Services; Environmental Services; and Planning Office in the MDOT. Most had never met. Their job was to advise the negotiating team and report back to their departments. They were the communication link within MDOT. Their first challenge was learning about each other and each other's departments.

Most of the MDOT group attended early T-PAC sessions. As the meetings progressed it became clear that the major changes would be in the process by which a project was chosen. Many of MDOT's concerns and some individual involvement in T-PAC faded. For those continuing, T-PAC became nearly a full-time job. For the others, "check in" meetings became the norm. Although the intention was to have this group within MDOT be a formal reporting group, the pace and time demands made that impossible. The three from the original group who continued to advise their negotiators met three times a week if not daily toward the end.

Implementation within MDOT

I talked to most of the original MDOT group in January of 1993, immediately after the final approval of the rules. They had a cautious attitude and concerns as to how they were going to implement the new rules. As one of them said, "civil engineers look for civil engineering solutions." These were problems for planners and economists. MDOT was being asked to do things that they hadn't done before and couldn't necessarily carry out with resources within the department. The real cost figures were unknown. MDOT was were expected to have a draft plan by January 1994 and a final state plan by 1995.

Those inside MDOT understood what a huge undertaking implementing the new rules would be: new systems and new procedures would be required. The law had changed, but the culture inside MDOT had not. Although Commissioner Connors was committed, the organization as a whole was not structured in a way to allow change to happen easily.

Cultural change within MDOT. T-PAC pushed MDOT to improve the planning process and become a more pro-active organization. In the past, MDOT had been mainly a technical outfit, a group of engineering specialists. It tended not to coordinate issues between departments, but rather to pass a project on through the various departments. MDOT is now initiating use of an integrated design team. There will be one project manager responsible for an entire project, who will follow it from beginning to end. MDOT is looking at new ways to present its projects and to develop better communication skills and better public relations.

Perhaps the cultural change that has taken place is best exemplified in the MDOT's negotiations with contractors. The chief engineer, in talking about past relationships, said "there have always been conflicts—they want to do less for more, we want more for less. We just assumed conflict was a necessary ingredient—a healthy sign." Now, MDOT has hired facilitators, including Gosline and Reitman, and is sitting down with their various contractors, inspectors, etc. before jobs start and working out expectations and common goals.

As MDOT has reorganized, it has relied on its participants in T-PAC to provide guidance and supervision. They have been able to help facilitate the transition, in part because they understand and were a part of the process that mandated the change. Members of the T-PAC advisory group have been more visible within MDOT. They have been willing and able to carry the experience of T-PAC into new responsibilities within MDOT.

Implementation Problem Areas

The law creates an opportunity for more public involvement and provides a broader, more democratic process, but it is too early to assess the result. How effectively public participation will work remains to be seen. The new inclusion of public input before plans are made has led to criticism that MDOT is now too vague. Public suspicion still remains. The design staff gets frustrated with the on-going public input and response system. To be efficient, MDOT needs closure, a point at which enough is enough. Where that point is, is still not clear.

Although MDOT has respect for the planning process, it is are primarily focused on results. The new process lengthens projects and makes them more cumbersome. The ten-year plan and two-year schedule mandated by T-PAC locks MDOT in, in a way it was not before. Projects need to begin earlier, and take longer. MDOT has lost some of its flexibility and ability to act.

The greatest obstacle to be overcome at this stage of implementation is the greater complexity of the new rules. The new rules increase the costs, introduce new relationships that need to be attended to, and require development of new skills. Although the prospect of getting projects approved and built has improved, there are new internal demands. This increased complexity has emerged in comparable cases across the country. "Although collaboration may make environments more predictable in some respects, they [sic] also cause new dependencies to be created, thus increasing environmental complexity and concurrently reducing participating organizations' control over the environment" (Wood and Grey, 1991:158).

SUMMARY AND CONCLUSIONS

The Maine Department of Transportation was mandated by public referendum to write multimodal, environmentally responsive transportation rules. The rule writing committee (T-PAC) of 58 stakeholders, under the guidance of two facilitators, arrived at new rules within a six month period.

T-PAC is an example of collaboration and consensus building producing innovative solutions. Its experience supports the contention that a mediated process can be a vehicle for change and new ideas. Not only was the process in itself a new way to write policy, the process itself generated innovation.

T-PAC isn't an end in itself, but rather the beginning of a new transportation policy. The group met its immediate objective of writing the new rules. The rules and the process have led to a reorganization and cultural change within MDOT and the greater Maine community. Some questions and hesitations remain. The ability of MDOT to operate under the new system will not be clear for some time. Whether consensus techniques and public participation can produce effective results over time remains in question. What is clear is that its success has bolstered the use of and understanding of consensus techniques, which makes the transportation policy's ultimate success that much more likely.

Perhaps T-PAC's most important contribution will be in its transformation from a temporary process to a permanent structure. The relative importance of individual group interests has shifted to a broader domain of state transportation policy. Over time that new consciousness will change the context of the way people in Maine approach other policy issues.

CHAPTER 12

The Ethics of Environmental Mediation

William O. Stephens, John B. Stephens, and Frank Dukes

The ethics of designing, convening, and mediating negotiated environmental decisions is of critical importance as one reflects on the developments cited elsewhere in this book. The growth of the practice of mediating environmental disputes which affect human economies and natural ecosystems, along with recent thinking in environmental ethics, raises new questions about what interests can be negotiated. *Who can and should speak for the environment?*

Two dialogues of significance for these questions and for decision making on environmental issues have, for the most part, been carried on independently. One is the philosophical and political discussion about the ethics of humankind's decisions which affect proximate and global ecosystems. Stewardship, sustainable development, and the rights of nonhuman creatures have been central factors in this dialogue. The other dialogue comes from those involved in mediated negotiations of environmental disputes. Issues such as disputed data, projections of resource use on ecosystems, property rights, and governmental regulation have been the subjects of this dialogue.

We see a need to bring together the reflections of thoughtful third party practitioners with the principles of environmental ethicists, in a new examination of the ethics of environmental mediation. The ethical precepts from philosophy can inform, and be tested in, the nuts and bolts of actual decision making. The ideals of participation, collaboration, and a balanced representation of interests in dispute resolution are challenged by different principles of environmental ethics.

INTRODUCTION TO ENVIRONMENTAL ETHICS

One challenge that arises in the attempt to construct ethical guidelines for mediated negotiations is that there is much disagreement among environmental philosophers about which things are worthy of moral consideration, and thus which entities can and should have their "interests" represented. Who *can* speak for the interests of the environment? How can the environment itself, or some particular part of it, be a party to the dispute which will undoubtedly affect it? The disagreements among environmental philosophers tend to result from two pairs of conceptual opposition. These oppositions are the conflict between anthropocentrism and various forms of nonanthropocentrism on the one hand, and the conflict between an individualistic approach and a holistic approach to environmental issues on the other.

Anthropocentrism

The dominant, though not exclusive, approach to moral philosophy in the Western tradition has been that all and only human beings have moral value. In this view, nonhuman entities do not have any moral standing whatsoever. For the anthropocentrist, nonhuman entities have merely instrumental value *for us*. As mere things, nonhumans cannot be harmed or abused; they are simply tools or resources for human use. Thus, humans have no direct moral obligations to the environment itself, but only to other human beings.

Criticisms of Anthropocentrism: Animal Welfare Ethics

The criticism advanced against anthropocentrism is that humans are not the only beings worthy of moral concern. Contemporary philosophers (Rachels, 1990; Regan, 1983; Singer, 1975) have argued that the capacity for conscious experience (i.e., the ability to feel pleasure and pain) is the only satisfactory, nonarbitrary criterion for moral standing. The view that all and only human beings are worthy of moral concern simply because of their membership in the species *Homo sapiens* has been called "speciesism" and has been likened to racism and sexism in being unacceptably arbitrary (Singer, 1990). The simple fact that a being can be made to suffer means that it is possible to be cruel to it, and cruelty is morally objectionable. Practices such as hunting and trapping for sport (in contrast to hunting as the only way to survive), experimentation on animals for cosmetic testing, and factory farming animals for food instead of adopting a vegetarian diet have been condemned by Singer for the reason that the interests sentient animals have in not suffering from these practices are not being given consideration equal to our own interests in not being treated similarly. Regan rejects Singer's utilitarian principle and instead argues that all animals which are experiencing subjects of a life—at least all mammals (Regan, 1983)—have equal inherent worth and thus certain rights.

Criticisms of Animal Welfare Ethics

Some environmental ethicists have rejected both Singer's utilitarian approach and Regan's rights-based approach to animal ethics. In addition to criticizing Regan for failing to give greater moral weight to members of endangered species than to members of nonendangered species (Regan, 1983), these environmental ethicists fault both Regan and Singer for failing to give moral consideration to non sentient organisms like plants and other organisms which are "low" on the evolutionary scale of being (i.e., those organisms which lack central nervous systems and thus lack the capacity for sensations of pain and pleasure). In effect, the criticism of sentientism is that, despite its attempt to arrive at a nonarbitrary criterion of moral standing which is not anthropocentric, it settles on a criterion, namely sentience, which *is* nonetheless anthropocentric. Why do sentient animals deserve moral consideration while plants and other nonsentient organisms (like many marine animals) do not? The criticism is that sentience, while not being *as* arbitrary a criterion of moral standing as membership in *Homo sapiens*, is still unacceptably arbitrary since it ranks sentient beings above nonsentient ones in a hierarchy which unfairly favors those organisms "higher" on the evolutionary scale.

Biocentrism

An ethical system is "biocentric" if it views all life as possessing inherent worth. Paul Taylor has developed a systematic and philosophically sophisticated defense of a biocentric ethics (Taylor, 1986). Taylor argues that it is meaningful to say that all living things have a good of their own. By this Taylor means that an entity's life and well-being can be enhanced and preserved or damaged and destroyed. Since every living entity has this good of itself, Taylor reasons that every living thing has inherent worth. For Taylor, a mulberry bush or a butterfly is a "teleological center of life" which grows, develops, sustains itself, and propagates its species. In displaying such purposive activity, it distinguishes itself as having inherent worth. In contrast, a pile of sand or a rock exhibits no such purposive activity and so has no good of its own and no inherent worth. Thus Taylor's concept of "teleological center of life" is broader and more inclusive than Regan's "subject of a life" criterion for moral standing. Taylor's system confers moral standing on *individual* organisms and seeks to adjudicate conflicts among *individual* living entities.

Criticisms of Biocentrism

Since Taylor holds that inherent worth resides only in individual organisms, then according to his biocentric ethics we have no *direct* duties to any ecosystems as a whole, to any species or group of individuals, or to any nonliving features of the environment such as mountains, valleys, lakes, and rivers. Basically, the criticism of biocentrism is that although it is nonanthropocentric, its individualistic bias fails to appreciate the *holistic* perspective of ecological science. Taylor's ethics tend to assume an adversarial relationship among living things in which each organism vies against all others in the pursuit of its *telos* (goal). Thus ecological relationships are characterized by conflict and competition. The problem with this model is that other environmental philosophers emphasize the cooperation and mutual dependencies (e.g., symbioses) among individuals within ecosystems. Exerting our moral energies to promote and protect the well-being of individual organisms is misguided because it betrays an ignorance of the nature of complex ecological communities. Proponents of a holistic approach to the environment argue that it is not individual entities which ought to be the center of our moral concern, but the entire ecological community itself.

Ecocentrism

Aldo Leopold is the founding father of ecocentrism. He presents what he calls "The Land Ethic," according to which the "land" is conceived of not as a mere object to be used, as a dead thing to be owned as property. Rather, the "land" is viewed as a living organism that can be healthy and thriving or unhealthy, injured, or killed. Ecocentrism shifts the focus of moral consideration away from the rights, interests, and claims of individuals to the whole "land community" of which every living thing is a "biotic citizen." In this view, ecological wisdom would dictate that we preserve all species of life forms in all their diversity in order to maintain the stability of the whole interconnected system. When changes occur within the system at a slow (i.e., evolutionary) rate, the system is self-regulating and maintains balance and integrity. Abrupt and violent changes, such as those caused by human intervention, in contrast, can be catastrophic. Consequently, Leopold concludes that "a thing is right when it tends to preserve the integrity, stability, and beauty of the biotic community. It is wrong when it tends otherwise" (Leopold, 1966:262).

Criticisms of Ecocentrism

The sharpest criticism of ecocentric ethics is that, according to the Land Ethic, human *individuals* simply have no moral status whatsoever. This criticism points to the frightening truth that ecosystems could be made much more integrated and stable if the human population were reduced by billions of individuals. Since the human species is just one species among thousands of others, in Leopold's biotic community *Homo sapiens* is not a privileged species. Such ethical holism has been called "environmental fascism" (Regan, 1983) and "totalitarian," since it subverts respect for individuals (Katz, 1985; Kheel, 1985).

A second criticism of ecocentrism is the difficulty of establishing from a *non*anthropocentric perspective what would count as "beautiful" land. Are forest fires "beautiful" if they promote the ecological cycles of renewal of a forest? Is the process of desertification "beautiful"? It would seem impossible to give content to this aesthetic concept without presupposing a human orientation. In short, it seems impossible for us to "think like a mountain" (Leopold, 1966), as the ecocentric approach requires.

Deep Ecology

Unlike Leopold's ecocentric ethics, *deep ecology* has been a movement which has not arisen out of one primary source and does not refer to one systematic philosophy. In recent years, however, the phrase "deep ecology" has come to refer primarily to the ideas developed in the writings of Arne Naess (1989) and Bill Devall and George Sessions (1985).

Whereas the "shallow" approach to environmental problems focuses on issues like pollution and resource depletion and looks only at the immediate effects of the environmental crisis, Naess characterizes the "deep" approach as investigating a wider field of the social, economic, and cultural causes of the environmental crisis. A "cure" for our present environmental ills, Naess argues, can only come from radical personal and cultural transformations (Naess, 1984). Deep ecologists hold what they call the "dominant worldview" as responsible for global environmental degradation and destruction and construct their own alternative philosophical worldview. The strategies which deep ecologists employ to escape from the ideology of the dominant worldview include varied ideas from poetry, Buddhism, Taoism, spiritualism, and Druidic nature worship. For those involved in radical environmentalism as a political movement, like David Foreman and members of Earth First!, deep ecology seems to offer the ideological justification which sanctions their militant activism.

Deep ecologists reject the dominant metaphysics of modern industrial societies because it is fundamentally individualistic and reductionistic. Deep ecologists view individuals as existing only in relationships within a system (Fox, 1974). Deep ecology yields two ultimate norms, *self-realization* and *biocentric equality*, derived from rejecting the strong distinctions between individuals and nature on the one hand and objectivity and subjectivity on the other. Self-realization is a process through which people come to see themselves as deeply interconnected with the rest of nature. Biocentric equality is the judgment that since all organisms are equally members of an interrelated whole, all organisms possess equal intrinsic value.

Criticisms of Deep Ecology

Articulating precise criticisms of deep ecology is especially difficult given its diffuse hodgepodge of ideas.

> In some ways, the claims of deep ecology are so sweeping and general as to become empty. A "movement" that can claim inspiration from such diverse sources as Taoism, Heraclitus, Spinoza, Whitehead, Gandhi, Buddhism, Native American cultures, Thomas Jefferson, Thoreau, and Woody Guthrie is certainly eclectic at best. At worst, it becomes unintelligible. (DesJardins, 1993:231)

Ecofeminism

Ecological feminism, or "ecofeminism," "is the position that there are important connections—historical, experiential, symbolic, theoretical—between the domination of women and the domination of nature, an understanding of which is crucial to both feminism and environmental ethics" (Warren, 1990). Warren has described a "logic of domination" in which a distinction is drawn between two groups (men and women) on the basis of purported characteristics (men are rational, women are emotional), and then a hierarchy of value is imposed on these characteristics (reason is superior to emotion) and consequently the subordination of the one group is claimed to be justified by appeal to this imposed hierarchical evaluation (men ought to be in positions of power and authority because of their superior rationality).

It is this dichotomous pattern and value-hierarchical thinking which ecofeminists reject. Ecofeminists see the need to scrutinize a constellation of dualisms, such as masculine/feminine, human/nature, reason/emotion, mind/body, and objectivity/subjectivity, that have traditionally been used to support men's domination of women and nature. The alternative conceptual framework suggested by ecofeminists is relational, contextualistic, diverse, inclusive, holistic, and *nonhierarchical*.

Criticisms of Ecofeminism

While there certainly appears to be some truth to the claim that there is a connection between the domination of *some* women by *some* men and the domination of nature by *some* men, this overgeneralizes the relationship between women and men by failing to differentiate among different social, political, economic, and cultural conditions. For example, it seems wrong to blame men in poor, third world countries for the exploitation of the natural world when it is men *and* women in wealthy Western countries who consume a much larger share of natural resources and energy. Ecofeminism identifies only one kind of domination: the domination of women by men. There are many other forms of social domination at work which can be seen as contributing to environmental degradation. The causes are more complex and varied than simply sexual domination.

Social Ecology

In addition to articulating the sharpest, most cogent criticisms of deep ecology (1988), in *The Ecology of Freedom* (1991), Murray Bookchin has presented a compelling history of the diverse forms of hierarchy and domination that have existed in societies from the Paleolithic era to the modern day. In stark contrast to biocentrists, ecocentrists, and deep ecologists, Bookchin sees humans as a *unique* species which has emerged from the long evolutionary process of biological diversification and physiological development toward greater and greater subjectivity, rationality, freedom, and self-determination.

Bookchin, following Cicero, describes what he calls "first nature" as the relatively unconscious biological nature found in the fossil record prior to the development of conscious, mammalian life (1990). This process of biological evolution thus has produced in humanity a natural capacity to intervene consciously into, and deliberately act upon "first nature" (1990). Consequently, "first nature" has given rise to a human-created, cultural, social, political, and societal "second nature." Bookchin sees humans as "extraordinary" and unique life forms because of the extent to which we have *participated in our own evolution*. First nature, which developed in a process of biological evolution, gradually transforms itself into second nature, which emerges through social evolution.

This salutary social evolution of organic societies with nonhierarchical and egalitarian forms of social organization was halted by certain hierarchical institutions. These institutions *include* patriarchal institutions of domination of men over women and *also* social, economic, and political "class" structures in which a powerful class dominates a powerless class, as described by Marxist analysis. Bookchin's social theory is more comprehensive than ecofeminism since he argues that hierarchy and domination could easily continue to exist in a "classless" or "Stateless" society in the form of "elders" dominating the young, one ethnic group dominating another, the town dominating the countryside, and bureaucrats who profess to speak of "higher social interests" dominating the ignorant "masses" (1991). In short, social ecology is the view that the domination of nature has stemmed from the domination of certain humans by other humans.

Bookchin conceives of the commodification of nature and human activities as subverting the possibility of a genuinely participatory, democratic, and egalitarian society. In contrast to this market society, Bookchin sees a truly ecological society as something which

> would be a transcendence of both first nature and second nature into the new domain
> of a *free* nature, a nature that could reach the level of conceptual thought—in short,

a nature that would wilfully and thinkingly cope with conflict, contingency, waste, and compulsion. . . . Humanity, far from diminishing the integrity of nature, would add the dimension of freedom, reason, and ethics to first nature and raise evolution to a level of self-reflexivity that has always been latent in the very emergence of the natural world. (1990:182-183)

Conclusion

Each of the approaches to environmental ethics surveyed in this section has contributed important ideas to the ongoing development of this field. Later in this chapter we will return to this idea of including such guardians to represent the interests of the environment as parties to a mediated environmental negotiation.

ENVIRONMENTAL MEDIATION

The second element of our approach to the ethics of environmental mediation is more historical and practical. A brief review of the rationale for environmental mediation, assumptions about its practice, the variety of choices mediators make, and the minimal understanding of measuring "success" of mediations helps frame ethical concerns as developed from within the dispute resolution field.

Gerald Cormick and Jane McCarthy's mediation of a dispute over the construction of the Snoqualmie River dam constitutes the first effort to apply dispute resolution techniques to environmental issues (Bingham, 1986; Goldman, 1980). This mediation was part of a deliberate effort sponsored primarily by the Ford Foundation to expand the range of applications of dispute resolution procedures from the labor-management arena to neighborhoods and communities. The project begun in Washington State in 1974 launched an experiment which, in greatly diversified forms, continues today.

Many of the first applications of environmental dispute resolution were conceived as "showcase" examples, intended to demonstrate the feasibility of conflict resolution in fields not familiar with its philosophy or practices. These were efforts to introduce the concepts of consensus, participation, integration, and interest-based negotiation to individuals and institutions accustomed solely to adversarial modes of thinking and practice.

The practice has expanded from mediated negotiations of site-specific disputes to a wide array of applications, including formal and informal policy dialogues at local, state, regional, national, and international levels; regulatory negotiations for states and federal agencies; strategic planning for public and private organizations; facilitation for retreats and workshops; training and education; and assisting in many kinds of public participation, including task forces, visioning processes, and ordinary public hearings.

What Is Mediation?

Environmental mediation involves the use of an impartial or independent (we prefer not to use the term *neutral*) third party who helps to convene and facilitate discussions and dialogue among parties in conflict over issues concerning the use, allocation, protection, or enhancement of natural resources. Mediation has slowly, often grudgingly, become an increasingly used tool that supplements the familiar processes of legislation, administrative rule making, and litigation, not to mention back-room dealing, power plays, and gridlock.

The basic concept behind environmental mediation is to create and sustain an attitude of joint problem solving which replaces the adversarial climate typical of disputes. Typically disputes are characterized by a number of elements which discourage productive mutual problem solving:

- There is a win/lose mentality that is blind to possibilities of mutual gain.
- Effort is put into beating the opponent instead of getting what is needed.
- The focus is on the personalities of opponents rather than on the substance of issues.
- The more a position is defended or attacked the more hardened it becomes, and the less open parties are to exploring other options.
- Misunderstanding and miscommunication, which are problems even in relatively benign issues, become exacerbated.

The intervention of a skilled mediator can do many things to counter these obstacles. The mediator's presence, as well as the mediation structure, can encourage the parties to examine their negotiation style and preparations, which in turn leads to changes in attitude and format. The focus of the dispute can be withdrawn from personalities of adversaries and placed upon the issues. Parties are offered an opportunity to explore the interests underlying their stated positions. Attention is paid to opening up clear lines of communication, clarifying issues, and differentiating the substantive differences from what are simply misunderstandings. Outside expertise acceptable to all parties can be made available.

The Mediation Process

While each case is unique, some aspects of the mediation process always require attention. Each of these points requires many judgments by the mediator *and* the parties. These judgments have both practical and ethical implications. Among the most important considerations are the following:

Convening the mediation. The mediator often conducts thorough interviews with the parties to determine whether the issues may be appropriate for mediation, whether the parties are truly interested in engaging in good faith negotiations, whether or not the dispute is "ripe"—that is, whether the issues are of enough significance to the parties, and they are sufficiently frustrated with current settlement efforts, to be motivated to seek resolution.

As a practical matter independent of ethical considerations, representation of competing interests must be inclusive of parties with sufficient interest and power, to ensure that any agreement will not be blocked by a party left out of the process. The influence of who is providing the resources (i.e., funding) for the mediation is an area of concern for both the third party and the process. The third party must also deal with how the funding arrangement is interpreted by the disputants, and indeed by the funder.

Ethically, how can nonhuman interests be interviewed? How can representatives for those interests contribute to the resources (i.e., paying for the third party's services) when nonhuman species are not part of the human cash economy?

Facilitating the negotiations. Every mediation actually involves several sets of negotiations. Of course, the parties at the table are negotiating with one another. But in environmental disputes most parties are negotiating on behalf of a larger constituency than themselves. Various interest groups—industry, public interest organizations, citizens, or regulators—often have considerable internal differences. Members of the business community are often competitors, of course, but less attention is paid to the fact that public interest organizations, citizens, and regulators are often competing as well for limited funds, status, and power.

Individual participants must also satisfy their organizational interests. Staff from organizations must satisfy their supervisors, boards of directors, and professional colleagues. Corporate participants are responsible to their corporate hierarchy. Other participants have varying responsibilities to constituencies as well.

In many mediations, "caucuses" of participants who share primary interests, such as industry or citizens, are formed in order to keep group members working together. Tensions internal to the interest group, such as differences over leadership or willingness to compromise, can be expressed in caucus without appearing as a weakness to the other parties. Mediators may have a modest or significant role in the formation and operation of caucuses.

Besides facilitating the direct talks among the disputants and the interest-group caucuses, a mediator must make judgments about issues such as recruitment of new participants, telephone or in-person discussions with individual disputants, preparing and distributing minutes from meetings, dealing with the media, and keeping up to date with relevant technical and political issues. Finally, a mediator should consider the likely effects of the negotiation on parties not directly involved in the dispute, such as legislators and interested regulatory agencies.

A multitude of ethical concerns arise in the judgments made in facilitating a negotiation. Three important ones are (1) How are caucuses determined and related to the general negotiation? (2) How are the values of confidentiality of information and representatives informing their constituencies/superiors balanced? (3) What kind and degree of "outside information" is important for a mediator to provide competent service without being biased by the necessarily limited time to consider the information?

Implementing agreements. Reaching agreements is only part of a negotiation's purpose. Often implementation, monitoring, and providing for needed adjustments in agreements is more difficult than getting the disputants to agree in the first place. New legislation may be needed, new responsibilities may be placed upon unwilling regulatory agencies, unrepresented parties may find fault with the process, and the public may be asked to accept something which seems less than ideal.

Again, the ethical and practical considerations are complex and consequential. What are the responsibilities upon the mediator and the parties to a negotiation to support a mediated agreement? How public must such support be? What constitutes a violation of the agreement, and who makes that judgment?

INTRODUCTION TO THE ETHICS OF ENVIRONMENTAL MEDIATION

Within the field of dispute resolution, attention to ethical concerns has been scattered. This is to be expected in an area in which substantial growth and experimentation has yet to plateau. The two largest professional organizations catering to environmental dispute resolution practitioners are the International Association of Public Participation Practitioners (IAP3) and the Society of Professionals in Dispute Resolution (SPIDR).

IAP3 is a relatively new organization, and it is just beginning to develop standards of conduct for its members. SPIDR adopted its "Ethical Standards of Professional Responsibility" in 1986, and its members are required to subscribe to those standards. Four main areas dominate the standards: responsibility to the parties, background and qualifications of a "neutral" party, fee disclosure, and support of the profession. The responsibility to the parties falls under six categories: impartiality, informed consent, confidentiality, conflict of interest, promptness, and the consequences of settlement.

For the purposes of exploring the ramifications of new thinking about environmental ethics, the two most important topics are "unrepresented interests" and the consequences of settlement.

The SPIDR standards focus on the circumstances of interests not being represented and the recognition of those interests by the negotiators at the table. The facilitator is obligated to make certain such interests have been considered by the principal parties (Thomas, 1991). Most conveners or mediators consider a fair or useful negotiation to be one in which parties combine relevant interests with some form of power to pursue those interests. The main concern is one of *not excluding* some party that can significantly diminish or prevent a solution from being implemented. Considering the power of parties in deciding how interests will be represented in a mediated negotiation is an important instrumental value. However, we will pursue the representation question by bringing the force of the aforementioned ethical arguments to other practical questions of third party behavior.

The consequences of an agreement concerning large-scale environmental issues implicitly involve the worth of different uses of land, water, air and the effects on living beings. Yet guidance provided by SPIDR standards is limited to recognition that the "process belongs to the parties." The standards allow a mediator to express concern about possible consequences of an agreement if "the needs of the parties dictate" (Thomas, 1991:4). Under these standards, a third party concerned about the consequences of settlement on nonhuman beings would have recourse to one action only: relaying those concerns to the negotiating parties. We will offer other options in the next section.

This analysis is not meant to criticize the ethical standards, which were designed for general purposes. Indeed, the SPIDR standards acknowledge that ethical considerations relevant to some disciplines are not covered by the standards. Our concern is to indicate the gap which exists between environmental mediation practice and attention to ethical concerns.

Early Ethical Concerns

In order to understand this gap and the state of environmental mediation ethics, it is important to recall the origins of the field in labor relations practice. Early efforts to resolve public disputes drew their inspiration from several sources, including social psychology, small group dynamics, social activism, and, most notably, the labor-management experience (Bellman, Sampson, and Cormick, 1982).

Lee (Lee, 1982), in an article entitled "Defining Success in Environmental Dispute Resolution," offers several criteria of "orderly" dispute resolution transferable from the labor relations experience to the environmental arena. These include the mutual recognition of parties, legal and administrative procedures, and the continuing relationship among parties. Other elements have lessons for implementation, including recognition of the importance of joint action, participation, and continuing oversight.

Cormick and Patton (Lake, 1980) describe environmental mediation principally by its deviation from labor-management mediation. Lentz (Lentz, 1986) even argues that a "revisionist" mediator who abandons labor model standards alters the mediator role so much that the practice can no longer be called mediation.

But long-standing ethical standards and ideals such as neutrality cannot be readily transferred from existing fields of practice such as labor mediation to the environmental arena. The two arenas differ significantly, with environmental disputes involving multiple parties, multiple and changing issues, visibility, public impact, and so forth (Lentz, 1986). Those differences between the environmental and labor arenas provided the main points of contention during the early years of environmental mediation. The crux of the matter was pointed out by Susskind and Weinstein (Susskind and Weinstein, 1980): the long-term ecological effects which might be irreversible were at stake.

The debate centered around the question of mediator accountability for results, and it involved issues such as the mediator's role in balancing power, the substantive knowledge and experience of the mediator, and the mediator's impact on any agreement. This debate reached its most elegant manifestation in the exchange involving Susskind, Stulberg, and McCrory (McCrory, 1981; Stulberg, 1981; Susskind, 1981). Susskind argued that the demands of the environmental disputes called for a more active response by the mediator than McCrory and Stulberg believed was workable and ethical. For those coming from a labor neutral background and for others as well, what Susskind and his supporters were suggesting was heretical, unworkable, and damaging to the profession as a whole.

The debate never concluded. It was simply set aside, lost to the demands of practice, while attention moved to other issues. Current practice indicates that Susskind and his supporters have had the better of it, but less by virtue of philosophical agreement than by the seemingly unavoidable bowing to the practical imperatives of conducting negotiations in the public arena. And the important questions of ecological effects, community acceptance, and representation remain not only unanswered but, in fact, rarely asked.

IMPLICATIONS FOR THE ETHICS OF ENVIRONMENTAL MEDIATION

Many ethical issues involving environmental mediation remain worthy of further consideration. For instance, the whole area of third party accountability for the implementation of agreements deserves exploration well beyond the boundaries of current SPIDR ethical standards. And many choices third parties make subtly but significantly reflect values about participation, compromise, efficiency, power, and so forth, as was implied in the general ethical questions discussed earlier in this chapter.

However, consistent with the aim of this chapter, we will focus on the idea of "the environment" as a party whose interests may require different forms of representation than are currently provided. Thus, we pursue only one strand, albeit an important and provocative one: the garment of the ethics of environmental mediation.

"The Environment" as an Interested Party

The rhetoric of dispute resolution points to some kind of moral standing and/or consideration of nonhuman interests. First, all "affected parties" should have input into a decision-making process which has an impact on their well-being. Second, drawing from the general values in ascendence on many economic and ecologic agendas—sustainability and lessening the impact of human living on ecosystems—the question of who is *not* at the table when important environmental decisions are being made is crucial from an ethical point of view.

We explore the issue of enhanced representation for the environment within the context of two questions. First, do purely nonhuman concerns deserve some kind of representation and/or protection within the practice of environmental mediation? Second, what is a third party's responsibility for drawing attention to these concerns?

Certainly many interest groups claim a special relationship with environmental concerns. Some focus on particular geographical areas for preservation. Others focus on particular species for protection. Some are only concerned with the health of human beings. Others advocate broader ecosystemic or biospheric values. Yet, upon reflection of direct involvement with these groups in problem-solving settings and discussions with other environmental mediators, many such groups have fallen short on the professed focus on long-term ecological integrity.

We have observed that the programs of established environmental organizations are driven in some instances less by perceived need for environmental protection than by demands of institutional imperatives. These include several very real needs: increasing membership (which leads to increased influence, prestige, funding, and staff); and attracting foundation support, with similar advantages; attracting and retaining political support. These pressures combine to encourage compromise, selective prosecution or persecution of perceived violators of environmental standards, and a tilt towards what is politic as opposed to scientifically defensible. Furthermore, environmental organizations often compete with each other for scarce resources to fulfill these needs.

Moreover, few environmental advocacy organizations claim to speak for nonhuman life forms *per se*. This is not a criticism, but only an elaboration of the competing moral visions about the relationship between humans and the environment developed earlier in this chapter. Science can help us understand some ideas that enhance or degrade environments with concomitant gain or loss of livable habitats for plant and animal species. But very few people could plausibly claim to know the mind of a bison or the preferences of a field of daisies. It would be absurd to claim to be the *duly selected* representative of a nonhuman life or a whole ecosystem.

What Can a Third Party Do?

A mediator of large-scale environmental disputes is not in the same position as a mediator of private disputes. Issues of fairness and foresight might charge a third party to take active roles—to learn more, to raise questions with the parties, or even to warn participants if an agreement is developing that would greatly hurt unrepresented parties. The final challenge is deciding whether a third party should withdraw from a mediation gone awry.

Many environmental negotiations occur in circumstance in which the concerns of environmental ethicists are likely to have little practical relevance. For example, the connection between issues such as cleanup or cost recovery at a Superfund site, or siting of a new landfill, or adoption of new regulations about end uses of tires and concern for nonsentient beings is tenuous at best. But take, for example, a dispute over habitat and species protection for a national park and jurisdictions adjacent to the park. What can a third party confronted in actual practice with substantial concerns of environmental ethics do? Is there some alternative to remaining silent, on the one hand, and complete withdrawal from negotiations, on the other?

We outline five possible measures for consideration of the environment as worthy of enhanced representation. These are presented in order ranging from least intrusive on the mediation process to most activist on the part of the third party. They are

- *Education of the third party*;
- *Education of the disputants*;
- *Active "reality testing" by the third party* about consequences of action on the environment;
- *Diversifying representation* to include parties who might represent the "environment as worthy of representation" views;
- *Appointment of a special representative for environmental interests and education of the third party*. At the least, a mediator can become better educated in several areas. A third party can investigate long-term ecological effects of past decisions, whether those decisions were mediated or not, to see what subjects merit concern. A mediator versed in scientific, legal, and policy issues who understands environmental ethical foundations and fault lines will be, at a minimum, better prepared to identify risky territory and take steps to steer clear of dangerous areas. This measure is not likely to be controversial or to suggest bias. It is consistent with SPIDR's standards for continuing development of professional skills (Thomas, 1991). It is also a necessary precursor for measure 2.

Education of the disputants. Mutual education about the issues under dispute is always part of some level of cooperation and exchange in negotiations. However, enhanced representation might require more deliberate efforts on the part of the mediator to explore what is truly at stake in negotiations. This action still does not vary far from the traditional third party role. Controversy among practitioners would probably come in the purpose, scope, and details of this measure.

Active "reality testing" by the third party. The third measure on the scale of intervention is active "reality testing" by the third party about consequences of potential actions on the environment. This measure moves beyond the traditional third party role of providing procedural advice and direction to prodding or cautioning parties about substantive issues. We doubt that many mediators refrain from all such substantive counsel. Most mediators serve as virtual conflict analysts by helping each party (in private caucus, if need be) identify options, interests, dangers, and opportunities during the course of the negotiations. Again, the degree of action would determine how far this option is seen as straying from the traditional mediator role. While this may be a logical extension of measures 1 and 2, anything more than minimal activity would certainly be controversial with practitioners and analysts of the field.

Diversifying representation. The fourth measure is to diversify representation to include parties who might represent the "environment as worthy of representation" views. Part of most third parties' preparation for mediating environmental negotiations includes gathering data (i.e., the "thorough interviews" discussed earlier) to understand the history of the conflict, the issues, the parties, and who needs to participate. This information gathering task can include exploration of the parties' understanding and consideration of the interests and needs of nonhuman beings. In this area, scientific evidence and advocacy can easily blur. A third party's more involved preparation with one or more parties before and between joint meetings simply extends the ideas of Laue and Cormick (Bermant, Kelman, and Warwick, 1978:205-232) from community disputes to the environmental realm.

Appointment of a special representative for environmental interests. This last measure, as we envision it, is likely to be not only the most controversial among practitioners, but also the most difficult to realize in practice. If it seems out-of-step with human-centered problem-solving models and if it seems to usurp the role of environmental activist organizations, it is nonetheless an extension of the logic of certain environmental ethical frameworks.

The Difficulties of Representing the Environment

At present, there appear to be insurmountable practical barriers to implementing the idea of representing nonhuman life in environmental mediation. Yet there already exist models of having one human speak for another who is deemed incapable of self-representation. First, power of attorney or trusteeship is a legal transference of power for one person acting in the best interests of an underage, incompetent, or incapacitated person. Second, guardian *ad litem* is another legal device for representing a minor child in an unstable, abusive, or transitional family situation. At least one environmental ethicist has recommended a "special representative" for the environment (Stone, 1974). Stone proposes that when an interested party perceives a natural object to be endangered, we should have a system in which that party can petition a court for the creation of a guardianship.

Different third party roles—the ombuds and governmental public advocates—are given standing without specific authorization from the interests they are representing. Ombuds' goals include being a convener, fact-finder, protector of multiple interests, and advocate for changes that are mutually beneficial for the people in conflict (Burton and Dukes, 1990). Many states have offices that are given the duty of representing ratepayers/consumers in the public utility regulatory process.

There are several arguments against designating a representative for some or all nonhuman interests:

1. Despite the political exigencies faced by environmental pressure groups, "representing species/ecosystems" is what they are all about. The environmental groups base their legitimacy on their knowledgeable representation of nonhuman values and/or longer-term interests of nonhuman beings and on the size and power of their membership. Adding a different representative of "the environment" presumes that the new party would have some kind of unusual expertise that other well-organized environmental groups do not. Also, it could easily lead to an automatic bias for mediation agreements to have no or low impact on the existing flora and fauna.

2. There cannot be a single representative acting for nonhuman interests because those interests are diverse and often incompatible among different *species* in the same habitat and among different *individuals* in the same habitat. "The environment" is hardly static, unified, predictable, or harmonious. All kinds of decisions affect the populations of various species and the qualities of life of various individual specimens. Any naturally occurring or human-directed transformation of the environment will benefit some species and certain individuals and hurt others. Which animals and plants are to be represented? Are threatened and endangered species preferred over others? If so, to what degree? Environmental ethicists who advocate the individual-sentientist approach (e.g., Regan) would certainly disagree with the holistic-approach thinkers (e.g., Leopold) about the answers to these questions. In short, it is all too evident that "pro-environment" values are not singular; they are hotly debated among activists and ethicists, not to mention negotiators and third parties.

3. It is presumptuous to set up any one person or group as privileged to speak for an interest that did not and cannot choose that person or group to be its representative(s). If informed consent is important in the SPIDR Code of Ethics, it seems to rule out the notion of a human speaking on behalf of a nonhuman until we have a common language with most members of the food chain.

Nonetheless, there may be ways that appointment of a special representative might be acceptable for disputants. Mediations often include "resource" representatives with expertise in key areas who sit in on meetings but who do not participate in decisions, and the special representative might be invited within this context. Or, in mediations open to the public, such a representative might be invited to "shadow" the negotiations by attending meetings as a spectator. Other participants would then be free to discuss issues with this individual.

CONCLUSION

Due to the diversity of perspectives on the central moral questions about humankind's relation to the environment, there is no clear direction for those involved in facilitated negotiations on environmental decisions. We hope we have moved the debate forward in one important area: how nonhuman interests are constituted and considered in human negotiations. But just as the fields of environmental science and environmental ethics continue to evolve, so too, we suspect, will the field of the ethics of environmental mediation.

Chapter 13

Assuring Justice in Cross-Cultural Environmental Mediation

Carolyn Blackford and Hirini Matunga

"Te manu e kai ana i te miro, nona te Kahere
Te manu e kai ana i te matauraka nona te ao"

["The bird that eats of the miro inherits the forest. The bird that seeks education inherits the world." (In Maori mythology a bird is a personification of a person.)]

In recent times New Zealand has undertaken a major reform in the area of environmental, planning, and resource management legislation. One of the main outcomes has been the Resource Management Act 1991 with the purpose of promoting "the sustainable management of natural and physical resources." This Act has made some notable advances in attempting to recognize Maori (New Zealand's first people) tribal values and rights associated with the environment.

It also acknowledges, for the first time in New Zealand environmental legislation, the value of specifying mediation as one of several techniques that can be used to seek resolution of conflict in site-specific disputes. Environmental mediation is therefore being looked to by both Maori and non-Maori as an important mechanism for dealing with resource conflict.

Although a wealth of experience on environmental mediation is recorded in the North American literature in particular, we want to see the development of a practice that is appropriate to New Zealand's cultural context: a practice that is likely to ensure justice for Maori participants. In order to move some way toward that goal, there is a need to delineate the characteristics of a just cross-cultural mediation process, from a Maori perspective, as well as to know something of recent experiences of Maori people in processes resembling mediation. The overall objective of our research was to find ways of improving Maori effectiveness in environmental mediation as a preliminary step toward a bicultural mediation process (Blackford and Matunga, 1991). The remainder of this chapter describes the research process involved in developing two distinct approaches to promote Maori tribal effectiveness in environmental mediation.

THE CONTEXT

A number of Maori proverbs emphasize the importance of looking to the past to understand the present in order to find the answers for the future. Within the context of environmental decision making, the more we move into the future the more important become the messages from the past. A number of phases which are pertinent to any discussion on Maori rights and environmental decision making in New Zealand form the context within which environmental mediation is taking place today and will continue to take place in the future.

Pretreaty of "Waitaki" (Pre-1840)

Prior to the signing of the Treaty of "Waitaki" in 1840, "Aotearoa"/New Zealand was under the jurisdiction of numerous Maori tribes, who had sovereignty over defined lands, waters, and other natural resources within their tribal territories. Decisions about resource management, use, and allocation within their territories were under the control of the particular tribe.

The Treaty of "Waitaki": A Promise of Justice (1840-1975)

The Treaty of "Waitaki," which was signed in 1840, was supposed to ensure that the resource management rights of the various Maori tribes would be protected by the new settler government, established by the British Crown. There were, however, two versions of the Treaty: an English version and a Maori version and one was not a direct translation of the other. The English version ceded sovereignty from the Maori tribes to the British Crown on the proviso that the Maori chiefs were guaranteed "the full exclusive and undisturbed possession of the Lands and Estates, Forests, Fisheries and other properties which they may. . . possess, so long as it (was) their wish and desire." The Maori version, on the other hand (and which the majority of Maori chiefs signed), ceded only "kawanataka" (governance or the right to govern and make laws) to the Crown. This was on the understanding that the Maori tribes would still retain "tino rakatirataka" (sovereignty or higher authority) over their lands, villages, and "o ratou taoka katoa" (everything which they valued).

Despite the ensuing debate over what was promised and what was not, both versions of the Treaty at least promised Maori a primacy in any environmental decision-making process that was to be established. Maori, therefore, could reasonably expect that their resource management rights would be protected and they would be assured of justice in the process. However, as history has shown the Treaty was honored more in the breach than in the compliance with its provisions. Quite soon after it was signed, until at least the mid-1970s, Maori were the recipients of an extraordinarily unjust environmental decision-making system which, in light of original Treaty guarantees, was all the more inequitable.

The First Glimmers of Justice? (1975-1991)

In the mid-1970s and in the midst of increasingly vehement Maori criticism of its continuing breaches of the Treaty, the New Zealand Government established the "Waitaki" Tribunal to examine breaches of the Treaty by the Crown, to recommend fair and equitable redress for these breaches, and to define Crown obligations to Maori under the Treaty. However, the Crown has not acted on the majority of recommendations made by the Tribunal to date.

The Town and Country Planning Act, which was enacted in 1977, for the first time gave limited statutory recognition to Maori rights and values in resource use planning. This Act recognized, for the first time in New Zealand law, the relationship between Maori and their culture and traditions with their ancestral lands as a matter of national importance.

A New Era of Justice? (1991 and Beyond)

The passing of the Resource Management Act in 1991 built on gains made in the late 1980s and signaled a new era for Maori in environmental management in New Zealand. Almost 150 years after the signing of the Treaty of "Waitaki," environmental law was taking the first real yet tentative steps in recognizing that Maori tribes had the authority to make decisions about natural resources within their tribal territories, and Maori had a legitimate Treaty right to expect that their interests in the environment would be recognized and provided for. Some of the more significant provisions in the Act for Maori include requirements that resource management agencies recognize and provide for the relationship of Maori people and their culture and traditions with their ancestral lands, waters, sites, "waahi tapu" (sacred sites), and other "taoka" (treasures); take into account the principles of the Treaty of "Waitaki" ("Te Tiritio Waitaki"); and allow that certain powers be transferable to "iwi" (Maori tribal) authorities.

ENVIRONMENTAL MEDIATION:
ITS POTENTIAL AND ITS LIMITATIONS

The context within which environmental mediation will take place is one which is characterized by the domination of one Treaty party over the other. We now turn our attention to the nature of environmental mediation as it has developed in North America over the past two decades or so in order to assess its appropriateness for New Zealand's cultural environment.

Environmental mediation is one of a number of consensual approaches to what is referred to as alternative dispute resolution (ADR) or environmental dispute settlement (EDS). It is generally a voluntary, collaborative, joint problem-solving approach to decision making that is based on face-to-face dialogue and communication. This approach may be adopted in instances when parties in dispute may be unable to reach agreement unassisted, when a large number of parties are involved in a dispute, or when the dispute is of a complex nature (Susskind and Cruikshank, 1987). However,

> [m]ediation does not lead to a resolution of the basic differences that separate the parties in conflict. Rather, in situations where none of the parties perceives that it is able to gain its goals unilaterally, mediation can help the parties agree on how to make the accommodations that will enable them to co-exist despite their continued differences. (Cormick, 1987:307)

A major assumption inherent in the mediation approach is that the parties are likely to be the best judges of the real issues at stake and whether an adequate resolution has been achieved. Broader attention can be devoted to the real issues because the parties negotiate their agenda as well as deciding on the terms of the agreement (Bingham, 1986). The involvement of the intermediary is considerably more substantial in environmental mediation than in other forms of assisted negotiation, such as facilitation and conciliation.

Is Mediation Likely to Appeal to Maori Disputants?

Consensus decision making, which characterizes alternative dispute resolution approaches, characterizes Maori decision-making approaches. The principle of "kotahitaka" (Maori political process) "is directed toward the necessity of reaching unity through consensus. . . . Maori political process is designed to recognize individuals and include all their concerns even if in the end they do not get their own way" (Ritchie, 1986:30).

Mediation implies an approach that may be appropriate to New Zealand's cultural environment. It offers a forum for the expression of Maori cultural and spiritual values that may not be available during formal resource consent application (local authority) and appeal (Planning Tribunal) hearings. Processes can be negotiated that meet the needs of all the parties and could include co-mediators of sufficient "mana" (standing, authority, prestige) to provide legitimacy and credibility to the process (Ministry for the Environment, 1988). Further, the face-to-face dialogue that is an integral part of the mediation process mirrors that of the traditional Maori decision-making process (Gray, 1990, personal communication).

Although mediation may appear to be an attractive option, the fundamental power differentials that exist in the wider political, social, and economic spheres cannot be eliminated in the dispute resolution forum. Government organizations and private corporations come to the negotiating table with all the power and influence endowed by the existing political/economic system. Other groups have to attempt to secure power resources on a situation-by-situation basis (Cormick, 1987).

When inexperienced negotiators face highly experienced and sophisticated opponents in the informal atmosphere of mediation, some parties may be seduced into compromising their values and accepting unjust settlements they might not have supported in a more adversarial setting. Unequal access to scientific and technical expertise and information may place some parties at a distinct advantage. Those who can best mobilize relevant expertise and research are likely to find themselves in a powerful position at the negotiating table (Amy, 1990).

Criteria for Assuring Justice to Maori

Criteria expressing Maori notions of justice which could be applicable to any decision-making or consensus-building process, such as mediation, are needed to assess whether the Maori participants have been treated in a manner which is just and to guide any recommendations arising from that analysis. Two broad criteria are applicable and can be applied to any environmental mediation process to assess its justness from a Maori perspective. These include

- "Hei mihi atu ki te manawhenua" (Recognition of manawhenua)
- "Hei mihi atu ki ka tikaka" (Recognition of "tikaka").

"Hei mihi atu ki te manawhenua" (Recognition of "manawhenua"). The concept of "manawhenua" and recognition of "mana" is central to assessing the justness or otherwise of any decision-making process from a Maori perspective. In short, it determines who has the right to participate in the process, be it mediation or otherwise. A just process, therefore, is one which includes all Maori groups who have the right through their "mana" to participate. "Manawhenua" denotes rights to particular lands or resources over which an "iwi" (tribe) or "hapu" (subtribe) has customary authority. While the concept is sometimes applied to "iwi," it is most applicable at a "hapu" level and denotes rights to specific areas and

resources within an "'iwi's' territories" (Blackford and Matunga, 1991:46). "Manawhenua" is a pivotal determinant of Maori land rights and denotes customary rights to oversee and regulate land and water resources within the tribal territory. It is generally expressed by organizational groups such as "hapu" (tribal subdivisions) and "whanau" (family units) and is bestowed by "whakapapa" (genealogical linkages to ancestors associated with the resource or area). It can be exercised regardless of whether legal title to the resource or area is held; that is, it cannot be extinguished as it rests upon the authority deriving from an ancestor or ancestors who remain the same, regardless of current "ownership" of the resource or area (Blackford and Smith, 1993).

"Hei mihi atu ki ka tikaka" (recognition of "tikaka"). A second criterion for assessing the justness of a particular process is the extent to which it recognizes the "tikaka" of those Maori participating in the process.

"Tikaka" can mean different things depending on the context, and its usage in Maoridom is quite extensive. In a general sense, however, it can mean reason, cause, or motive for thinking or acting in a particular way. It can also mean custom, belief, tradition, values, and attitudes. Its usage also extends to those things which determine what is right, normal, correct, and usual (Minhinnick, 1991, personal communication). It can also be used in quite specific cases to denote specific customs or rules covering a particular aspect of Maori tribal life. The essential requirement is that the group whoever the group is (i.e., tribe, subtribe, or family), determine what the "tikaka" is and how it should be expressed.

Many tribes are defining what they mean by "tikaka" in their tribal management plans. For instance, the "Ngaati Te Ata" tribe defines "tikaka" as its "inherent rights as an 'iwi.'" This includes the right of "Ngaati Te Ata" to define its own reasons for anything, to have its own methods or logic for determining what is significant, to have the authority and control to determine what is right, correct and normal for it, and to have its own customs, habits and values independently of others (Awaroa ki Manuka, 1991).

In short, therefore, "manawhenua" determines who has the right to participate, and "tikaka" identifies how they may choose to participate and the values, beliefs, customs, and attitudes they may bring to the process because of their history, their present-day reality, and their aspirations for the future.

THE CASE STUDIES: SOME EXPERIENCE TO DATE

With the context in which mediation takes place in New Zealand and a brief outline of the potential and the limitations of environmental mediation for Maori, we now look at the experience of participants in three case studies involving Maori cultural and spiritual values and concerns.

When choosing cases in which mediation has been used to resolve disputes involving Maori cultural and spiritual values, it became apparent that very few examples of "pure" mediation, as described above. The three cases finally chosen have been described as mediation by some involved in those processes but appear to be hybrid processes involving elements of facilitation, negotiation, mediation, and, in some instances, arbitration at different stages in their decision-making processes (Blackford and Matunga, 1991).

The first is a land/resource ownership claim by the "Ruapuha hapu" (Ngati Maniopoto) that had been filed with the "Waitaki" Tribunal in 1987 and subsequently went to mediation. A compensation settlement was eventually mediated, but the details remain confidential.

The second case represents an attempt to develop policy guidelines for allocating state-owned indigenous forests of South Westland (south of the Cook River) to wood production or protection. Although the working party was able to reach agreement on a number of resource management issues, it was unable to reach consensus on the most contentious issues regarding the allocation of forest land for protection or production.

The third case is a site-specific conflict in which the "Te Atiawa hapu of Taranaki" have been trying to protect their shellfish beds from local pollution for over 20 years. In addition to concerns over the disposal of both industrial and human wastes, these people became very concerned at the proposal to site two petrochemical projects in the area. The government eventually agreed substantially to subsidize the upgrading of an existing outfall and the provision of secondary treatment. Some argue that a number of surrounding issues have not been satisfactorily resolved.

The Participants' Experience

The most practical framework within which to consider the experience of case-study participants seemed to be that of a generic model of a mediation process (Moore, 1986; Susskind and Cruikshank, 1987). The Maori and many of the non-Maori participants in the case studies were contacted, and all except two (who responded by mail) were personally interviewed.

Prenegotiation phase. A fundamental issue for Maori in mediation (and in any resource management decision-making process, for that matter) is who has the "mana" to participate. Directly related to this issue is the situation in which ownership of a particular piece of land is in dispute; more than one "iwi," "hapu," or "whanau" may claim the right to be involved. Alternatively a second group may attempt to join the mediation on the grounds that the group that has the "mana" to participate is not but should be seeking to protect traditional Maori values relating to the resource at the basis of the dispute. Further issues are (a) who has the right to determine which Maori interests should participate and (b) the inability of some non-Maori to recognize inter-"iwi" and intra-"iwi" complexity and diversity and that several groups, not just one, may have a legitimate place at the table.

Maori participants may not be allowed sufficient time to choose their representatives in the appropriate way, and this can lead to groups later claiming that their interests were not represented. Credible representatives chosen appropriately have the support of their elders. It may be too much for one Maori person to cope with all the issues that arise, particularly when there are particular ways of doing things depending on the way a person is brought up. Difficulties may arise when representatives are not allowed to have advisors or others with them.

Little attention appeared to be given to establishing protocols, particularly with regard to venue, costs of participation, and voting procedures. When "hui" (meetings) are held on a "marae" (village, meeting house complex), some opportunities exist to redress power imbalances that may exist, and cultural perspectives can be more readily expressed. The relative informality is preferred to the formal courtroom situation, and everybody is free to say what they wish. In non-Maori settings, attitudes of people can change; others may become condescending, patronizing and insincere to Maori. Communication can be mostly one-way, and Maori protocols may not be practiced.

The costs of participating were not equal; most Maori representatives had to meet their expenses themselves. The self-employed had to bear a loss of income to attend meetings, while others took time off work without pay. This situation was in stark contrast to many of the non-Maori representatives, who had organizational or departmental backup. There also appeared to be few limits on the amount of money available to bring scientific and technical information to the negotiation table.

The process of defining the issues gave rise to a number of problems. Crown institutions generally attempt to separate resource issues in a way that is incompatible with Maori views of the interconnectedness of the natural world. Issues of concern to the "takata whenua" (people of the land) may be discarded in favor of issues that are more compelling for the non-Maori participants.

Information gathered was sometimes meaningless in Maori terms, particularly when apparently irrelevant technical solutions were offered to address cultural and spiritual concerns. There were also disparities in the resources available to each of the parties to prepare their cases.

Negotiation phase. "Pakeha" (non-Maori) attitudes toward information presented by Maori parties varied from very considerate to paternalistic to scornful and uninterested. At the same time, some Maori participants became tired of being talked down to by technical people and academics. At times parties on both sides were unable to understand either technical and engineering concepts or Maori cultural values.

A major challenge facing non-Maori parties is instances in which they are asked to accept and respect Maori spiritual beliefs that they cannot understand as well as recognizing the necessity of finding options that are compatible with those beliefs. Parties promoting an engineering perspective appeared to believe that with a perfect technical solution everything else would fall into place. They were attempting to present solutions to a cultural perception they were unable to understand.

At times insufficient time was made available to both Maori and other representatives to consult with their constituents. Representatives faced difficulties when pressed for an immediate response to an issue and were not given the opportunity to discuss it with their "iwi," "hapu," or "whanau" group. Problems also arose for Maori representatives when they were required to be loyal to a "pakeha" process that may demand secrecy during the negotiations and were then criticized by their people for not sharing information.

Implementation phase. Agreements can break down after the mediator has left, particularly if he or she is unaware of underlying problems. Parties will understandably feel bitter when agreements reached or recommendations made are not implemented, particularly if issues that appeared to be of particular concern to the intermediary are 'actioned. Parties resent changes being made to the final agreement or deviations from the intent of that agreement without their participation or consent.

Issues that arose with regard to the mediator or intermediary related to his or her appointment/selection, his or her role, and the skills and qualities expected of a mediator. Parties resent having an intermediary imposed on them, particularly if they have no choice over his or her selection. They are also concerned if he or she does not appear to be neutral or independent. The mediator may not always have sufficient knowledge of Maori structures and "tikaka" (culture) and in consequence may encounter difficulties understanding Maori concerns if they are not expressed in scientific or technical terms. Parties may be willing to transgress aspects of their protocols temporarily if the mediator is respected.

DISPUTE RESOLUTION STRATEGIES

In light of the experience recounted in the case studies we developed two distinct strategies which Maori groups might adopt when they find themselves facing an environmental dispute. First, we emphasize the importance of preparing a dispute resolution strategy (DRS) for any Maori group or individuals involved in any kind of environmental dispute as a precursor to even deciding on the appropriateness or otherwise of environmental mediation as an resolution approach. The two main reasons for preparing such a strategy (DRS) are

- To identify a range of dispute resolution options which may be appropriate to the particular dispute; and

- To identify the relevant factors which need to be taken into account when making choices as to which dispute resolution options to utilize for the dispute (including where appropriate, mediation).

There are many reasons why a dispute resolution strategy should be prepared (Blackford and Matunga, 1991). We identify the more important of these as

1. To focus on an agreed Maori objective
2. To encourage a proactive stance
3. To empower the group
4. To evaluate consistency with other environmental objectives
5. To evaluate consistency with other social, cultural and economic objectives
6. To consider potential alliances that could help to achieve group aspirations
7. To consider costs and access

Here we define a basic seven-phase procedure which could be followed but could be amended to suit the particular dispute and the particular group or individuals needs. We define seven main phases.

Phase 1: Define a Desired Maori Outcome or Objective

A DRS needs to state the desired Maori outcome or objective to be achieved from the particular dispute. Sufficient time needs to be given to allow discussion within the group to seek either agreement or a common understanding of this desired outcome. This needs to be clearly stated so that all within the group are in no doubt as to what the desired outcome is and can therefore work toward this with a unity of purpose and organization.

Phase 2: Devise a Checklist of Factors That May Assist in or Detract from Achieving the Desired Outcome

The aim of this phase is to consider all internal (those which are largely under the control of the particular Maori group or which reflect its "tikaka," values, experiences, etc.) and external (such things as relevant statute, legal precedent, relevant national, regional, or local government policy, or relevant management plan which may support the group's defined desired outcome) constraints and opportunities.

Phase 3: Define the Bottom Line or the Best Alternative to the Desired Maori Outcome

Having worked through its checklist of relevant factors which may have an impact on the dispute and then evaluated for itself the extent to which its desired outcome is achievable or not achievable, the group should then attempt to define a bottom line or best alternative.

Phase 4: Identify a Range of Dispute Resolution Options

The group should also identify a range of dispute resolution options which are available, accessible, appropriate, and affordable and which suit the group and particular dispute.

Phase 5: Evaluate the Costs and Benefits of the Various Dispute Resolution Options

Having worked through a checklist of relevant factors and considered the various dispute resolution options, the group then needs to evaluate each resolution option in terms of potential costs and benefits to itself.

Phase 6: Choose the Most Appropriate Dispute Resolution Options and the Sequence for their Usage

Having defined a preferred outcome, devised and worked through relevant factors, assessed the various dispute resolution options, and weighed the relative costs and benefits of each, the group should then decide which dispute resolution options to take and the sequence for their usage.

Phase 7: Identify a Process to Implement and Then to Review the DRS

The DRS is then implemented and continually reviewed to ensure it pursues the desired Maori outcome. Review is also necessary to cope with changing or unexpected circumstances that may arise during its implementation. For example, new legislation or policy may be passed that could significantly enhance or inhibit pursuit of the objective. Alternatively, the group may run out of money, time, or personnel (Blackford and Matunga, 1991).

ENVIRONMENTAL MEDIATION STRATEGIES

While the preparation of a Dispute Resolution Strategy is one means of assuring justice to Maori, when Maori decide to use mediation as part of this strategy there is still a need to ensure that from an equity point of view they are able to participate effectively in any environmental mediation process established. The concept of a Maori environmental mediation strategy (EMS), therefore, is a further means of providing for more effective participation of Maori once environmental mediation is chosen as part of a strategy to seek resolution of the dispute.

The aim of an EMS is to ensure that before Maori interface with non-Maori, they have at least discussed collectively and where possible struck internal agreements on a number of factors that will be crucial to assuring justice for themselves in the mediation itself.

Pre-Prenegotiation Phase

The specific issues that arose in the case studies were grouped into four main categories—participation, representation, process, and the mediator. In order to participate effectively, Maori groups need to do a lot of preparation with regard to these issues in what we have termed a pre-prenegotiation stage before they interface with non-Maori parties to the dispute.

Using the first broad criterion referred to earlier, the notion of "Hei mihi atu ki te manawhenua" (recognition of "manawhenua") includes within it Maori concepts of "tino rakatirataka" (full authority), "kaitiakitaka" (guardianship obligation), and "ahi kaa" (occupation and use). Taken collectively, these provide the basis for Maori participation in environmental mediation because they determine who has the right to be involved, the grounds on which that right is claimed, and the nature of that right.

The second broad criterion referred to earlier for assessing the justness of the process—that is, "Hei mihi atu ki ka tikaka" (recognition of "tikaka")—determines or defines how that right should be allowed to be exercised during the actual mediation process itself, beginning with the choice of mediator, choice of the Maori representatives or negotiators, and the importance of "whanaukataka" (obligation or accountability to the group) through the extent to which Maori "kawa" (or protocol) is incorporated into the mediation process.

The reasoning we have followed is that encouraging more effective participation by Maori through the preparation of an environmental mediation strategy will provide greater assurances that a more just process will result for Maori.

Who Has the Right to Participate?
"Rakatirataka, Kaitiakitaka, Ahi Kaa"

As discussed already, the Maori concept of "tino rakatirataka" referred to in the "Treaty of Waitaki" implies a state of absolute authority over one's natural resources. In a contemporary context, however, Maori tribes have in reality not retained anything close to the authority they believed they were simply affirming within the Treaty over their natural resources, and the majority of these resources are no longer in Maori legal title but may still be valued by them for many reasons.

While mediation, therefore, may try to deal with specific issues, in the background such things as tribal and colonial history, impacts sustained as a result of colonization, development pressures, pollution or confiscation of resources, and so on will always shape the manner in which Maori approach mediation. "Rakatirataka," however, denotes the authority or chieftainship to participate in the mediation process because of the tribe's authority within that tribal territory.

The concept of "kaitiakitaka" is, however, associated more with the obligation to manage the resource wisely than it is with the notion of one's authority. This authority must be managed wisely so that the well-being of the tribe ("iwi") or subtribe ("hapu") is protected and enhanced.

"Kaitiakitaka" stresses the need for accountability back to the constituency (whether "iwi," "hapu," or "whanau" in the present, to "tupuna" in the past, and to generations in the future). "Kaitiaki" must have "manawhenua" and "ahi kaa" status, and their authority is given (or invoked) by "iwi" or "hapu," "kaumatua," "kuia," or "tohuka." "Kaitiakitaka" acts as a discipline or check on the wise use or otherwise of one's authority.

"Kaitiaki" have been given a specific responsibility to carry out as guardians and custodians of a resource and should be involved as a priority in any dispute affecting "taoka" over which they have responsibility. It also means that areas over which "kaitiaki" have responsibility may not necessarily be in Maori ownership. This does not diminish their right to be involved in any mediation affecting these resources.

"Ahi kaa," however, is the highest expression of "manawhenua" status as it denotes not only genealogical linkage to the ancestors associated with the resource or place but also occupation of the place, either by residency or continuing use of the resource. Any claim of "ahi kaa" must be supported by the act of occupation or continuing association with the particular area or resource, and the group (i.e., "hapu" or "whanau") who can legitimately claim "ahi kaa" over an area or resource has an unquestionable right to be party to any mediation which affects such areas or resources.

The primary aim during this stage of preparing the environmental mediation strategy is to be clear about why the particular Maori group is claiming (and also able to substantiate if challenged) its right to participate.

How should that right be exercised? There are a number of crucial issues that the "iwi," "hapu," "whanau," or other Maori group needs to sort out before it interfaces with any of the other parties. These issues include who the representatives or negotiators should be and how much time is needed to choose them, an accountability process with their people (including whether there is a requirement that representatives maintain confidences, for example), the mediation approach they prefer, the protocols they wish to follow, the issues they want to see on the agenda, choosing a lawyer, and what kind of knowledge and information they want to present and in what manner. They also include such things as choice of mediator, the importance of "whanaukataka," and the extent to which Maori "kawa" (protocol) should be incorporated into the mediation.

Choosing the mediator. The choice of the mediator depends on the individual and the issue. Obviously the choice must lie with the Maori tribes and the other parties. It is important, however, for the Maori groups to identify where possible the characteristics they would prefer in a mediator and even more preferably identify potential mediators themselves. In traditional Maori society, the mediator was often a "kaumatua," "tohuka," or "rakatira," who had the "mana" and respect of the various parties to the dispute. Today the mediator is still generally a person or group of persons who have demonstrated skill, wisdom, political acuity, a sense of fairness and "whakapapa" linkages and who command respect.

Some believe it is imperative that the mediator has knowledge of "tikaka" Maori or at least be amenable to calling on this advice if needed. Some believe that knowledge of tribally specific "tikaka" is just as important so that the mediator is familiar with tribal nuance and idiosyncrasy, tribal history and experiences, etc. For some, the mediator may be of any race. Others argue that only Maori mediators fully comprehend the depth of the spiritual relationship "iwi" have with their resources. Maori parties will expect the mediator to have a good understanding of Maori structures and processes.

Choosing the Maori representatives or negotiators. In traditional society, leadership was based on hereditary right (i.e., "rakatira"). Each "hapu" had its "rakatira," who acted as trustee or representative for the group. In contemporary society, leadership is often based on a mixture of hereditary right, power of oratory, demonstrated skill, proven track record, commitment, education, debating skills, political acuity, and (probably most important) the continuing support of the Maori group being represented.

The main issue for "iwi" in respect to environmental mediation is to choose the representatives or negotiators who singly or collectively can best represent its interests and have a proven track record in doing so. Choosing the wrong representatives obviously diminishes the chance of getting the outcome most desired by "iwi." Desired traits include an understanding of the aspirations of the "iwi"; a commitment to achieving these aspirations; the ability to listen, articulate thoughts clearly, analyze situations; and have a good understanding of all the issues surrounding the dispute, and familiarity with all the parties to the mediation and their interests.

In the event that these skills are not found in one person, "iwi" may wish to establish a negotiation team who collectively possess these skills. The overriding principle is that "iwi" or "hapu" choose their own representative(s) for the mediation. Once this decision has been made, it should not be undermined by any of the other parties to the mediation.

"Whanaukataka." Once chosen, representatives must seek a mandate from their people on a number of key aspects. This notion of obligation to the group or "whanau" who have chosen you to act on their behalf is covered by the concept of "whanaukataka." For instance, there may be crucial points in the mediation at which key decisions are being made on the agreement, and representatives need to report back to their people.

The intergenerational component of "whanaukataka" brings an immense pressure to perform. Bad decisions or unwise compromises as a result of mediation will not only affect the "mana" of the "whanau" in the present but also potentially incur the disfavor of and, even worse, have a negative impact on future generations of the group.

Effective mediation can only take place if there is recognition of the importance of loyalty and accountability to members of the group. Conflict can arise when Maori representatives are torn between observing the need for secrecy at some stages of a mediation process and accountability to their tribal group. Maori representatives should discuss this issue with their people before the mediation and state their position during the protocol-setting stage on keeping aspects of the mediation confidential from their people partway through the process.

Maori parties may require that other members of their "whanau" be present to give moral support and/or request sufficient time to consult with their people when considering options. These issues need to be discussed at the pre-prenegotiation stage in order that the preferred method/manner for expressing "whanaukataka" obligations can be discussed when protocols are set.

"Kawa." The next step is for the representatives to secure agreement with their people on the preferred approach to the mediation. This will include such things as preferred venue for the mediation, including how important it is that the mediation be held on a "marae" (traditional Maori setting). It may also be important to be able to speak "Te reo" Maori (Maori language) at the mediation. "Te reo" Maori is a "taoka" (treasured possession) and it is the only way in which many Maori concepts can be fully understood and articulated. Many will have Maori as their first and preferred language of expression. The speaking of Maori is a right and not just a privilege. Those wishing to use "Te reo" Maori should seek to have provision built into the protocols for interpretation services.

The Maori group should also consider how it wishes to describe/express its concerns and to present its views to the other parties to the best advantage. "Iwi" must identify the kind of information/knowledge, such as history, culture, values, and "wahi tapu," it needs to present its case. In doing so, it needs to ascertain what information is not directly available and how this could be made accessible.

The use of information has to be negotiated. This is the "iwi's" choice. However, when "iwi" clearly refuse to disclose sensitive information—for example, the site of an "urupa" (burial ground)—they need to weigh the potential consequences of nondisclosure. If they do not want to disclose certain information, the mediation may fail and the dispute would then go to a court hearing, at which the "iwi" may feel they could be forced to disclose it.

When the Maori group involved has made decisions on all the issues outlined above, they could then expect to meet with the other parties to negotiate the mediation approach, protocols, and process and to set objectives for the overall mediation.

SUMMARY AND CONCLUSIONS

The purpose of this chapter has been to contribute to the development of an approach to environmental mediation that assures justice for Maori participants. In order to achieve this goal, we looked briefly at the historical backdrop for contemporary resource management and environmental decision making, at the potential and limitations of mediation (as it has been practiced in North America over the past two decades), particularly for Maori participants in light of that historical context, and at recent practice in New Zealand to see how Maori groups have fared.

Based on the findings of that experience and on Maori process criteria, we proposed two distinct approaches to improving Maori effectiveness in environmental mediation as a preliminary step toward the development of a just bicultural mediation process. The first is a dispute resolution strategy that is designed to help "iwi" groups both to evaluate the dispute resolution options that are available to them and to choose the option that is most likely to achieve a desired Maori outcome. The second approach is a Maori environmental mediation strategy that "iwi" groups can use in the event that mediation emerges as the preferred dispute resolution option. The main thrust of the latter approach is for those groups to prepare themselves adequately in what we have termed a pre-prenegotiation phase before they interface with non-Maori groups.

These approaches suggest ways in which "iwi" groups can go some way toward empowering themselves within a mediation process. However, it is apparent from the case studies that Maori participants did not receive just treatment at all times or in all cases. Broader societal power imbalances are inherent in dispute resolution processes such as mediation. There is a need to address these power imbalances within the broader environmental/resource management decision-making environment to increase the probability of success for the strategies we propose above. We therefore recommend a number of substantive actions that will further assist Maori in achieving justice when they participate in environmental mediation. These include

1. Investigate the feasibility of establishing a nationalized conflict resolution information service for "iwi."

2. Investigate the feasibility of establishing a regional and local service that offers independent advice to "iwi" on conflict resolution.

3. Investigate means by which people can find out the grounds on which Maori groups are claiming the right to participate, and the nature of that right.

4. Prepare a guide for "iwi" on opportunities for participation in resource management decision making that are provided in legislation.

5. Investigate potential sources of funding to enable "iwi" to participate effectively in environmental mediation.

6. Investigate changes that are needed in the Resource Management Act to ensure Maori effectiveness in mediation.

7. Prepare guides on mediation for agencies and individuals that interface with "iwi" (e.g., government departments, regional councils, local authorities, consent use applicants, mediators, etc.).

8. Investigate methods of cross-cultural environmental information exchange in New Zealand, the United States, Canada, and Australia.

Chapter 14

Regulatory Negotiation:
Learning from Experiences at the
U.S. Environmental Protection Agency

Clare M. Ryan

Our goal is to make the entire federal government both less expensive and more efficient, and to change the culture of our national bureaucracy away from complacency and entitlement toward initiative and empowerment. We intend to redesign, to reinvent, to reinvigorate the entire national government. (President Bill Clinton, remarks announcing the *National Performance Review*, March 3, 1993)

The Clinton Administration's *National Performance Review* presents a number of recommendations intended to improve government in general and the process of federal agency rule making in particular. The "reinventing government" report urges federal agencies to make greater use of regulatory negotiation as well as to expand their use of alternative dispute resolution (ADR) techniques. The U.S. Environmental Protection Agency (EPA) is cited as a model agency, having successfully conducted a number of regulatory negotiation activities and saved money in the process (Gore, 1993). In addition, recent legislative initiatives such as the *Administrative Dispute Resolution Act* and the *Negotiated Rulemaking Act* encourage agencies to consider using ADR techniques in their administrative procedures. The two laws establish uniform procedures for certain formal actions such as rule making and adjudication and direct agencies to conduct specific activities throughout the decision-making process. Most recently, Executive Order 12866 requires federal agencies to identify potential rules for negotiation and investigate the feasibility of conducting a regulatory negotiation within the next year.

Clearly, federal agencies will continue to be encouraged to use negotiation and consensus building as a rule making technique. Thus, the question addressed in this chapter is not whether the encouragement is appropriate but how federal agencies new to regulatory negotiation can learn from EPA's experiences and adapt the technique for their specific purposes. This chapter discusses conventional and regulatory negotiation procedures, illustrates links with alternative dispute resolution theory, and provides an in-depth discussion of regulatory negotiation in practice. Finally, EPA's experiences with the technique are examined, along with benefits and drawbacks of the technique. The intent of this chapter is to explain the regulatory negotiation process, raise several key issues and questions, and address them in the context of EPA's experience. Other federal agencies, as they begin to use regulatory negotiation, will then be more knowledgeable about the process and prepared to use it more effectively.

THE ADMINISTRATIVE FUNCTIONS OF A FEDERAL AGENCY

The regulatory activities of a federal agency are governed by overarching statutes that have been developed and approved by Congress. Statutes provide the standards for agency decision making, and while virtually every administrative agency varies in its function, most agencies find it useful to adopt general principles governing the performance of its functions—that is, rules. Rule making is an agency action that regulates the future conduct of persons, through formulation and issuance of an agency statement (the rule) designed to implement, interpret or prescribe law or policy. Administrative agencies such as EPA are created to deal with and address contemporary crises as well as a variety of social problems. The EPA was created in 1970 to deal with increased public concern about risks to human health and safety and threats to the natural environment. EPA is responsible for implementing statutes that regulate the quality of the air, water, and soil and treatment and disposal of hazardous wastes, to name just a few.

Federal regulatory agencies rely heavily on rule making as a means of formulating policy, and a major impetus for agencies to make use of rule making comes directly from Congress. For example, Congress has assigned to federal agencies the responsibility of defining regulatory policy in the environmental area. Many environmental statutes enacted during the 1970s contain grants of rule making authority and instruct agencies to proceed by general rule. Congress created programs under which administrative officials at EPA are responsible for regulating hundreds of thousands of workplaces and pollution sources. The agency cannot hope to accomplish its mission unless it makes broad use of its rule making authority. In addition, the public and other interested parties have an interest and a right to be involved in determining that policy. In many environmental policy decisions, conflicts between competing interest groups arise, and policy making is often delayed, incomplete, or subject to lengthy litigation.

The Conventional Rule Making Process

EPA faces a variety of challenges as it attempts to develop and implement regulations to protect the environment and public health. One of those challenges involves the relationship between the agency and "outside" parties affected by the regulation or policy decision, be they regulated industries, environmental groups, other interested parties, or the general public. Traditionally, agency decision-making procedures are governed by the requirements of the *Administrative Procedure Act* (APA). The APA establishes uniform procedures for certain formal actions such as rule making and adjudication by any federal administrative tribunal or official. Three primary requirements for rule making are included in the Act: (1) Notice that rule making is going to take place; (2) opportunity to participate; and (3) a concise general statement of the basis and purpose for the rule. A major objective of the APA is to provide an opportunity for all affected interests formally to submit comments on proposed rules. The Act requires the agency to conduct information gathering and sharing activities (such as publication of significant decisions in the *Federal Register*) and to hold hearings to obtain public comment prior to specific decision points.

The conventional rule making process under the APA is known as "notice-and-comment" rule making. In other words, the agency gathers data from various sources and may have informal meetings with interested or affected groups to seek information and test ideas. The agency then decides on the content of a proposed rule and publishes a notice of the proposed rule in the *Federal Register*. All interested parties may submit written comments; in addition, the agency may hold public hearings on the proposed rule. After reviewing the comments and any testimony presented at hearings or submitted in writing, the agency must prepare and publish a final rule at least 30 days before it becomes effective. At EPA, the process of developing and finalizing a rule takes several months, often years. Because of this and other problems with the conventional process, federal agencies have been encouraged through legislation and Executive Order to use alternative means to develop rules.

The *Negotiated Rule Making Act* establishes a framework for federal agencies to use regulatory negotiation to develop proposed regulations and clarifies the agencies' authority to use this consensual technique. The Act does not *require* the use of regulatory negotiation but allows each agency discretion in deciding whether or not to use it. Regulatory negotiation, also called "Reg-Neg," entered the scene in the 1980s as an alternative to traditional procedures for drafting proposed regulations. The technique is based on the assumption that it is possible to bring the affected interest groups together to negotiate the text of a proposed rule. If the negotiators achieve consensus, the resulting rule is likely to be easier to implement and the possibility of litigation is reduced. Even without consensus on a draft rule, the process is valuable as a means of better informing the regulatory agency regarding the issues and concerns of the interested parties.

Alternative means of dispute resolution have been used increasingly by states, courts, and private entities in the past decade. The *Administrative Dispute Resolution Act* grants federal agencies the authority to use mediation, arbitration, and other consensual methods of dispute resolution in resolving cases under the APA. The Act establishes a federal policy of encouraging alternative dispute resolution (ADR) instead of more costly, time-consuming adjudication or litigation. The legislation is based on Congress' findings that ADR can lead to more creative, efficient, stable, and sensible outcomes and authorizes and encourages all federal agencies to use consensual procedures. Each agency must designate a senior official as the "dispute resolution specialist" of the agency. In addition, each agency is expected to make training available to its specialist and other employees involved in dispute resolution activities. The Administrative Conference of the United States (ACUS) has published an extremely helpful handbook (*Sourcebook: Federal Agency Use of Alternative Means of Dispute Resolution*, 1987) which outlines a variety of ADR techniques and alternatives. ACUS continues to encourage federal agencies to use ADR procedures based on the experiences of the Environmental Protection Agency, the U.S. Army Corps of Engineers, and a few other federal agencies that have successfully used similar procedures.

Advantages of alternative dispute resolution processes. Increasing interest in and use of ADR techniques such as Reg-Neg have come in response to criticism that the traditional regulatory process is slow, cumbersome, and excessively adversarial. Advocates for ADR point out the shortcomings of litigation as a method of resolving environmental conflict and that the increasing number of environmental disputes adds to the burden of a seriously overcrowded court system. Because litigation is aimed at very narrow, or "shadow" issues (generally procedural in nature), the key policy issues are not debated. The scope of judicial review is limited; adjudication is focused on rights, duties, and remedies; little attention is paid to cost; and the system is not as creative as ADR in looking at alternatives. In addition, the court system precludes direct participation by the principal parties to a dispute, and the adversarial nature of litigation tends to polarize disputants as well as discourage open communication, sharing of information, and joint problem solving (Susskind and McMahon, 1985). The court process is a win-lose approach, and these types of decisions encourage the losing party to keep pursuing its case through appeals or other legal action (Fisher and Ury, 1981). As a result, legal decisions often fail to resolve the controversy (Harter, 1982). Proponents of ADR claim significant procedural benefits associated with the use of ADR. ADR is claimed to be cheaper and faster than litigation; court cases lasting several years are well documented (Bacow and Wheeler, 1984; Bingham, 1986; Talbot, 1983). ADR is credited with yielding better results and rules than current decision making procedures; the cooperative procedure is expected to produce better final rules and to diminish the number of challenges to them (Harter, 1982; Rodwin, 1982). ADR allows for compromise agreements that satisfy all the parties involved and allow parties to see conflict in terms of interests, thus encouraging creative trade-offs and compromises that constitute a "win-win" approach (Fisher and Ury, 1981).

Because ADR processes bring all parties together to consider all parts of a dispute at once, the process can better accommodate all the claims. ADR allows for more direct and meaningful participation by interest groups in the decision-making process and can produce longer lasting and more satisfying solutions to difficult policy disputes and increased acceptance of the outcome (Harter, 1982; Ozawa, 1991). Institutionalization of ADR may give citizen groups greater power and influence in the decision-making process through greater access to key decision makers and important information and the potential to influence or control meeting agendas to their advantage (Bingham, 1986; Crowfoot and Wondolleck, 1990; Ozawa, 1991). The process can empower environmentalists or other less powerful groups and constrain the most powerful, keeping some parties in check (Susskind and McMahon, 1985). Improved communication and working relationships develop as well (U.S. EPA, 1987).

Disadvantages of alternative dispute resolution processes. A number of important drawbacks to ADR processes have been pointed out. Legitimate concerns have been raised regarding power imbalances among participants in terms of experience and skills in negotiation, as well as scientific and technical expertise (Amy, 1987; Crowfoot and Wondolleck, 1990; Ozawa, 1991). Questions relating to participation, identifying adequate representation for all parties, ensuring that all parties have sufficient resources, and bounding the scope of analysis (Fisher and Ury, 1981) present additional problems. Other issues regarding when and how ADR should be initiated, who participates and how they are identified, the scope of the issues, use of outside mediators, time required, and how to implement the agreements (U.S. EPA, 1987) have been raised as well.

Many critics point to deeper concerns with the process, noting the fact that participants may not fully trust the process of negotiation as well as the availability of reliable information regarding scientific, economic, and social aspects of a policy (Rabe, 1988). These issues present significant barriers for agencies attempting to use the techniques. Additional questions arise relating to whether the process really delivers better public health or environmental protection outcomes or dramatically reduced costs; whether agencies are properly equipped to play a viable role of mediator; and the belief that agencies have failed to gain the public trust that is fundamental to any effort they might make to play a genuinely mediative role.

An important issue in the debate is whether ADR is necessarily faster or cheaper than traditional processes. No systematic studies exist that demonstrate that mediation efforts in rule making take less time than the traditional process. Mediation often goes on at the same time as litigation; groups may be spending more time and money on the maintenance of two concurrent processes. Adequate participation requires research and time for travel and negotiation sessions; these can use more of an organization's time and resources than submitting comments or filing a brief in court. Federal provisions often allow environmental groups to recoup attorney's fees; this is not usually possible in mediation cases (*Dispute Resolution Forum*, 1986).

WHAT IS REGULATORY NEGOTIATION?

Recently, as a result of problems with the traditional process (lawsuits, delays, difficulty implementing decisions) as well as legislative initiatives, EPA and other agencies have begun to use a variety of different consultative decision-making processes, all of which involve more face-to-face contact with interested parties than ever before. One technique, called regulatory negotiation, or "Reg-Neg," is used to develop proposed rules. Reg-Neg is an alternative dispute resolution process which brings together representatives of various interest groups and a federal agency, with the goal of negotiating and reaching consensus on the text of a proposed rule.

Regulatory negotiation differs from the traditional rule making process. In Reg-Neg, a balanced group representing the regulated community, public and environmental interest groups, state and local governments, and other interests joins with the federal agency in a federally chartered advisory committee to negotiate the text of a rule before it is published as a proposed rule. EPA or the appropriate federal agency participates as an interested party in the negotiations. If the committee reaches consensus on the text of the rule, then the federal agency may use this consensus as the basis for its proposed rule. The consensus agreement is still subject to public comment, however, and Reg-Neg should be viewed as a *supplement* to the rule making requirements of the APA. Thus, the negotiation sessions take place *prior to* the issuance of the notice of proposed rule making and the opportunities for the public to comment required by the APA.

Reg-Neg is also different from other forms of environmental mediation that have been researched and described extensively in the environmental mediation literature. The controversies that it attempts to resolve extend beyond specific geographic sites and have very broad policy applicability. Its primary purpose is to define general rules that will influence later behavior, not to resolve site specific disputes. Finally, Reg-Neg is more like the legislative than the judicial process as a framework for making policy (Fiorino, 1988).

Regulatory Negotiation at the Environmental Protection Agency

Although several federal agencies are currently using Reg-Neg processes, EPA was selected as the agency of interest for this chapter because EPA has more experience using the process and has successfully completed more Reg-Neg cases (approximately 12) than any other federal agency. At any one time, EPA may be in the process of developing from 200 to 250 rules, nearly 80 percent of which are challenged in court (U.S. EPA, 1987).

In 1982, the Administrative Conference of the United States set forth criteria for identifying rule making situations for which Reg-Neg is likely to be successful. In early 1983, EPA began a demonstration project to attempt to develop two proposed rules using regulatory negotiation. The project's purpose was to investigate the value of developing regulations by negotiation, the types of regulations which were most appropriate for this process, and the procedures and circumstances which best fostered negotiations (Kirtz, 1990). As a result of the pilot project, subsequent experiences with the technique, and reviewing the literature on environmental dispute resolution, EPA further refined the selection criteria for use within the agency. EPA developed the following selection criteria for selecting rules to be negotiated, as well as for evaluating potential participants in the process (Source: *EPA Negotiated Rule Making Selection Criteria Fact Sheet*).

Criteria for the Rule To Be Negotiated:

- The proposal should require the resolution of a limited number of interdependent or related issues, none of which involve fundamental questions of value or extremely controversial national policy. The policy implications of the issues to be resolved are more or less limited programmatically (i.e., the rule making will not establish binding precedents in program areas not encompassed by the negotiations). Complex multi-media issues may be difficult to resolve.
- There must be a sufficiently well-developed factual base to permit meaningful discussion and resolution of the issues.
- There should be several ways in which the issues can be resolved.
- There should be a firm deadline imposed upon the negotiations by EPA due to some statutory, judicial, or programmatic mechanism. The deadline should provide adequate time for negotiation of the issues.

Criteria for Participants in Regulatory Negotiation

- Those participants interested in or affected by the outcome of the development process should be readily identifiable and relatively few in number. Participants should be able to represent and reflect the interests of their constituencies.

- The parties should have common goals. They should be in good faith about wanting to participate in the negotiations and should feel themselves as likely, if not more likely, to achieve their overall goals using negotiations as they would through traditional rule making.

- Some of the parties should have common positions on one or more of the issues to be resolved which might serve as a basis for agreement during the course of negotiations.

- The parties should view themselves as having an ongoing relationship with the agency beyond the item under consideration. Any ongoing litigation does not inhibit the parties' willingness or ability to engage in genuine give and take.

EPA's Reg-Neg process. As a result of increasing encouragement to use Reg-Neg, agencies unfamiliar with the technique may wonder what specific steps are involved in conducting a Reg-Neg process. The following is a brief outline of the steps involved in a typical Reg-Neg process at EPA. More general details are provided in the Administrative Conference's *Negotiated Rule Making Sourcebook,* a step-by-step guide to the conduct of Reg-Neg activities. The volume contains a discussion of when and how to use the procedure, along with sample notices and other documents that may be needed by an agency using the process. Numerous articles, both analytical and practical, are reprinted in the book, along with an extensive bibliography.

Timing. As soon as the office responsible for developing a rule can determine (i.e., the item may meet the criteria proposed by EPA and/or the Administrative Conference) that it might benefit from regulatory negotiation, it raises the issue internally and begins what is called the Convening Stage. This means that there are a limited number of interests, the issues are ripe for decision, no fundamental value conflicts exist, there is a diversity of issues involved, potential parties view it as in their interest to negotiate, the agency is willing to use the process and participate in it, no one interest will dominate the proceedings, and a clear deadline for achieving consensus exists. Proposals for rules to be negotiated may originate with agency staff, external parties, or Congressional direction.

Convening. Convening determines whether an item is "ripe" for negotiation by identifying issues and potentially affected interested parties. The lead office staff work to see if the item meets EPA's threshold criteria, discussed earlier. A convenor, or outside mediation specialist, is selected and contracted with to identify and initiate contact with potential participants. After discussions with the potential participants, the convenor advises the agency whether the item is a likely candidate for negotiations and may recommend bringing the parties together for that purpose. EPA has established a contract with a professional dispute resolution organization for the purpose of convening and facilitating negotiations. The majority of EPA's convenors and facilitators are private, outside professionals in the mediation field.

The process of convening includes evaluating the feasibility of negotiating a rule, designing the structure of the negotiating committee, and identifying a preliminary set of issues to be negotiated. Convenors are persons or organizations that are able to carry out these tasks and discuss the results with agency officials. Convenors may be agency personnel or private contractors skilled in bringing parties together to negotiate and are neutral with respect to substantive issues. Representation of all potentially affected interests in the negotiation is critical if the rule is to be successfully developed and implemented. About 25 is the maximum number of participants for which the process can be kept manageable. The convenor identifies all interests that may be affected by a rule, contacts the parties to interview them in an effort to identify interests and issues, and determines whether it is possible to obtain commitments to negotiate from representative parties and agency personnel. The convenor attempts to assemble a balanced committee that is willing and able to work toward the goal of consensus on a rule.

Once the agency decides to proceed with Reg-Neg, potential participants then give their firm commitments to the convenor to proceed with the process and their assurances that they can represent their constituencies. EPA publishes a *Federal Register* notice announcing its intent to conduct a negotiated rule making. An organizational meeting is held for potential participants to review the scope, timing and procedures for negotiations, to make a joint commitment to go forward, and to submit comments on the negotiation plan.

Chartering a FACA committee. The *Federal Advisory Committee Act* (86 Stat. 770), or FACA, regulates the formation and operation of advisory committees by federal agencies in the Executive Branch. Because the Reg-Neg group meets on a regular basis as a "preferred source" of advice or recommendations to the agency, the committee must be chartered under FACA. An Advisory Committee is defined to include any committee or similar group (1) established by statute or organization plan, (2) established or utilized in the interest of obtaining advice or recommendations, and (3) not composed wholly of full-time federal officers or employees. FACA committees may be established only after public notice and a determination that establishment is in the public interest; that each advisory committee has a clearly defined purpose and that its membership is balanced in terms of points of view represented and the functions to be performed; and that meetings of the advisory committee are open to public observation. All negotiation sessions are held in a public forum, and interested parties who are not directly participating in the negotiations may attend and observe the meetings.

Facilitation. Facilitation helps parties reach a decision or a satisfactory resolution of the matter being addressed. EPA's Reg-Negs are chaired and facilitated by a neutral outside party, usually a professional mediator. Other agencies have used in-house staff trained in facilitation techniques. The facilitator, or "mediator," conducts meetings and coordinates discussions but normally does not become involved in the substantive issues. Facilitators also record and distribute meeting summaries. The Administrative Conference has created a roster with information on mediators and facilitators who are available to assist in Reg-Neg efforts.

Prenegotiation training. Participants may or may not have experience in negotiation or negotiation training. Training sessions provide an opportunity for participants to augment and update their negotiation skills; become acquainted with each other; demonstrate consensus building techniques; allow facilitators to observe the dynamics of interaction among participants; and provide a common vocabulary and procedures for consensus building behavior. The sessions are usually conducted before the first regular negotiation session and vary from a half to a full day in length.

Costs. EPA has a small resource fund to assist participants with few resources to participate in Reg-Neg. Funds are usually reserved for environmental group or state and local representatives, who traditionally operate with more limited resources than industrial or manufacturer representatives. Reg-Neg expenses include fees for facilitators, travel costs for participants, as well as rental of rooms if the agency does not have appropriate meeting facilities. Additional costs are incurred in staff time for data collection and analysis, training, and administrative support to the committee.

Protocols or ground rules. EPA and/or the facilitator submits draft protocols of operation to the committee for consideration and approval. Protocols address such procedural agreements as operating by consensus, a party's right to leave the table at any time, and facilitation, among other issues.

Negotiations. Negotiation is a form of communication among parties in an effort to reach agreement. Negotiations are chaired by a neutral facilitator whose task is to keep the negotiations moving toward consensus. The total time spent negotiating depends on the specifics of each case, and can vary widely. Often, if the agency has a clear deadline for when agreement must be reached, the negotiations are planned working backward from that date. Negotiations are normally conducted on a monthly basis for one to two days, with one day for a general session and one day for work or task group meetings. Documents may be exchanged and conference calls held in the time between meetings. Negotiations at EPA have taken from 4 to 18 months, depending on deadlines set by the program office.

Closure of negotiations. At the end of the negotiation period, the committee has reached consensus on the actual language of a proposed rule or a set of recommendations or advises that consensus cannot be met on all issues. In the case in which a complete consensus is not reached, a recommendation is made for those issues that have been resolved through consensus agreements. At EPA, the consensus agreement is used as the basis for the proposed rule (the agreement must be within EPA's statutory authority), which is subject to the regular administrative procedure rule making requirements for notice and public comment. Even if complete consensus is not achieved, the records from the process provide a valuable source of information for the agency to use in proposing the rule.

Lessons from EPA's Experiences with Reg-Neg

Since the first negotiation in 1984, EPA has initiated approximately 12 regulatory negotiation processes, with varying degrees of success (U.S. EPA, 1991b). EPA has made a firm institutional commitment to using Reg-Neg, and will continue to pursue opportunities for successful Reg-Neg activities. The Office of Policy, Planning and Evaluation (OPPE) at EPA has full-time professional staff assigned to evaluate rule making candidates and manage the process, who are also responsible for a systematic evaluation of rules under development for possible negotiated rule making. In addition, OPPE provides staff and contract assistance to rule making offices in setting up and managing Reg-Neg proceedings. As with any procedure under development, there are benefits as well as drawbacks to using the technique; several key issues are discussed below.

Regulatory outcome. A primary benefit of Reg-Neg for EPA is that the rule it is required by law to promulgate actually gets developed and promulgated, often with little or no litigation by industrial or environmental groups. At times, the agency has experienced *early* implementation and compliance with the regulation. This is because the regulated community, state and environmental interests have been involved in the process all along and know what the contents and requirements of the rule will be. Most parties agree that a rule developed under Reg-Neg is better than a rule that EPA develops in the traditional manner, because more of the affected parties are involved, allowing more issues to be addressed.

Participants from state agencies and environmental groups see regulatory benefits as well. Often, state and environmental groups' primary interests are to have a rule in place that mandates specific requirements for the reduction of a variety of pollutants. With a successful Reg-Neg, such a rule is developed. Often the Reg-Neg rule is more readily implemented and enforced than a traditionally developed rule, which may be litigated for years. Thus, the environmental benefits of specific pollution reduction goals are achieved on schedule and sometimes much earlier.

Finally, the regulated community experiences benefits from Reg-Neg as well. By participating in Reg-Neg, it is able to transmit and analyze critical data upon which regulatory decisions will be made. Participation allows the regulated community to have input into the design of the final regulation, which gives it certainty regarding what the regulation will require. This certainty often results in earlier and more consistent implementation and enforcement of the final rule.

Participation and communication. Reg-Neg involves more of the key parties in the early stages of rule making and increases their participation and communication with other parties. Traditionally, industrial or manufacturing representatives are often the only "interested" parties in contact with the agency during the early stages of rule development. As a result, EPA attempts to represent the interests of those parties not as actively involved (states, environmental groups, and public health organizations), or those interests do not typically get involved until very late in the process. Reg-Neg ensures that other parties *are* involved early on, and allows the agency to pursue its own interests, with less worry about representing an absent party. Thus, the importance of carefully assessing and selecting Reg-Neg participants is critical.

There are constraints to participation, however, especially for environmental groups and state and local government representatives. For example, environmental groups, as well as state and local governments, are quite limited in terms of numbers of staff who are able to participate in a Reg-Neg and thus cannot participate in an unlimited number of such activities. Representatives for these groups must therefore evaluate and participate in those Reg-Neg activities that will meet their goals and interests to the greatest degree. Industrial representatives, who typically have more resources at their disposal, could potentially participate in many more Reg-Negs.

Reg-Neg can legitimize and enhance communication between all parties, simply by ensuring that a key contact person is identified for each interest group. All participants know who is involved and can communicate openly with less of a "political" problem than they might have had in the past (i.e., an environmental representative talking with an industrial representative, or an EPA staff person calling up an environmental group representative). While not all communication is friendly and in fact can be quite hostile at times, most participants believe that by the end of the process, they have improved communication with the various interest group representatives.

Future conflict and litigation. One of EPA's primary reasons for conducting Reg-Neg was to reduce the amount of conflict and litigation that the agency was subject to as it developed and implemented rules. Dispute resolution theory posits that because all of the interested parties are involved in the development of the rule, less conflict and litigation over promulgation and implementation will result because all of the key issues have been raised and addressed. EPA's experience to date suggests that fewer rules are litigated when Reg-Neg is used, although the number of completed cases is still quite small. Approximately 20 percent of the rules developed using Reg-Neg have been litigated, which is a vast improvement over the 80 percent that EPA experienced previously. Finally, it is unclear whether Reg-Neg leads to "better" policy outcomes in terms of public health or national environmental policy. More completed cases, in addition to an in-depth comparative study, are needed before it can be conclusively stated that Reg-Neg reduces litigation or conflict and produces superior policy outcomes.

Costs. Participating in a Reg-Neg process is costly for all parties in terms of staff time and other organizational resources. The sponsoring agency must fund participants, the facilitator, and many other aspects of the process, in addition to participating as an interested party. For example, EPA managers who have been the agency's negotiators have devoted far more time to the negotiations in which they were involved than they would ordinarily spend on a single rule making effort. In one case (the Noncompliance Penalty negotiations), a division director and two branch chiefs put in significant time (U.S. EPA, 1987). Other parties must spend time familiarizing themselves with technical issues and materials, communicating with constituents, and preparing for and participating in the negotiation sessions.

Reg-Neg will not enable EPA or other parties to cut back on pre-proposal data collection and analysis. In a recent wood stove negotiation, EPA spent more than $1 million gathering and analyzing data before the negotiations began (U.S. EPA, 1987). The advance work was critical, however, because it enabled EPA staff to evaluate negotiation discussions and to respond to questions concerning technical and economic issues.

Little research has been conducted regarding the amount and types of costs that have accrued for Reg-Neg processes. A more comprehensive analysis of time and other resources spent on Reg-Neg must be completed and compared to figures from the conventional rule making process in order to determine whether Reg-Neg does in fact save time and money.

Chartering a FACA committee. If a rule is to be developed using Reg-Neg, a FACA committee must be chartered, which at times has become a barrier to the process. During the later years of the Bush administration, a moratorium on FACA committee charters was issued, making it nearly impossible to conduct a Reg-Neg. The Clinton administration has abolished the moratorium and encourages the use of Reg-Neg. Environmentalists, states, and others with limited resources tend to favor the formation of a FACA committee, as that is the only way they can be reimbursed for their participation. Industrial representatives tend to agree to participate on FACA committees more reluctantly, with reasons that are less evident. All parties sense that they have more influence over the final outcome if they are allowed and encouraged formally to participate in the rule development process via a FACA committee. An additional concern for the sponsoring agency is ensuring a balanced membership on the committee. Several of the constraints on participation discussed earlier could present barriers to formation of a balanced committee or could limit the number of committees formed.

SUMMARY AND CONCLUSIONS

Encouragement to use Reg-Neg as a rule making process in federal agencies will undoubtedly continue, and perhaps increase. In order successfully to use and further develop the process, federal agencies must be aware of the steps involved and anticipate the potential benefits and problems that are likely to result when using the process. Although EPA has a conducted a relatively small number of Reg-Neg processes, it has more experience using the technique than most other federal agencies. EPA's experience suggests that critical areas include issues surrounding regulatory outcomes; participation and communication; future conflict and litigation; costs; and chartering a committee to conduct a Reg-Neg. More experience using the technique, a greater number of successful cases to analyze, and additional data on costs are necessary before definitive conclusions regarding the success or failure of Reg-Neg can be drawn. However, EPA views the experience as successful and continues to use Reg-Neg in rule making. Other agencies considering the use of Reg-Neg should view the benefits of the process as encouragement to experiment with the technique and view the drawbacks as an opportunity to anticipate and perhaps avoid some of the pitfalls EPA has experienced. Finally, as more agencies use the technique, we will continue to add to our knowledge of the process and further refine and develop the technique into an effective rule making procedure.

ACKNOWLEDGMENTS

The author would like to thank Dr. James E. Crowfoot and Dr. Julia M. Wondolleck for providing valuable advice and comments on early drafts of this chapter.

Chapter 15

Environmental Mediation:
Keys to Success
at the Local Government Level

J. Lynn Wood and Mary E. Guy

Public works initiatives that have a potential to affect the environment adversely are born in conflict. The methods that local governments have used, or could use, to address disagreement among stakeholders and achieve consensus are worth noting because they forestall bitter conflict and expensive litigation. While seeming to delay implementation in the short run, these methods speed it in the long run by avoiding public outcry, prejudicial court decrees, and political stalls.

PUBLIC WORKS AND ENVIRONMENTAL ACTIVISM

One of the primary functions of local government is to provide services to citizens. These services are designed to enhance the quality of life within towns, cities, and counties. Adequate roadways, water service, sewer service, garbage collection and other local government services are necessary to maintain an acceptable standard of living. Indeed, virtually everyone expects water to run from the faucet when it is opened and then flow properly down the drain for disposal. They expect their garbage and trash to be collected routinely and removed from the neighborhood, and they expect to travel passable thoroughfares regardless of the weather.

In order for these services to be rendered, water filtering plants, wastewater treatment facilities, and landfills must be sited, constructed, and operated. Transport systems, such as roadways and pipelines, must be built and maintained. Local government officials are responsible for deciding when and where such projects are to be implemented and what form they will take. These decision makers are accountable to a citizenry who are increasingly sensitive to environmental issues and the disruption of ecosystems, as well as disturbances to the aesthetics of a community or to real property value.

Safety, attractive environments, and the preservation of natural habitats have begun to figure prominently in a community's perceived quality of life. In the past, such undertakings were planned, designed, and constructed largely from within the engineering departments of local government or by engineering consultants and contractors hired by local governments. As a result of sensitivity to environmental issues, engineers and local government administrators do not have the luxury of planning projects and designing facilities based purely on measures of cost efficiency and ease of engineering. Since construction of service facilities and their accompanying infrastructure has the potential to cause environmental problems such as erosion, siltation, habitat destruction, and non point source pollutant loading, these types of projects have become focal points for environmental activism.

Recently we have seen an emergence of a new list of players who are active participants in decision making about projects that affect the environment. These new players include planners, scientists, politicians, attorneys, engineers, and others from within local government as well as external players, such as business interests, environmental groups, land developers, and residents who live near the planned project. Moreover, public awareness has precipitated local environmental watchdog groups that keep a close watch on any public works projects that have the potential to affect the ecosystem adversely. The membership of such groups typically consists of well-educated and sophisticated citizens who donate their time, attention, and expertise in order to protect and maintain environmental quality. They want to insure that adequate safeguards are in place to minimize environmental hazards.

One of the primary functions of local environmental groups is informational. They want to keep their membership, as well as the general public, informed about environmental quality. Consequently, it is not uncommon to find environmental specialists as full-time, paid staff members of these organizations. These specialists routinely monitor environmentally sensitive areas. Construction projects and facility operations which do not adhere to safeguards may suddenly find themselves on the evening television news when the watchdog group identifies a threat. If the threat escalates, litigation is likely to occur through citizen-filed lawsuits, which are provided for in most federal environmental regulations.

An additional concern is that the membership of such groups represents an active voting public. Since environmental quality has become a hot political issue, elected officials consider not only the most cost-effective means to implement projects but also the most environmentally sound and politically viable means of implementation. Support for public works projects is dependent on many, or all, of the aforementioned interests listed.

STRATEGIES FOR SUCCESSFUL IMPLEMENTATION

There are several strategies for reaching a consensus regarding projects that are environmentally sensitive. These strategies are based primarily upon the following elements: having a key contact person to serve as a liaison to all interests; ensuring timely and effective communication; being sensitive to environmental concerns; and identifying stakeholders early in the planning process. Each of these elements is discussed, followed by a case study showing how they contributed to the successful implementation of a wastewater treatment project in Jefferson County, Alabama. Essential steps for attaining project goals may be derived from these four basic components. The following discussion explains how the key contact person, effective communication, environmental sensitivity, and working with, rather than against, stakeholders contribute to successful implementation.

Choose the Right Individual as the Key Contact Person

Designating an individual to work specifically with environmental matters has proven to be advantageous for local government. Communication is perhaps the most important factor in any mediation process. Adept presentation of ideas, plans, and proposals figures prominently in gaining acceptance for environmentally sensitive projects. This key person should have technical knowledge about environmental issues and be able to speak effectively to citizens' groups and the media.

The person in this position should be a part of the internal configuration of the local government—ideally it is an employee with some degree of longevity within the agency that is spearheading the project. This provides an established familiarity with the organization and enhances the probability of understanding the basis for activities within the jurisdiction. Someone within local government who has dealt with environmental projects, or permitting and compliance, is well positioned to fill this role. Experience in these areas provides a basis for evaluating and assessing planned projects, especially as they pertain to requirements for compliance with applicable regulations.

Even if technical consultants or a public relations firm from outside the organization is hired, there remains the necessity for someone within the local government structure to act as a liaison. This person becomes an information hub for the agency and for the community, where all environmentally relevant matters can be directed. This avoids the frustration that will occur when someone who has questions or concerns about a specific project contacts one office, only to be given erroneous information or to be referred to someone else, who is likely to refer them to someone else. This holds true for stakeholders both within the organization and for those who are external.

Technical expertise. Technical knowledge of environmental quality is an important factor to consider when selecting this key contact person. This individual will serve as a liaison among often divergent interests and needs to be knowledgeable of their different perspectives. In spite of his or her technical expertise, however, the most important attributes may be those of effective communication, credibility, and tactfulness. The designated liaison must be able to communicate with project planners and designers in such a manner as to gain an understanding of the goals of the project and its implementation. This person must also be capable of communicating this information to other interested parties who may understand little about civil engineering. The manner in which the initial information concerning the project is disseminated will prejudice stakeholders toward acceptance of, or opposition to, the project.

Credibility. Another important attribute which the liaison must possess is credibility. Effective communication often depends upon the credibility afforded the messenger. Blind faith in government's actions does not exist. It is imperative that government agencies establish credibility in their activities. This is why the key contact person must be a good listener to the concerns of all stakeholders. The liaison must be seen as credible by those who care about the project, including the environmental, business, and political communities.

Establish Contact and Build Credibility with the Community

Once a person has been designated as the liaison for the project, ongoing contacts with stakeholders should be established. Stakeholders are viewed as anyone who can place a claim on an organization's attention, resources, or activities or are affected by an organization's activities. The external stakeholders include anyone outside the local government organization or, on a more specific scale, outside a department or division of local government. These may be citizens, taxpayers, service recipients, unions, interest groups, political parties, the financial community, and/or other governments (Bryson and Roering, 1988).

The next step is to make contact with those individuals who are instrumental in representing the ideas and opinions of the stakeholders. Notices in local newspapers that list meeting times and dates for local organizations is a good place to start. Identify those groups who are effective in expressing their positions regarding issues. Most groups, such as the Sierra Club and other environmentally oriented organizations, will hold regular public meetings. Periodic attendance at these meetings by the liaison provides insights pertaining to issues that may arise on upcoming projects.

Attendance should not be limited to occasions when controversial topics are "hot." Approaching such groups only when their support is needed or when controversial situations arise is too late and makes project officials appear as insincere and having ulterior motives. Occasional attendance helps build credibility for the liaison and the organization on an informal basis. Often the acquaintances established through these informal contacts create the foundation for consensus building later.

Environmental groups are not the only organizations upon which to focus, although they may be the most vocal and attract the most media attention. The community or communities in which initiatives may be planned are also important. The community sentiment and the political atmosphere foretell the projects' likelihood of success. Often local government projects alter opportunities for development. The business community should be informed when projects may expand existing land use or even when they may curtail development, such as in the case of wilderness areas or greenways.

The liaison should identify the property owners and any businesses located in the area of proposed activities. These stakeholders should be contacted personally and provided with an account of the project to be implemented. Later, a meeting with those affected should be arranged to obtain their feedback. From the standpoint of the liaison, the meetings may be more informative and less confusing if they are held separately (i.e., meeting with the business community at one time, and meeting with local residents at another time). This serves more narrowly to define the range of issues at each meeting and facilitates better communication with the liaison.

Public awareness program. Public awareness programs contribute to consensus building. Rothstein and Jones (1993:137-138) list seven recommendations that worked for involving the public on a project in Austin, Texas, which involved wastewater rate increases and facility construction projects. Public concern about planned increases in water rates and environmental protection were addressed by the following.

First, the people of Austin, Texas began at the beginning. They started planning and executing a public involvement program before the project was too far advanced to make changes. Second, they outlined exactly what the public involvement program would entail, delineated the roles and responsibilities of each individual, and established a proposed calendar of events. This created a roadmap for the entire program. Third, they established a "party line." They practiced word-for-word responses to the questions they anticipated. And they developed a one-phrase summary of their position. Fourth, they committed to a "no-surprises" policy so that the news media and opinion leaders were advised of developments early in the process. Fifth, they involved their enemies because they knew that their credibility rested on being reasonable and solution-oriented in the face of opposition. Sixth, they lowered people's expectations by avoiding taking a "promotional" approach to the project, for it is the gap between expectations and perceptions that results in dissatisfaction. Finally, they tolerated disagreement and declared victory: at hearings they let everybody talk at once and stubbornly clung to their positions, while they behaved as though this is a normal part of public discourse (it is).

These seven recommendations rest on two foundations: the reputation of the local government through its established credibility and goodwill, and recognition of the importance of communication in meeting the needs of the public. The objective of these recommendations is to build the government's reputation as an honest, competent service provider and to encourage the growth and development of constructive public involvement.

Public participation. Deister and Tice (1993) used a "Public Participation Model" to gain public support for a reclaimed water seasonal storage project in the Las Virgenes Municipal Water District and Triunfo Sanitation District in California. The model is designed to develop a public-supported decision making program. It has three phases: conceptualization, graduated building blocks, and implementation.

The conceptualization phase sets the stage for the process. Here officials who will be involved in determining the type and degree of public involvement sought must reach agreement. Measures for defining success, evaluating results, and setting guiding principles for the project are established. Deister and Tice (1993) recommend a multidisciplinary approach that includes people from departments of engineering, operations, planning, environmental compliance, community outreach, and public relations. They point out that the conceptualization team must incorporate these diverse perspectives into the project plan. In the California case, consensus on the conceptualization phase was based on the following affirmative principles:

1. The public participation program will be meaningful and useful;
2. The process of engaging the public to participate is an inclusionary one, seeking to involve as many interests and stakeholders as possible;
3. The program has an active intergovernmental coordination element, especially regarding the local governmental agencies within the service area as well as the environmental regulatory agents;
4. The information flow process will feature accurate, timely, user-friendly materials and messages;
5. The program will be based on a public-engineering joint decision-making process using facilitation and consensus building techniques and activities (Deister and Tice, 1993:133).

The second phase of the model is called the building block phase. Three building blocks are used to facilitate the progression from conceptualization to program development. The first building block is comprised of a "brainstorming" identification procedure by consultants and agency staff. Target groups are identified who can help distribute the message to the larger community. The middle building block proceeds further with public outreach. The goal at this stage is to engage a variety of viewpoints, with an emphasis on soliciting criticism from the community. The third building block provides a mechanism for decision making via two-way interaction. Here roles are defined and interaction begins between the agency staff, its consultants, and "formal" multi-represented bodies of public interests.

The last phase of the model is the implementation phase. Implementation is based on the level of public involvement designated in the final stage of the building block phase. Agency personnel and consultants must convey the level of involvement expected from the public to ensure effective decision making. Deister and Tice (1993) state that implementation should be designed with flexibility that accommodates concerns, interests, and perspectives while also providing information to all involved regarding what is planned and when and what is expected of the program. This plan incorporates feedback mechanisms so that the plan can be modified in each of the phases based on information gained while using the process. This flexibility is an important aspect in establishing a partnership for decision making based on consensus.

Community meetings. Public involvement requires community meetings. R. L. Harper (1993) recommends holding these in a setting that is conducive to speaking personally about matters of concern to residents. She warns against focusing on the technical attributes of proposed projects when the citizens may be more concerned about neighborhood safety, traffic problems, noise, odors, or other impacts to the neighborhood as a result of the proposed activity. "In presenting your case to the community, translate everything into 'How will it affect ME?' Answer questions in terms that are relevant and understandable to each individual in the audience, not in terms of your priorities or those of your agency" (Harper, 1993:118).

Another tip given by Harper (1993) is to be willing to admit the disadvantages of the proposal. Because all projects will have a downside to their implementation, project officials should not try to hide such facts. Rather, they should provide answers regarding the measures which will be taken to minimize the problems. Show that a deliberative process was used during the planning stages and that the proposal presented, while perhaps not perfect, is the best after considering many factors. Also, assure the community that someone who is both responsible and responsive has been designated to handle problems and complaints.

These approaches to soliciting citizen input highlight the importance of the project liaison as we described earlier. The probability of success while incorporating the above practices will be enhanced by frequent contact with all involved parties. An effective liaison is one who can present issues and alternately listen and evaluate the concerns of proponents and opponents. The liaison has a better chance of winning the respect of conflicting interests if the parties feel that their views have been heard and offered equal consideration. Attention to the manner in which issues are raised and discussed can give insight to the motivation of interested parties. An understanding of the external stakeholders' motivation for their stance on various issues is invaluable when working toward consensus.

Gain Support for Activities by Using Independent Organizations Such as Universities, Research Foundations, and Professional Organizations

Often the planning of local government activities must rely on technical data and professional opinion. This is especially true when environmental impact assessments are to be made. The environmental impact assessment evaluates the existing environmental conditions and estimates the effect that certain types of activities, such as construction, will have on the area. These studies also assess the predicted environmental impact that facility operations, such as the operation of wastewater treatment facilities, will have over a period of time. The assessment may include recommendations for certain practices to be incorporated into the proposed activity to minimize adverse effects. Such studies have typically been performed by the local government or its paid consultants. When particularly sensitive environmental areas are involved, the integrity of the data collected and assessments made may be more widely accepted if the study is performed by an academic institution or research foundation. Even if funding is provided to the institution by the local government, academicians and researchers may still offer a higher degree of credibility with certain special interest groups. Again in the use of this practice, the importance of the local government liaison is apparent.

The liaison should identify any colleges and universities or research centers in the area and establish contacts with the departments likely to employ expertise in activities performed by the local government. These may include such disciplines as civil and environmental engineering, environmental science, biology, chemistry, public administration, and schools of law. Even if the local government collects its own data or uses a private consultant, certain circumstances may lend credence to a review of the information by a recognized expert.

Professional organizations can also provide information and assistance for the evaluation and support of proposed activities by local government. Conferences, workshops, and other seminars held by such organizations as the American Society of Civil Engineers, the Water Environment Federation, the International City/County Management Association, the American Society for Public Administration, and others offer current information regarding accepted practices and methods for implementing projects. Results of applications of the latest technologies and strategies to comparable situations faced by other local governments also can be beneficial. The contacts made through memberships in these types of organizations have proven to be an invaluable way to network with others who are faced with similar tasks. Evaluating the success or failure of practices and ideas used in other areas may help to define methods of consensus building for use in one's own jurisdiction.

Keep in Touch with Regulatory Agencies

Environmental regulation is a major factor in the successful implementation of most public works projects. Mandates dictate methods of planning, construction, and operation. Local government must have a comprehensive understanding of regulations pertaining to the specific activities characteristic of their public service duties. Provisions of the Clean Water Act, the Clean Air Act, the Resource Conservation Recovery Act, and other federal and state regulations may apply. One of the best ways to assure that local government projects comply with applicable environmental regulations is to establish a communications network with the regulatory agencies.

Most regulatory agencies will have an individual assigned to oversee permitting for a particular local government area. The local government liaison should view this individual as one of the most important people in the consensus building network. Regulatory personnel can give insight concerning what current regulations will apply to given projects and what, if any, proposed regulations may become effective during the life of the project.

Periodic contact through informal meetings and telephone conversations helps provide a familiarity between the local government liaison and the regulatory agency personnel. For projects which will require some form of permitting, this familiarity may aid in negotiating terms during the draft and comment stage of permit writing. Apprising regulatory agencies at the beginning of the planning stage of projects can initiate an informal continuing review of the plans and facilitate their formal approval. This progression of communication during the planning process will alert engineers and others to faulty proposals which would not be in compliance with environmental regulations.

Informal contacts with the regulatory agency personnel set the stage for meeting environmental regulations and acquiring formal approval for projects. This, in turn, becomes a cornerstone upon which to build consensus with other stakeholders. If projects have obtained approval for meeting the criteria established by the regulatory agencies for the protection of the environment, then a major step in acquiring justification for the design and implementation of projects has been accomplished. This provides evidence to other stakeholders that the local government is concerned about environmental factors and has involved the regulatory experts in the planning process. A cooperative effort between the local government and the regulatory agencies helps to insure that the desired goals are achieved in the most environmentally sound manner.

This chapter has included four strategies to successful consensus building. These include using a key contact person from within local government as the project liaison, building credibility, involving regulatory agencies in the planning process, and identifying stakeholders who have concerns regarding the project. When these strategies are combined, they serve to minimize opposition to the project and ensure that it is as safe to the ecosystem as possible. The following case study demonstrates how such a pattern leads to successful implementation.

CASE IN POINT

A scenario involving the use of the methods recommended occurred in Jefferson County, Alabama. Jefferson County is the most densely populated county in the State of Alabama, containing the city of Birmingham and many suburban municipalities. The county government owns and operates several wastewater treatment facilities. The county geography and topography is such that a large regional wastewater treatment facility is not feasible. As a result, several treatment facilities have been constructed over the years in the small stream basins within the county. Most of these facilities were designed over twenty years ago, and during the time since their construction, an increase has occurred in many suburban populations. In some areas, facility capacity and design have become inadequate to provide the necessary treatment.

A typical example of such a situation occurred in a suburb which utilized a "trickling filter" treatment design. Under changing, more restrictive regulatory requirements, this treatment design began to offer borderline treatment during dry weather periods. The receiving stream for the treated wastewater experienced extreme low flows during the driest period of the year. The discharge limitations for the facility were based on the waste load assimilative capacity of the receiving stream at its lowest sustained flow over a seven-year period. In order to protect the ambient stream water quality as designated by environmental regulations, an upgrade of the existing facility was necessary. But a simple decision to upgrade the facility and move forward with design and implementation was not an acceptable course of action. There were several complicating circumstances.

A local environmental group existed whose purpose was to insure the protection of the water quality in the specific basin in which the facility was located. The group was concerned with any construction activity within the basin. The group also was concerned about how the county set priorities in funding different wastewater treatment projects. It felt that projects to reduce infiltration and inflow in the sewer collection systems should have priority over existing facility upgrades. It feared that facility upgrades would be done solely to increase the facility capacity and thereby encourage further development in the basin. The group advocates carefully controlled low-density growth and development in the basin. This environmental group was identified as an important stakeholder because of its history of political activism and the need for its approval of this and future projects within the stream basin.

Other issues also had to be addressed. The proposed facility upgrade would require the acquisition of additional property adjacent to the existing facility site. Another factor was the existence of a lake downstream of the facility discharge point which was apparently showing signs of the early stages of eutrophication. (Eutrophication can be caused from an excess of nutrients such as nitrogen and phosphorus which are common constituents of wastewater.) New regulatory requirements would also have to be met for the proposed upgrade.

An approach which incorporated the steps to successful consensus building was initiated. A liaison had been establishing a communication network for some time before this particular project had been proposed. The liaison had been involved in environmental water quality matters for a number of years and had worked for the local government on environmental matters in the basin for fifteen years. During this time he had formed effective working relationships with the agencies which were charged with determining and enforcing environmental regulations. The liaison had also attended meetings of the local environmental group over the years and had shared with them water quality information obtained by the county government. In addition, a working relationship had also been established over the years with the owners of the lake downstream of the county facility. The liaison also discussed the proposal with faculty experts in environmental quality at the local university. The professors were well respected by most of the stakeholders and assisted by contributing ideas as independent observers.

The county's original proposal had incorporated emergency high-flow holding basins to reduce the immediate effects of infiltration and inflow on the receiving stream. The original upgrade proposal utilized an extended aeration oxidation ditch design which has proven to be very effective in the removal of the nutrient nitrogen. In order to achieve even greater treatment efficiency, modifications were made to include phosphorus nutrient removal. In addition, the disinfection process was changed from chlorination followed by dechlorination to an ultraviolet radiation disinfection process. These modifications were applauded by both the environmental group and the lake owners. As a result of the feedback gained through the use of several of the processes described in this chapter, a consensus was reached among the stakeholders regarding the modifications to the existing facility in order that the water quality in the basin could be protected.

This case demonstrates the key steps for consensus building. A liaison working for the local government had an established communication network built upon informal contacts. Credibility both for the individual and the local government had been gained in the past through professional contacts and the opportunities to share information regarding environmental issues with these stakeholders. An independent observation group from the local university, well known to all parties, offered an assessment of the situation. During the planning process, design modifications had been made to accommodate the concerns of the environmental group and the lake owners. These modifications were then substantiated by the regulatory agency. The regulatory agency had been involved early in the planning process and had informally reviewed the project proposal. This facilitated the review and approval of the formal application process by the regulatory agency.

SUMMARY AND CONCLUSIONS

We have presented what we have found to be effective strategies that local governments can use to achieve consensus on projects that have the potential adversely to affect the environment. Local governments cannot rely solely on traditional engineering methods based on function and service. The various stakeholders must be taken into consideration when contemplating public works projects, especially in sensitive environmental arenas. The perception of citizens regarding the construction and operation of public works facilities is extremely important. Identifying the key contact person, involving the public and regulatory agencies, and establishing communication channels early in the process are useful ingredients for making projects work smoothly.

Chapter 16

Mediating the Idaho Wilderness Controversy

Dennis Baird, Ralph Maughan, and Douglas Nilson

Some environmental conflicts seem utterly resistant to settlement. An example is the 15-year controversy over congressional designation of permanent "wilderness" areas from among the roadless, undeveloped lands in the national forests in the state of Idaho.

After a decade of congressional attempts to impose a legislative solution to the Idaho wilderness controversy, the 1990 Idaho legislature appropriated $150,000 to hire a mediator to facilitate negotiations among the warring groups.

This chapter describes and analyzes the issue, the failure of mediation to bring a solution, the aftermath of the attempt to mediate the conflict, and lessons that can be learned from the Idaho experience.

WILDERNESS PRESERVATION IN THE UNITED STATES

The formal preservation of wilderness by the U.S. Forest Service began in 1924 when the district forester designated a wilderness area on the Gila National Forest in New Mexico. Soon several more wilderness areas were designated by Service officials, and in 1928 regulations were issued to standardize the establishment of these areas: only the Chief of the Forest Service would have this authority (the Chief could also abolish or modify them). These protected lands would be called "primitive" areas. By 1933, 63 primitive areas had been established.

In 1939, the Service announced new regulations requiring a review and reclassification of all the primitive areas to what would now be called "wilderness" or "wild" areas.[1] The Reclassification was to bring stricter management. Road-building, commercial timbering, and the construction of resorts would be expressly forbidden in the wilderness areas. However, officials were also directed to pare areas of commercial value from the boundaries (Robinson, 1975).

Reclassification proceeded slowly, in part due to World War II, but as time passed, advocates of natural preservation became increasingly dissatisfied with the Service's actions. The Forest Service frequently reduced the size of the protected areas and removed acreages of productive timber before reclassification.

Because the permanent protection from development embodied in the concept of wilderness preservation required a strong barrier to development threats, statutory protection of wilderness areas rather than administrative designation became the goal of wilderness advocates. They recognized that once an area was protected by law, the inertia of the legislative process would be a greater barrier to development than the demonstrated impermanence of the Forest Service's administrative wilderness protection.

In the mid-1950s wilderness proponents began to press Congress for a law that would create a wilderness system, and after much conflict in the western states over the issue, supporters were finally successful in 1964. The National Wilderness Preservation System (NWPS) was created. Initially the NWPS consisted of just those areas the Forest Service had previously reclassified from "primitive" to "wilderness." However, the act directed a review and recommendation to Congress of all remaining "primitive" areas for possible statutory wilderness designation.

THE ROADLESS AREA REVIEWS

The mandated review of the leftover primitive areas moved forward as specified by the Wilderness Act, as did congressional passage of bills adding newly reviewed primitive areas one-by-one to the NWPS. Meanwhile, the growing environmental movement had success getting Congress to add undeveloped, unroaded, and previously unclassified national forest land directly to the NWPS, by-passing any Forest Service review. This independent success propelled the Forest Service into conducting its first "Roadless Area Review and Evaluation" (RARE I) in 1971-1972.

The RARE I process, which identified 56 million acres of roadless lands in addition to previously designated primitive and wilderness areas, was beset by controversy and hostility from the start. Environmentalists regarded it as flawed because of a shoddy inventory of roadless areas and because the "wilderness study areas" selected by the process were too small and too few. RARE I was also greeted with hostility from traditional Western public land interests such as mining, logging, and grazing and by rural western elites who had traditionally opposed the reservation of public land from development.

Eventually political and legal pressure from dissatisfied environmentalists led the relatively friendly Carter Administration to conduct RARE II, the second roadless area review in 1977-1978.

THE ORIGIN OF THE IDAHO IMPASSE

A RARE II inventory and evaluation was conducted for each of the public land (western) states in 1977. Tens of thousands of public comments were received. Forest Service wilderness recommendations and a final environmental impact statement (FEIS) were released in 1978, but continuing dissatisfaction with the process and its results led to a legal challenge of the RARE II FEIS. In 1980 a federal court in *California v. Bergland* determined that procedural errors had flawed the RARE II process. An appeal of this decision in 1982 (*California v. Block*) resulted in a ruling that a site-specific EIS was needed before *any* of the roadless areas inventoried in RARE II could be developed. This ruling meant that all 62 million acres of inventoried roadless area in the national forests were barred from development until time-consuming EISs could be conducted for each roadless area in order to "release" it for uses not compatible with eventual wilderness designation.

The *de facto* moratorium on development resulting from *California v. Block* led Congress to begin crafting state-by-state (RARE II) wilderness bills in the early 1980s. By 1990, 21 state wilderness bills had become law. However, two states, Idaho and Montana, had not been able to overcome the political difficulties and pass state wilderness bills. These two states were the most rural of the western states and both possessed very large acreages of roadless, undeveloped lands.

Each state wilderness bill not only designated new wilderness areas, it also "released" for possible development the roadless areas not designated as wilderness. A pattern was set with the passage of the California Wilderness Act of 1984. The California act said the RARE II EIS for California was "sufficient" and no longer subject to judicial review. Roadless lands not designated as wilderness were said to be "released" from wilderness consideration. However, the interpretation of what "release" meant became increasingly controversial with the passage of more bills; and the phrasing of "release language" increasingly beset the Idaho and Montana wilderness debates.

Meanwhile, each national forest developed a forest plan (as mandated by the National Forest Management Act of 1976, PL 94-588). These forest plans again reviewed the roadless areas in states without state RARE II bills and made recommendations for wilderness designations. These replaced Service RARE II recommendations. However, these new recommendations turned out to be quite similar to those of RARE II. The roadless areas not recommended for wilderness through the forest plan were released for the uses specified for it in the plan.[2] As with previous recommendations, wilderness advocates argued more wilderness should have been recommended. In Idaho they appealed most of the forest plans. When their appeals failed, they litigated many of the plans. As a result, the "release" of roadless areas by the administrative process, sought by the timber industry, was often long delayed.

CONGRESSIONAL ATTEMPTS TO SETTLE THE
ROADLESS AREA CONTROVERSY IN IDAHO

RARE II identified more than 9 million acres (14,000 square miles) of roadless, undeveloped land in the national forests of Idaho—more than any other state.[3] The Forest Service recommended only slightly more than a million acres of this for congressional designation. After the forest plans were completed, the Service's proposals for Idaho wilderness stood at about 1.3 million acres.

In contrast, wilderness advocates advanced several proposals of their own. These were much larger. The major proposal was that of the Idaho Wildlands Defense Coalition (IWDC). The Wilderness Society, Sierra Club, and Idaho Conservation League were the major components of coalition. With time the IWDC's proposal underwent several iterations. It gradually increased from about 4.5 million to over 5.7 million acres. Throughout the 1980s the IWDC proposal was widely regarded as the environmentalists' proposal. Peter Kostmeyer (D., PA) introduced it in Congress several times, but it failed to move due to opposition from Idaho's congressional delegation. Nor did Idaho environmental groups mount a serious effort to move it. They generally treated it as a bargaining device and concentrated their efforts on securing congressional co-sponsors nationwide.

Idaho's senior senator, Republican James McClure, attempted to resolve the wilderness dispute in 1984. His bill would have protected just 526,000 out of the 9 million plus acres of roadless land. The rest would have been opened to timbering under "hard" release. Environmentalist resistance was swift in the House. Powerful chair of the Subcommittee on Public Lands, John Seiblerling (D., OH), blocked McClure's bill.

In an attempt at bipartisanship, Senator McClure convinced Idaho's governor, Democrat Cecil Andrus, to participate in a joint effort. Andrus had been President Carter's Secretary of Interior. This, and his opposition to an open pit mine in Idaho's scenic White Cloud Mountains in the early 1970s, gave Andrus some conservation credentials.

The joint legislation would have classified 1.3 million acres of wilderness. It would also have established a number of special management areas—some for roadless recreation; others for mandated timbering.

Opposition from environmental groups led Andrus to withdraw his support in 1990. Senator McClure retired that year.

THE INTERESTS ENGAGED IN THE
IDAHO WILDERNESS CONTROVERSY

Over the years in many engagements, the same interest groups emerged: conservationists/environmentalists, native Americans, and outfitters and guides in favor of more wilderness; livestock, irrigation, mining, timber, and off-road vehicles opposed. Elites in rural areas usually opposed wilderness, as did Idaho's Republican leaders. Democratic Party leaders did favor modest wilderness proposals, but Idaho's congressional delegation was predominantly Republican. So was the state legislature. GOP congressional members were in a position to block passage of a wilderness bill they did not like.

The strength of environmental groups was in Idaho's cities and resort areas such as Sun Valley/Ketchum and McCall. Matching the congressional delegation, Idaho wilderness groups held their own veto over wilderness/release legislation they did not like. Their veto power stemmed from their association with national environmental groups who could persuade the House Interior Committee to block legislation they opposed.

Because both pro- and antiwilderness sides checked one another and both sides could possibly gain from a settlement, it is not surprising that negotiations were finally proposed after years of stalemate.

THE BEGINNING OF THE WILDERNESS MEDIATION

Responding to an initiative by the timber industry, in March 1990 the Idaho Legislature appropriated $150,000 to try mediating the controversy. Nine organizations applied to mediate the issue. In December the Mediation Institute in Seattle was selected to facilitate the discussions.

Initially the IWDC balked at participating. The overwhelming control of the state legislature by Republicans who had not given the IWDC advance notice of the idea made the IWDC suspicious. Also, failure of the congressional delegation firmly to support the negotiations coupled with environmentalists' perennial hope that the 1992 elections would result in a more wilderness-friendly delegation led them to demur. However, quiet pressure, concern about public relations, and potential loss of their veto over wilderness legislation in Congress finally led wilderness advocates to join the effort.

The next two sections describe mediation experience in both northern and southern Idaho.

IN THE NORTH

Unlike much of the Rocky Mountain West, in north Idaho wilderness allocation is a matter of real jobs. Almost one third of all employment is timber-related, even more in some counties. Moreover, salaries tend to be higher than the Idaho average.

The determination to try mediation in north Idaho faced this question: "where?"

- Three large river valleys define north Idaho geographically and politically. The Clearwater, Lewis and Clark's route, is the most southerly, joining the Snake River at Lewiston on the Idaho/Washington border. In the center lies the St. Joe River, flowing into Lake Coeur d' Alene near the logging town of St. Maries. Finally, the Pend Oreille River, which drains the deep lake of the same name near the resort community of Sandpoint, flows near the Canadian border.

- Several sawmills exist in the Pend Oreille country, each with its own economic constituency. Conservation politics is similarly fragmented, although many groups fall under the umbrella of the Idaho Conservation League. Nearby Spokane, Washington, is a major influence. It is the true capital, with over 370,000 people in the metropolitan area. Spokane is the home of a large Sierra Club regional group as well as the influential conservation group, Inland Empire Public Lands Council.

- Passage of a wilderness bill in northernmost north Idaho would not put to rest the acrimonious controversy over forest management because of the environmental damage and roadless area fragmentation from mining and logging over the past century. Even the grandest wilderness vision for the area would place less than 10 per cent of the public lands in the NWPS.

- The central part of north Idaho, around St. Maries and the St. Joe River, enjoys a reputation of being a tough and unwelcome spot for environmental initiatives.

- Timber industry employment is especially high, and many local political elites derive their income from the industry. The area was the scene of a bruising battle in the mid-1970s over dredge mining and the classification of the St. Joe as a federal Wild and Scenic Rivers. In spring 1991, time did not seem ripe for compromise in this heavily forested valley.

- The valley of the Clearwater River, which contains two large national forests, the Nez Pierce and the Clearwater, remained as a location for beginning mediations. To the Legislature and the mediators, past history and some unique circumstances joined to make this area the start of the mediation process.

The scars of past Idaho wilderness fights had, surprisingly perhaps, not left a legacy of bitterness. True, the ranks of the protagonists had been thinned somewhat, but the survivors knew, valued, and appreciated one another.

The Clearwater valley has little public lands grazing. There are few private agricultural inholdings within national forest boundaries. Although use of off-road vehicles (ORVs) is increasing, horse and foot use of the unroaded backcountry is far more common.

The timber industry is dominated by the huge Potlatch Corporation saw-mill and paper plant at Lewiston. Smaller mills exist upstream at Orofino and Kooskia, at remote Elk City, and high up on the Camas Prairie at Grangeville. While fiercely competitive for timber supply, representatives of the timber industry in the area know and trust one another.

As of 1991, about one million acres remained roadless in the Clearwater National Forest. About 200,000 acres were in contention in the Nez Perce, all of this in one tract, Meadow Creek, considered by many to be the key ecological component of the adjacent Selway-Bitterroot Wilderness.[4] These roadless lands also contain lots of trees, and many residents view the areas as linked to their economic survival.

Early in 1991, a large crowd gathered in Lewiston for the first meeting of the north Idaho mediation, a public meeting. While under pressure from the Legislature to do otherwise, the "delegates" were essentially self-selected, a practice that also occurred in the southern Idaho mediations.

Unwritten rules emerged—appearance was limited to those who knew the land; who had proven and tested records of past involvement; and, above all, had the power in Washington to block enactment of a settlement. This rule was fully supported by timber, outfitting and hunting, and wilderness leaders. It effectively eliminated farming, ranching, and ORV groups. The ultimate test was, do you have the power to sink an agreement?

Mediation literature makes it clear that to succeed, negotiations must take place in private if grandstanding and posturing are to be avoided (Blackburn, 1990). But Idaho had a state open meetings law, and public funds were paying for the mediation. The media insisted on attending, threatening lawsuits. In the end, citizen participants determined they would attend private gatherings at their own expense and on their own time and do as they pleased. These gatherings were closed to the public and the media.

Out of the view of the media, it became apparent that progress would have to come from a still smaller group. Hunting, environmental, recreational, and outfitting interests decided that two people could represent them (one a co-author of this chapter). Timber and other commercial groups reached a similar conclusion. The successes and ultimate failure rested with these four negotiators.

The four negotiators worked closely with the professional mediator, benefiting from his skill. Real progress was made when the small body determined that general forest management, as well as wilderness classification, needed to be addressed. There was tacit understanding that a settlement had to offer tangible benefits to all of the key players. Broad resolution was reached on about 85 percent of the likely additions to the wilderness system. These were real breakthroughs. So valuable were they that the Idaho congressional delegation, working in 1993 on the same issue, incorporated much of the language in its deliberation.

By the autumn of 1991, however, the early optimism died and the negotiations ended. Two problems arose, both of which bear on the general topic of environmental mediation. First, for citizen negotiators such as the co-author, the process proved to be far too time-consuming. A paid, full-time conservation negotiator would have been hard-pressed to adequately inform and seek guidance from constituents. The two people representing conservation interests had full time jobs and many other interests. This probably doomed from the start the essential function of keeping their constituencies informed about the negotiations. The process was further hindered by the several-hundred-mile distances between the negotiators and all calls being long distance.

Second, successful mediators of forest issues must also possess the skill and political power to resolve very complex issues. The skill was present, but the political power was lacking. There was the power to settle wilderness matters purely within Idaho, but once broader forest management issues were discussed, the political arena grew. Management of the national forests is a national concern. An Idaho solution to these would make a national precedent, and Idaho negotiators could not guarantee any locally reached agreement in the national arena. This led to the end of the negotiations.

IN THE SOUTH

After the north Idaho negotiations began with some progress, hope arose that negotiations in some part of southern Idaho would yield success. Here the economy and culture were quite different. The forest products industry, while present, was much less prominent. Instead, there were millions of acres of public range land. Ranching was a major interest. Beginning in the mid-1970s, oil and gas interests emerged to oppose wilderness designation. The mining industry was also influential. The only constant between northern and southern Idaho was a large amount of unprotected roadless area.

South central Idaho was finally selected as the domain for the beginning of southern Idaho negotiations. The vast mountain area of south central Idaho is a focus of recreation for three of Idaho's five population centers: Boise, Pocatello, and Twin Falls. The area has stunning scenery and the cities are nearby, although none is actually in the area. Most of south central Idaho is sparsely populated mountains, high desert, or irrigated farmland. There is one center of strong wilderness support, Blaine County, the location of Sun Valley, Ketchum, and Hailey. The remaining small towns tend to rely on farming, ranching, and marginal mining and timber. They are traditionally antiwilderness.

The attempt to negotiate began with the Challis and Sawtooth National Forests. The two forests cover much of south central Idaho and possess all of Idaho's highest mountain ranges and many scenically acknowledged areas. RARE II discovered 80 percent of the huge Challis National Forest to be roadless.

Prior to the first meeting, environmentalists tried to get off-road vehicle groups (ORVs) excluded because they perceived that ORVs lacked power to derail a wilderness bill in Washington (although their influence was on the increase there). Additionally, ORVs appeared to have little incentive to reach an agreement since under the status quo they could ride their machines in most of the roadless areas, including the wilderness proposals selected through their forest planning process. With wilderness classification, all use of recreational vehicles would cease.

The first meeting was held in May 1991 in Arco, Idaho, a declining agricultural community on the edge of the central Idaho mountains. One of the co-authors of this chapter was a key participant.

Those attending on the wilderness side were self-selected, although conservation groups had asked certain key leaders to attend. On the nonwilderness side, the dominant players were the cattle industry and ORV enthusiasts loosely associated with the Blue Ribbon Coalition whose motto is, "Preserving our natural resources for the public instead of from the public."

The interest of ORVs in the outcome of wilderness allocation was obvious. The intense interest of ranchers in the issue was puzzling because the Wilderness Act (Sec. 4[d]) specifically allows grazing to continue in designated wilderness areas to the degree it occurred before classification. Moreover, the Colorado Wilderness Act of 1980 had established firm legal guidelines for the Forest Service insuring that wilderness classification could not be used to reduce the number of grazing animals or hinder vehicular access by ranchers to their herds.

The sawmill in Salmon, Idaho sent one representative to the first meeting. Oddly, oil and gas interests and mining, so prominent in earlier Idaho wilderness debates, were not officially represented.

The location of the meeting was not announced to the media, but the location was leaked, probably by both sides. Press from the *Twin Falls Times News* and the *Post Register* (Idaho Falls) arrived. The press said it was a public meeting due to funding by the state legislature and subject to Idaho's open meetings law. After some discussion, the press agreed to remain outside because it was evident the meeting otherwise would be canceled. Despite this, negotiators spent much of the time talking to the press on the steps of the building. Appreciating the futility of keeping the press out, negotiators invited the press in during the afternoon session.

Wilderness advocates, anticipating hostility, engaged in proactive patriotic symbol garnishment (i.e., they sported American flags on foot-long poles in their sport jacket pockets—this was a few months after the Gulf War).

Surprisingly, some progress was made negotiating with ORV enthusiasts, but representatives from the ranching interests seemed to have little specific knowledge of the Wilderness Act, the IWDC proposal, or even the roadless areas. They generally got in the way. Because some progress was made with ORV interests, a private negotiating session was held between the Blue Ribbon Coalition, an ORV advocacy group, and the Sierra Club, a month later at Idaho State University (ISU) in Pocatello.

At the private ISU session in which two of the co-authors of this chapter participated, substantial progress was made negotiating with the Blue Ribbon Coalition. Blue Ribbon was offered some favorite trails into several scenic roadless areas. In turn they agreed to support a wilderness proposal as large as the one IWDC proposed for the Challis National Forest. A public meeting for the Challis National Forest was then scheduled for late September at a small lodge near Sun Valley (Sun Valley Cabin).

Representatives from ranching,[5] farming, mining, oil and gas, ORVs, and wilderness appeared. A large and unexpected audience of tight-lipped ranchers filled the room to capacity. Numerous media with lights and cameras were on hand.

Negotiations did not fare well in front of a hostile audience and TV cameras. Environmentalists outlined the agreement struck with Blue Ribbon at ISU a month earlier, but Blue Ribbon disavowed the agreement. Environmentalists asked the ranching interests what they might support as an alternative to the agreement. After a caucus, the ranching delegation proposed 5000 acres of wilderness in one area above timberline where no grazing occurred (this out of a national forest containing over a million acres of roadless area).

Environmentalists believed they had been doublecrossed by Blue Ribbon and that the proposal by the livestock interests was an insult rather than a counterproposal. They stated this publicly. Next, the Blue Ribbon representative said the interests at the table were not fully representative of all interests and pushed forward a person in a wheelchair. At this point, insults about access to wilderness and those with disabilities were traded. A representative from the Idaho Conservation League noted that few ranchers present were in compliance with their allotment management plans and indicated that there might be litigation on grazing allotments. A representative from the cattle association said they would not be intimidated. The meeting broke up. Ranchers muttered threats to one co-author.

The wilderness mediation process for southern Idaho was finished.

THE AFTERMATH

So the mediation process ground to a halt. The heated Sun Valley session was a one day story in the major Idaho newspapers. Little was said in public about the meeting after the news reports. Nevertheless, bad feelings lingered among conservationists toward Blue Ribbon and, especially, the livestock interests.

1992 was an election year. Larry LaRocco, a first-term Democrat representing northern and western Idaho, campaigned that summer as a problem solver and won an easy reelection victory. Just after the election, he told the media he would introduce a wilderness bill for *his district* in 1993. Moving with remarkable energy, he held seven "town meetings" and listened to the comments of over 1600 people before Christmas 1992!

LaRocco's momentum caught senior Senator Larry Craig by surprise. Republican Craig, with close ties to timber, mining, and livestock, moved quickly to gain a share of the rising interest in a new legislative solution to the wilderness issue.

Working with Governor Andrus and negotiating with LaRocco, Craig called a meeting of the state's congressional delegation. The meeting was held on January 1993 in Boise. Here the delegates discussed using prescriptive land allocation language in a statewide wilderness bill.[6] Then the delegation held a follow-up meeting in Washington, D.C., at which they decided to first settle "basic principles," including impacts on private property, job loss, and state water rights. The delegation also agreed to conduct visits to the roadless areas and vicinities in the summer of 1993.

Representative LaRocco participated fully in this but nevertheless introduced his own first district wilderness bill (H.R. 1570) at the end of March. His bill would classify about 1.3 million acres as wilderness, release 2.5 million acres, and manage another 500,000 acres for various other uses. Most of his bill reflected the near-agreements made in the North Idaho mediation meetings. As with past Idaho wilderness bills, his bill received criticism from all sides. That, and criticism that the delegation should present a united front, resulted in LaRocco's temporary abandonment of a separate legislative track.

The congressional delegation visited the roadless areas in a series of quick "fly-overs," followed by meetings with invited interests that mostly rehashed old arguments. Governor Andrus declined to participate, expressing cynicism about the prospects of the new effort.

Public efforts in 1993 to move a wilderness bill were limited to three formal hearings in Idaho by Representative LaRocco that autumn. Timber industry spokespeople wondered aloud what was in a bill for them. Testimony by wilderness advocates was mostly about areas left out of H.R. 1570. If the congressman was seeking gratitude, compromise, or good will at the hearings, he failed to find it.

Early in 1994, a campaign letter emerged from Senator Craig's office urging the electoral defeat of Representative LaRocco in the 1994 election. As a result, LaRocco withdrew from the Republican-dominated Idaho delegation's wilderness process and introduced a slightly revised version of his earlier bill, H.R. 1570. This time he worked exclusively with House Democrats to try to move his legislation. Senator Craig announced in March 1994 that he would not support LaRocco's bill if it passed the House.

MEDIATION FAILURE LED TO EXPANSION OF THE ISSUE

The one common feature of the failed mediation process and all the years' struggle over Idaho wilderness is the list of players. Not only have most of the names been the same, but all have been from Idaho. Congressional action following the achievement of near consensus within a state congressional delegation has been the normal means of disposing of wilderness questions (Roth, 1988).[7] But in

July 1993, two members of Congress (later joined by 58 more) introduced the Northern Rockies Ecosystem Protection Act (NREPA). This sweeping legislation would designate about 14 million acres of wilderness in Idaho, Montana, and Wyoming (essentially all the remaining roadless areas, plus connecting corridors and "wilderness recovery areas"). None of NREPA's sponsors were from the three states involved. However, the proposal was written in Missoula, Montana, by the Alliance for the Wild Rockies. After much internal controversy, NREPA was endorsed by some major national environmental groups in 1994.

The intended effect of NREPA is to nationalize the wilderness issue; to take it out of the hands of Idahoans, perhaps as did the Alaska lands act to Alaskans in 1980. The promises and pitfalls of expanding an issue to a larger political arena are well known.

ANALYSIS OF THE CASES

The attempt to mediate the Idaho wilderness controversy failed in southern Idaho. Progress was made in the north, however. Representative LaRocco included many of the agreements in his first district bill, H.R. 1570. He settled the unresolved disputes himself. We cannot foretell the fate of his bill.

Lessons to be drawn from the Idaho mediation are discussed below, in light of a template drawn from recent environmental mediation literature (Jacobs and Rubino, 1988b). Expressed as questions, the issues addressed include

1. How neutral and fair was the mediator?
2. What role did the mediator assume?
3. How clearly defined were the issues under mediation?
4. Was pressure put on the participants to reach a decision?
5. What was the relative power distribution among the parties at the bargaining table?
6. Did important situational or personality factors influence participant willingness/ability to compromise?
7. Was the size of the bargaining unit conducive to serious negotiation?
8. Did bargainers have sufficient authority to commit their organizations?

How neutral and fair was the mediator? (Train and Busterud, 1978). No one actively engaged in the mediations questioned the competence or character of the mediators. In northern Idaho the mediator and negotiators quickly established rapport. Indeed, the professionalism of all of the participants characterized these deliberations.

In southern Idaho, environmental negotiators recommended excluding the Blue Ribbon Coalition because they believed that Blue Ribbon had insufficient congressional support to deserve to participate.

The mediator did not exclude the Coalition. Additional information available to the mediator convinced him to include a Blue Ribbon spokesman in the deliberations. If initially exasperated with this decision, conservationists did not allow these sentiments to blur their perceptions of the mediator. He was viewed as a neutral, but perhaps he was even neutral to a fault. He was reluctant to sanction violations of bargaining rules (albeit often implicit and informal rules.) But this attribute did not translate into beliefs that he favored one side over the other.

What role did the mediator assume? (Kettering Foundation, 1985). Experienced mediators often play nondirective roles. This worked well in northern Idaho, where negotiators diligently confronted the issues at hand. In southern Idaho a low-keyed approach might well have lost opportunities to enhance the quality of interactions. A mediator may have served as an unobtrusive socialization agent in helping some inexperienced negotiators learn their roles. A principled unwillingness to intervene had the unintended effect of not discouraging a grandstanding play by livestock interests: they packed the Sun Valley meeting with an audience of friendly cowboys.

Although hindered by Idaho's open meetings law, the mediators might have played more assertive roles in managing the media. Media inclusion at negotiating sessions complicated attempts to engage in negotiating behavior, particularly in southern Idaho.

How clearly defined were the issues under mediation? (Susskind and Weinstein, 1980). Negotiators and mediators tried to be very careful about issue delineation in north Idaho. However, the sheer complexity coupled with the power of outside interests overwhelmed the participants. They could not just develop and employ criteria for designating wilderness and timber lands. Southern Idaho discussions were complicated by public posturing. The Blue Ribbon leadership used its enhanced status—status conferred by the negotiating seat—to try to expand its organization. Cattlemen, a group with no specific stakes at risk, tried to use the process to reinforce a long-articulated opposition to any more wilderness designation.

Was pressure put on the participants to reach a decision? (McCracken, O'Laughlin, and Merrill, 1993). The long history of failure to settle the wilderness disputes probably decreased pressure to resolve the controversy. All sides could reason that they had waited for years to get a bill that they could tolerate. While annoying, the premediation context was not intolerable to anyone involved, although it was least tolerable to the timber industry, because it pressured the legislature to appropriate funds for mediation.

Both sides could look to the 1992 elections with some optimism. Conservationists thought that they would replace an antienvironmental Republican U.S. Senator (Steve Symms). The industry proponents expected to re-elect a friendly Republican President. The years of Republican domination had discouraged the environmental activism of Forest Service employees considerably. Industry expected to find the Service increasingly compliant in the future. The fact that neither side's electoral optimism was justified does not invalidate early perceptions. Both sides seemed under the impression that their own interests would fare better in the future. Thus neither side was eager to accept even a reasonable alternative. So 1991 talks were not held under an immense amount of pressure to reach a settlement.

To add perspective, however, uncertainty over harvest levels was starting to bother the forest products industry. It had much to gain from settling the roadless area issue because that way it could guarantee a supply of timber. Still, any settlement had to resolve complex access issues in favor of allowing lumber interests to cut in much of the nonwilderness roadless areas. Assuredly, timber representatives pursued these access goals with great vigor.

What was the relative power distribution of the parties at the bargaining table? (Taylor and Harp, 1985). Ascertaining power balances is usually difficult. Not only are influence resources important, but comparative stakes and local contextual factors must be considered. Timber and ranching interests probably control more political capital than environmental interests. Still, disposition of diminishing roadless areas is a high stakes issue for preservationists. Furthermore, a "consideration for wilderness" inclination is built into any determination of the future status of roadless lands. These considerations equalize power balances. Finally, in a complex political process with many decision points, defeating a measure is usually easier than passing one. In both northern and southern Idaho, each side to the dispute was capable of marshaling sufficient resources to stop an objectionable bill. In fact, this threshold of political influence—ability to kill a bill—became the initial criterion for selecting negotiating participants.

Did important situational or personality factors influence participants' willingness/ability to compromise? (White, 1985). North Idaho negotiations were not thwarted by temperamental factors. Neither were they handicapped by a clash of principles. Agreement was not reached because of the multitude and complexity of issues—many beyond the scope of the original bargaining framework. Sufficient time, sophisticated issue framing, and drawing lessons from the 1991 experience might have overcome impasses to resolution in the North.

The major players in southern Idaho were also capable of being pragmatic politicians. When specifically representing his "core" constituency—all-terrain vehicle users—the Blue Ribbon spokesman achieved agreement with conservation representatives on wilderness and trail usage. This agreement dissolved after it was opposed by prominent livestock spokesmen. When confronted with division within their own alliance, cattlemen reasserted opposition to any additional wilderness below the timber line. Environmental representatives perceived this assertion to be an uncompromising position on wilderness designation. The Blue Ribbon negotiator seemed to respond to this cue. An earlier willingness to bargain was followed by a marked reluctance to respond to the specific proposals of his adversaries.

Was the size of the bargaining unit conducive to serious negotiation? (Bingham, 1986). Some complaints were received about too many people participating in bargaining in the South. Deliberations often became tedious because some participants did not know the land, the applicable laws and proposal specifics. Power, stakes, and personal/organizational commitment criteria seem more important in these contexts than number of participants in the mediation. Nevertheless, a plethora of extractive industry representatives was invited to the negotiations. There was but one environmental seat. The psychological atmosphere that this created did not bode well for negotiations in the South.

Did bargainers have sufficient authority to commit their organizations? (Bingham, 1986). Participants in both the North and South were generally prominent representatives of their core mainstream organizations. Neither their capability nor their dedication was questioned by those who worked with them. Frequently, intraorganizational policy disagreement did not translate into loss of trust. Group trust of these spokespeople tended to be high on wilderness-specific issues. Geographic considerations posed only minor internal difficulties for the cohesive forest products industry. That simplified representation. The environmental delegates, however, spoke for a broader and more diffuse coalition of groups (whether formally or informally). This diversity in values and interests created a problem in terms of substantially "committing" the environmental community to back common proposals. While conservationists were as forthright about who they did not represent as they were about who they specifically represented, the possibility of misunderstandings and recriminations among their constituencies remained high.

The issue movement in north Idaho to topics transcending the drawing of lines on maps posed tough representational quandaries for negotiators. They were asked to make decisions on subjects about which they were underprepared—and ones on which they had no mandates from their constituent organizations. This was especially difficult for bargainers from the politically heterogeneous, geographically dispersed conservation community. Coping with such extraordinary problems can yield stresses which contribute to burnout.

LESSONS FOR ACTIVISTS

The northern Idaho mediation provided lessons that affected congressional behavior; southern Idaho mediations showed pitfalls to avoid. Due in large part to the single major stumbling block, actors currently crafting a prospective solution to the wilderness impasse are forging agreements in principle about issues other than actual land designations. This isn't easy. Complex water rights issues are among those which have to be confronted. Yet this illustration shows how the 1991 mediations were not for naught.

A second issue for mediators and negotiators to confront is the determination of legitimate and illegitimate media access to the proceedings. This determination will guide rulemaking about press contacts with participants. Then mechanisms must be established to encourage journalist and participant compliance with these rules. It is important not to be naive. Media remain a political resource for both sides. The threat to escalate an issue—usually through the media—is a time-honored tactic. But there is a time to posture and a time to bargain. These should not be confused. Effective bargaining cannot take place under the glare of the media.

Finally, mediation is not the proper forum for securing support for sweeping symbolic statements. This is not because these statements are unimportant. The problem lies in the nature of the statement. Often such declarations are couched in either/or terms. Mediation proceeds more smoothly when either/or dichotomies are converted into continua. This allows "more" or "less" thinking. Such thinking facilitates compromise. Hence, a sensitive mediator will suggest techniques for creating continua out of less flexible constructions.

LESSONS FOR STUDENTS

Students of mediation should pay more attention to the clarity-complexity trade-off. The very proper concern for clarity can lead to issue over-simplification. Unlike hortatorical and legal language, bargaining language demands specificity and detail (Edelman, 1974). This reflects a character of bargaining behavior: participants inventory their needs and desires closely. Too much constriction of their room to maneuver hampers chances of a mutually beneficial outcome.

Mediators also need latitude for maneuvering. Experiences of the authors suggest that different approaches to mediation in the two cases may have been appropriate. Scholars should be careful to avoid general statements endorsing the superiority of a particular mediation style. Of course, there are many effective ways to mediate. However, a promising approach may lie in categorizing or typologizing mediation goals and settings. Hypotheses which link type of mediation structure and appropriate mediation style might be helpful.

A final lesson emerging from the experiences reported here involves some special problems to explore in representation. Indeed, environmental mediation might represent a distinctive case. A manageable number of negotiators is necessary; but this implies that two or three people may be representing ten or twelve similar, but distinct, groups. Normally participants will share substantial agreement on very general premises but disagree on details. In such instances the spokespeople must contrive the right mix of leader discretion and popular consult-

ation styles of representation. A mediator aware of the duality required of environmental group leaders might adjust processes to take account of the special communication requirements facing these representatives.

SUMMARY AND CONCLUSIONS

Idaho wilderness negotiations provided an opportunity to look at two very
different experiences with environmental mediation. In north Idaho the failure to
come to an agreement rests with neither the mediator nor the negotiators. The
conflict they were trying to resolve was too complex politically and technically.
The work that these bargainers did was built into one subsequent congressional
attempt to resolve the dispute. In south Idaho the mediation replicated a textbook
case of why many mediations do not achieve their objectives. But even in this case
the outcome probably would have been improved had more attention been paid to
representation matters.

The Idaho wilderness issue still defies resolution. Now the conflict seems to be
expanding into the national political arena.

NOTES

1. Those areas over 100,000 acres in extent would be designated as "wilderness." Those
under would be named "wild" areas.

2. Quite often such release meant timber management which would result in the
complete development of an undeveloped area. Very often, however, the plan specified only
partial development or management that would probably result in no development over the
ten-year life span of the forest plan. This led to insistence by environmentalists that any
release last only for the life of a forest plan. This became known as "soft" release. Industry
typically wanted permanent release and no further roadless reviews—"hard" release.

3. In addition to the 9 million acres of roadless lands inventoried in RARE II, over 4
million acres of public lands in Idaho have been designated wilderness under the original
Wilderness Act, the subsequent review of primitive areas, and the Endangered American
Wilderness Act of 1978.

4. The Selway-Bitterroot Wilderness is one of America's largest such areas. It sprawls
over 1.5 million acres of Idaho and Montana. It is separated from the Frank Church/River
of No Return Wilderness to its south by just one dirt road. The Frank Church wilderness is
over 2.3 million acres, the largest in the lower 48 states.

5. Ranching had two representatives at the table, one for sheep and one for cattle. We
were told that sheep and cattle did not trust one another.

6. Prescriptive allocation language could solve questions about "release" of areas,
"certainty," and make available land protection classifications less restrictive than wilderness. The great difficulty with them was that national environmental groups didn't like them
since the result would be a different system of protection in every state rather than a national
system such as the NWPS.

7. One important exception to this generalization was the Alaska Native Land and Wilderness Act of 1980. Much of the bill's contents came from outside Alaska, as did its support. The issue was nationalized. Bluntly, the Alaska delegation "was rolled." This was due to the magnitude of land allocation involved—its national and international significance.

Chapter 17

The Inland Northwest Field Burning Summit: A Case Study

Mollie K. Mangerich and Larry S. Luton

The mediation of an Inland Northwest field burning environmental conflict serves as a case study in this chapter. The Inland Northwest is part of the Pacific Northwest and includes "a vast area extending from southeastern British Columbia on the north to northeastern Oregon on the south, and from the Cascade Range in the west to the Rocky Mountains on the east" (Stratton, 1991:xiv). The case may be considered somewhat representative of a history of mediated alternative dispute resolutions within the Pacific Northwest. Due to historically rich reservoirs of timber, fish, water resources, and other natural resources, the region has shared its bounty with people who have harvested, extracted, and protected its resources. Over the past twenty years, the increasing population of the Pacific Northwest has also increased the demands on natural resources.

Naturally, the increased demands have led to conflicts. One of the first environmental dispute resolutions that was fully implemented and documented is now widely cited as the hallmark case study within the Pacific Northwest. Because of a fifteen-year dispute involving flood control and recreation on the Snoqualmie River in Washington State, the governor appointed Gerald Cormick and colleague Jane McCarthy to conduct a mediation effort. Within one year the stakeholders developed and signed a set of joint recommendations that were endorsed by the governor (Cormick and McCarthy, 1974).

After this successful beginning, environmental conflict mediation has established itself in the Pacific Northwest as a viable alternative to institutionalized conflict resolution. More recent mediated cases include the Portage Island dispute (Amy, 1987), the Interstate 90 dispute (Cormick and Patton, 1990), and the Timber/Fish/Wildlife agreement (Protasel, 1991).

While these cases build optimism regarding the efficacy of alternative dispute techniques, what has been reported is a very rosy view of the process—a one-sided view that has emphasized the potential advantages of this new approach. Still, several questions remain: How successful have environmental dispute resolution processes been? How is their success measured? What are the assumptions behind environmental conflict resolutions?

This chapter has three sections. The first is a brief definition and description of environmental dispute resolution (EDR) and its connection to traditional environmental decision-making processes. Environmental and natural resource disputes have special characteristics that distinguish efforts to settle them from processes used to resolve public policy disputes more generally. Within this section criteria are established by which we evaluate the success of the selected case study.

The second section presents a case study of a particular period in a mediated environmental dispute that continues to this day: the Inland Northwest Field Burning Summit. The case centers on the practice of open field burning of Kentucky bluegrass. The smoke generated by these burns, and its intrusion on urban areas, has escalated the level of conflict between the tourism industry, clean air advocates, local health authorities, citizens, and the grass seed industry.

The final section is a discussion, focusing on the case study, of the important issues and questions raised earlier regarding the degree of success to be attributed to the dispute resolution process in solving environmental conflicts.

For two decades, voluntary dispute resolution alternatives have been used in settling environmental disputes. It remains to be seen, however, whether face-to-face negotiation is more likely than litigation to produce fair and efficient outcomes that serve the interests of all sides. While no single case study can produce a final answer to the questions regarding dispute resolution, it can add to the existing body of documentation regarding what role alternative dispute resolutions serve in creating solutions to environmental conflicts.

THE ENVIRONMENTAL DISPUTE RESOLUTION (EDR) PROCESS

According to Gail Bingham (1986), the term *environmental dispute resolution* (EDR) refers collectively to a variety of approaches that allow the parties to meet face to face to reach a mutually acceptable resolution of the issues in a dispute or potentially controversial situation. All are voluntary processes that involve some form of consensus building, joint problem solving, or negotiation. Litigation, administrative procedures, and arbitration are not included in this definition because the objective in those approaches is not a consensus among the parties.

A form of EDR, environmental mediation, does not rely on one person understanding all of the various interests involved. Instead, it relies on the participants themselves, who are assumed to be best qualified to understand and negotiate concerning their interests. Susskind and Ozawa write, "Proponents [of mediation] claim that direct participation also allows for a better understanding and treatment of the scientific and technical complexities of environmental controversies" (1984:27). As will be seen in the following case study, disagreements occurred over the exact effects of the smoke generated by grass seed field burning, so stakeholders initiated a fact-finding effort to ascertain the adverse health effects of agricultural burning.

This interest in alternative approaches for resolving environmental disputes arises largely from dissatisfaction with the ability of more traditional decision-making processes to deal with the real issues in dispute. According to Douglas Amy (1987), when a dispute is not adequately resolved, dissatisfied parties may attempt to prolong the dispute, hoping to change the outcome and using other means available through the legislature, the bureaucracy, and the courts. In environmental disputes, parties often take actions within these institutions—through political action, administrative appeals, and litigation.

Advocates of environmental mediation argue that these actions are far from an ideal way to resolve environmental disputes. Amy (1987) states that these courses of action often result in court delays, deplete the financial resources of the parties, and result in a win-lose decision that may be counterproductive. Crowfoot and Wondolleck (1990) found that other approaches often kept citizens interests from being served. Processes by which citizens participate in government (public hearings, for instance) are often designed to elicit support for the decisions and plans that those in power are promoting. Rabe (1991) and Fuller (1981) have argued that courts are poorly equipped to sort out the competing claims of more than two parties—and environmental disputes commonly involve more than two parties.

The problem with litigation and administrative proceedings, however, is not that decisions are not reached but "that those decisions frequently are appealed. In theory, if the parties themselves have voluntarily agreed to a decision, they are more likely to be satisfied with it" (Bingham, 1986:xxii). Thus, agreements reached through an environmental mediation process could be more likely to be implemented.

While many scholars and practitioners tout the benefits of consensus-based decision making and often characterize environmental mediation as superior to litigation, a caveat is in order. Litigation and other traditional decision-making processes remain important options. Disputes over environmental issues vary so much that no one dispute resolution process is likely to be successful in all situations.

Though litigation and other approaches may be inappropriate in many environmental disputes, it is necessary to establish what types of conflict are best suited for a collaborative dispute resolution process. Mediation practitioners have mediated a number of environmental disputes with an impressive record of successes (e.g., Bingham, 1986; Blackburn, 1991; Cormick and McCarthy, 1974), and a variety of claims have been made about the advantages of environmental mediation over litigation.

A few researchers have begun establishing an identification process by which to target the practices and conditions which favor successful outcomes of conflict management efforts. A document published by the Bureau of Governmental Research and Service (Anonymous, 1990) maintains that eight factors, if analyzed prior to mediation, will assist in the selection of a collaborative dispute resolution process as a viable alternative to more traditional methods of conflict resolution:

1. The issues in the dispute can be clearly defined;
2. The issues do not focus primarily on constitutional rights;
3. There are a number of underlying interests, allowing room for trade-offs;
4. The primary parties involved in the conflict are readily identifiable;
5. Each party has, or could designate, a legitimate spokesperson;
6. There is a relative balance of power between the parties (if one party can get what it wants unilaterally, it has little incentive to negotiate);
7. The parties are likely to have continuing relations; and
8. It is likely that a realistic deadline will be set.

The mediators of the Inland Northwest Field Burning Summit used an "interest-based" problem-solving approach to the EDR process. In brief, this approach focuses on solving problems instead of arguing over positions or solutions. A guiding principle used by these mediators is, "get tough on the problem and not on the participants." The theory behind interest-based problem-solving models states that success lies in achieving workable and durable agreements. Following Hackman (1987), these mediators believe that three elements must be met in order to resolve conflict: (1) a contribution to the personal needs of the group, (2) enhancement of interpersonal relationships, and (3) enhancement of the quality of their products (i.e., solutions).

This "people, process, product" sequence is similar to another theoretical model (National Center Associates, 1989), which states that three types of satisfaction must be met to obtain that "workable agreement." Stakeholders must (1) achieve a sense that they got what they came for (substantive), (2) agree that the process was fair (procedural), and (3) have felt they were heard and respected (psychological). Determining whether these criteria have been met can be difficult, so some mediators find it sufficient for stakeholders, based on their perceptions of the issues, to have acted upon implementing the solution.

Two researchers have developed more specific guidelines by which qualitatively to evaluate the effectiveness and success of environmental conflict resolutions. This chapter uses a combination of the within-process criteria from Blackburn (1991) and the post-process criteria from Bingham (1986). Blackburn's theory is based on sixty-three propositions about the conditions, activities, and processes that are vital to successful outcomes of mediation. Condensed, they form a ten-stage model in which the emphasis is placed on the steps necessary for a successful outcome on issues dealing with the environment.

Four additional measures of success are based upon Bingham's research

(1986). The first criterion is whether an agreement has been reached among the participants. Second is whether the participants' constituent groups have ratified the agreement. Third is how stable the agreement is (the extent to which the parties have implemented agreements after reaching them). Finally, the fourth criterion is whether the participants report that the process itself was valuable. Combined with Blackburn's criteria, the Bingham criteria comprise a checklist that we used to evaluate the Inland Northwest Field Burning Summit:

Environmental Mediation Checklist

Within-process criteria

1. Mediator: Person or persons with no stake in the outcome.
2. Preconditions for Mediation: Dispute is suitable for mediation.
3. Recruitment of Participants: Participants have substantial interest and are educated on the mediation process.
4. Design of the Mediation Process: Participants design and approve mediation process, ground rules, etc.
5. Identification of the Issues: Issues at the center of the dispute are clearly identified.
6. Establishing the Information Base: Parties understand the relevant facts; issues broken into logical pieces for consideration.
7. Development of Preliminary Agreement: Alternatives generated; preliminary agreement written; follow-through assured.
8. Consulting Constituents on Appropriateness of Agreement: Parties meet, consult, and receive approval of preliminary agreement from constituents.
9. Making the Agreement Final: Modifications incorporated and approved by all parties.
10. Assuring the Implementation of the Agreement: Constituent approval; means to monitor and redecide the agreement if necessary.

Post-process criteria

1. Agreement reached.
2. Agreement ratified by constituent groups.
3. Agreement implemented.
4. Process reported valuable by parties.

CASE STUDY: INLAND NORTHWEST FIELD BURNING SUMMIT

In this section we describe an environmental dispute mediation conducted in the vicinity of Spokane, Washington. The case study covers the period between November 20, 1990 and August 10, 1992, in which time the stakeholders met monthly (sometimes more frequently) and came to a consensus-based solution to their particular conflict. During this time, the parties in dispute agreed to allow a researcher to be present. Information was derived from a literature review, interviews, site visits, news clips, correspondence, and participation in conflict resolution training. While this case study covers a two-year period, the mediation efforts continue to this date.

The case study will be represented in the following sequence: (1) general introduction and background to the case; (2) description of the conflict; (3) identification of the stakeholders and their interests; (4) a discussion of the mediation process; and (5) an analysis using the measures established within the previous section.

Background

The open burning of Kentucky bluegrass after harvest of the seed is conducted in areas of the United States where it is cultivated. Northeast Washington and northern Idaho (part of an area commonly called the Inland Northwest) grass growers are the number one producers of bluegrass seed in the nation. Bluegrass is a turf grass that is used for golf courses and residential lawns. Due to its quality and pure strains, this region's bluegrass is exported world wide. In Washington State, 42,000 acres are dedicated to bluegrass seed production; over two thirds of these fields (30,500 acres) are located in Spokane County, in northeastern Washington. The balance of the Inland Northwest's bluegrass production is in neighboring Kootenai and Benewah counties of Idaho (28,000) (METCO, 1990).

Open field burning was introduced and adopted in the mid-1940s to control disease and pests. Prior to this "sanitizing" practice, grass producers often lost entire harvests to these elements. Numerous types of diseases, fungi, grasshoppers, and mites can cause devastating damage to bluegrass fields if not controlled. Field burning reduces the need for application of pesticides or other treatments for their control (Lundgren, 1989).

Burning also produces greater yields in the following years of harvest and helps to prolong the life of the bluegrass stand. After harvesting the seed, the remaining bluegrass stubble is burned, which stimulates abundant new growth for the next cultivating season. The burning of grass seed fields is so important to the current competitive production of grass seed that an Intermountain Grass Growers Association (IGGA) report states that positive net return on investment is not possible without this annual post-harvest treatment (METCO, 1990).

Open field burning continued unregulated until the early 1970s, when the nation started becoming more "environmentally aware." The resulting social movement pressed for stricter laws and regulations to protect our natural resources. In response, the Washington Clean Air Act of 1973 addressed the problem of smoke-generated air pollution from grass field burning. It acknowledged the problem of obtaining clean air but allowed the grass seed industry to retain the practice of burning stubble through the provision of interim regulation until economical and practical alternative agricultural practices are found (RCW 70.94.656). Growers recognized that tightening regulations and growing negative sentiment by the surrounding communities would continue. To address the increasing problems, in 1969 the IGGA was formed to promote the benefits of grass production, support and fund research for alternatives to field burning, and coordinate smoke management efforts.

Through the next two decades, resistance to grass seed field burning increased. Mitigative efforts by the farmers to reduce smoke intrusions on urban areas through voluntary smoke management programs were not reducing the level of conflict. An increasing number of disputes arose over the emotional, legal, and scientific aspects of field burning.

Many citizens believed the current field burning policy failed to protect their right to breathe clean air. Citizens were coalescing and voicing their grievances to the media. The issue of grass seed field burning became increasingly salient among citizens, health professionals, and government officials, who said the burning degrades air quality and affects health, and farmers, who said no reasonable alternative exists.

The Conflict

One event represents a critical moment in this field burning conflict and the resulting movement toward an environmental mediation process. In early autumn of 1989, unfavorable atmospheric conditions caused smoke from just-burned fields to lay like a soot-covered blanket over two major urban areas: Spokane, Washington and Coeur d'Alene, Idaho. Christened "Black Wednesday" by local media, that incident helped to mobilize opponents of field burning through marches and pickets, generated scathing editorials, and increased membership in local clean air advocacy organizations (Gray, 1991).

The demonstration of public sentiment incited action by elected officials. Solutions were needed, but as is often the case in environmental conflicts, the traditional legal, technical, and bureaucratic channels were unable to provide an acceptable solution.

Most of the citizen complaints toward field burning centered on the adverse health effects experienced during smoke intrusions. A spokesperson for the Kootenai County (Idaho) Clean Air Coalition said, "You look at the sky, and you say the whole world must be on fire. . . .Your next comment is, this must be illegal. It can't be that any one group of people can subject another group to this type of abuse" (Ashton, 1991:B7).

Local government officials were sympathetic to the citizens' complaints. The mayor of Sandpoint, Idaho, complained, "It is unfortunate that the grass growing industry has so little regard for the health and quality of life of those in the path of their profit-making activity" (Keating and Taggert, 1991:B3).

Citizens and local governments turned to the scientific community both to justify their concerns and to seek answers to the question, can't something be done? The director of the Spokane Chapter of the American Lung Association said, "There is no safe level of exposure to smoke." Noting calls to her office tripled during the burn season, she added, "They call us because they're choking, they can't breathe" (Sullivan, 1989:B1).

But there is often a significant difference between technical answers regarding acceptable levels of pollution and the threats to their health as perceived by citizens. According to Krimsky and Plough (1988), environmental risk events are composed partly of physical processes and partly of socially constructed phenomena. As a result, risk assessment and communication must incorporate the cultural and socioeconomic elements of the situation, as well as the technical elements, because they may be of equal or greater importance than the technical components in mitigating conflict and misunderstanding. The scientific data are not currently sufficient to predict accurately negative health effects caused by field-generated smoke. There are three primary reasons: (1) measurement technology, (2) reporting criteria, and (3) insufficient evidence to attribute causal relationships between field burning smoke and negative health impacts.

The 1970 Clean Air Act listed six "criteria" air pollutants. The Environmental Protection Agency (EPA) designates non attainment status to communities based on pollution measurements exceeding a 24-hour standard or within an annual arithmetic mean. Non attainment means that the EPA has identified a clearly delineated geographic area as exceeding a national ambient air quality standard or standards for one or more of the criteria pollutants. In 1980 the EPA revised the standards regarding particulates to include only particulate matter with an aerodynamic diameter less than or equal to a nominal ten microns (PM_{10}).

While Spokane County has been cited for non attainment on the PM_{10} standard, non attainment was not attributed to field burning. According to an environmental planner for the Washington State Department of Ecology, "the problem is that two to three dust storms every year skew the annual average" (McBride, 1991:B1). According to a Spokane County Air Pollution Control Authority (SCAPCA) chemist, "As long as smoke is managed well, its impact on the non attainment status of Spokane County is minimal or nonmeasurable." However, he is quick to add, "that fact does not minimize the impact on individuals with health problems in any way."

Little empirical evidence currently exists on the specific health risks imposed by inhaling smoke from the burning of field grass. Other pollutants such as acid aerosols, sulfur dioxides, wood smoke and agricultural and ambient dust combine to make it difficult and expensive to isolate field burning smoke particulates and extract their adverse health effects.

Still, there can be little doubt that burning grass fields is potentially harmful to people's health. According to SCAPCA's chemist, the burning of grass fields is known to emit carbon monoxide, ash, and CO_2. In addition, he cautions, "some strange hydrocarbons are formed when the residue of chlorinated pesticides/herbicides are burned. Many of these hydrocarbons provide for the formation of dioxins and furans—some of the most lethal chemical ingredients to man." A Washington State University Cooperative Extension Officer confirmed that such materials are used on the region's grass crops. "I think growers use some kind of weed control on their seedling bluegrass" . . . [but he cautions that use of such products]. . . "should not be blown up like the Alar issue" (Bond, 1991).

Jurisdictional responsibility over smoke emission during the grass seed field burning season has also been a complex affair. In 1986, the Idaho State Legislature transferred the responsibility for controlling the air pollution effects of field burning from the state's Air Quality Bureau to the seed growers. Following that change in the statutes, in order to monitor and control smoke generated by field burning, Idaho growers formed the Panhandle Area Council to represent north Idaho counties, major cities, and tribes.

The air quality regulatory body responsible for Spokane County, Washington, saw this situation as a problem. The Spokane County Air Pollution Control Authority (SCAPCA) was formed in compliance with the 1973 Washington Clean Air Act's mandates. Its function is to regulate compliance of Washington State's Clean Air Law. Included among its main goals is reducing emissions from grass seed field burning. While Spokane County growers were required to comply with SCAPCA's regulations, there was no comparable legislatively designated air control authority in Idaho. As a result, though the two states shared the same air pollution sources and problems, they operated under very different sets of rules, regulations and guidelines.

At a meeting to explore the potential for a bistate effort to reduce smoke impacts, a SCAPCA member said, "our feeling is that we have a very good set of regulations, while Idaho has nothing. . . . [If Washington and Idaho were jointly to tackle the grass seed field burning issue] SCAPCA would only be willing to change its rules and regulations as long as Idaho gets an air quality authority." SCAPCA was interested only in dealing with either the Idaho State Legislature or a parallel authority, not with the growers. This compounded the difficulty in reaching resolution to the Inland Northwest field burning conflict.

The social, legal, bureaucratic, and technical components of the Inland Northwest field burning issue combined to form a complex environmental conflict. Further complicating the issue were the multiple issues and interests that were reflected in the diversity of stakeholders invested in its outcome.

The Stakeholders and Their Interests

Several days after "Black Wednesday," a local chapter of the Soil and Water Conservation Society organized a well-attended and media-covered public forum on regional grass burning. The results produced a position paper that recommended the establishment of a "regional committee representing all relevant interests, and vested with authority to collect and disseminate facts and to devise solutions" (Peterson et al., 1990:4). The Spokane Area Chamber of Commerce contacted mediators within Cooperative Extension at Washington State University to facilitate the resolution process. In the fall of 1990, the Inland Northwest Field Burning Summit got underway.

Included among the agricultural interests were grass seed producers (Cenex Full-Circle, Heart Seed Company, Jacklin Seed Company), Coeur d'Alene Tribal authorities, and their constituency group, the Intermountain Grass Growers Association (IGGA). Also included were area wheat producers, represented by the Washington Association of Wheat Growers and the Kootenai County (Idaho) Wheat Growers. They recognized that smoke was perceived as a growing problem within their industry as well.

The grass seed industry strongly felt that there were no viable alternatives to open field burning. The industry saw itself as justified in taking this position, since it had invested considerable sums of money over the years in researching alternatives to burning. The growers viewed themselves as a beleaguered group besieged by the press, the regulators, and the clean air proponents who were calling for an end to burning. "We are sick of it [the threats]. . . . Besides, we get the blame for slash burning and other field burning [i.e., wheat stubble]. We burn 5 percent of the days and the other 95 percent have clean air because of grass production. If we do away with the grass seed industry, the smoke won't go away."

Tribal interests were represented by the Coeur d'Alene Tribe of Idaho. They had several thousand acres in grass seed production and were exempt from state air quality regulatory authorities. The Tribe's smoke management program coordinator exerted total control over all burning practices on tribal land. The Tribe did not intend to relinquish its right to designate when, where, and how burning was to take place on the Coeur d'Alene reservation.

Another coalition of interests involved in the mediation was a combination of organized interest groups focused on environmental and health issues. These included the Clean Air Coalition (Idaho); the Kootenai County Clean Air Coalition (Idaho); the Kootenai County Environmental Alliance (Idaho); and the Spokane County Clean Air Coalition (Washington). Although their memberships' opinions varied on specific issues, they shared the perspective that "field burning is detrimental to the health of those who are forced, unwillingly, to breathe the smoke" (Gray, 1991:4).

Many environmentalists saw this conflict not as a right to farm issue, but a right to pollute issue. They expressed the desire to see the grass fields put into housing instead of continuing in agriculture, since "farmers just go to the bank and are getting rich off our pain" (Gray, 1991:4). Environmentalists strongly felt that there must be an alternative to releasing smoke into the air during the late summer/early fall burning season.

The Spokane Chapter of the American Lung Association of Washington represented the health concerns and felt a strong obligation to those members of the society that are most vulnerable to air pollution. The Lung Association wanted to see a "time certain" progression in resolving the issues and advocated a systematic study to evaluate the long-term health effects of field burning.

The tourism sector was represented by Post Falls (Idaho) Tourism, Incorporated. They believed that open field burning was harmful to their industry as well. To support their concerns, they cited an unscientific survey conducted by the Sandpoint Chamber of Commerce (Idaho): "9,600 visitor hours may have been lost to the smoke . . . that's more than $400,000 lost to the Bonner County economy . . . and we get none of the benefits . . . from the grass-growing industry" (McBride, 1989:B1).

Governmental and regulatory interests were represented by the Idaho Division of Environmental Quality, the Spokane County (Washington) Air Pollution Control Authority (SCAPCA), and the Washington State Department of Ecology. This coalition saw its role as enforcing laws to safeguard the public. As discussed previously, enforcement power varied greatly between Washington and Idaho. The Idaho Division of Environmental Quality was empowered by few enabling statutes and did not enforce any smoke management rules. The Washington State Department of Ecology had enforcement authority and was gearing up to enforce more stringently the state's Clean Air Act's provisions that restricted slash burning, eliminated most cereal stubble burning, and reduced the allowable acreage for grass seed production.

With the possible exception of the regulators, the one thing that all stakeholders seemed to hold in common was a sense of vulnerability. An author in a farmer's trade journal expressed the agricultural interests' sense of vulnerability: "In my belief, the two greatest forces that threaten our survival are the economy and the public's acceptance of our products as environmentally safe, combined with the public's view of accepting farmers as good stewards of the [natural] resources." He went on to say, "Never before in modern history have we been faced with such a tenuous economic situation, which is also so vulnerable to the environmental agenda" (Rustemeyer, 1991:5).

The Mediation

Any mediation would have to address the stakeholders' sense of vulnerability and create a sense of trust that their needs would be met. The facilitators' guiding principle throughout their involvement in the grass burning conflict was to create group processes that allowed participants' needs to be addressed on three levels: the personal (by providing a group experience that contributed to the growth and personal well-being of each member); the interpersonal (by designing a group experience that built trust and the members' willingness to work together interdependently in the future); and substantive results (by achieving an outcome that gained the support and commitment of each interest) (Fiske and Gray, 1992).

The first two Summit meetings were dedicated to identifying stakeholders, clarifying the roles of the negotiators and mediators, and arriving at procedural agreements by which to conduct the sessions (See Appendix: Proposed Ground Rules). Summit participants also identified questions they wanted addressed during time set aside for presentations from each interest. The facilitators estimated that 50 percent of the time would be devoted to defining the problem (through individual stakeholder presentations), 20 percent to deriving the criteria by which any alternative solution could be evaluated, and 30 percent to development of an agreement based upon those criteria (Fiske and Gray, 1992).

The first task was for stakeholders to prepare and present their perception of the problem to the other members. As might be expected, with fifteen Summit participants, fifteen different definitions of the problem were presented. Depending on who was talking, the "problem" was perceived narrowly (e.g., as grass and/or field burning; smoke; air pollution) or broadly (e.g., as damage to public health; the negative impact on economic growth and tourism).

Through this give-and-take discussion the participating interests came to understand that the problem was multifaceted and that each interest's perspective was legitimate. Summit members agreed that the "problem" was broader than previously defined by any one interest.

The next several meetings were dedicated exclusively to providing each interest with the opportunity to educate others about how it viewed the problem. Through this increasingly open interchange among participants, a series of written "understandings" resulted. They formed the basis for a set of criteria by which alternative solutions would be evaluated. With these criteria in hand, Summit participants could better evaluate each alternative solution.

Inland Northwest Field Burning Summit

Criteria for proposed solutions

Does the proposed solution

- Establish baseline data?
- Reduce the number of complaints?

- Reduce contaminant emissions?
- Reduce visual smoke?
- Reduce the number of people exposed?
- Provide for ongoing monitoring?
- Contain an educational component?
- Promote economic viability and cost effectiveness?
- Generate member commitment to implement?
- Specify a timetable for implementation?

Summit participants then divided themselves into self-selected and representative groups to develop alternative solutions to the field burning problem. After several weeks of research and discussion, four components were identified as essential ingredients of an acceptable agreement: (1) a smoke management plan (including penalties) with a specified short-term burn program, (2) establishment of baseline data information and complaint tracking system that addressed health effects, (3) a long-term emissions reduction program; and (4) an education/outreach program.

At this point, Summit participants again self-selected into workgroups on one or more of the above topics and worked as committees to draft detailed plans that could be shared with their constituents. The draft agreement went through six revisions over the next three months as it was honed into an "acceptable" document.

During this fine-tuning phase, several major obstacles had to be overcome. The first hurdle dealt with how best to measure a decrease in smoke—should it be through acreage reduction (easily measured) or emissions reduction (much more difficult to measure)? The grass seed industry agreed to a 20 percent reduction in acreage because current economic conditions had already prompted growers to plow up 20 percent of their grass-producing stock.

The second obstacle centered on the "recognition" of the grass growers' situation. Environmental interests were concerned that through signing the agreement, they were explicitly accepting the grass growers' view of the problem and its solution. This impasse was satisfactorily resolved through footnoting the "recognition" in the agreement and defining it in a way that allowed each interest to have a "varying level of belief/conviction in the statements."

At the end of one year the stakeholders of the Inland Northwest Field Burning Summit signed an agreement before a packed press conference held at the Spokane Area Chamber of Commerce. A plan that specified how each interest would implement that agreement was also developed. That plan was successfully followed by Summit participants during the 1991 and 1992 burning seasons, and in 1993 was reviewed for possible revision.

SUMMARY ANALYSIS

Using the "Environmental Mediation Checklist" the EDR process of the Inland Northwest Field Burning Summit obtained reasonable success in meeting both within-process and post-process criteria. The within-process criteria were met in the following fashion:

1. Mediators were identified and recruited who did not stand to reap personal gain (other than enhanced professional reputation) from the outcome of the dispute.

2. The mediators assessed the situation as a suitable candidate for mediation (i.e., there was sufficient incentive for parties to participate and significant uncertainty regarding possible outcomes through traditional bureaucratic, technical, or legal channels).

3. The participants were carefully selected. They demonstrated long-term commitment and involvement throughout the EDR process. No one defected from the Summit, which seems to mean that those most able to resolve the conflict were indeed at the table.

4. Careful attention was given to designing the process so that interests could be clearly stated without leading to disruptive emotional displays. The development of ground rules by the stakeholders, the provision of adequate time given for individual presentation, and a well-delineated problem-solving planning process assured that the participants shared "ownership" in the process.

5. This environmental dispute involved issues with many dimensions with great complexity. The facilitators allowed each of the participants ample time to present the issues as they saw them, thus assuring that no salient issues were left out.

6. Facilitators then assisted the group in breaking the issues into logical pieces for consideration. That step facilitated the establishment of a comprehensive and interest-relevant information base from which to develop criteria for solutions. As a result, misperceptions based on an inadequate grasp of the facts were avoided.

7. The preliminary agreement in this case was the "Inland Northwest Field Burning Summit Criteria for Proposed Solutions," which was created as a by-product of the fact-finding stage and established a common foundation for further work.

8. The preliminary agreement allowed the stakeholders of the field burning mediation to consult with their constituents before moving toward a final settlement. The acceptance of the ten criteria by the constituent groups provided assurance that the terms of any final agreement would be in accord with their interests and concerns.

9. As evidenced by the six revisions necessary to make the agreement final, adequate care was given to incorporate modifications so that all interests would be accommodated.

10. Once signed and ratified by all the stakeholders, the final agreement incorporated measures that assured its implementation. The agreement was limited to the 1991 and 1992 burn seasons, which assured that a review of its effectiveness would take place prior to the 1993 burn season. Members had to take steps during the 1991-1992 period to fulfill their responsibilities in implementing the four major elements of the final agreement, which included monitoring the impact of the agreement.

Summit Resolution: Elements of Implementation

1. A Regional Smoke Management Plan that
   a. eliminated burning on Fridays, weekends, and holidays;
   b. designated three smoke management regions and reduced the number of allowable burn days during an expanded burning "window" in each region; and
   c. established fines for burning without permits or outside of the designated burn period.

2. An Emissions Monitoring and Complaint Tracking Program that
   a. established a process for collecting baseline data on smoke, opacity, and particulate levels;
   b. utilized mobile emission monitoring equipment;
   c. proposed that a data gathering and complaint tracking system be developed to identify the impacts of open field burning on human health; and
   d. requested the Idaho and Washington smoke management advisory committees to designate fees to support research on toxicity, risk analysis, and impacts of alternative farming methods.

3. An Emissions Reduction Program that
   a. prohibited the burning of first year grass plantings;
   b. decreased the burning of planned tear-out fields;
   c. reduced by 20 percent the number of acres burned during 1991 and 1992; and
   d. requested tri-state (Idaho, Oregon, and Washington) legislative support for research on alternatives to burning.

4. An Education and Outreach Program that
   a. provides Summit participants and the general public with ongoing information regarding the problem and progress being made; and
   b. monitors agreement implementation (Fiske and Gray, 1992).

The four post-process criteria were met as well. The Bi-State Regional Smoke Management Plan documented (1) the reaching of an agreement, (2) the ratification and signing-off by constituent groups, and (3) a detailed agreement on implementation measures. To make an evaluation using the final criterion set forth in this chapter, interviews were conducted with Summit participants. These resulted in generally positive, but qualified, responses to the query, "Do you feel the mediation process was valuable?" One respondent stated that all participants have continued to work hard to hammer out solutions but noted that he was still "standing firm on the issue of fighting for clean air . . . whatever the polluting source." Another participant believed the process to be valuable but felt that much work remained toward developing and funding a comprehensive study on the health effects of inhaling smoke from field burning. A third stated, "I've grown to respect the others [Summit members] over the years . . . and the experience working together as a group was worthwhile . . . [but I will] continue to work toward initiating legislation [in Idaho] that would protect the quality of the air."

CONCLUSIONS

The process appears to have been valuable to the stakeholders. Agreements were enacted that eased the conflict and improved smoke management methods, but the pollution problems still existed and further work would be necessary before that aspect of the problem would be solved.

At a 1993 meeting, stakeholders undertook the challenge of meeting this environmental problem. The Idaho Clean Air Coalition was concentrating on several air quality and monitoring issues. The Idaho Division of Environmental Quality was looking at a joint smoke management plan between Idaho and Washington that would require rewriting current legislation. An IGGA representative was serving on an Agricultural Burning Task Force, a regulation advisory board formed to establish best management practices, permit fees, and to recommend research project alternatives to field burning. The Washington State Department of Ecology was about to begin a comprehensive inventory of the air quality issues in Washington State.

If the participants expected to stop grass seed field burning, the EDR process would have been an unequivocal failure. However, by bringing together representatives from state regulatory agencies, the grass seed industry, Indian tribes, health authorities, and environmental groups, a remarkable degree of consensus was achieved on how better to protect the environment while meeting to a degree the interests of the stakeholders.

This was both a symbolic and substantive move forward. Symbolic in that the meetings represented and promoted cooperation, which is a missing element in the resolution of many environmental problems. Substantive through the development of a signed, ratified, and implemented agreement that allowed consideration of a comprehensive range of expertise and technical data affecting the environmental decisions. It was a cooperative effort by former battle-weary adversaries to forge agreements where none were thought to exist.

Because the Inland Northwest Field Burning Summit mediation continued beyond the conclusion of this research, it would be premature to draw summary conclusions on how well the EDR process resolved the air quality issues of the Northwest. In fact, improvements in air quality may not be the best measure of success in this case. The Summit addressed several issues, each related to the air quality issue but distinct in its own social, technical, and legal components.

While this makes it difficult to reach definitive conclusions, two points can be made that support the effectiveness of the environmental mediation process in the field burning conflict. First, substantive measures, based on a signed and ratified agreement, were implemented to reduce the emissions of smoke. Second, a by-product of this agreement has been the continuation of efforts by Summit participants to work together to tackle the various and complex issues surrounding the broader air quality issue. If they thought they could better meet their interests through other venues or actions, they probably would have done so by now.

Problems, barriers, and conflicts remain. Any long-term solutions will need to be broad-based and backed by statutory language. What once may have been conceived as a site-specific environmental conflict (growers vs. tourism) has grown to include the larger issue of airshed quality across state boundaries.

While the mediation process in this case appears to offer many advantages for the interest groups involved, environmental mediation should not be viewed as a panacea or cure-all. It may be advantageous in some circumstances and disadvantageous in others. Group problem-solving techniques can be very time-consuming. There are often large amounts of information replete with legal and technical jargon to assimilate. Citizen organizations may initially not have the necessary negotiating and problem-solving skills to participate effectively in an EDR process. Part of the organizational cost of an alternative process is the time and energy spent to maintain interaction with constituents. Representatives from interest groups have to devote their energies not only to participating in the actual problem-solving sessions but also to maintaining group cohesiveness and support for negotiated agreements within their organizations.

Despite the hard work involved, if an environmental conflict seems suitable for a collaborative process, EDR's strengths and benefits may be of use. Stakeholders may find the process gives them greater power and influence in the decision-making process. The confidence, credibility, negotiation skills, and political savvy gained by individual members can translate into greater effectiveness and legitimacy of the group as a whole. Perhaps one of the greatest ongoing benefits of an environmental mediation process is improvement of communications and working relationships. Better communication creates a more positive environment for implementation of agreements and for future cooperation on other issues.

Research on the practice of environmental mediation is beginning to identify the practices and conditions which favor successful outcomes of conflict management efforts. Given the variation among environmental disputes, variation in dispute resolution approaches is also to be expected. While this chapter does not attempt to evaluate the host of styles, objectives, and characteristics of mediators' practices, it does describe and assess the track record of one singular mediated event. In doing so, we hope to support the growing body of academicians, practitioners, citizens and interest groups who are finding that environmental mediation processes may assist in solving the controversial issues and complex problems that arise around environmental conflicts.

Appendix 17A

Proposed Ground Rules for the Inland Northwest Field Burning Summit

Each of the participants in the Summit agrees to the following ground rules:

1. *Legitimacy and respect*. Summit participants are representative of a broad range of interests, each having concerns about the outcome of the issue at hand. All parties recognize the legitimacy of the interest and concerns of others and expect that their interest will be respected as well.

2. *Active listening and involvement*. Participants commit to listen carefully to each other, to recognize each person's concerns and feeling about the topic, to ask questions for clarification, and to make statements that attempt to educate or explain. Participants should not assume that any one person knows the answers.

3. *Responsibility*. Each of us takes responsibility for getting our individual needs met and for getting the needs of Summit participants met. Participants commit to keeping their colleagues and constituents informed about the progress of these discussions and to do so in a timely manner.

4. *Honesty and openness*. Constructive candor is a little used but effective tool. Participants commit to stating needs, problems, and opportunities—not positions.

5. *Creativity*. Participants commit to search for opportunities and alternatives. The creativity of the group can often find the best solution.

6. *Demilitarized discussion*. Participants commit to leave their weapons of war at home (or at least outside the room).

7. *Consensus*. Participants agree that any decisions will be reached by consensus.

8. *Separability*. This Summit is in no way meant to detract from, or interfere with, current efforts regarding field burning.

9. *Media*. Participants agree that to get maximum benefit from the Summit, a climate that encourages candid and open discussion should be created. In order to create and sustain this climate, participants commit to not attributing suggestions, comments, or ideas of another participant to the news media or nonparticipants. We encourage the participants to use good faith in dealing with the media, and to refer questions to Bill Justus at the Spokane Chamber of Commerce, Ag Bureau. No media will be invited to attend unless cleared with participants prior to the meeting.

10. *Freedom to disagree*. Participants agree to disagree. The point of this Summit is to foster open discussion of issues; and in order to facilitate this we need to respect each other's right to disagree.

11. *Commitment*. Participants agree that this effort is a priority in terms of time and/or resource commitment. Each participant will provide the name of an alternate. The

alternate will attend in the absence of the participant. It is the responsibility of the member and alternate to keep each other up to date.

12. *Rumors*. Participants agree to verify rumors at the meeting before accepting them as fact.

13. *Freedom to leave*. Participants agree that anyone may leave this process and disavow the above ground rules, but only after telling the entire group why and seeing if the problem(s) can be addressed by the group.

14. *Dispute resolution*. Participants agree that in the event this effort is unsuccessful, all are free to pursue their interest in other dispute resolution forums without prejudice.

Chapter 18

Environmental Mediation Theory and Practice: Challenges, Issues, and Needed Research and Theory Development

J. Walton Blackburn

The practice of environmental mediation is very strong, but theory development is very weak. The literature on environmental mediation and the contributions to this book indicate that many mediation practitioners from all over the nation, and even abroad, are engaged in a great variety of mediation efforts. Yet apparently the only recent comprehensive development of environmental mediation theory is mine, which is the "Eclectic Theory of Environmental Mediation." (According to Dr. Bruce Clary, Professor and Acting Director, Graduate Program in Public Policy and Management, Edmund S. Muskie Institute of Public Affairs, University of Southern Maine, my theory has yet to be improved upon.)

Nothing is as practical as a good theory. The challenge is spelled out by O'Leary in her chapter in this book when she states the need for "theoretically informed case studies, surveys, interviews, and statistical analyses of quantitative data." But the theory which is indeed available is difficult to locate. While I did develop a very comprehensive "grounded theory" by testing 63 propositions through interviews with 30 environmental mediators and conducting statistical analyses of the responses, my report of this theory development is found in two edited volumes (Blackburn 1990, 1991) which do not focus specifically on environmental mediation. Thus, the very fugitive nature of the literature on environmental mediation continues to be a barrier to the diffusion of what little recent theory has been available. In addition, the flow of books which address environmental mediation specifically appears to have diminished. While several books appeared in the early and mid-1980s, few volumes have appeared since that time.

Further theory development is needed in environmental mediation to provide a framework for advancing mediation practice. The tremendous variety of different techniques, practices and approaches which are in use need to be evaluated within a theoretical framework. The great variety of conceptual frameworks in use in the literature on environmental mediation and in case studies results in assessments of mediation practice using many different evaluation criteria.

The very interdisciplinary nature of environmental mediation and its general relevance to many interests and perspectives result in a very wide dispersion of the literature and create substantial obstacles to the identification of sources. The fugitive nature of the literature on environmental mediation is clearly evident from an analysis of two bibliographies. In one developed by O'Leary for her contribution to this volume, only five journals contained more than two contributions on environmental mediation since 1978—these were the *Environmental Impact Assessment Review* (16 contributions), the *Environmental Law Reporter* (four contributions), the *Boston College Environmental Affairs Law Review* (four contributions), the *Arbitration Journal* (three contributions), and the *Policy Studies Journal* (three contributions). Two journals, the *Journal of Planning Literature* and the *Natural Resources Journal*, each had two contributions. Twenty-two other journals had one contribution each. These included such periodicals as the *Ecological Law Quarterly,* the *EPA Journal, Environmental Management,* the *Annual Review of Public Health,* the *Georgetown Law Journal,* the *Administrative Law Review,* the *Journal of Policy Analysis and Management, Environmental Management,* the *Journal of Social Issues, Environments,* the *Air Force Law Review,* and the *Northwest Environmental Journal.*

Another bibliography of literature since 1987 which I developed had nine journals not found in the O'Leary list, with one citation each. Included were such titles as the *Engineering News Record, Environmental Affairs,* the *Journal of Water Resources Planning and Management,* and the *Western Political Quarterly.*

The task of searching the literature on environmental mediation is greatly complicated by the varied terminologies in use. Such combinations of terms as "environmental conflict management," "environmental dispute settlement," "environmental dispute resolution," and "environmental negotiation" and different combinations of these terms are in wide use. In addition, such conflict management strategies as the "Negotiated Investment Strategy," "Policy Dialogue," and "Regulatory Negotiation" are relevant to environmental mediation and further diffuse the literature.

The task of theory development is challenging not only because of the fugitive nature of the environmental mediation literature but also because there is a great abundance of literature on social conflict and on community mediation, most of which is not directly relevant to environmental mediation but which may need to be reviewed to locate the few environmental mediation gems available. Expanding the scope of theory development to include the broad literature on "alternative dispute resolution (ADR)," however, would greatly enrich the theory of environmental mediation. O'Leary has cited many useful ADR works in her chapter in this book. The literature on citizen participation, the stages of group development, and group decision process management also would enrich theory development.

Perhaps a major impediment to the development of environmental mediation theory has been that those who are theory-oriented are different individuals than those process-oriented people who are out conducting mediation. The challenges of mediation practice may leave little energy for theory development, and the mind-set and personality types of effective practitioners are usually very different from those of theoreticians. An exception is the contribution to this volume by John Allen.

A challenge to theory development is the problem of defining "success" in mediation efforts. O'Leary (this volume) and Crofoot and Wondolleck (1990) report that participants often report an appreciation for the process and a feeling of empowerment through gaining public involvement skills, even when no written agreement results from a mediation effort. O'Leary questions the empirical bases for the claims of success of many mediation practitioners.

A variety of specific challenges to the development of the theory of environmental mediation can be identified within the framework of my "Eclectic Theory." These are presented in the next section. Even this listing of theoretical issues is not comprehensive due to the complexity of environmental mediation. O'Leary's chapter also articulates many of these issues in relation to the mediation practitioner literature. Theory development in environmental mediation deserves substantial attention if the practice of mediation is to continue advancing systematically. A theoretical framework is a compact and efficient means of testing and communicating best practices.

SOME CHALLENGES TO THEORY DEVELOPMENT WITHIN THE FRAMEWORK OF "THE ECLECTIC THEORY OF ENVIRONMENTAL MEDIATION"

"The Eclectic Theory of Environmental Mediation," which I developed (Blackburn 1988, 1990, 1991), is organized in the framework of "ten stages" of mediation for the sake of convenience, even though some of the activities and considerations presented in the propositions of the theory are relevant to more than one stage. The "ten stages" provide a framework for further theory development.

A few of the more broadly applicable propositions are presented below as mediation issues which need further theoretical refinement and empirical testing. Related issues are presented. Much of the evidence of the need for theory elaboration comes from personal conversations at professional conferences, conference panel discussions, and experience working with the literature over the years—consequently few sources of evidence will be cited.

The Appendix at the end of this chapter presents the key propositions of the "Eclectic Theory" within the framework of the ten stages.

Stage I—Identify the Mediator

The objectivity of the mediator. Concern with the objectivity of the mediator—
that is, that "the mediator should not have an interest in the outcome of the
dispute" (Proposition 1 of the Eclectic Theory)—received the highest importance
rating by mediation practitioners (of any of the propositions in the theory) as
critical to successful mediation results. Yet its importance rating was only 2.8 out
of a possible 3.0. Perhaps this widely accepted concept needs further testing, and
the proposition may need to be refined. Maybe it should be "not have a *personal*
interest" in the outcome. Yet "personal interest" may need to be defined. In
actuality, maybe no mediator can be absolutely neutral or the individual would not
even be concerned to find a settlement of the dispute.

The technical expertise of the mediator concerns whether the mediator needs
technical sophistication to understand the issues in dispute (Proposition 2). It has
been argued that great technical expertise on the part of the mediator may lead to
too much focus on technical solutions at the expense of relationship-building and
careful process development. Arguments over data often conceal differences truly
founded in values differences or relationship conflicts, resulting in "going around
in circles" with no conflict resolution being achieved. Evidence from the literature
and from conference discussions, however, suggests that a moderate level of
technical expertise can very helpful to the mediator so that this individual understands at least the essence of points in contention. Yet the mediation effort must not
focus exclusively on data or differences in data interpretation.

*The active or passive involvement of the mediator in controlling the process
and substance of mediation.* Among mediation practitioners there is substantial
disagreement on how aggressive mediators should be in the structuring and managing of mediation efforts. My personal position is that very active interventions
are appropriate in the management of structure and processes, which is entirely
distinct from interventions in matters of substance. In addition, mediators may
need to be more active in creating structure and managing group processes at some
stages than at others. Evidence from research for the development of the Eclectic
Theory indicates that some mediators involve themselves in substance—at a
moderate level—when they take an active part in drafting the wording of mediation agreements. Some of the trade-offs of more or less active mediator involvement in controlling the process is addressed briefly in the Idaho wilderness
designation controversy chapter in this volume.

*Is there a need for mediator training? to produce mediators who thoroughly
understand the most advanced principles and practices of mediation?* Because
environmental disputes vary so widely in scope, substance, context, complexity,
and in the nature and number of participants, it can be argued that training
mediators in "standard" approaches to mediation management might produce an
unfortunate rigidity in approach. I would argue, on the contrary, that although

flexibility and adaptability are important in mediation, training is very much needed and should accommodate a diversity of approaches to mediation management. Two chapters in this book are relevant to mediator training.

Stage II—Assess the Preconditions

Types of disputes appropriate for mediation. (This concern is related to Proposition 5.) Some argue that issues which are vague and undefined may not be suitable for mediation. Other authorities maintain that disputes which involve issues related to deeply held values may be unsuitable for mediation due to the intransigence of interests. Disputes which can set important nationwide legal precedents may not be appropriate because the results of a court battle may be more effective in advancing a particular position than a locally mediated agreement. Disputes which lack deadlines or time pressures may be unsuitable. While failed mediation efforts are often very instructive in advancing the art and science of mediation, they expend scarce resources on efforts which often produce substantial frustration. Research is needed on the types of conflicts which are suitable for mediation.

Conditions under which mediation is appropriate. Various observers have argued that a variety of different conditions should be met before mediation efforts can be expected to succeed (see propositions 3-4, 6-11). This is a complex area of concern which needs extensive exploration. Many of these propositions may need to be refined—for example, how can a "balance of power" among contending parties be measured or defined? (Proposition 6.)

Stage III—Recruit Participants

The identification and appropriate representation of interested parties in mediation. (Propositions 12-13, 15-16 deal with issues of recruitment and representation.) In environmental conflicts which involve complex issues and potentially extensive environmental impacts, the identification of potentially affected interest groups who should participate in a mediation process can be a major challenge. Similar or identical interests may be represented by several different groups—consequently, difficult choices may need to be made to avoid having unwieldy numbers of representatives involved. Hunters and fisher sportspersons may have similar, but not identical, concerns, just as sheep and cattle interests may have some similar and other different concerns. Various environmental groups may focus upon both similar and divergent problems. Other difficult questions may arise concerning how representative particular spokespersons are of the groups they claim to represent. Mediators may confront difficult questions of who determines which groups shall participate in mediation according to which criteria. Extensive research is needed on the best methods of obtaining effective representation. Another issue concerns regular participation in mediation sessions when mediation efforts last for extended periods of time, to assure adequate representation of particular perspectives throughout the mediation effort.

Appropriate numbers of participants in mediation. Authorities in mediation differ on whether there are practical maximum or minimum numbers of participants for effective mediation. Some argue that large numbers of participants slow the proceedings too much, while others argue that skillful process management can overcome the disadvantages of large numbers. O'Leary examines this question in her chapter.

The addition of other interests during mediation. Mediation authorities disagree on whether interests identified after mediation has been in process for a time should be included. Some argue that the risk of lawsuits by unrepresented parties necessitates the addition of interests late in the process, while others argue that the disruption of processes in motion, from the late addition of new parties, can be detrimental to reaching a mediated settlement.

Stage IV—Design the Mediation Process

Process and content issues in mediation. In designing mediation efforts, both process and content issues must be addressed. Processes must be designed so that all participants are treated fairly, all perspectives receive a fair hearing, and the parties in mediation develop a commitment to reaching an agreement. Content issues concern how information on the subject of the dispute is gathered, processed, disseminated, and analyzed. Extensive research is needed on which processes and information management techniques are most effective and efficient in producing results satisfactory to all perspectives. Overemphasis on either process or content, to the neglect of the other, can be very detrimental to reaching mediated settlements.

The management of group decision processes. (Propositions 17-20, 22-23.) Many techniques of group decision making are available. Research is needed to explore which techniques are most appropriate for mediation efforts. Different techniques may be appropriate at different times in mediation, depending upon how well the different interest know each other, and how many individuals are involved in decision making.

The stages of group development. Mediators need to be aware of the literature on the stages of group development. Premature emphasis on reaching agreement, before groups have worked through the stages, can have negative results. Research is needed on the importance of working through the stages of group development in relation to reaching mediated agreements.

The quality of relationships among mediation participants and with the mediator. (Propositions 21, 24-25.) Some authorities argue that positive relationships among the participants in mediation are an important contribution to reaching mediated settlements. In my interviews with mediators (Blackburn, 1990), I found that mediators rated positive relationships of much less important than many other considerations. Research is needed on how important positive relationships are to achieving settlements, how they can be fostered, and the extent to which resources and time need to be dedicated to developing such relationships.

Social justice and weaker parties in mediation. A literature is emerging (Douglas Amy is a key spokesperson) which addresses the concern about whether representatives (often nonexpert laypersons) in mediation who are less sophisticated than the representatives of formal organizations are at a disadvantage in maintaining support for their positions. An argument has been made that they are often co-opted into taking positions which more experienced and knowledgeable individuals would be reluctant to accept. This subject needs continued exploration. Two chapters in this book address ethical issues related to these concerns.

The involvement of private citizens and the demands on their resources. Private citizens may be at a tremendous disadvantage relative to representatives of corporations, governmental entities or organized interest groups in the practical limitations on their time and resources available for participation in mediation (Crowfoot and Wondolleck, 1990). Many typically fund their participation out of their own pockets.

Stage V—Identify the Issues

The identification of the issues in mediation. (Proposition 26.) In some environmental disputes, the identification of issues is very challenging due to the sometimes unknown past or future effects of environmental changes. The complexity of interrelated interests and concerns and the broad geographical scope of some disputes may make issues identification a substantial challenge. Research is needed to evaluate the effectiveness of different approaches to issue identification.

The expansion of issues in mediation. Once a mediation process is in progress, research on the issues often reveals other unsuspected environmental problems which fall within the scope of the dispute. Research is needed on how this expansion can be done most effectively and efficiently.

Stage VI—Establish an Information Base

The technical understanding of nonexpert participants. Nonexpert participants in mediation may be at a substantial disadvantage in participating actively in mediation efforts. Lack of understanding may make them reluctant to take positions based on technical arguments. My research suggests that a level of trust built up among different parties in mediation may mean that nonexpert participants may not feel the need for a complete understanding of some technical issues. An "adequate understanding" of the issues may be sufficient, while actual agreement on the facts may not be necessary. The Richardson chapter in this book describes some practical processes by which nonexpert participants can gain the level of understanding of technical issues which they feel they need.

The processing and comprehension of technical data. In complex environmental disputes, technical information may need to be summarized and interpreted for ease of understanding by all participants or perspectives. Research is needed on the best methods of communicating sufficient, but not overwhelming, amounts of technical information.

Stage VII—Develop a Preliminary Agreement

The importance of consensus in mediation. Most mediation practitioners seem to favor consensus decisions (that is, without voting). Consensus reduces the threat of lawsuits from parties which were outvoted in reaching agreements. Research needs to be conducted on the value of consensus decisions and whether voting may be acceptable under certain circumstances.

Stage VIII—Consult Constituents on the Suitability of the Preliminary Agreement

Getting constituents to agree to positions in mediation, and not feel that they have been sold out by their representative in mediation. Because constituents of representatives in mediation do not experience the "give and take" involved in reaching mediated agreements and may not appreciate the legitimacy of opposition interests, they may feel "sold out" by their representatives by an agreement reached through mediation. Research is needed on how to bring constituents along with an understanding of the mediation processes, to reduce the threat of a backlash of opposition to mediated agreements.

Getting interest group members, or coalitions of interest groups, to reach agreement on positions. In order to advance positions effectively, representatives of interest groups, or coalitions of interest groups, may need to obtain agreement on positions among their constituents. This can be a substantial challenge with widely dispersed groups and groups with individuals with greatly varied and strongly held opinions. Some authorities suggest that assisting groups to develop unified positions is an important activity for the mediator to undertake. This subject needs research.

Stage IX—Finalize the Agreement

A variety of process issues need to be addressed on the mechanics of achieving an agreement which will be approved by all parties to mediation.

Stage X—Assure the Implementation of the Agreement

The costs and benefits of involvement of governmental agencies, or other organizations associated with implementation, in mediation. In many environmental disputes, governmental agencies will be responsible for implementing mediated agreements. Some authorities recommend involving governmental agencies directly in mediation to assure their understanding and support of a mediated settlement, which they will then be more likely to implement faithfully. Other authorities argue that their participation is inappropriate because they may compromise, or give the appearance of compromising, their responsibilities to the general public by becoming parties to a mediated settlement. This subject needs extensive research.

The circumstances and situations which may require remaking, or redeciding, an agreement. Because mediated agreements often cannot encompass or address all environmental circumstances and changes which may accompany the implementation of an agreement, flexibility is needed for remaking or redeciding an agreement after implementation has been initiated. The issue of when this follow-up phase is appropriate and how it can be conducted effectively to the satisfaction of all interests in disputes needs extensive research.

Appendix 18A

Key Propositions of Blackburn's Eclectic Theory of Environmental Mediation

In the development of "The Eclectic Theory of Environmental Mediation," I conducted an extensive search of the literature to identify the activities mediation practitioners performed and the conditions they claimed were conducive to successful mediation efforts. In this search, 63 elements, considerations and activities were found that were evident in or had been used in different mediation efforts. These components of mediation were shaped into 63 propositions about which activities and conditions favored successful mediation outcomes.

The 63 propositions were tested through interviews with environmental mediation practitioners. From 40 practitioners contacted, 30 interviews were completed.

For presentation purposes and ease of understanding, the 63 propositions were organized into ten "stages of mediation." This does not mean, however, that the activities or conditions are relevant only within the time context of any particular stage. Many mediation activities are iterative, and re-iterative. Many conditions are relevant both early and late in a mediation effort.

Propositions which were rated as "Critically Important" or "Very Important" to mediation success by the mediation practitioners interviewed are identified with "(1)" after the statement of the proposition. Propositions which were rated as less important are identified with "(2)" after the proposition.

I. Identify the Mediator

1. The mediator should not have an interest in the outcome of the dispute (1).
2. The mediator should not have great technical expertise in the subject of the dispute (2).

II. Assess the Preconditions

3. There should be real consequences to the parties if mediation is not attempted which makes mediation the best alternative (1).
4. There should be uncertainty about possible outcomes of the dispute in a context other than mediation (i.e., in the courts, before a regulatory body, etc.) (1).
5. The issues in dispute should be concrete and specific (2).
6. There should be perceived balance of power among contending parties (2).
7. It should be clear that the parties to the dispute had reached a stalemate or an impasse (2).
8. Contending parties should have the potential to experience economic costs if a mediated settlement was not reached (2).
9. The dispute should not have potential to set important legal precedents (2).
10. The dispute should not center on strongly held ideological or philosophical differences (2).
11. The opposing parties should not have a history of contentious relationships (2).

III. Recruit Participants

12. Particular effort and attention should be devoted to the selection of participants (1).

13. All parties with a substantial interest in the dispute should be represented (1).

14. The mediator should educate the contending parties on the mediation process (2).

15. Participants in mediation should have clearly identifiable constituencies (2).

16. New parties should be added as the mediation process evolves and new issues are identified (2).

IV. Design the Mediation Process

17. Contending parties should participate in designing the mediation process (1).

18. The participants and the mediator should develop ground rules for the process (1).

19. The ground rules for mediation should be approved by all participants (1).

20. Ground rules should be developed for dealing with the news media (1).

21. The mediator should obtain the trust of the contending parties (1).

22. Clear and enforceable deadlines should be developed to provide an impetus for a mediated settlement (2).

23. Contending parties and the mediator should hold regularly scheduled meetings (2).

24. Positive attitudes and interaction should develop among representatives of contending parties to mediation (2).

25. The opposing parties should not have a history of contentious relationships (2).

V. Identify the Issues

26. The issues in dispute should be clearly identified (1).

27. Agreement should be reached among contending parties on the geographical boundaries and time horizons of the issues in dispute (2).

VI. Establish an Information Base

28. Efforts should be made to be sure that all representatives of parties to mediation have an adequate understanding of the facts relevant to the dispute (1).

29. The issues in dispute should be broken into logical pieces for consideration (2).

30. Agreement should be reached among participants in mediation on the facts and data relevant to the dispute (2).

VII. Develop a Preliminary Agreement

31. A variety of alternative solutions should be generated by the participants (1).

32. The contending parties and the mediator should hold informal meetings (1).

33. The contending parties should hold their own caucus sessions (1).

34. The mediator should spend time interacting with participants on a one-on-one basis (1).

35. Communication should be maintained with those who would be responsible for implementing the agreement (1).

36. Parties responsible for implementing the agreement should provide assurances that they will follow through (1).

37. Clear means should exist for binding the parties to the agreement (1).

38. A preliminary agreement should be reached (1).

39. A preliminary agreement should be put into writing (1).

40. The mediator should assist the participants in mediation who represent a particular side to reach agreement within their membership on positions to be put forward in mediation (2).

41. The mediator should assist in drafting the wording of the preliminary agreement (2).

42. The mediator should put forth trial solutions (2).

VIII. Consult Constituents on the Suitability of the Preliminary Agreement

43. Participants should maintain regular contact with their constituents (1).

44. The participants should consult with their constituents on the suitability of the preliminary agreement (1).

45. The constituents consulted should approve the preliminary agreement (1).

46. No major group of constituents should oppose the preliminary agreement (1).

IX. Finalize the Agreement

47. Modifications recommended by constituents of representatives to mediation should be incorporated into the final agreement (1).

48. An agreement should be reached which is approved by all parties to mediation (1).

49. The mediator should assist in drafting the final agreement (2).

X. Assure the Implementation of the Agreement

50. The agreement should be ratified, or approved, by the constituents of the representatives to mediation (1).

51. Means should be provided for monitoring the agreement (1).

52. Means should be provided to remake or redecide the agreement, if necessary (1).

Bibliography

Administrative Conference of the United States. *Negotiated Rulemaking Sourcebook.* Washington: Administrative Conference, Office of the Chairman, 1990.

Administrative Conference of the United States. *Sourcebook: Federal Agency Use of Alternative Means of Dispute Resolution.* Washington: Administrative Conference, Office of the Chairman, 1987.

Aiken, "Ethical Issues in Agriculture." In Tom Reagan, ed., *Earthbound: New Introductory Essays in Environmental Ethics.* New York: Random House, 1984: 277-78.

Aleshire, Robert, A. "Planning and Citizen Participation Costs, Benefits and Approaches." *Urban Affairs Quarterly* (June 1970): 369-93.

Allen, John C. "Managing Community Conflict: Strategies for Resolving Community Level Disagreements." Cooperative Extension Publication, G92-1122-A, Institute of Agriculture and Natural Resources, University of Nebraska-Lincoln, Lincoln, Nebraska, December, 1992.

Amy, Douglas. *The Politics of Environmental Mediation.* New York: Columbia University Press, 1987.

Amy, Douglas J. "The Politics of Environmental Mediation." *Ecological Law Quarterly*, 11 (1983a): 1-19.

Amy, Douglas J. "Environmental Mediation: An Alternative Approach to Policy Stalemates." *Policy Sciences*, 15 (1983b): 345-65.

Amy, Douglas J. "Environmental Dispute Resolution: The Promise and the Pitfalls." In N. J. Vig and M. E. Kraft, eds., *Environmental Policy in the 1990s: Towards a New Agenda.* Washington, D.C.: Congressional Quarterly Press, 1990.

Anonymous. *Dispute Resolution—A Handbook for Land Use Planners and Resource Managers.* University of Oregon: Bureau of Governmental Research and Service, October 1990.

Arnstein, Sherry "A Ladder of Citizen Participation." *Journal of the American Institute of Planners*, 35 (July 1969): 216-24.

Ashton, L. "Farmers Hope Burning Reductions Will Improve Image." *The Spokesman-Review*, (April 21, 1991): B7.

Awaroa ka Manuka. *Ngas tikanga o ngasti ata (Tribal policy statement).* Awaroa ka Manuka, Waiukup. New Zealand, 1991.

Bacharach, Samuel B. and Edward J. Lawler. "Power Dependence and Power Paradoxes in Bargaining." *Negotiation Journal*, 2 (April 1986): 167-74.

Bacow, L. and J. Milkey, "Overcoming Opposition to Hazardous Waste Facilities: The Massachusetts Approach." *Harvard Environmental Law Review*, 6, (1982): 265-305.

Bacow, Lawrence S. and Michael Wheeler. *Environmental Dispute Resolution.* New York: Plenum Press, 1987.

Baldwin, J. H. *Environmental Planning and Management.* Boulder, Colo.: Westview Press, 1985.

Bankert, Lynne S. and R. Warren Flint, eds., *Environmental Dispute Resolution in the Great Lakes Region: A Critical Appraisal.* Buffalo, N.Y.: State University of New York at Buffalo, 1988.

Barber, Benjamin R. "Liberal Democracy and the Costs of Consent." In Nancy L. Rosenblum, ed., *Liberalism and the Moral Life.* Cambridge, Mass.: Harvard University Press, 1989.

Barker, Rocky, Editor *Post Register*, Idaho Falls, Idaho. Personal interview, 1993.

Bazerman, Max H. "Negotiator Judgment." *American Behavioral Scientist*, 27 (November/December, 1983): 211-28.

Beatty, Kathleen M. "Public Opinion Data for Environmental Decision Making: The Case of Colorado Springs." *Environmental Impact Assessment Review*, 11 (March 1991): 29-37.

Bellman, Howard S., Cynthia S. Sampson, and Gerald W. Cormick. *Using Mediation when Siting Hazardous Waste Management Facilities: A Hand Book.* Washington, D.C.: U.S. Environmental Protection Agency, 1982.

Benford, Robert D., Helen A. Moore, and J. Allen Williams, Jr. "In Whose Backyard? Concern About Siting a Nuclear Waste Facility." *Sociological Inquiry*, 63, no. 1 (Winter 1993): 30-48.

Bermont, Gordan; Herbert Kelman; and Donald Warwick. *The Ethics of Social Intervention.* Washington D.C.: Hemisphere Publishing Corp., 1978.

Bingham, G. and L. Haygood, "Environmental Dispute Resolution: The First Ten Years." *The Arbitration Journal,* 41 (1986): 3-14.

Bingham, Gail. *Resolving Environmental Disputes. A Decade of Experience.* Washington, D.C.: The Conservation Foundation, 1986.

Bingham, Gail, Frederick R. Anderson, R. Gaull Silberman, F. Henry Habicht, David F. Zoll, and Richard H. Mays. "Applying Alternative Dispute Resolution to Government Litigation and Enforcement Cases." *Administrative Law Review*, 1 (Fall 1987): 527-51.

Blackburn, J. W. "Environmental Mediation as an Alternative to Litigation: The Emerging Practice and Limitations." In M. K. Mills, ed., *Alternative Dispute Resolution in the Public Sector.* Chicago: Nelson-Hall Publishers, 1991: 123-42.

Blackburn, J. Walton. "Environmental Mediation as an Alternative to Litigation." *Policy Studies Journal*, 16, no. 3 (Spring 1988): 562-74.

Blackburn, J. Walton. "Theoretical Dimensions of Environmental Mediation." In M. Afzalur Rahim, ed., *Theory and Research in Conflict Management.* New York: Praeger, 1990.

Blackford, C. *Guidelines for Monitoring Additional Dispute Resolution Processes within the Resource Management Act.* Lincoln, New Zealand: Lincoln University, 1992.

Blackford, C. and H. Matunga. *Maori Participation in Environmental Mediation*. Information paper. Lincoln, New Zealand: Centre for Resource Management, Lincoln University, 1991.

Blackford, C. and A. Smith. *Cross Cultural Mediation: Guidelines for Those Who Interface with Iwi*. Information paper. Lincoln, New Zealand: Centre for Resource Management, Lincoln University, 1993.

Blair, George S. *Government at the Grassroots*, 4th edition. Pacific Palisades, Calif: Palisades Publishers, 1986.

Bleiker, Hans and A. Bleiker. *Citizen Participation Handbook*. Laramie, Wyo: Institute for Participatory Planning, 1981.

Bond, D. "Grass Chemicals: The Unknown in Burning Equation." *The Coeur d'Alene Press* (August 16, 1991).

Bookchin, Murray. *The Ecology of Freedom: The Emergence and Dissolution of Hierarchy*, revised edition. Montreal: Black Rose Books, 1991.

Bookchin, Murray. *The Philosophy of Social Ecology: Essays on Dialectical Naturalism*. Montreal: Black Rose Books, 1990.

Bookchin, Murray, "Social Ecology Versus Deep Ecology." *Socialist Review*, 18, nos. 1-2 (July/Sept. 1988): 11-29.

Boulding, K. *Ecodynamics*. Beverly Hills: Sage, 1978.

Brunet, Edward. "The Costs of Environmental Alternative Dispute Resolution." *Environmental Law Reporter*, 18 (December 1988): 10515-17.

Bryson, John M. and William D. Roering, "Applying Private Sector Strategic Planning in the Public Sector." In J. Bryson and R. Einsweiler, eds., *Strategic Planning: Threats and Opportunities for Planning*. Chicago, Ill: Planners Press, American Planning Assoc., 1988.

Buckle, Leonard G. and Suzann R. Thomas-Buckle, "Placing Environmental Mediation in Context: Lessons from 'Failed' Mediations." *Environmental Impact Assessment Review*, 6 (March 1986): 55-70.

Burgess, Guy. "Current Challenges in Environmental Dispute Resolution." Working paper #89-6. Boulder, Colo.: Conflict Resolution Consortium, University of Colorado, October, 22, 1988.

Burns, Michael E. *Low-Level Radioactive Waste Regulation: Science, Politics and Fear*. Chelsea, Mich.: Lewis Publishers, 1988.

Burton, John and Frank Dukes. *Conflict: Practices in Management, Settlement and Resolution*. New York: St. Martin's Press, 1990.

Burton, Lloyd. "Ethical Discontinuities in Public-Private Sector Negotiation." *Journal of Policy Analysis and Management*, 9 (Winter 1990): 23-40.

Bush, Robert A. "Efficiency and Protection, or Empowerment and Recognition?: The Mediator's Role and Ethical Standards in Mediation." *University of Florida Law Review*, 41 (1989): 253-86.

Bush, Robert A. "The Dilemmas of Mediation Practice: A Study of Ethical Dilemmas and Policy Implications." A Report on a Study for the National Institute for Dispute Resolution, 1992.

Carley, Michael and Ian Christie. *Managing Sustainable Development*. Minneapolis, Minn.: University of Minnesota Press, 1993.

Carlson, John E., Marie L. Lassey, and William R. Lassey. *Rural Society and Environment in America*. New York: McGraw-Hill Book Company, 1981.

Carpenter, Susan and W. Kennedy. *Managing Public Disputes: A Practical Guide to Handling Conflict and Reaching Agreements*, #14. San Francisco: Jossey-Bass, 1988.

Carpenter, Susan and W. J. D. Kennedy. "Managing Environmental Conflict By Applying Common Sense." *Negotiation Journal*, 1 (April 1985): 149-61.

Clary, Bruce. "The Enactment of the Nuclear Waste Policy Act of 1982: A Multiple Perspectives Explanation." *Policy Studies Review*, 10, 4 (Winter 1991): 90-102.

Colosi, Thomas. "Negotiating in the Public and Private Sectors." *American Behavioral Scientist*, 27 (November/December 1983): 229-53.

Cormick, G. W. "Intervention and Self-Determination in Environmental Disputes: A Mediator's Perspective." *Resolve* (Winter 1982): 1-3.

Cormick, G. W. "Strategic Issues in Structuring Multi-Party Public Policy Negotiations." *Negotiation Journal*, 5 (April, 1989): 125-32.

Cormick, G. W. "The Theory and Practice of Environmental Mediation." *The Environmental Professional*, 2 (1980): 24-33.

Cormick, G. W. "Environmental Mediation." In R. W. Lake, ed., *Resolving Locational Conflict*. New Brunswick, N.J.: Center for Urban Policy Research, Rutgers University, 1987.

Cormick, G. W. and J. McCarthy. *Environmental Mediation: A First Dispute*. St. Louis, Mo.: Community Crisis Intervention Center, Environmental Mediation Project, Washington University, 1974.

Cormick, G. W. and L. K. Patton. "Environmental Mediation: Defining the Process through Experience." In L. M. Lake, ed., *Environmental Mediation: The Search for Consensus*. Boulder, Colo.: Westview Press, 1990: 76-97.

Coulson, Robert. "Must Mediated Settlements Be Fair?" *Negotiation Journal*, 4 (January 1988): 15-17.

Crable, S. "ADR: A Solution to Environmental Disputes." *The Arbitration Journal*, 48, 1 (1993): 24-38.

Creighton, J. *Public Involvement Manual*. Washington, D.C.: Government Printing Office, 1980.

Croce, Cynthia. "Negotiation Instead of Confrontation." *EPA Journal*, 11 (April 1985): 23-4.

Crowfoot, James E. and Julia M. Wondolleck. *Environmental Disputes: Community Involvement in Conflict Resolution*. Washington, D.C.: Island Press, 1990.

Daly, Herman E. and John B. Cobb, Jr. *For the Common Good*. Boston, Mass.: Beacon Press, 1980.

Deister, A. D. and C.A. Tice. "Building a Public Supported Project: A Working Organizational Model Applied to a Reclaimed Water Seasonal Storage Project." Paper presented at the 66th Annual Meeting of the Water Environment Federation, 1993.

Denke, Gregory A., M. Garcia and J. Prescolli. *Public Involvement and Social Impact Assessment*. Boulder, Colo.: Westview Press, 1981.

DesJardins, Joseph R. *Environmental Ethics: An Introduction to Environmental Philosophy*. Belmont, Calif.: Wadsworth Publishing, 1993.

Devall, Bill and George Sessions. *Deep Ecology: Living as If Nature Mattered*. Salt Lake City: Peregrine Smith Books, 1985.

Dinkins, Carol E. "Shall We Fight or Will We Finish: Environmental Dispute Resolution in a Litigious Society." *Environmental Law Reporter*, 14 (November 1984): 10398-401.

Dispute Resolution Forum. Regulatory Negotiation Issue (January 1986).

Doniger, David D. "Negotiated Rulemaking at the EPA: Examples of Wood Stove Emissions and Truck Engine Emissions." *Environmental Law Reporter*, 17 (July 1987): 10251-54.

Dotson, Bruce. "No-go Negotiations." Paper presented to the Conference of the American Schools of Collegiate Planning, October 29, 1993.

Dotson, Bruce. "Who and How? Participation in Environmental Negotiation." *Environmental Impact Assessment Review*, 4 (June 1983): 203-17.

Druckman, Daniel, ed. *Negotiations.* Beverly Hills: Sage, 1977.

Druckman, Daniel, Benjamin J. Brome, and Susan H. Korper. "Value Differences and Conflict Resolution." *Journal of Conflict Resolution*, 32 (September 1988): 489-510.

Dryzek, John S. and Susan Hunter. "Environmental Mediation for International Problems." *International Studies Quarterly*, 31 (March 1987): 87-102.

Ebbin, S. and R. Kasper. *Citizen Groups and the Nuclear Power Controversy.* Cambridge, Mass.: MIT Press, 1974.

Edelman, Murray. *The Symbolic Uses of Politics.* Urbana: University of Illinois Press, 1974.

Egan, Timothy "Land Deal Leaves Montana Logged and Hurt." *New York Times* (October 19, 1993a): A-1, 7.

Egan, Timothy "Upheaval in the Forests." *New York Times* (June 30, 1993b): A-1, 9.

Eisenberg, Melvin Aron. "Private Ordering Through Negotiation: Dispute-Settlement and Rulemaking." *Harvard Law Review*, 89 (February 1976): 637-81.

Executive Order No. 12866 in "4." *Federal Register*, Vol. 58, October 4, 1993: 51735.

Fine, Gary A. and Sherryl Kleinman. "Rethinking Subculture: An Interactionist Analysis," *American Journal of Sociology*, 85 (1979): 1-20.

Fiorino, Daniel J. "Can Problems Shape Priorities?: The Case of Risk-Based Environmental Planning." *Public Administration Review*, 50, no. 1 (January/February 1990): 82-90.

Fiorino, Daniel J. "Regulatory Negotiation as a Policy Process." *Public Administration Review*, 48, no. 4 (1988): 764-72.

Fisher, Roger. "Beyond Yes." *Negotiation Journal*, 1 (January 1985): 67-70.

Fisher, Roger. "Negotiating Power." *American Behavioral Scientist*, 27 (November/December 1983): 149-66.

Fisher, Roger. *Some Notes on Criteria for Judging the Negotiation Process.* Presented at the Negotiation Seminar of the Harvard Negotiation Project, Harvard Law School, 1979.

Fisher, Roger. "The Structure of Negotiation: An Alternative Model." *Negotiation Journal*, 2 (July 1986): 233-35.

Fisher, Roger and Loraleigh Keashly. "Third Party Interventions in Intergroup Conflict: Consultation Is *Not* Mediation." *Negotiation Journal*, 4 (October 1988): 381-93.

Fisher, Roger and Scott Brown. *Getting Together: Building a Relationship That Gets to Yes.* Boston: Houghton Mifflin, 1988.

Fisher, Roger and W. Ury. *Getting to Yes: Negotiating Agreement without Giving In.* Boston: Houghton Mifflin, 1981.

Fisher, Roger and W. Ury. *Getting to Yes: Negotiating Agreement without Giving In.* New York: Penguin Books, 1991.

Fisher, Roger and Wayne H. Davis. "Six Basic Interpersonal Skills for a Negotiator's Repertoire." *Negotiation Journal*, 3 (April 1987): 117-22.

Fisher, Ronald J. "Third Party Consultation as a Method of Intergroup Conflict Resolution." *Journal of Conflict Resolution*, 27 (June 1983): 301-34.

Fiske, E. and K. Gray. "The Inland Northwest Field Burning Summit: A Case Study in Interest-based Facilitation of an Environmental Conflict." Paper presented at the regional training session for Cooperative Extension faculty. Portland, Ore., February, 1992.

Flora, Cornelia Butler, Jan L. Flora, Jacqueline D. Spears, and Louis E. Swanson. *Rural Communities: Legacy and Change.* Boulder, Colo.: Westview Press, 1992.

Folk-Williams, J. "The Use of Negotiated Agreements to Resolve Water Disputes Involving Indian Rights." *Natural Resource Journal,* 28 (1988): 63-103.

Forester, John. "Envisioning the Politics of Public Sector Dispute Resolution." Prepared for the Council of the Fund for Research on Dispute Resolution, 1989.

Forester, John. "Envisioning the Politics of Public Sector Dispute Resolution." *Studies in Law, Politics, and Society,* 12 (1992): 247-86.

Forester, John and David Stitzel. "Beyond Neutrality: The Possibilities of Activist Mediation in Public Sector Conflicts." *Negotiation Journal*, 5 (July 1989): 251-64.

Fox, Warwick. "Deep Ecology: A New Philosophy for Our Time?" *Ecologist*, 14, no. 5-6 (1974): 194-200.

Fragile Foundations: A Report on America's Public Works—Final Report to the President and the Congress. Washington, D.C.: U.S. Government Printing Office, 1988.

Frankena, Frederick. *Environmental Mediation: A Bibliography.* Monticello, Ill.: Vance Bibliographies, 1988.

Frankena, Frederick and Joanne Koelin Frankena. *Citizen Participation in Environmental Affairs, 1970-1986: A Bibliography.* New York: AMS Press 1988.

Freudenburg, W. R. "Social Scientists' Contributions to Environmental Management." *Journal of Social Issues*, 45, no. 1 (1989): 133-52.

Fuller, L. L. "Forms and Limits of Adjudication." In K. I. Winston, ed., *The Principles of Social Order.* Durham: Duke University Press, 1981: 87-124.

Fuller, Lon L. "Mediation—Its Forms and Functions." *Southern California Law Review*, 44 (Winter 1971): 305-39.

Gaffney, Frank and Robert Loeffler. "State-Sponsored Environmental Mediation: The Alaska Forest Practices Act." *Environmental Impact Assessment Review*, 11 (December 1991).

Galanter, Marc. "Reading the Landscape of Disputes: What We Know and Don't Know (And Think We Know) About Our Allegedly Contentious and Litigious Society." *UCLA Law Review*, 31 (October 1983): 4-71.

Garrett, B. *The Territorial Architecture of Prescott, Arizona.* Prescott, Ariz.: Javapai Heritage Foundation, 1978.

Gellhorne, Walter, John T. Dunlop, Harry T. Edwards, and Carolyn B. Kuhl. "Alternative Means of Dispute Resolution in Government: A Sense of Perspective." *The Administrative Law Review*, 1 (Fall 1987): 459-77.

Gilford, Dorothy M., Glenn L. Nelson, and Linda Ingram, eds., *Rural America in Passage: Statistics for Policy.* Washington, D.C.: National Academy Press, 1981: 18-24.

Gillroy, John Martin. "Moral Considerations and Public Policy Choice:Individual Autonomy and the NIMBY Problem." Paper presented at the annual meeting of the Midwest Political Science Association, Chicago, April 1990.

Goldberg, Stephen B., Eric D. Green, and Frank E. A. Sander. *Dispute Resolution*. Boston: Little, Brown and Co., 1985.

Goldman, R. B. ed. *Roundtable Justice: Case Studies in Conflict Resolution. Reports to the Ford Foundation*. Boulder, Colo.: Westview Press, 1980.

Gore, Albert. *Creating a Government That Works Better and Costs Less. Report of the National Performance Review*. September 7, 1993.

Gore, Albert. *Earth in the Balance*. Boston, Mass: Houghton Mifflin, 1992.

Granovetter, Mark. "The Strength of Weak Ties." *American Journal of Sociology*, 78, no. 6 (1973): 1360-80.

Gray, K. "Case Study: Inland Northwest Grass Burning Environmental Conflict Intervention." Unpublished manuscript, 1991.

Greenhalgh, Leonard. "The Case Against Winning in Negotiations." *Negotiation Journal*, 3 (April 1987a): 167-73.

Greenhalgh, Leonard. "Relationships in Negotiations." *Negotiation Journal*, 3 (July 1987b): 235-43.

Grey, Barbara. *Collaborating: Finding Common Ground for Multiparty Problems*. San Francisco: Jossey-Bass, 1989.

Grey, Barbara and Donna Wood, eds., *The Journal of Applied Behavioral Science*, Special Issue: Collaborative Alliances: Moving From Practice to Theory, Part 1 & 2, 27, no. 1 & 2 (June 1991 and March 1991).

Gunton, T. and S. Flynn. "Resolving Environmental Conflicts: The Role of Mediation and Negotiation." *Environments*, 21, no. 3 (1992): 12-16.

Gusman, Sam. "Selecting Participants for a Regulatory Negotiation." *Environmental Impact Assessment Review*, 4 (1983): 195-202.

Gusman, Sam and Philip J. Harter. "Mediating Solutions to Environmental Risks." *Annual Review of Public Health*, 7 (1986): 293-312.

Hackman, J. R. "The Design of Work Teams." In J. W. Lorsch, ed., *Handbook of Organizational Behavior*. Englewood Cliffs, N. J.: Prentice-Hall, 1987.

Halbert, Cindy L. and Kai N. Lee. "The Timber, Fish and Wildlife Agreement: Implementing Alternative Dispute Resolution in Washington State." *The Northwest Environmental Journal*, 6 (Spring 1990).

Harper, R. L. "Ten Tips for More Successful Community Meetings." Paper presented at the 66th Annual Meeting of the Water Environment Federation. Anaheim, California, October 3-7, 1993.

Harter, Philip J. "Negotiated Rulemaking: An Overview." *Environmental Law Reporter* 17 (July 1987): 10245-47.

Harter, Philip. "Negotiating Regulations: A Cure for Malaise." *Administrative Law and Regulatory Policy* (1985).

Harter, Philip J. "Negotiating Regulations: A Cure for Malaise." *Georgetown Law Journal*, 71, no. 1 (October 1982): 100-118.

Harter, Philip J. "Points on a Continuum: Dispute Resolution Procedures and the Administrative Process." *The Administrative Law Journal*, 4, no. 1 (Summer 1987): 141-211.

Harter, Philip J., Lee M. Thomas, Kay McMurray, Robben W. Fleming, and Marguerite Millhauser. "Institutionalizing Alternative Dispute Resolution: Where Does the Government Go From Here?" *The Administrative Law Journal*, 1 (Fall 1987): 509-25.

Hassinger, Edward W. and James R. Pinkerton. *The Human Community*. New York: Macmillan, 1986.

Hensler, Deborah R. "Science in the Court: Is There a Role for Alternative Dispute Resolution?" *Law and Contemporary Problems*, 54 (Summer 1991): 171-93.

Hettwer, R. "Ethical Factors in Environmental Negotiation." *Environmental Assessment Review*, 11, no. 3 (1991).

Hilgendorf, Lucy, M. "A Brief Summary of the Scoping Process." Internal Project Memorandum. The Western Network, Santa Fe, New Mexico, January 1989a.

Hilgendorf, Lucy, M. "Description of the Public Participation Activities." Report to the United States Forest Service. February 1989b.

Hill, Barry E. "Negotiating Superfund Mixed Funding Settlements." *Environmental Law Reporter*, 21 (November 1991): 10651-57.

Hill, Jeffrey S. and Carol S. Weissert. "Interstate Compacts and the Irony of Congressional Delegation." Paper presented at the Annual Meeting of the Association for Public Policy and Management, 1992, Denver, Colorado.

Hoard, Major E. David and Terrence M. Lyons. "Negotiating with Environmental Regulatory Agencies: Working Towards Harmony." *The Air Force Law Review*, 7 (1989): 201-23.

Hollister, R. and T. Lee. "Front End Impact Assessment." *Development Politics: Private Development and the Public Interest*. Washington, D.C.: Council of State Planning Agencies, 1979

Holznagle, Bernard. "Negotiation and Mediation: The Newest Approach to Hazardous Waste Facility Siting." *Boston College Environmental Affairs Law Review*, 13 (1986): 329-78.

Honadle, Beth Walter. "Defining and Doing Capacity Building: Perspectives and Experiences." in B. W. Honadle and A. M. Howitt, eds., *Perspectives on Management Capacity Building*. Albany, N.Y.: State University of New York Press, 1986: 9-23.

Honadle, Beth Walter. "The Federal Government's Role in Community Infrastructure in the 1980s and Beyond." In T. G. Johnson, B. J. Deaton, and E. Segarra, eds., *Local Infrastructure Investment in Rural America*. Boulder, Colo.: Westview Press, 1988: 257-59.

Honadle, Beth Walter. *Public Administration in Rural Areas and Small Jurisdictions: A Guide to the Literature*. New York: Garland Publishing, Inc., 1983.

Huelsberg, Nancy A. and William F. Lincoln, eds., *Successful Negotiating in Local Government*. Washington, D.C.: International City Management Association, 1985: 1430-60.

Hunter, Floyd. *Community Power Succession: Atlanta's Policy-Makers Revisited*. Chapel Hill: University of North Carolina Press, 1980.

Institute of Cultural Affairs. "Facilitation Methods: An Introduction to Small Group Leadership Skills." Seattle, Wash.: Institute of Cultural Affairs, 1980.

Jacobs, David C. "The Concept of Adversary Participation." *Negotiation Journal*, 4 (April 1988): 137-42.

Jacobs, Harvey M. and Richard Rubino. *Environmental Mediation: An Annotated Bibliography*. Council of Planning Librarians Bibliography No. 189, 1987.

Jacobs, Harvey Martin. *Predicting the Utility of Environmental Mediation: Natural Resource and Conflict Typologies as a Guide to Environmental Conflict Assessment.* Madison, Wisc.: Institute for Legal Studies, University of Wisconsin School of Law, 1988.

Jaggar, Alison. *Feminist Politics and Human Nature.* Totowa, N.J.: Rowman & Allanheld, 1983.

Johnson, Jeffrey Paul. "Negotiating Environmental and Development Disputes." *Journal of Planning Literature,* 1 (Autumn 1986): 509-21.

Johnson, Peter T. "How I Turned a Critical Public into Useful Consultants." *Harvard Business Review* (January-February 1993): 56-66.

Kartez, Jack D. "Planning for Cooperation in Environmental Dilemmas." *Journal of Planning Literature*, 5 (February 1991): 226-37.

Kathlene, Lyn and John A. Martin. "Enhancing Citizen Participation: Panel Designs, Perspectives, and Policy Formation." *Journal of Policy Analysis and Management*, 10, no. 1 (Winter 1991): 46-63.

Katz, Eric. "Organicism, Community, and the Substitution Problem." *Environmental Ethics,* 7 (Fall 1985): 241-56.

Kaufman, Harold F. "Toward an Interactional Conception of Community." *Social Forces*, 38, no. 1 (1959): 8-17.

Kearney, Richard C. and John J. Stucker. "Interstate Compacts and the Management of Low Level Radioactive Wastes." *Public Administration Review*, 42, no. 1 (January/ February 1985): 210-20.

Keating, K. and C. Taggert. "Where Smoke Wafts, Anger Sure to Follow." *The Spokesman-Review* (August 31, 1991): B3.

Kettering Foundation. "The Basics in Negotiation and Mediation." in N. A. Huelsberg and W. F. Lincoln eds., *Successful Negotiating in Local Government.* Washington, D.C.: International City Management Association, 1985: 27-34.

Kheel, Marti. "The Liberation of Nature: A Circular Affair." *Environmental Ethics* 7 (Summer 1985): 135-49.

Kingdon, John W. *Agendas, Alternatives and Public Policies.* Boston, Mass.: Little, Brown and Co., 1984, and Minneapolis, Minn.: University of Minnesota Press, 1993.

Kirtz, Chris. "EPA's Regulatory Negotiation and Other Consensual Activities." *Environmental Hazards,* 2, no. 2 (February 1990).

Klase, Kenneth. *Small Community Characteristics and Human Resources Affecting Environmental Management: Building the Capacity of Small Communities Through Training.* Morgantown, W.Va.: National Environmental Training Center for Small Communities, May 1993.

Kolb, Deborah M. "Corporate Ombudsman and Organization Conflict Resolution." *Journal of Conflict Resolution*, 31 (December 1987): 673-91.

Kraft, Michael E. and Bruce B. Clary. "Citizen Participation and the NIMBY Syndrome: Public Response to Radioactive Waste Disposal." *Western Political Quarterly*, 44, no. 2 (June 1991): 299-328.

Krimsky, S. and A. Plough. *Environmental Hazards: Communicating Risks as Social Process.* Dover, Mass: Auburn House Publishing Company, 1988.

Kubasek, Nancy. "Environmental Mediation." *American Business Law Journal*, 26 (1988): 533-55.

Lake, Laura M. *Environmental Mediation: The Search for Consensus*. Boulder, Colo.: Westview Press, 1980.

Lake, Robert W., ed. *Resolving Locational Conflict*. New Brunswick, N.J.: Rutgers University Center for Urban Policy Research, 1987.

Landis-Stamp, Paul. "The Mediation of Environmental Conflicts." In Tom Woodhouse, ed., *Peacemaking in a Troubled World*. New York: Berg, 1991.

Langbein, Laura and Cornelius M. Kerwin. "Implementation, Negotiation and Compliance in Environmental and Safety Regulation." *The Journal of Politics*, 47 (August 1985): 854-80.

Lapping, Mark, Thomas L. Daniels, and John W. Keller. *Rural Planning and Development in the United States*. New York: The Guilford Press, 1989.

Lax, David A. and James K. Sebenius. "Interests: The Measure of Negotiation." *Negotiation Journal*, 2 (January 1986a): 73-92.

Lax, David A. and James K. Sebenius. "Three Ethical Issues in Negotiation." *Negotiation Journal*, 2 (October 1986b): 363-69.

Lee, Kai N. "Defining Success in Environmental Dispute Resolution." *Resolve*, 1, no. 12 (Spring 1982).

Lentz, Sydney Solberg. "The Labor Model for Mediation and Its Application to the Resolution of Environmental Disputes." *Journal of Applied Behavioral Science*, 22, no. 2 (1986): 127-39.

Leopold, A. *A Sand County Almanac with Essays on Conservation from Round River*. New York: Oxford University Press, 1966.

Levinson, Alfred. "Environmental Dispute Resolution and Policy Making." *Policy Studies Journal*, 16 (Spring 1988): 575-84.

Levitt, Rachelle L. and J. Kirlin. *Managing Development through Public/Private Negotiations*. Washington, D.C.: ULI—The Urban Land Institute, 1985.

Liepmann, Karen L. "Confidentiality in Environmental Mediation: Should Third Parties Have Access to the Process?" *Boston College Environmental Affairs Law Review*, 14 (1986): 93-129.

Lobel, Ira B. "Addressing Environmental Disputes with Labor Mediation Skills." *Arbitration Journal*, 47, no. 3 (September 1992): 48-56.

Luke, Jeffrey, C. Ventriss, B J. Reed, and Christine Reed. *Managing Economic Development*. San Francisco: Jossey-Bass, 1988.

Lundgren, M. *To Burn or Not to Burn: The Bluegrass Issue*. (Pamphlet produced for the Spokane County Conservation District [SCCD], 1989. Available from Monica Lundgren, SCCD, N. 222 Havana Street, Spokane, WA 99202.)

Lyden, Fremont J., Ben W. Twight, and E. Thomas Tuchmann. "Citizen Participation in Long-Range Planning: The RPA Experience." *Natural Resources Journal*, 30 (Winter 1990): 123-38.

MacDonnell, Lawrence J. "Environmental Dispute Resolution: An Overview." *Natural Resources Journal*, 28 (Winter 1988): 5-19.

Macklin, Laura. "Promoting Settlement, Foregoing the Facts." *Review of Law and Social Change*, 14 (1986): 575-612.

Magazine, Alan H. *Environmental Management in Local Government: A Study of Local Response to Federal Mandate*. New York: Praeger Publishers, 1977.

Maine Low Level Radioactive Waste Authority. *Summary of Points of Agreement and Disagreement*, Citizens Advisory Group Meeting no. 1, November 2, 1989.

Manik, Roy, "Pollution Prevention, Organization Culture and Social Learning." *Environmental Law*, 22 (November 1, 1992): 189-252.

Mank, Bradford C. "The Two-Headed Dragon of Siting and Cleaning Up Hazardous Waste Dumps: Can Economic Incentives or Mediation Slay the Monster?" *Boston College Environmental Affairs Law Review*, 19 (Fall/Winter 1991): 239-85.

Manring, Nancy J. "Reconciling Science and Politics in Forest Service Decision Making: New Tools for Public Administrators." *American Review of Public Administration*, 23, no.4 (December 1993): 343-59.

Manring, Nancy, Patrick C. West, and Patricia Bidol. "Social Impact Assessment and Environmental Conflict Management: Potential for Integration and Application." *Environmental Impact Assessment Review*, 10 (September 1990): 253.

Mansbridge, Jane J. "The Rise and Fall of Self-Interest in the Explanation of Political Life." In Jane J. Mansbridge, ed., *Beyond Self-Interest*. Chicago: University of Chicago Press, 1990.

Marcus, Alfred A., Mark V. Nadel, and Karen Merrikin. "The Applicability of Regulatory Negotiation to Disputes Involving the Nuclear Regulatory Commission." *Administrative Law Review*, 36 (Summer 1984): 213-38.

Martin, Geoffrey R. "The Practical and the Theoretical Split in Modern Negotiation Literature." *Negotiation Journal*, 4 (January 1988): 45-54.

Martin, Michael, "Ecosabotage and Civil Disobedience." *Environmental Ethics* 12 (Winter 1990): 291-310.

Massachusetts Bureau of Solid Waste Disposal. *Municipal Recycling Ordinances*. Boston: Massachusetts Bureau of Solid Waste Disposal, 1986.

Mays, Richard H. "Alternative Dispute Resolution and Environmental Enforcement: A Noble Experiment or a Lost Cause?" *Environmental Law Reporter*, 18 (March 1988): 10087-97.

Mays, Richard H. "The Need for Innovative Environmental Enforcement." *Environmental Forum*, 4 (March 1986): 7-14.

McBride, K. "Burning Brings Ill Wind Protestors Say." *The Spokesman-Review*, (August 9 1989): B1.

McCarthy, Jane and Alice Shorett. *Negotiating Settlements: A Guide to Environmental Mediation*. New York: American Arbitration Association, 1984.

McCracken, James G., Jay O'Laughlin, and Troy Merrill. *Idaho Roadless Areas and Wilderness Proposals*. Moscow, Idaho: Forest, Wildlife and Range Policy Analysis Group, University of Idaho, 1993.

McCrory, John, "Environmental Mediation—Another Piece for the Puzzle." *Vermont Law Review*, 6 (Spring 1981): 49-84.

McGinnis, Michael V. "Low-Level Radioactive Waste Compacts: Cases in the Illogic of Collective Action." in Eric B. Herzik and Alvin H. Mushkatel, eds., *Problems and Prospects for Nuclear Waste Disposal*. Westport, Conn.: Greenwood Press, 1993.

Mediation Quarterly, San Francisco: Jossey-Bass. Vol. 20 (Summer 1988).

METCO Environmental Report on the 1990 Smoke Management Program. (Prepared for the Intermountain Grass Growers Association) Salem, Ore.: METCO, 1990.

Meyers, Gary D. "Old-Growth Forests, the Owl, and Yew: Environmental Ethics Versus Traditional Dispute Resolution under the Endangered Species Act and Other Public Lands and Resources Laws." *Boston College Environmental Affairs Law Review*, 18 (1990).

Miller, Jeffrey G. *Fundamentals of Negotiation: A Guide for Environmental Professionals.* Washington, D.C.: Environmental Law Institute, 1989.

Miller, Richard E. and Austin Sarat. "Grievances, Claims, and Disputes:Assessing the Adversary Culture." *Law and Society Review*, 15 (1980-1981): 525-65.

Mills, Miriam K. *Conflict Resolution and Public Policy.* Westport, Conn.: Greenwood Press, 1990.

Ministry for the Environment. "Resource Management Disputes: Part B: Mediation." *Resource Management Law Reform*, working paper 31. Wellington, New Zealand: Ministry for the Environment, 1988.

Mintz, Joel A. "Agencies, Congress and Regulatory Enforcement: A Review of EPA's Hazardous Waste Enforcement Effort, 1970-1987." *Environmental Law*, 18 (1988): 683-777.

Moore, Christopher. *The Mediation Process: Practical Strategies for Resolving Conflict.* San Francisco: Jossey-Bass, 1986.

Mosher, Lawrence. "EPA, Looking for Better Way to Settle Rules Disputes, Tries Some Mediation." *National Journal* (March 5, 1983): 504-6.

Murray, John S. "Understanding Competing Theories of Negotiation." *Negotiation Journal*, 2 (April 1986): 179-86.

Nachmias, David and Chava Nachmias. *Research Methods in the Social Sciences.* 3rd edition. New York: St. Martin's Press, 1987.

Nader, Laura. "Disputing without the Force of Law." *The Yale Law Journal*, 88 (April 1979): 998-1021.

Naess, Arne. "A Defense of the Deep Ecology Movement." *Environmental Ethics*, 6 (Fall 1984).

Naess, Arne. *Ecology, Community, and Lifestyle*, tr. and rev. by David Rothenberg, Cambridge, England: Cambridge University Press, 1989.

Naess, Arne. "The Shallow and the Deep, Long-Range Ecology Movement." *Inquiry*, 16 (1973): 95-100.

Nakamura, Robert T., Thomas W. Church, Jr., and Phillip J.Cooper. "Environmental Dispute Resolution and Hazardous Waste Cleanups: A Cautionary Tale of Policy Implementation." *Journal of Policy Analysis and Management*, 10, no. 2 (Spring 1991): 204-21.

Nash, Jennifer and Lawrence E. Susskind. "Mediating Conflict over Dioxin Risks of Resource Recycling: Lessons From a Flawed Process." *Environmental Impact Assessment Review*, 7 (March 1987): 79-83.

National Center Associates, Inc. and Center for Dispute Resolution. *Willamette University College of Law. The Course in Collaborative Negotiation.* Willamette, 1989.

National Commission on the Environment. *Choosing a Sustainable Future.* Washington, D.C.: Island Press, 1993.

National Environmental Policy Act. "Implementation of Procedural Provisions; Final Regulations." *Federal Register*, November 29, 1989.

Nelkin, Dorothy. *Controversy: Politics of Technical Decisions,* 2nd ed. Beverly Hills, Calif.: Sage, 1984.

North Central Regional Center for Rural Development. *Coping with Conflict: Strategies for Extension Community Development and Public Policy Professionals.* Ames, Iowa: University of Iowa, 1979.

Norton, Bryan G. *Toward Unity Among Environmentalists.* New York: Oxford University Press, 1991.

Nyhart, J. D. "Negotiating Conflict Over Marine Resources: The Use of Multiparty Models." *Environmental Impact Assessment Review,* 4 (December 1983): 557-60.

Nyhart, J. D. and E. A. Dauer. "A Preliminary Analysis of the Uses of Scientific Models in Dispute Prevention, Management and Resolution." *Journal of Dispute Resolution* (1986): 29-53.

O'Connor, David. "Environmental Mediation: The State-of-the-Art?" *Environmental Impact Assessment Review,* 2 (October, 1978): 9-17.

Olpin, Owen, David Doniger, Madeleine Crohn, Steven Schatzow, Terry Calvani, and Neil R. Eisner. "Applying Alternative Dispute Resolution to Rulemaking." *The Administrative Law Journal,* 1 (Fall 1987): 575-88.

Olsen, Marvin E. *Viewing the World Ecologically.* Boulder, Colo.: Westview Press, 1992.

Olson, Erik D. "The Quiet Shift of Power: Office of Management and Budget Supervision of Environmental Protection Agency Rulemaking Under Executive Order 12291." *Virginia Journal of Natural Resources Law,* 4 (Fall 1984): 1-83.

Ozawa, Connie. *Recasting Science. Consensual Procedures in Public Policy Making.* Boulder, Colo.: Westview Press, 1991.

Paehelke, Robert C. *Environmentalism and the Future of Progressive Politics.* New Haven, Conn.: Yale University Press, 1989.

Painter, A. "The Future of Environmental Dispute Resolution." *Natural Resources Journal,* 28 (Winter 1988): 145-70.

Perritt, Henry H. "Negotiated Rulemaking before Federal Agencies: Evaluation of Recommendations by the Administrative Conference of the United States." *The Georgetown Law Journal,* 74 (1986a): 1625-717.

Perritt, Henry H., Jr. "Negotiated Rulemaking in Practice." *Journal of Policy Analysis and Management,* 5 (Spring 1986b): 482-95.

Peterson, W. A., D.R. Dole, J. Gady, J. M. Sours, G. Storment, and D. E. White. *The Issue of Open Field Burning of Grass Seed Production Residue in Northeastern Washington and Northern Idaho.* Spokane, Wash.: Soil Conservation Service, January 1990.

Phillips, B. and A. Piazza. "The Role of Mediation in Public Interest Disputes." *Hastings Law Journal,* 34 (1983): 1231-44.

Pitkin, Hannah. *The Concept of Representation.* Berkeley, Calif.: University of California Press, 1967.

Plumwood, Val. "Current Trends in Ecofeminism." *The Ecologist,* 22, no. 1 (January-February 1992).

Plumwood, Val. "Feminism and Ecofeminism." *The Ecologist,* 22, no. 1 (January-February 1992).

Polinsky, A. *An Introduction to Law and Economics,* 2nd ed. Boston: Little, Brown and Company, 1989.

Porter, Richard. C. "Environmental Negotiation: Its Potential and Its Economic Efficiency." *Journal of Environmental Economics and Management* 15 (1988): 129-42.

Posner, Richard A. *Economic Analysis of Law.* Boston: Little, Brown and Company, 1972.

Posner, Richard. *Law and Literature: A Misunderstood Relationship.* Cambridge, Mass.: Harvard University Press, 1988.

Potapchuk, William and Chris Carlson. "Using Conflict Analysis to Determine Intervention Techniques." *Mediation Quarterly,* 16 (Summer 1987): 31-43.

Powers, Ronald C. and Edward O. Moe. "The Policy Context for Rural-Oriented Research." In D. A. Dillman and D. J. Hobbs, eds., *Rural Society in the U.S.: Issues for the 1980s.* Boulder, Colo.: Westview Press, 1982: 10-20.

Prescott Planning and Zoning Department. "The Prescott Comprehensive Plan." Prescott, Ariz.: City of Prescott, 1986.

Priscoli, Jerome Delli, "Conflict Resolution for Water Resource Projects: Using Facilitation and Mediation to Write Section 404 General Permits." *Environmental Impact Assessment Review,* 7 (December 1987): 313-26.

Protasel, G. J. "Resolving environmental conflicts: Neocorporatism, Negotiated Rulemaking, and the Timber/Fish/Wildlife Coalition in the State of Washington." In M. Mills, ed., *Alternative Dispute Resolution in the Public Sector.* Chicago: Nelson-Hall Publishers, 1991: 188-205.

Pruitt, Dean G. "Strategic Choice in Negotiation." *American Behavioral Scientist,* 27 (November/December 1983): 167-94.

Pruitt, Dean G. "Trends in the Scientific Study of Negotiation and Mediation." *Negotiation Journal,* 2 (July 1986): 237-44.

Pruitt, Dean G. and Jeffrey Rubin. *Social Conflict: Escalation, Stalemate, and Settlement.* New York: Random House, 1986.

Rabe, B. G. "Impediments to Environmental Dispute Resolution in the American Political Context." In M. Mills, ed., *Alternative Dispute Resolution in the Public Sector.* Chicago: Nelson-Hall Publishers, 1991.

Rabe, Barry G. "The Politics of Environmental Dispute Resolution." *Policy Studies Journal,* 16, no. 3 (1988): 585-601.

Rachels, James. *Created from Animals: The Moral Implications of Darwinism.* New York: Oxford University Press, 1990.

Rahim, M. Afzalur. *Theory and Research in Conflict Management.* New York: Praeger, 1990.

Raiffa, Howard. "Mediation of Conflicts." *American Behavioral Scientist* 27 (November/December 1983): 195-210.

Reed, Christine M. and B. J. Reed. "Assessing Readiness for Economic Development Strategic Planning." *American Planning Association Journal,* 53, no.4 (Autumn 1987): 521-30.

Regan, Tom. *The Case for Animal Rights.* University of California Press, 1983.

Reid, J. Norman. "Building Capacity in Rural Places: Local View of Needs." In B. W. Honadle and A. M. Howitt, eds., *Perspectives on Management Capacity Building.* Albany, N.Y.: State University of New York Press, 1986: 74-75.

Rennie, S. "Kindling the Environmental Flame: Use of Mediation and Arbitration in Federal Planning, Permitting, and Enforcement." *Environmental Law Review,* 19 (1989): 10479-84.

Richardson, James R. "Overcoming Obstacles to Negotiating Electric Utility Industry Regulations." *Negotiation Journal* (January 1991): 51-53.

Riesel, Daniel. "Negotiation and Mediation of Environmental Disputes." *Journal on Dispute Resolution,* 1 (Fall 1985): 99-111.

Riggs, Douglas A. and Elizabeth K. Dorminey. "Federal Agencies' Use of Alternative Means of Dispute Resolution." *The Administrative Law Journal,* 1 (Fall 1987): 125-39.

Ritchie, J. "Planning: A Perspective on the Maori World." *Planning Quarterly,* 82 (1986).

Robbins, Stephen. "Conflict Management and Conflict Resolution Are Not Synonymous Terms." *California Management Review*, 21 (Winter 1978): 67-75.

Robinson, Glen O. *The Forest Service: A Study in Public Land Management.* Baltimore: Johns Hopkins Press, 1975.

Rodwin, Marc A. "Can Bargaining and Negotiation Change the Administrative Process?" *Environmental Impact Assessment Review,* 3 (December 1982): 373-86.

Ross, Monique and J. Owen Saunders, eds. *Growing Demands on a Shrinking Heritage.* Calgary: Canadian Institute of Resources Law, 1992.

Ross, William H., Jr. "Situational Factors and Alternative Dispute Resolution." *The Journal of Applied Behavioral Science,* 24 (1988): 251-62.

Roth, Dennis M. *The Wilderness Movement and The National Forests: 1980-1984.* Washington, D.C.: U.S. Government Printing Office, 1988.

Rothstein, E. and E. Jones. "Utility Public Involvement Strategies That Work: A Case Study in Austin, Texas." Paper presented at the 66th Annual Meeting of the Water Environment Federation, Anaheim, California, October 3-7, 1993.

Rubin, Jeffrey Z. and Frank E. A. Sander. "When Should We Use Agents? Direct vs. Representative Negotiation." *Negotiation Journal,* 4 (October 1988): 395-401.

Rubino, Richard G. *Mediation and Negotiation for Planning, Land Use Management, and Environmental Protection: An Annotated Bibliography of Materials, 1980-1989.* Chicago: Council of Planning Librarians, 1990.

Rustemeyer, A. "Tradition versus Change in Agriculture in the New Age of the 1990s." *Wheat Life,* 34 (1991): 5-6.

Sachs, Andy. "Nationwide Study Identifies Barriers to EnvironmentalNegotiation." *Environmental Impact Assessment Review,* 3 (March 1982): 95-100.

Sandole, Dennis J. D. and Ingrid Sandole-Staroste. *Conflict Management and Problem Solving: Interpersonal and International Applications.* New York: New York University Press, 1987.

Saunders, Harold H. "We Need a Larger Theory of Negotiation: The Importance of Pre-Negotiating Phases." *Negotiation Journal,* 1 (July 1985): 249-62.

Schneider, Keith. "Accord Is Reached to Aid Forest Bird." *New York Times* (April 14, 1993): A-1, 9.

Schneider, Peter and Ellen Tohn. "Success in Negotiating Environmental Regulations." *Environmental Impact Assessment Review,* 5 (March 1985): 67-77.

Schoenbrod, David. "Limits and Dangers of Environmental Mediation: A Review Essay." *New York University Law Review,* 58 (December 1983): 1453-76.

Seroka, Jim. "Rural Public Administration Research: An Assessment." In Jim Seroka, ed., *Rural Public Administration: Problems and Prospects.* Westport, Conn.: Greenwood Press, 1986: 191-93.

Singer, David. "Arbitration Journal Report: The Use of ADR Methods in Environmental Disputes." *The Arbitration Journal,* 47 (March 1992): 55-59.

Singer, Peter. "All Animals Are Equal." *Philosophical Exchange,* 1, no. 5 (Summer 1974).

Singer, Peter. *Animal Liberation: A New Ethics for Our Treatment of Animals.* New York: Random House, 1975.

Singer, Peter. *Animal Liberation.* New York: Avon Books, 1990.

Sjostedt, Gunnar, ed. *International Environmental Negotiation.* Newbury Park, Calif.: Sage, 1993.

Slovic, Paul and Baruch Fischhoff. "How Safe Is Safe Enough? Determinants of Perceived and Acceptable Risk." In C. A. Walker, L. C. Gould, and E. J. Woodhouse, eds., *Too Hot to Handle? Social and Policy Issues in the Management of Radioactive Wastes*. New Haven, Conn.: Yale University Press, 1983: 112-50.

Smith, R. "Citizens Take Action in Court." *Prescott Courier*. Prescott,Ariz. (December 13 and 14, 1984).

Smith, Zachary A. *The Environmental Policy Paradox*. Englewood Cliffs, N.J.: Prentice Hall, 1992.

Sorensen, John H., Jon Soderstrom, and Sam A. Carnes. "Sweet for the Sour: Incentives for Environmental Mediation." *Environmental Management*, 8 (July 1984): 287-94.

Stephenson, Max O. and Gerald M. Pops. "Conflict Resolution Methods and the Policy Process." *Public Administration Review*, 49 (September/ October 1989): 463-73.

Sternberg, Robert J. and Lawrence J. Soriano. "Styles of Conflict Resolution." *Journal of Personality and Social Psychology*, 47 (1984): 115-26.

Stewart, R. "The Reformation of American Administrative Law." *Harvard Law Review*, 88, no. 8 (1975): 1667-1813.

Stodolsky, David. "Automatic Mediation in Group Problem Solving." *Environmental Impact Assessment Review*, 1 (March 1980): 80-90.

Stone, Christopher D. *Should Trees Have Standing? Toward Legal Rights for Natural Objects*. Los Altos: William Kaufmann, Inc., 1974, partially reprinted in *People, Penguins, and Plastic Trees: Basic Issues in Environmental Ethics*, D. VanDeVeer and C. Pierce, eds., Belmont, Calif.: Wadsworth, 1986: 87-88.

Stratton. D. H. *Spokane and the Inland Empire: An Interior Pacific Northwest Anthology*. Pullman, Wash.: Washington State University Press, 1991.

Stulberg, Joseph B. "The Theory and Practice of Mediation: A Reply to Professor Susskind." *Vermont Law Review*, no. 6, (1981).

Sullivan, J. "Grass Growers Defend Burning at Air Meeting." *The Spokesman-Review*, (October 6, 1989): B1, B3.

Sullivan, Timothy. *Negotiation-Based Review Processes for Facility Siting*. Cambridge, Mass.: Kennedy School of Government, 1979.

Sullivan, Timothy J. *Resolving Development Disputes through Negotiations*. New York: Plenum Press, 1984.

Susskind, Lawrence. "Environmental Mediation and the AccountabilityProblem." *Vermont Law Review*, no. 6 (1981).

Susskind, Lawrence. "Mediating Public Disputes." *Negotiation Journal*, 1(1985): 19-22.

Susskind, Lawrence. "It's Time to Shift Our Attention from Impact Assessment to Strategies for Resolving Environmental Disputes." *Environmental Impact Assessment Review*, 2 (October 1978): 4-8.

Susskind, Lawrence and Connie Ozawa. "Mediated Negotiation in the Public Sector." *American Behavioral Scientist*, 27 (November/December 1983): 255-79.

Susskind, Lawrence and Gerald McMahon. "The Theory and Practice of Negotiated Rulemaking." *Yale Journal on Regulation*, 3, no. 1 (1985): 133-65.

Susskind, Lawrence, Gerard McMahon and Stephanie Rolley. "Mediating Development Disputes: Some Barriers and Bridges to Successful Negotiation." *Environmental Impact Assessment Review*, 7 (June 1987): 127-38.

Susskind, Lawrence and Jeffrey Cruikshank. *Breaking the Impasse: Consensual Approaches to Resolving Public Disputes*. New York: Basic Books, 1987.

Susskind, Lawrence E., J. Richardson, and K. Hildebrand. *ResolvingEnvironmental Disputes: Approaches to Intervention, Negotiation and Conflict Resolution.* Cambridge, Mass.: Department of Urban Studies and Planning, Laboratory of Architecture and Planning, 1978.

Susskind, Lawrence E. and L. Dunlap. "The Importance of Nonobjective Judgements." *Environmental Impact Assessment Review* (1981): 335-66.

Susskind, Lawrence and Alan Weinstein. "Toward a Theory of Environmental Dispute Resolution." *Environmental Affairs* 9, no. 3 (1980): 311-57.

Susskind, L. and C. Ozawa. *Mediated Negotiation in the Public Sector: Objectives, Procedures and the Difficulties of Measuring Success.* Cambridge, Mass.: Harvard Law School Negotiation Project, 1984.

Susskind, Lawrence and Connie Ozawa. "Mediating Public Disputes: Obstacles and Possibilities." *Journal of Social Issues,* 41 (1985): 145-59.

Syme, G. J., C. Seligman, and D. K. MacPherson. "Environmental Planning and Management: An Introduction." *The Journal of Social Issues,* 45, no. 1 (1989): 1-15.

Talbot, Allan. *Settling Things: Six Case Studies in Environmental Mediation.* Washington, D.C.: Conservation Foundation/Ford Foundation, 1983.

Taylor, Bob Pepperman. *Our Limits Transgressed.* Lawrence, Kans.: University of Kansas Press, 1992.

Taylor, Paul. "The Ethics of Respect for Nature." In D. VanDeVeer and C. Pierce, eds., *People, Penguins, and Plastic Trees: Basic Issues in Environmental Ethics.* Belmont, Calif.: Wadsworth Publishing, 1986; original source: *Environmental Ethics,* 3 (Fall 1981): 197-218.

Taylor, Paul. *Respect for Nature.* Princeton, N.J.: Princeton University Press, 1986.

Taylor, Thomas E. and Marilyn Harp. "David and Goliath: Shuttle Diplomacy in a Water Rate Dispute." In N. A. Huelsberg and W. F. Lincoln, eds. *Successful Negotiating in Local Government.* Washington, D.C.: International City Management Association, 1985: 143-60.

Thomas, Anne B., ed. *Making the Tough Calls: Ethical Exercises for Neutral Dispute Resolvers.* Washington, D.C.: Society for Professionals in Dispute Resolution, 1991.

Tobin, Richard. *The Expendable Future: U.S. Politics and the Protection of Biological Diversity.* Durham, N.C.: Duke University Press, 1990.

Tolba, Mostafa K. *Saving Our Planet: Challenges and Hopes.* New York: Chapman and Hall, 1992.

Touval, Saadia. "Multilateral Negotiation: An Analytic Approach." *Negotiation Journal,* 5 (April 1989): 159-73.

Train, Russell E. and John Busterud. *Environmental Mediation: An Effective Alternative.* Palo Alto: Resolve, 1978.

Tremblay, Kenneth R., Jr. and Riley E. Dunlap. "Rural-Urban Residence and Concern with Environmental Quality: A Replication and Extension." *Rural Sociology,* 43 (1978): 474-91.

U.S. Environmental Protection Agency. *An Assessment of EPA's Negotiated Rulemaking Activities.* Washington, D.C.: Program Evaluation Division, Office of Policy, Planning and Evaluation, 1987.

U.S. Forest Service. "Copper Basin Land Exchange and Mine Proposals Orientation Summary." Prescott, Ariz.: Prescott National Forest, Southwestern Region, January 1989.

U.S. Forest Service. "Memorandum of Understanding." Prescott, Ariz.: Prescott National Forest, Southwest Region, March 1987.

U.S. Forest Service. "Request for Proposals: Copper Basin Land Exchange and Mine Plan Proposal." Prescott, Ariz.: Prescott National Forest, Southwest Region, July 1988.

Ury, W. *Getting Past No*. New York: Bantam Books, 1991.

Vig, Norman J. and Michael E. Kraft. "Conclusion: The New Environmental Agenda." In N. J. Vig and M. E. Kraft, eds., *Environmental Policy in the 1990s*. Washington, D.C.: CQ Press, 1994.

Wald, Patricia M., Robert Coulson, Gerald W. Cormick, Richard K. Willard, Alan B. Morrison, and Harold H. Bruff. "Uses for Alternative Dispute Resolution: Better Ways to Resolve Some Public Sector Controversies." *The Administrative Law Review*, 1 (Fall 1987): 479-507.

Warren, Karen. "The Power and Promise of Ecological Feminism." *Environmental Ethics*, 12 (Summer 1990).

Watson, J. and L. Danielson. "Environmental Mediation." *Natural Resources Lawyer*, 4 (1982): 687-719

Weisbord, Marvin. *Discovering Common Ground*. San Francisco: Berrett-Koehler, 1992.

White, Orion. "The Dynamics of Negotiations." In N. A. Huelsberg and W. F. Lincoln, eds., *Successful Negotiating in Local Government*. Washington, D.C.: International City Management Association, 1985.

Wilkinson, Kenneth. "The Community as a Social Field." *Social Forces*, 48, no. 3 (1970): 311-22.

Wilkinson, Kenneth. *The Community in Rural America*. Westport, Conn.: Greenwood, 1991.

Windsor, M. "Prescott, Everybody's Home Town." *Arizona Highways* (August 1985): 15-22.

Wondolleck, Julia. "The Importance of Process in Resolving Environmental Disputes." *Environmental Impact Assessment Review*, 5 (December 1985): 341-56.

Wondolleck, Julia. *Public Lands Conflict and Resolution: Managing National Forest Disputes*. New York: Plenum Press, 1988a.

Wondolleck, Julia. "The Role of Training in Providing Opportunities for Environmental and Natural Resource Dispute Resolution." *Environmental Impact Assessment Review*, 8 (September 1988b): 233-48.

Wood, Donna and Barbara Grey. "Toward a Comprehensive Theory of Collaboration." *The Journal of Applied Behavioral Science*, 27, no. 2 (June 1991): 158.

Zartman, William. "Common Elements in the Analysis of the Negotiation Process." *Negotiation Journal*, 4 (January 1988): 31-43.

Index

About the Contributors

John C. Allen is Assistant Professor of Rural Sociology in the Department of Agricultural Economics at the University of Nebraska-Lincoln. Dr. Allen has been a farmer and a journalist. His research has been published in journals ranging from *Futures Research Quarterly* and *The Community Development Journal* to *Teaching Sociology*. His primary area of interest is community response to institutional change. He has worked as a mediator in community disputes in Oregon, Washington, Idaho, Maine and Nebraska.

Dennis Baird is Social Science Librarian at the University of Idaho. He has served several times as head of the Idaho Chapter of the Sierra Club and is currently Co-Chair of the National Forest Committee of the entire Sierra Club. He is author of several articles on Idaho environmental history and has testified before Congress on over ten occasions concerning public lands management.

Carolyn Blackford is Research Officer for the Centre for Resource Management, Lincoln University, New Zealand. Her main activity is research in resource management and environmental decision making, with a particular focus on conflict resolution. The outputs of this research assist central and local government resource management policy makers.

J. Walton Blackburn is a Quality Development Coordinator for the Nebraska Department of Social Services. Dr. Blackburn directed strategic planning at Creighton University, and has taught public administration, political science, business management, urban studies, urban planning and health services management at various universities. He has published widely on environmental mediation, and co-authored, with Willa Bruce, *Balancing Job Satisfaction and Performance: A Guide for Human Resource Professionals*.

Sondra Bogdonoff directs the Maine Sustainability Project at the Muskie Institute of Public Affairs and co-teaches a graduate class on "Leadership, Ethics, and Diversity." She has been a professional weaver for fifteen years. She recently returned to school and received her MA in Public Policy and Management in 1994. As graduate assistant to the Director of the Muskie Institute of Public Affairs, she helped conduct the conference, "Toward a Sustainable Maine."

Willa Marie Bruce is Professor of Public Administration at the University of Nebraska at Omaha, where she is a Faculty Fellow and Fellow of the Center for Great Plains Studies. Dr. Bruce teaches administrative ethics, and organization behavior, development, and theory. Her research interests are in public service ethics, implications of workplace changes on public employees, and ecclesiology. She has published numerous books and articles, and was co-winner, with Christine Reed, of the James E. Webb award for the best paper at the 1990 ASPA conference. She is a member of the Board of Editors of three national journals and listed in *Who's Who in the Mid-West* and *Who's Who of American Women*.

Guy Burgess is Co-Director of the Conflict Resolution Consortium at the University of Colorado and Co-Coordinator of conflict resolution projects in intractable conflict, justice without violence, and environmental problem solving. Dr. Burgess was co-founder of Public Science, a consulting firm, and helped a joint industry, government, and university team develop a $27 million dollar plan to investigate environmental issues. He has published numerous books and articles.

Heidi Burgess is Co-Director of the Conflict Resolution Consortium at the University of Colorado, and was co-founder of the consulting firm, Public Science. In addition to her work with Guy Burgess in the Conflict resolution consortium, Dr. Burgess has been a Professional Research Associate at the University of Colorado School of Nursing and Senior Associate to ACCORD Associates, formerly ROMCOE, Center for Environmental Problem Solving. She has published numerous articles.

Bruce B. Clary is Professor of Public Policy and Management at the Edmund S. Muskie Institute of Public Affairs, University of Southern Maine. Presently Dr. Clary is Acting Director of the Program. Besides his interest in environmental mediation, he has published in the policy areas of nuclear waste, natural hazards, and environmental pollution.

Frank Dukes is Senior Associate at the Institute for Environmental Negotiation and a Lecturer in the Department of Urban and Environmental Planning at the University of Virginia. His work includes designing dispute resolution and public participation processes, mediation and facilitation, and teaching and training for a wide range of public issues.

James B. Dworkin is Associate Dean and Professor of Organizational Behavior and Human Resources Management at the Krannert Graduate School of Management at Purdue University. Collective bargaining, labor relations, and research methods are Dr. Dworkin's main teaching interests. His current research interests include unionism in professional sports, codetermination, worker participation in management, why workers join unions, and how arbitrators decide cases.

Mary E. Guy is Professor and Chair of the Department of Political Science and Public Administration at the University of Alabama at Birmingham. Dr. Guy specializes in public management. She is the author of numerous publications. Her recent books include *Ethical Decision Making in Everyday Work Situations* and *Women and Men of the States: Public Administrators at the State Level.*

Regan Hornney is a graduate assistant in Public Policy and Management, Edmund S. Muskie Institute of Public Affairs, University of Southern Maine. She is also a student in the University of Maine School of Law, and has particular interest in environmental mediation as an alternative to litigation.

G. Logan Jordan is Assistant Dean at the Krannert Graduate School of Management at Purdue University. He is currently a doctoral student in strategic management. His teaching interests include business policy and organizational theory. His current research interests include strategic planning in the not-for-profit sector, the management of change and innovation, organizational issues in technology transfer, and the management of complex organizations.

Kenneth A. Klase is Assistant Professor of Public Administration at West Virginia University where he teaches public budgeting and public financial management. Dr. Klase's research has focused on local government financial management.

Larry S. Luton is Associate Professor of Public Administration at Eastern Washington University. Dr. Luton's research interests include citizen-administrator relations, and public administration theory and environmental policy. He is currently working on a book on the politics of solid waste management.

Peter R. Maida is Director of Mediation Services and Training at Key Bridge Therapy and Mediation Center in Arlington, Virginia. He is a mediator, trainer, group facilitator, and editor of *Mediation Quarterly*. Dr. Maida is on the Qualifications Commission of the Society of Professionals in Dispute Resolution.

Mollie K. Mangerich spent two years tracking the process and progress of Summit participants and mediators as the subject of her graduate thesis at Eastern Washington University. Her interests lie in the field of mediation and environmental policy.

Hirini Matunga is Associate Director and Lecturer at the Centre for Maori Studies and Research, Lincoln University, New Zealand. He was Convener of the Indigenous Committee of the Executive Council of the World Archaeological

Congress, and has been extensively involved with local, regional, and central government cross-cultural environmental disputes, and Maori policy making and planning in resource management. His tribal affiliations are Kai Tahu, Ngati Kahungungu, and Ngati Porou.

Ralph Maughan is Associate Professor of Political Science at Idaho State University. His present research is the "Wise Use" movement (with Douglas Nilson). Dr. Maughan was co-author of many of the wilderness proposals by the Idaho Wildlands Defense Coalition. He is a regional Sierra Club Officer and co-author of *The Hiker's Guide to Idaho.*

Douglas Nilson is an Associate Professor of Political Science at Idaho State University. Dr. Nilson's research interests include environmental politics. He is currently studying nuclear waste storage at a DOE site. Another project examines the support of and political rhetoric of "Wise Use" organizations. He is a local Sierra Club officer.

Rosemary O'Leary is an attorney and Associate Professor at the School of Public and Environmental Affairs at Indiana University. Dr. O'Leary has served as Director of Policy and Planning for an environmental agency. She has over 30 publications in the areas of environmental policy, law, and public policy, and has won five national awards for her research in the last five years. She was a recipient (with Charles Wise) of the 1991 and 1992 William E. Mosher and Frederick C. Mosher Awards for Best Article by an Academician in *Public Administration Review.* Her book, *Environmental Change: Federal Courts and the EPA,* was published in 1993. She is a member of the Board of Editors of four national journals.

Christine M. Reed is a Professor of Public Administration at the University of Nebraska at Omaha. Dr. Reed teaches public and environmental policy, and administrative law. Her research interests are in strategic planning and community development, work and family policy, and the relationship between public policy and ethics. She has published numerous books and articles, and was co-winner, with Willa Bruce, of the James E. Webb award for the best paper at the 1990 ASPA conference.

James R. Richardson is an Associate Professor and Director of the Community and Regional Planning Program at the University of New Mexico. His field of expertise is negotiation and public dispute resolution. He is an experienced mediator with extensive practice in facilitating citizens, developers, and regulators in face-to-face negotiations on development issues.

Clare M. Ryan is a Ph.D. candidate at the University of Michigan School of Natural Resources and Environment, focusing on natural resource and environmental policy. Her research interests address environmental regulatory policy, public administration, and dispute resolution and conflict management. She has worked as an environmental specialist and manager in state and federal natural resource agencies, dealing with a variety of water quality and hazardous waste issues.

John B. Stephens has been Research Director for the Ohio Commission on Dispute Resolution and Conflict Management since 1991. He is a Ph.D. candidate at the Institute for Conflict Analysis and Resolution at George Mason University, and received an MPhil in Systems Science from the City University, London.

William O. Stephens is Assistant Professor of Philosophy at Creighton University where he teaches courses in Ancient and Hellenistic philosophy, the history of ethics, and environmental ethics. Dr. Stephens' research includes works on Stoic naturalism, rationalism, ecology, the concept of fate, and a translation of *Die Ethik des Stoikers Epictet.*

J. Lynn Wood is Environmental Laboratory Administrator for Jefferson County, Alabama. He oversees the implementation of federal and state pollution control programs for the Jefferson County Department of Environmental Services. He also serves as the primary contact between the Department, federal and state environmental agencies, and local environmental agencies.

ISBN 0-89930-846-5

EAN

9 780899 308463

HARDCOVER BAR CODE